Confessions of a Banffshire Loon

The Ancestors and Early Life of a Bad Boy
from the Boondocks

Relations are simply a tedious pack of people who haven't the remotest
knowledge of how to live, nor the remotest instinct about when to die.
Oscar Wide *(1854-1900) The Importance of Being Earnest*

AuthorHouse™ UK Ltd.
1663 Liberty Drive
Bloomington, IN 47403 USA
www.authorhouse.co.uk
Phone: 0800.197.4150

Published by AuthorHouse   10/18/2013

ISBN: 978-1-4817-6851-1 (sc)
ISBN: 978-1-4817-6850-4 (hc)
ISBN: 978-1-4817-6852-8 (e)

Confessions of a Banffshire Loon

Being an Historical Account of the Ancestors and the Strange and Surprising Early Life and Adolescence of a Bad Boy from the Boondocks of Banffshire, now Sadly Known as Aberdeenshire, in the Country of Scotland, and Containing a Full and Frank Confession of his Misadventures and Misdemeanours Written by Himself and here

Revealed to the Public for the Very First Time.

4-11-2016

To Gillian
with best wishes.
Lovely to see you again
after sixty years...
David

DAVID M. ADDISON

authorHOUSE®

By the same author

An Italian Journey
A Meander in Menorca
Sometime in Sorrento
Bananas about La Palma
Misadventures in Tuscany
An Innocent Abroad

For my grandchildren

Bless them every one.

In order of appearance: Leon, Finn, Zara, Eimear and Orla.

I am their past; they are my future.

Acknowledgements

I would like to thank the following for their help and without whose help this book would not have appeared in its present form:

Judith Legg, Marjory Nicholson and Pat Lyon of Aberdeenshire Library Services and Dr MJC Mills of Northern Health Services Archives.

Isobel MacPherson, Jenny Morrison, Gordon Geddes, John Mitchell, Jane Addison, Kitty and Edie Crow, Edie Tate, Margaret and Michael Elstob, Georgina Ingram, Marjorie Gunn, Jim Leslie, Martin Green, Robert Orledge, Ornella Volta, Willie Addison, Tim Addison and Betty Gray.

Special thanks to Iain Gray, my advisor, chief contributor and mentor on the Munros and without whose help that chapter would have been much shorter. Likewise Sandy Addison for his information on the Portknockie Addisons, Al Somers for his on one lot of Canadian Addisons and Peter Addison for his on the other lot.

I would also like to offer special thanks to George and Evelyn Addison who provided me with a base during my researches and pointed me in the right direction. Last and certainly not least, Fiona Addison, whose patience, tolerance and help in trudging around wet, windy and sometimes snowy cemeteries in search of dead people and photographing their headstones goes well beyond the call of wifely duties.

Contents

Foreword: the genealogist's plea

I have a confession to make. In the course of this book I get quite a few others off my chest but it's best to get this one out of the way at the very start: I am a committed taphophile. It may not be a word that you are familiar with, but fear not, it's not the sort of thing which would result in the long arm of the law feeling the back of your collar. I'm not sure when I was smitten with this affliction exactly, but I do remember my six-year old daughter presenting me with a birthday card she had made herself, the irregular and gaily-coloured letters that said "Happy Birthday" surrounded by gravestones in the same jolly hues.

I am no ordinary taphophile however. Just as some philatelists have a special interest in certain countries or subjects, say birds for example, my special delight is to track down the graves of famous literary figures—which brings me to my next confession.

In my teenage years I was much addicted to the novels of, amongst others, Dennis Wheatley and Leslie Charteris, much to the despair of my parents, who thought they were "tripe" although I am perfectly certain they never read a single word of their works, apparently judging the books by their covers, which, as everyone knows, you should never do, either in the literal or metaphorical sense.

Amongst my treasures I have letters from both these literati. Leslie Charteris bemoaned the fact that critics accused him of constructing far-fetched plots, whereas, he said, he got them from the newspapers. Please remember this when you come across the amazing coincidences in this work of non-fiction.

As for Dennis Wheatley, whilst he may have been an old Tory, well actually, no doubt about it at all—he *was*, but don't hold that against him, he couldn't help it: it was the way he was brought up and who amongst us cannot say that that is why we are the way we are now? You may never have heard of him if you are of a certain generation, or of a certain nationality, but in the Second World War, Dennis was one of the select number known as the London Controlling Section which, amongst other things, was engaged in the deception and cover plans for Operation Overlord, the Allied invasion of Normandy.

His ashes are interred in Brookwood, Surrey, a cemetery so vast that at one time it had *two* railway lines delivering the dead from London. It has the distinction of being the largest cemetery in the United Kingdom and one of the largest in Europe. And if there are a lot of people living in London now, just think how many people who have lived and died there since Victorian times. As you would expect, it is teeming with the good, the bad, the ordinary, and the famous.

I had gone primarily looking for Dennis Wheatley and it was only when I got there that the enormity of the task came home to me. Although I knew he was in a particular area, it nevertheless seemed such a monumental task to track him down that it seemed rooted in futility. Imagine my delight therefore, when after searching increasingly in vain, so it seemed, and on the point of giving up, my excellent wife happened to stumble upon him where he had apparently been kicked into the long grass. A heart-shaped piece of pink granite about a foot square with the following etched upon it in black letters: *Dennis Wheatley Prince of Thriller Writers 1897-1977*. And that, literally, is it!

I picked it up. It didn't weigh that much. If you were expecting another confession here, expecting to hear that Dennis's stone now has pride of place beneath a cherry tree in my garden (where it would receive much more respect), you will be sadly disappointed. But perhaps it wouldn't have been such a bad thing to do after all. The stone may not even be anywhere near Dennis anyway as it might depend on how many people did as I did, picked up the stone but didn't quite put it back in the same place . . .

Was this his wish, to be buried in some insignificant plot, like some "inglorious Milton"? If so, he certainly got his wish and how incredibly modest! Surely such genius deserves a headstone as least as big as Wordsworth's (and that is modest enough, God knows) for a wordsmith such as Dennis who served his country in a way that is impossible to calculate, to say nothing of the pleasure he brought his legions of fans.

That I am grateful to my ancestors for my existence goes without saying, but I also bless them for the way many of them are clustered together in the cemeteries of Fordyce, Alvah and Portknockie: grandmothers, grandfathers, uncles and aunts. Having said that, I came to learn that just because it is written in stone, it does not mean that what you read on their headstones is completely accurate, nevertheless they make a very useful springboard for anyone delving into one's roots. And that is how this book began, many, many years ago.

I also realise all too well that this book is bound to appeal more to family members than the wider public.

That is understandable, but don't dismiss this book just because you are not genetically connected to me and you have never even heard of me before. There are plenty stories here to interest you: sad stories and tragic tales, stories of sex and violence and yes, even murder. And I hope you like mystery stories because there are a number of these too. Some I have solved; some may be solved in the years to come as more documents become available; some will always remain a mystery—but that does not preclude you from having a pretty good guess based on the balance of probability.

And if all that sounds too sensational or gloomy, on the happier side of life, there are a good number of births, naturally, and also a great deal of mirth, not forgetting a good helping of love and romance.

And don't forget those astonishing coincidences that I mentioned earlier.

Falkirk 2013

The Author's Addison Ancestors

Chapter One

Stormy Weather

"Hurry up, George! I can't hold on much longer!"

The voice sounds desperate, frightened and although I do not yet know the word, I would describe it as having more than a hint of panic about it. I am only five and although I do not fully realise it, I am facing the most dangerous time of my life since I was born. In those first few hours and days of life I was far too young to be aware of how serious my situation was, but this time I know something is wrong—very seriously wrong.

My mother is holding a tea tray to the small, four-paned window in the gable end of our little cottage in Crovie (pronounced Crivie), Banffshire, in a way rather reminiscent of that apocryphal tale about the Dutch boy who put his finger in the dyke and saved his town from drowning. But unlike him, whose finger fortunately happened to be of just the right dimensions, the tray is smaller than the window and furthermore, although she is pressing it against the window with all her strength, she is powerless to repel the forces of Nature and still the sea comes surging in. Canute could have told her.

Where my sister of twenty months is, I don't remember. Probably in her cot in my parents' bedroom at the back of the house, relatively safe and quite possibly sleeping, totally unaware of the drama unfolding just yards away. She was born just too late to have any recollection of the dramatic events unfolding just a matter of yards away. As for me, I am on the floor, too shocked to cry, appalled by the sight of the blood pouring from my knee, soaked to the skin, sitting in inches of water, not understanding why my safe world has been turned upside down, why the sea is coming into my house, why my mummy is not attending to my wounded knee, feeling shocked and the beginning of fear.

A few moments previously, I had been kneeling on the shelf of the gable end window, awestruck and mesmerised at the power of the waves, mountainous grey monsters, gathering their strength, curling in a fury of white water before unleashing themselves like missiles from a medieval trebuchet for yet another remorseless attack on our defenceless little house. An unequal combat in which there seemed to be only one possible winner. And yet it did not occur to me just how serious and potentially dangerous that spectacle was. In those innocent years, the raging sea was just an incredible sight, and such a sight that I had never witnessed before and I gazed at it with wide-eyed fascination.

I can't say for certain if the wave that shattered the glass of the window and cut my knee (I still bear the scar today) had picked up a pebble and thrown it with malicious intent, or if it was merely the enormous force of the water itself which broke it, but suddenly I found myself hosed backwards from several times my height into the room, as if I were nothing more substantial than a cork. But there, amidst a deluge of seawater, the resemblance ended just as suddenly as it had begun, when I landed with a thump upon the floor. I was, you may say, more than somewhat surprised at this sudden turn of events and lucky that on my descent I did not strike my head on some offending hard object which caused damage to the brain. Or maybe it did and the effects are just beginning to emerge more than half a century later.

Up in my bedroom, in the attic, on this never-to-be-forgotten day, my father was putting the finishing touches to the shutters he had been making for the gable end window in anticipation of what had just happened, happening. And, if events were not already dramatic enough, as he went outside to fit this hastily assembled homemade device to the gaping window, we were not to know, my mother and I, that it could well have been the last time we were to see him— for he was swept off his feet by the enormous backwards surge and had he not managed to wrap his arms round a clothes pole which providentially happened to be there, he would certainly have been swept away and it is unlikely that his body would ever have been recovered.

I have no recollection of how long it took him to finish his handiwork or how long it took him to fit it in place, but I do seem to remember that there was a fish, a big fish, like a cod, swimming about in our living room. It could certainly have come in through the window in those minutes which must have seemed like hours, before the shutter was fitted, or it might even have come down the chimney, for it is certainly a fact that the waves were higher than the house, shooting cascades of water down it. And if a fatty like Santa Claus can get down a narrow chimney, then I see no reason why a fish, even a very large fish, in those extraordinary conditions, could not, by some extraordinary fluke, have done likewise. I can even see it now, though you might dismiss it as just childish embroidery, especially since the distinction between fantasy and fact can become blurred and fused at the best of times over events long in the past, particularly in the mind of a five-year-old child.

At some time after my father fitted the shutters, he set off in search of help. We would have to evacuate. With the telephone wires down, he borrowed a car from someone, somewhere, and drove to my Uncle Jimmy's farm at Clayfolds in Alvah some four miles on the other side of Banff which is itself about eight or nine miles from Crovie as the seagull flies. The most likely person from whom he would have borrowed the car was his friend Miller Murray who lived in nearby Gardenstown, a thriving metropolis by Crovie standards. He was a baker by profession and I couldn't say if his name had anything to do with that or not but I think it suited him very well. Well done Mr and Mrs Murray.

At that time, Crovie and Gardenstown, little more than a mile apart, were linked by a coastal path, only accessible when the tide was out because the cliff jutted out into the sea at one point, necessitating a detour across the shingle before you could pick the path up again on the other side. That route was of course impossible, so supposing Miller did provide the car, follow my father's nightmare journey as he set off in that howling gale and lashing rain. No raincoat could have been protection against that. He would have been soaked to the skin long before he had negotiated that perilous journey along the path in front of the houses where he had nearly been swept away just a short time previously. Then there would have been the 1-in-7 hill up to the top of the cliff to the T-junction at Bracoden. Then the relatively flat road to the main road before plunging down towards the sea again in Gardenstown—a total distance of five miles or more. And all the time not knowing for certain if he would be able to borrow the car, then the car journey in the teeth of the gale, not knowing if uprooted trees would block his path, not knowing what was happening to us . . .

For her part, my mother must have been worried sick in view of my father's narrow escape earlier, wondering if he had even made it as far as the end of the village. Did she plead with him not to go, or did she see that as the only option, not knowing if the house would withstand the onslaught as gallons of water continued to be flushed down the chimney as minute by minute, the water in the room rose and rose, and with no power and the shadows in the room lengthening imperceptibly.

I imagine, with the ground floor swimming in water, we retired to my garret bedroom, closing the door at the bottom of the stairs behind us. I can imagine us all huddled up there together, the light of a Tilley lamp throwing long and eerie shadows into the darkness, the crashing of the waves thundering on the tiles, my mother desperately hoping that the roof would not cave in, my sister and I crying for reasons we could not understand, but knowing that something extraordinary was going on and that was reason enough to cry. I can imagine my mother comforting us as best she could but more frightened than us because she was more fully aware of the danger and as time dragged on and on and still my father and rescue did not come, she would have been unable to banish the nightmarish thought from her mind that the worst had happened and she might at this very moment be a widow. The other nightmare, how she would cope with two small children and no income and no house was, no doubt, one which would insist on nagging away at her, despite her very best attempts to not even contemplate it.

I have been talking about the last day of January 1953, the year that was to go down in history as the year of The Great Storm. If it was bad for us, in the North-East of Scotland, at the outer edges of the freak tidal surge which swept like a tsunami down the eastern coast of the British Isles—it was much worse for the east coast of England, particularly Norfolk, where it claimed the lives of 307 people. But in the low-lying Netherlands which got the full force of the surge, more than six times that figure drowned—to say nothing of 30,000 animals, mainly dairy cattle. Nobody's finger in any dyke, only the hand of God, could have prevented this tragedy. Incredibly, an astonishing sixth of the entire land area of the Netherlands was inundated.

Many years later I was to see the extent of the destruction for myself on a video and photographic exhibition in Middelburg, the provincial capital of Zeeland, which, of all the Dutch provinces bordering the North Sea was the one most severely affected—breached dykes, farmhouses marooned, houses reduced to skeletal ribs, the rich green grass of fields under feet of salty water, the cattle dead and bloated, looking as if those huge bellies must explode at any moment, expelling God knows what into the already fetid atmosphere. And thousands upon thousands of people evacuated and rendered homeless and jobless in a region whose main occupation is primarily dedicated to dairy farming. It was nothing short of a disaster of Biblical proportions.

My father did make it through to Clayfolds, eventually, and later than evening, when the storm had abated somewhat, we were rescued by my Uncle Jimmy and his orra loon, Gordon Geddes. For those of you who do not have the Doric, that's a man-about-the-farm who is expected to turn his hand to anything, though never in his wildest dreams, did Gordon imagine that he would be called upon to undergo a mercy mission like this. They set off in two cars and Gordon relates how it took an absolute age to get to Crovie because of uprooted trees and fallen telegraph poles with their loose wires lashing the skies like whips.

They parked the cars at the bottom of the cliff and by the light of their torches, made their way like crabs along the narrow path keeping their backs to the walls of the houses. When they reached our house, Number Twenty-three, at one of the narrowest points, just where the path takes a bend away from the shore before it comes closer to the sea again, apart from a very relieved woman, they found the floor swimming in water, just as I remembered. But what Gordon remembers most was the astonishing sight of the table, flattened, with a huge boulder lying on top of it, heavier than he could lift. I could have been under that!

My parents put some clothes and some other essentials in suitcases and like refugees, we made our way to the cars.

Chapter Two

Crovie

Our tiny cottage consisted of two rooms downstairs plus a kitchen and an outside toilet up the close, bang up against the cliff. Upstairs, there was a general-purpose attic which, as I have already said, served as my bedroom and which was reached by a flight of steep wooden stairs concealed behind a door in the connecting passage. This door was held shut by a snib, which meant of course, that once I had retired to bed, I was effectively imprisoned there for the night until released by my parents the next morning. Very practical for the purposes of parental privacy, but the Health and Safety boys would have a field day today.

Crovie, like the better-known Pennan, which is only a few miles along the Buchan coast and known to millions thanks to the film *Local Hero*, is a fishing village strung out along the foot of sheer cliffs. The houses, with the exception of one small inlet, are only yards from the sea and are built gable-end on to the sea to present the smallest target to the sea as a precaution against the sort of thing that happened most spectacularly in 1953. It consists of something like sixty houses with a footpath running parallel to the shore, often festooned with washing, and a pier jutting out into Gamrie Bay. We lived at Number 23. The inhabitants were fishermen, naturally, and I'm not making any allegations about inbreeding, but nearly everyone was called West.

It was, as you can imagine, a tight, close-knit community and we were outsiders. For a start, my father was not a fisherman, who tended to be rather wealthy, but a poor teacher at Bracoden, a mile or so away at the top of the cliff. I hope you will not consider me too boastful, but I know from old photographs that until the age of about three, we were so poor that all my clothes were knitted by my mother (or someone else). I do seem to have had shoes however, or sandals at least, and I was certainly not lacking in toys.

I had a bogie my father made, a wooden box on wheels with a long handle and which I would put things in and tow behind me. For a change, I also had a sort of headless wooden horse on wheels which I pushed people about on. In one photo, a big, fat blonde boy about the same age as me but twice the girth, is astride the horse while my right foot is raised high with the effort required to push him. Apart from the rotundity of my passenger, the path along the front of the houses was not concreted as it is now but as rough and bumpy as the road to ruin. I also had a wheelbarrow which was probably also made by my father, resurrecting a discarded pram wheel, which for all I know, he might have found lying on the beach. There was another set of wheels I had, but not made by my father—a tricycle.

Later I graduated to a much bigger trike and my sister fell heir to the one I had broken in. Just one example of how coming second in the family actually means you finish first: most of your toys and most of your clothes have been tried and broken in first, especially if you happen to be of the same sex. Even better, you have more experienced parents who have learned from their mistakes. You reap the benefits of all the practicing they did on your older sibling: it was *you* they were preparing for. But that is by the way.

I had the sea and the shore on my doorstep and although there was no sand, I was as happy as the proverbial sandboy. I was also lucky to have such practical parents who could clothe me and provide the means of my own entertainment. By the time my sister was born and able to sit up on her own, times must have been a bit better. As the photographic evidence shows, she is wearing clothes that had come out of a shop. There is also one of me pushing her in a carrycot and I too am wearing clothes that had not been wrought by my mother's knitting needles.

In a place where it takes a generation for an incomer to *begin* to be accepted, we were not, firstly because of my father's profession as I said, secondly because my mother was English and thirdly, and probably most significantly, my parents were not religious in the narrow-minded, Bible-thumping, Sabbath-observing sense of the word as observed by the villagers—who were not slow to let us know the error of our ways.

One Sunday, a warm and sunny day it was, my mother was giving me an airing in my pram when she was stopped by a crone who transfixed her with a glittering eye.

"That child should be wearing a hat on the Sabbath day," she admonished my mother severely.

My mother tended to have a short fuse and did not take this advice kindly. "You try putting it on him then!" she returned, thrusting the offending garment at her. "See if you can make him wear it!"

She also fell foul of the village when her mother, my grandmother, died unexpectedly while she was staying with us. The custom in the village was for the open coffin to be paraded along the street so the villagers could take their final farewells. Although they scarcely knew my grandmother by sight, let alone as a person, it did not go down well in the village that my mother refused to have anything to do with this tradition: her with her snooty, southern, heathenish ways.

They claimed to be good Christians, fundamentalists who did all the Right Things, doing nothing on a Sunday except going to church and reading the Bible (not to mention policing blasphemous babies and keeping a sharp lookout for other possible transgressors). They also regarded modern technology as the invention of the Devil. Nevertheless, it was permitted to have shortwave radio on board *Maggie Jean* or whatever dame they named their fishing vessel after, by special arrangement with the Creator apparently.

Then there was the case of the family in Gardenstown, just along the bay, but a bigger community since the cliffs being less precipitous there, it permitted the construction of dwellings which clambered up the hill. The inhabitants of that community were nevertheless identical in their rigorous observance of their strict moral code. The story goes that the daughter of one particular family fell in love with a boy who was not of the persuasion and when she would not give him up, was ostracised by her parents and made to have her meals alone in her bedroom until she regained her wits.

There were some kind people in Crovie though: people who were kind to their own kind. Before the storm really broke, for instance, those who lived in the houses further back permitted the inhabitants of those closest to the shore to store precious items there, even furniture. It was not an offer that was extended to us however. In fact, probably because they were in radio contact with boats scrambling for shore, they knew of the approaching storm and its severity before us but no-one thought to mention it to us. Had they done so, perhaps my father would have had the window boarded up in time.

It is one thing to be ignored but another to be singled out for a puerile act of spite. One day a man came to the door requesting my father's help. His car would not start but he thought if my father gave him a push that would do the trick. Because there was no room to park at the bottom of the cliff, cars were kept at a space higher up and some even had wooden garages there. I suppose it might have occurred to my father to wonder why he was being singled out for help in this way rather than one of the Chosen Few, but in any case it was not an offer he could refuse, for to do so would be cited as evidence as how standoffish he was, unfriendly and unwilling to help a neighbour in need. On the other hand, to lend assistance in this way might be a favour returned in the future and even if it were not, at least the word would get about that heathen though he may be, at least he was a helpful heathen. Nor was it that small a request either, for it was quite a trek up that hill to where the garages were. In winter we used to sledge down it, my father and I, hurtling down the incline, with me terrified that he would not be able to make the sledge turn at the bottom and we would plunge straight on and down into the harbour.

I was accustomed to that walk every day to school, a long way for very short legs up such a steep gradient and

I accompanied my father that evening. I don't remember anything of the journey but I imagine my father and the man chatted amicably and even more strangely, I don't remember my father's reaction when he saw the car facing up, not down the hill, nor when the "benighted" motorist simply climbed into his car, started it up and drove away.

If that was a bad experience for my father, he had a worse one earlier in our Crovie days, though I think it is fair to say it was even worse for my mother and me. My mother was pregnant and I was a toddler, still unsteady on my feet when one day the village policeman came to call, not on a matter of duty I hasten to add, but because he was a friend and was just dropping in. He had his Alsatian with him and I tottered towards the dog with my newly-acquired walking skills and with my tiny hand outstretched.

"No, David, don't touch the doggie," was all my mother managed to get out before the next second, my head disappeared into the brute's mouth. Fortunately, I have no memory of this incident and unlike my knee, fortunately bear no scar as a souvenir, which is the right way to arrange it should you wish to have scars to remind you of your passage through life's traumas. Nor has the incident given me even a subconscious fear of dogs—possibly because we always had one throughout my childhood years and indeed even up to when I left to go to university.

The event did have a lasting effect on my mother however. The sight of her first-born being devoured like Granny in *Little Red Riding Hood* had such an alarming effect on her that she had a miscarriage. What's worse, it caused her to fail to conceive for some time thereafter due, it is believed, to a residual blood clot or a tear in her cervix. Thus, at a very early age, I was unwittingly responsible for the death of a sibling and the delayed arrival of another. As a matter of fact, my sister should be eternally grateful to me, for if it were not for me, she would not have been born at all.

She, like myself, was born in Banff, in Chalmers Hospital to be precise, and I think seeing her for the first time is my earliest memory. Like the storm, it was another shocking experience, though nothing like as traumatic. Never having been very good at Maths, I nevertheless am able to calculate, without pencil and paper even, since there are four years between us, that I was four years old when this event happened. She was lying in her cot in the hospital, probably a day young. I am not sure what I expected to see, but certainly not the sight that I now beheld. The birth must have been a difficult one for she was very badly bruised—black and blue all over as though someone had given her a right good hiding. Nevertheless, I remember overcoming my shock and gazing with tenderness at the poor mite as I slid a Rich Tea biscuit (which I had filched from home), between the bars of her cot and which I laid gently on her blanket so as not to disturb her beauty sleep which, even I could see, she needed a great deal of.

"That's for her cup of tea," I explained and couldn't understand why everyone was laughing at such an act of kindness.

It was not the only time that I provoked mirth in my early days at Crovie. One day I was walking along the shore, towards Gardenstown, where the bay broadened out to form a pebble beach. I suspect I was alone, that it was in my pre-school days and if so, then the story could only have got back to my parents by the fisherman—which might just go to show that the residents of Crovie were not all as unfriendly and bigoted as I have depicted.

The fisherman had dragged his rowing boat up onto the beach and was engaged upon painting it. I could not understand what he was doing, but I could see that the boat was changing colour with every stroke of his brush. It looked like an act of vandalism to me and I wanted to know what he was up to.

"Are you makin' a mess?" I asked.

Perhaps I had been painting one day and got the paint everywhere as toddlers tend to do, or perhaps I got the idea of a mess from being chastised for strewing my toys about the place, though in post-war Britain where everything was rationed, together with my parents' poverty, it is hard to imagine there could have been very many of them to create much of a clutter. With the exception of the tricycle, those other toys I mentioned would have remained outside. Maybe there were a few wooden bricks. You can create quite a good impression of chaos with a few of them if you leave them lying about. I have never been the tidiest of people: I just can't be bothered with it. And so, to my sins, you may add, if you wish, innate idleness.

And to that you can certainly add gross stupidity, or to be fair, naivety, which would be a kinder term. We had no such thing as a bathroom of course. I don't know anything about my parents' ablutions which they must have performed at the kitchen sink, but presumably once in a while they squeezed into the same tin bath as I did in front of the fire, with water they would have heated on it.

One evening I was just about to get into the bath when a visitor called and my parents were distracted. Unfortunately, it coincided with the very same time that my parents deemed me old enough to wear a watch. It seemed a symbol of, if not quite maturity itself, at least a passage from infancy into childhood. It might have been a present for my fifth birthday. It might not have been new, more than likely its provenance was from some family member and might have had some sentimental value. I wore it with pride, looking at it every few seconds though I doubt if I could even tell the time at that stage. I certainly couldn't tell it by that watch, at least, not after I had immersed it in the bath. I remember crying out to the company in surprise and alarm: "My watch isn't working!" Naturally I was very upset at the watch's demise and the backward step it represented in my development. It was not, I think, until I attained double figures that I was entrusted with my trusty Ingersoll.

As I said above, Crovie could have given me a craven fear of the canine race, especially big dogs and a special prejudice against German Shepherds, but it didn't. And it might have given me a fear of water, given that night of the Great Storm—my mother certainly claimed it did, citing my reluctance to go anywhere near soap and water, but the truth is it only did so to a slight extent. I do treat water with respect, nevertheless I taught myself to swim and often courageously venture out of my depth into the briny which I much prefer to swim in than a pool. But Crovie *did* leave me with one lasting legacy—a fear of feathers.

My mother's theory was that my phobia dates back to a time when someone tickled me with a feather. I was lying in my pram, helpless and perhaps hatless, who knows, especially if it was not the Sabbath. But who was that someone? Surely my mother must have known the perpetrator if that was her explanation—unless she found an abandoned feather in my pram (probably a white one from a seagull) like something out of the First World War where alleged cowards were given this symbol of their assumed cowardice, normally by middleclass women who knew nothing of the horrors of the trenches.

I put my hand up to being a coward if feathers has anything to do with it, particularly if there is blood mixed up with them and especially if they are on big, live birds with flapping wings. How large a part this episode in the pram played in my pteronophobia I can't be certain, but it was certainly reinforced when, some years later, when, as I was helping my Aunt Janet at Clayfolds to collect eggs, a hen flew from her perch, smack into my face.

The White Queen in *Through the Looking Glass* famously boasted that she could believe in six impossible things before breakfast, while I, on the other hand, (much more modestly) can think of four possible ways that eggs can be served up *for* breakfast. I thought I was merely collecting eggs, but the hen naturally had a different take on the proceedings and gave me a good slapping about the face with her wings for kidnapping her embryonic children, which of course, I thoroughly deserved for such a henous [sic] crime. Who would have thought that a hen brain could have shown such maternal instincts? But what I would *really* like to know is where was my mother when *her* chick, powerless in his pram, was being subjected to an attack of tickling by feather? Did she imagine I was screaming with laughter?

Anyway, ever since the Clayfolds incident, I have chickened out of all contact with poultry, apart from a dead hen on a plate, and of course I never touch the wings, though I marvel at how small and puny they are, like the absurd forearms of Tyrannosaurus Rex, and wonder why I should be so scared of them. But of course, denuded of feathers and perfectly still, there is nothing to be frightened of—yet to this day, I never choose chicken wings at a restaurant and when I am carving the Sunday roast chicken, I leave the wings alone.

It still sends shivers down my spine when I think about it. I can see it still, unreeling before my eyes like a horror movie, when one day my Aunt Janet happened to open a door in the kitchen which I knew led up a flight of stairs to my cousin George's bedroom, like mine in Crovie, only behind this door was a dead hen hanging upside down from a hook. How I pitied poor George having to pass this feathered corpse on his way to bed and his nightmares as he slept (if he could) with that *thing* down below. Even with the door shut, I gave it as wide a berth as possible as I knew what lay behind.

But of course, my sympathy was wasted. George was used to such sights. Just as on another occasion I marvelled when another cousin, Graham Chalmers (and of whom more later) who, looking for a pail for some reason, thought he had found one in his kitchen, but to his irritation, found it occupied by a dead hen which he picked up by the feet and unceremoniously dumped back in with a feathery plop, as if it were the most natural thing in the world to find feathered corpses in any convenient kitchen receptacle.

Nearly twenty years later, I took my fiancée, as she was then, on a visit to Crovie to let her see that I did not emerge from a swamp or from under a stone, but from here, from this picturesque little fishing village on the shores of the Moray Firth. Crovie, by this time, the fishermen, having mainly sailed away after the Great Storm, had turned into a place of bijou seaside residences, second homes for the rich and affluent of Banff, or white settlers from England, though one wonders why in the case of the former they would bother—it's hardly as if Banff is miles from the sea. Our dentist bought our house as a matter of fact. You will meet him later too.

As it happens, on this nostalgic trip back to the past, I had an encounter with a fisherman—not the "messy" one, I presume, but from the length of his white whiskers, I dare say there was an outside chance he might have been the same one. He certainly was not one of the foreigners from down south anyway.

As we were walking towards Gardenstown, my lady friend, a geography graduate, was admiring the finest example of puddingstone rock that it had ever been her good fortune to come across, when we came across a stricken gull. It did not appear to be in pain, but there was obviously something wrong with it, for instead of flying off as we approached, it just sat there watching us closely, opening its beak in a threatening way as we came even closer, though it uttered not a sound.

Imagine the courage it took for me to approach that bird with its fearsome yellow beak with the bright crimson spots, twisting its neck as I came nearer, ready to defend itself by stabbing that fearsome weapon right into my hand. Of course I could have walked on by, but for me that was not an option. I could not be like the Levite and cross to the other side of the street, for my conscience would not allow it. I have an innate love of animals, inherited from both my parents.

My father, the son and grandson of a farmer and who had three brothers who all became farmers, felt too much sympathy for the animals to follow in the family footsteps and went in for teaching instead. My mother was even more tender-hearted than that. Once, in Egypt, during the war, she came upon a donkey which an Arab was beating mercilessly with a stick in an effort to make the poor beast stand up. The problem was that it was an impossible task for the poor creature since it was so over-laden. My mother wrested the stick from the man and although she had no Arabic and he almost certainly had no English, she made him understand that he was to reduce the load to what she considered an acceptable size. He was so terrified of being beaten with his own stick by this mad, pint-sized Englishwoman, that he did as he was told. She also told him not to do it again in future.

Apart from having no desire to have my hand slashed open and because of my fear of feathers, I could not bear to touch the injured bird, so I dropped my jumper over it and picked it up, amazed at how light it was. But what now? I suppose I had some vague idea of taking it to a vet who could put it down humanely or something. On the way however, I encountered the aforementioned whiskery fisherman and showed him what I was carrying. Perhaps he would have some idea what to do with it.

"Aye, ah ken," he said philosophically, "she's been lyin' there for twa days noo." As he passed on he added, "She'll sail awa' the nicht."

I was struck with the appropriateness of the euphemism coming from the mouth of a fisherman and also with the wisdom of his words. Gently, I laid the bird down in the grass, just off the path, to let nature take its course.

Chapter Three

The War and Me

The invention of the internal combustion engine, followed by the jet engine, and now the Internet, where you need not travel any further (at least initially) than your computer chair, have all had a profound effect on widening the scope of possible choices from whom one might eventually chose a life-long partner. With this increased selection, one may have supposed there would be a better-than-ever chance of finding the perfect mate. In actual fact however, this does not appear to be the case: a prospective partner tends to be not so much for life but just a Christmas or two.

My paternal grandparents, being from farming stock, were always unlikely to move far from home and although they had rather more opportunity to travel even further afield than their parents, none of my father's brothers seem to have cast the net any further than a twenty-mile radius. My only uncle on my mother's side, Uncle Tommy, didn't even go that far. He literally married the girl next door. But now, with the facility to travel even further afield and more cheaply than ever before, what is surprising, at least to me, is how many of my cousins (I had 27 first cousins once upon a time but some are in heaven now) still seem to have met their fate within the same narrow radius as their forefathers.

My parents however, were the exception, travelling halfway round the world before their paths crossed.

Of course if it had not been for the war, it is extremely unlikely that they would ever have met. In fact, I don't know what my mother would have done without the war, for she at least, (I am not sure about my father) was convinced that there was one, and only one person, in the entire world with whom you could spend the rest of your life in connubial bliss—which makes the finding of the proverbial needle in the haystack sound like the sort of thing you could just dash off before lunch, after a long lie-in. Certainly I never ever heard my parents arguing. Not even once. Which is remarkable in any marriage, but astounding in my mother's case, since she was hardly patience personified.

They both happened to be assigned to the Middle East together. He was with Signals in the RAF, (Addison G.M. 1366459); she was a nurse in General Hospital No 41, El Qantara, on the east side of the Suez Canal, some thirty miles south of Port Said. On the platform of the railway station, there was a tall woman struggling with her luggage.

"Here, let me give you a hand with that," said my mother who was about half the size of the other, despite the fact that she had her own luggage to contend with too.

It was the start of a friendship that lasted all their lives and the tall woman turned out to be my father's sister, Georgina. That was her Sunday name and she never used it, not even then. To her colleagues she was known as "Addie" but after the war she was always known as "Gina" though she used the full handle when she signed her name including an L for Louisa. Through her, my mother met my father and the result, in due course, was me. But after the war, and with her biological clock ticking (she was nearly 36) my mother, it seems, was in no hurry to jump into marriage, nor was my father. Had it not been for the event I am just about to relate, who knows when they may have finally taken the plunge—and then where would I have been?

They were going to be meeting at and staying with my mother's brother and his wife, my future Uncle Tommy and Aunt Nan, but there was a problem. During their visit, Tommy and Nan were going to a wedding and would be staying away overnight, leaving my parents alone in the house unchaperoned. Tommy and Nan themselves were an old married couple: they were married in 1933.

To my parents this posed a knotty problem. No matter that they were strangers in this town, where no-one knew them and for all the neighbours knew or cared, they may well have *been* married. Furthermore, even if they *were* left alone, that did not automatically mean that they must succumb to temptation. But from my parents' point of view, *they* knew they were not married and could not bear the stigma of being labelled as "living in sin" as the phrase had it, with people looking at them in a knowing way, tut-tutting behind their backs, certain that they were at it like rabbits.

Amongst their generation they were not unique and it was a prudery that stayed with them all their lives. Because of their late start in the marriage stakes, it meant that my school friends' parents were considerably younger than mine and this narrow-minded attitude to sex meant that when it was "discovered" by me and others during the Swinging Sixties, I was the teenager with the most unliberated parents on the planet. Well, apart from my future fiancée's that is—but that comes later.

So what were my parents to do? Cancel their visit? Yet they were desperate to meet, my father being in the North-East of Scotland and my mother in the North-East of England. It was a huge dilemma until my Aunt came up with the solution.

"Why don't you two get married?" she suggested.

And so, like the eponymous protagonist, Jane Eyre, famously informed her reader, I can inform you they did indeed get married, though the manner of it was scandalous. Like young romantics, despite their ages, they ran away together and only informed their parents after the deed had been done, ironically giving rise to great speculation that they "had to get married"—so much sudden haste after this protracted romance which didn't look as if it was going anywhere very fast! How carefully my grandparents must have counted the months until I was born! Naturally, there was nothing shady about the circumstances of my conception, but perhaps it was just as well all the same that I was not born prematurely.

My mother never talked about her elopement, or the war. It was only in her latter years when she moved from Banffshire to be near my sister, that she leaked snippets which my sister gleaned and passed on to me. There are also masses of old photos, most of which mean nothing to me—lots of people, colleagues and patients, together with some faces I do recognise, like my father of course, and my Aunt Gina and Uncle Jack, and from which I have been able to piece together some of the story she never told me. But there is not a single photo of their wedding.

Happiness and war seem an oxymoron but I remember my Uncle Jack once telling me he had a good war and I can see why. Apart from meeting my Aunt Gina there, he was very musical and played in a band or maybe even an orchestra. It is good to know there was some culture amongst the carnage, though how much they saw of the latter I do not know but it was an occupational hazard for a nurse after all, especially one who worked in theatre, which to my mind at least, somewhat bizarrely, my mother said was the aspect of the job she liked best. In any case, amidst the slings and arrows of the outrageous fortunes of war, there seem to have been enough of Cupid's arrows flying about to re-enact the battle of Agincourt.

There is a photo of my mother in a dress next to a soldier in his regulation shorts. On the back is written, "The happy couple". Then there is another photo of her standing on the same man's shoulders. They are both wearing the same clothes. I hope, and remember this is my mother we are talking about, he was gentleman enough to resist the temptation to look up. On the back she has written, "High up in the world for a change".

Just about the only thing my mother did tell me about the war was that her fellow nurses (it's inconceivable that her patients would have been so rude) used to call her "duck arse" because her posterior was so near the ground. In yet another photo she is standing next to a very tall South African wearing a kilt. He has his left arm outstretched in a casual sort of way over my mother's head while she is following the slope of his arm upwards with her eyes. She fits under his oxter perfectly. He looks taller than the 6 foot 2 attributed to him but it does give you a sense of my mother's diminutive stature and also explains why I didn't have a snowball's chance in hell of being tall.

There are more photos of my mother and the man doing gymnastics on the beach and one of him throwing my mother backwards into the sea and then this one of them in the prow of a rowing boat, which is significant. He is looking up at her adoringly, whilst she is looking down at him. Unfortunately her face is in shadow and despite her having taken off her sunglasses, it's impossible to make out her expression. What is intriguing about this photo is that on the back she has written, "Can you see the supposed love light?" To whom was this question addressed? What is the significance of the crucial word "supposed"? Was the love on her part beginning to wane?

Your guess is as good as mine but you will have already guessed that this man was not my father, though he might have been had the love-light not waned. She did admit to being engaged to someone before my father but she called it off as it "just didn't feel right" and that's all she ever said on the matter.

Then there was another fellow who appears in lots of photos, a lot more than the other. I suppose many would call him handsome but he looks a bit flash to me with his neatly trimmed circumflex moustache, a sort of fairish Clark Gable in *Gone With the Wind*.

In fact there are so many of him that it wouldn't surprise me if *he* was the fiancé and not the other bloke who is not identified on any of the photos. "Clark Gable's" name was Jack Duncan R.E., known as "Jack the Dunk", so it says in my mother's rather challenging calligraphy on the back of several photos. They all seem to have had nicknames for each other. My mother's was

27

"Jet" (when it was not "duck arse") and had nothing to do with the colour of her hair; it was merely her initials which I remember seeing stencilled in thick black letters on a suitcase and which I once took to be the make of the case.

There are many, many photos of Jack and my mother. They seemed to have spent a lot of time together and in different places, whereas there are none at all with my father. I don't know when exactly she met him or how long after they met that they became "an item" as they say nowadays. It seems they met when he came on leave to visit Gina and it looks like it might have been a case of love at first sight and long distance after that. There is a photo of my father sitting in a canvas chair in exotic-looking gardens with less attractive buildings in the background. On the back he has written, "Writing to you from Tel Aviv. All my love. George". If the old adage that opposites attract is true, then their handwriting may well be the proof of that, for my father's handwriting was beautifully formed.

And then there is a snap of my mother and Jack the Dunk on which my mum has written, "Taken on the eve of his departure". Where? When? For how long? Did he return? Or was it sometime after this that she met my father and sent him a "Dear Jack" letter? Oh, the questions you wish you had asked when you had the opportunity—if you could have been assured of answers! I am sure after my mother was dead Gina would have told me, if only I had thought to ask, or had I been writing this book then.

One thing I didn't need to ask her, as anyone who has ever seen films set in the Forties knows very well, in those days just about everyone smoked like chimneys, enough to give that arch anti-smoking campaigner James I a fatal heart attack if he had not been dead for well over three hundred years already. My mother was no exception and there are some photos of her holding the pernicious weed but I never saw her with one in real life. That's because even before she ever clapped eyes on me, I made her feel sick. We know now the harm that can be done to the foetus in the womb by the mother smoking, but way back then, mother Nature told my mother and she gave it up, never to start again, unlike my father who smoked both cigarettes and a pipe until the day he died and it wasn't that that killed him either.

I don't know what happened to Jack. He is probably dead too now but I sincerely hope that he survived the war and his broken heart, and found happiness and another lady, some other time, some other place. There is a chance he might not have made it through the war though. On the back of a snap of some anonymous chap, my mother has written, "Killed by a mine in the desert".

Love-life apart, as the photographs show, (most of them almost certainly taken by that other Jack, Jack Ingram) when they were not working, my mother, Gina and Jack, all seemed to have had plenty of opportunities to enjoy themselves, swimming and fooling about in the water, larking in the sand or merely being lazy and lying in the sun for hours. Years and years later, Gina paid the price: she contracted melanoma and had to have a great chunk taken out of her leg so it was as thin as a peg leg that you associate with the pirates in children's stories.

They also swam in the Suez Canal and there was a lido at El Qantara where my mother won second prize for diving at a swimming gala, a skill I never knew she possessed and which she must have taught herself. I think she must have been a natural, took to it like a duck to water, but then being equipped with that aforementioned aquatic bird's nether regions, it gave her an unfair advantage when it came to this competition. It's surprising in fact that she wasn't disqualified or didn't win the damned thing outright.

I suppose you could argue that another good thing about Jack and Gina's war, and that of my parents, was the opportunity it gave them to travel. They saw places they would never ever, in their wildest dreams, have expected to visit had it not been for this world-wide conflict—far flung places such as Egypt, Palestine and Syria, to name but three. Like some people's lives, the history of this area is complicated and some of the places they visited are now in different countries. For instance, my mother, looking very tropical in her white uniform and pith helmet, was stationed at General Hospital No 23 at the exotically named Sarafand. Sarafand today is just south of Haifa, was in Palestine then and is in what we call Israel now, just like Herzliya, where she was also stationed, which is just south of Tel Aviv.

Not only did my mother travel far away but she did so in style, sailed on a Cunard liner, no less. Only it was wartime and it was not exactly a luxury cruise. The liner in question was the Queen Mary. I was lucky enough to visit the old lady at her retirement home at Long Beach, California, at the end of my year's teaching exchange to Montana in 1979. Knowing my mother's association with her, I was interested to see an exhibition of what she (the Queen) had looked like during the war when she was kitted out as a troop ship. No surprise at all to see it was not in the least luxurious, as you would expect in those circumstances, but it did come as a massive shock to me, just as it might have done to posh fare-paying passengers up to as late as 1967 when she was decommissioned—to discover that in exchange for a goodly number of their pounds and dollars, they could enjoy the experience of plumbing that looked as if Noah himself might have installed it, though in actual fact it was merely thirty-three years old, dating from the year the Queen Mary was built in 1934.

So not the high life on the high seas for my mother when she travelled to the theatre of war. Likewise life in the Kaiser's Palace in Jerusalem was not for her the epitome of gracious and luxurious living either: it was the 61st General Hospital. She also had connections with the Petit Palais in Kifisia, a northern suburb of Athens. How that had come down in the world too! It was the nurses' mess.

On the other hand, and this does sound a bit more swanky and sophisticated, when she was stationed at the 13th General Hospital in Suez, she attended a cocktail party hosted by Shell. But I suppose it all depends on what was available to make the cocktails. Since grapes would have been in short supply and figs plentiful in those parts, one trusts that Shell could come up with more than syrup of figs for her delectation.

There was even the opportunity to do a bit of sightseeing too. Once, she and three other nurses hired a car and a driver and went from Palestine to Syria. At the border, not a machine gun or a rifle or a single strand of barbed wire in sight, only a donkey which my mother and another nurse made a great deal of fuss over. Their destination was Baalbek, one of the best-preserved

Roman sites in the world, now a World Heritage site and now in Lebanon. In Roman times it was known as Heliopolis or Sun City and home to two of my favourite gods, Venus and Bacchus. They also worshipped Jupiter but I suppose they felt they had to, as being head honcho he would have got a bit upset if they had missed him out. Those gods were extremely puerile, took the strunts at the slightest thing.

She also visited Damascus, Bethlehem and Jericho. I remember once after Sunday school at Ternemny, the Reverend Dickie came in to see my parents' snaps of the religious sites in the Holy Land. And nearer to "home" in Egypt, my mother went to Cairo and Alexandria where she visited the zoo. She would. And goodness knows where they came from or who looked after them (though my mum is a likely suspect) but a number of dogs also feature in her photos. I would not have thought that a pet would have figured high in the priorities of Her Majesty's Government Forces or even been allowed, but there they are all the same, like unofficial mascots. Probably strays my mother rescued.

She and Gina also visited the gardens at Al Isma'iliya on Lake Timsah, one of the Bitter Lakes halfway between Port Said and Suez. Another swimming opportunity and on one occasion at least, a bunch of them drove the jeeps down there for a picnic.

There were the ubiquitous flies and fleas and the sand and the unremitting sun and we will pass hastily over the latrines except to say they seem to have been modelled on the communal Roman model, or at least the men's were. And there was the lack of basic home comforts, such as a bath in which you could stretch out. All my mother and her mates had for a bath was a canvas receptacle about two feet square and lucky if the water was six inches deep, with no such thing as a bathroom for privacy. No wonder they did so much swimming.

In addition to these inconveniences and others beyond my powers to conceive, I remember my mother telling me that before they bit into a biscuit, they tapped it on the table to get the weevils out—an image which makes you fear the worst as far as the quality of the mass-produced food they ate in the mess was concerned. Despite all that, it would not surprise me to learn, as my Uncle Jack hinted, and seen especially through the rose-tinted spectacles of nostalgia, that there was much they *did* enjoy about their war and they had the time of their lives.

One thing is certainly true—had it not been for the war, their lives would have turned out utterly differently, not least in the matter of meeting spouses from much further afield than the next parish, like generations of their ancestors had been accustomed to do. As Winston Churchill might have put it had he bothered to put his mighty mind to the phenomenon: *never have so many owed so much to the field of human conflict.* I include myself amongst that number. But for the war there would have been no me, at least not in my present form.

Chapter Four

The Sins of the Fathers

Children can be a severe disappointment to their parents. I should know. I was one. The fact is I was never very good at anything and yet I ended up being a very great disappointment without even trying. To be honest, I never *tried* to be good at anything and couldn't care less that I wasn't. I suppose you may say I lacked the competitive spirit, or I suppose you could say I was lazy. Both may be correct. Anyway, my parents never expressed their feelings about my shortcomings. Perhaps if they had, some shame might have goaded me into trying—I won't say harder, but just a little bit, at my schoolwork for instance.

Maybe it was the gods wreaking their revenge, for my father and my Aunt Gina were severe disappointments to *their* parents. A long, long time later, long after my father died, when my mother moved from Banffshire to Thurso, she confided to my sister that her mother-in-law hardly welcomed her with open arms, to put it mildly. Although the reasons were never voiced, they were not hard to seek.

For a start she was English but the main reason was that my grandparents were staunchly Presbyterian and not only was my mother brought up in the Church of England, (Low Church, mercifully) but horror of horrors, she had been educated at the illustrious-sounding—wait for it, you can just imagine my grandmother's hair standing on end—the Roman

Catholic Convent of the Canonesses of St Augustine
Boarding School in Hull. It had been founded in 1907
by a group of French nuns who, during the Third
Republic under the rabid anti-clerical Prime Minister,
Emile Combes (1902-1905), had fled from Versailles
as the government set about secularising state and
education. By 1904 almost 10,000 religious schools had
been closed down and thousands of nuns and priests
had fled the country.

I am sure my grandmother, at least, must have
thought my father could have chosen more wisely and
this perceived disapproval of my mother played no
small part in their decision to elope and avoid the fuss
of a wedding, apart from the time it would have taken
to arrange such an event, time they did not have if
they were to be together when my Uncle Tommy and
Aunt Nan abandoned them to attend the nuptials of
that other couple. Such a decision would hardly have
endeared the newly-weds to my grandparents and I
would have loved to have been present when my father
and his new bride met them for the first time after their
return. Was it twenty degrees of frost or a towering
volcano that greeted them?

One can only speculate therefore on the reaction
when Aunt Gina announced that she was marrying
Jack Ingram, an Englishman and a Catholic to boot.
At that time Jack was pretty devout although in an
amazing volte-face he later became as disenchanted as
he had been fervent about the Church. I think it had
something to do with his second daughter, my cousin
Frances, being Downs Syndrome. But of course my
grandparents could not have foreseen that scenario
which might have eased their minds a little, nor even

more reassuringly, that Gina would never "turn" though their granddaughter, Margaret, was brought up in the Old Religion and went on to marry an ardent Catholic herself, producing ten children, one, sadly, being a cot death. Margaret underwent not one, but two hip replacements, neither of which turned out to be in the least effective as a method of birth control. Like Queen Victoria, my Aunt Gina was not amused, accusing her son-in-law of treating Margaret "like a rabbit".

Jack and Gina were married soon after the war ended. My father was the best man; my Aunt Trixie, Gina's younger sister, the bridesmaid. Jack whisked his new bride off to Nottingham, which, although it was not at the end of the earth exactly, was a lot further away than it is today and certainly a lot further away than Crovie.

Similarly, my granny need not have worried about my mother's religious background for she was a member and regular attender of the Church of Scotland, at least from the time when she had to as the dominie's wife in Deskford. As for her education, Public schools (by which, somewhat confusingly, we are meant to understand "private") are a lot more common in England than north of the Border—with the exception of Edinburgh where they constitute a quarter of the provision.

I like to think that I went to a public school myself. In fact, all the schools I attended were public schools, following in the best traditions of 19th century Scottish education, where everyone from the laird's son to the son of a peasant crofter sat together in the same class and where the latter could aspire to be what was known as the "lad o' pairts" or all-round achiever, and who, despite his humble background, could attain dizzying heights of academic success. My mother's school was not a Public school in that sense, but neither was it loaded with the connotations of privilege and snobbery with which Public schools are associated in Scotland (or England for that matter)—it was just a Roman Catholic school that took in some non-Catholic girls for a bit of well-meaning indoctrination and lessons on how to be a lady. In both of these aims they failed spectacularly as far as my mother was concerned.

Being one of the "underprivileged", I have always felt a sense of sympathy for those poor kids who are packaged off at the age of six or thereabouts, or later, for a "better" education out of sight and sound of the parents, but such sympathy would have been wasted on my mother, for it was a relief for her to get away from home. It was not a happy place when my grandfather was back from the seas. Whether he had a girl in every port I couldn't say, but I would not lay any money against it.

When my grandmother died, he was living with his mistress, or not to put too fine a point on it, a "prostitute", as my mother put it more bluntly. She began as a maid in my grandparents' house which is how my grandfather came to know her in both the literal and Biblical sense. When he died, she inherited all his worldly goods, including all those curios he had picked up on his travels and which probably would be worth a fortune today. The maid, you could say, made good in the end.

She did not, however, inherit the grey parrot which was free to roam the house and which used to stick his head around the door and greet my grandfather with

"Hello, Alex," as it would have predeceased her long ago. Apart from it, there were a few articles which the lady did not get her hands on and which somehow my mother did: an armadillo transformed into a basket with a red lining, his tail tucked into his mouth to form the handle; an octagonal sewing table inlaid with various kinds of wood and ivory; a grandfather clock with a brass face; and a huge mahogany sideboard with a mirror on the top running its full length and which must have reflected both my grandparents, and possibly, as Macbeth was shown by the witches, ancestors going back for generations, depending on how old it was. If only there were some way that those reflections of the past could be viewed in the present!

Grandpa Tate was a chief engineer, descended from a long line of seafarers, just as my father's belonged to the land. He was a grandfather I would have loved to have known. I don't know how often he saw me but it could not have been often since we lived so far apart, he in Darley, near Harrogate, north Yorkshire and us in Crovie. I'm sorry to say I don't remember ever meeting him but it seems as if he might not have been favourably impressed by me. According to my mother, his words on first clapping eyes on me were: "He'll be a bad bugger, him!"

Time will be the judge and as I am already well stricken in years, the proof should already be out there. I admit I have not been perfect as you will see (who is?) but what gift of prescience did he have that he could come to this conclusion merely from looking at a babe in arms—or in my pram, as I happened to be? Perhaps I threw something out of it, but so what? That's what babies do and some grown-ups too, metaphorically speaking, who should know better. Perhaps I cried at the sight of *him* or at the unfamiliar smell of alcohol on his breath. Or, and this might just be nearer the mark, the answer might be it takes one to know one—for my grandfather, it seems, was a thoroughly bad egg, at least as far as my mother was concerned and lies apparently unlamented in an unknown grave probably in Harrogate—at least at the moment. I might yet be able to dig him up, so to speak. He died on January 2nd 1954 at 11, Stockwell Road, Knaresborough and left £526 9s 5d to my Uncle Tommy and my mother. It took until December 4th to settle the will. It makes me wonder if his girlfriend contested it. I wonder why she would have bothered since she had already got everything else.

My grandfathers were physical opposites and undoubtedly that applied to their personalities too. My paternal grandfather, Charles Addison, was big and bucolic and in the only photo I have ever seen of him, looks perfectly modern in his three-piece suit, apart perhaps, from the chain at the waistcoat which anchored his pocket watch. (Whatever became of that I wonder?) I have no firm evidence on which to base this supposition, but he does look of good, solid Presbyterian stock, as he was reputed to be, a child of Calvin through marriage at least, with one eye on his crops and the other on heaven. It amuses me to wonder when my granny married him, if she realised how not so long ago, the Addisons had been the staunchest of Catholics, much more than her daughter-in-law never was, but I doubt if she did: I doubt if my grandfather realised it himself. It certainly came as a great shock to me to discover my early Addison ancestors were Catholics. You will meet them later.

My other grandfather, Grandpa Tate, was small of stature, lean and wiry, and looks decidedly Edwardian with his trim goatee beard and high, stiff collar. Mind you, that was at his son's wedding and he would have been dressed up for the occasion. For some reason photographers make you swap partners when they record for posterity the moment of their off-springs' launching into matrimony and in the process no doubt confuse future genealogists no end if they forget this arcane rule. Thus the scary woman in the furs and cloche hat hanging on Grandpa Tate's arm is not his wife but my Aunt Nan's mother. Strange that she should have produced such a beautiful daughter with such a sense of humour. Aunt Nan was an aunt par excellence: this dame defies you to smile at your peril. I could imagine her getting on really well with my father's mother as together they tut-tutted and lamented and decried the modern ways of the world, just as my mother and Aunt Nan did towards the end of their lives. As I do now.

But perhaps I am being totally unreasonable to draw these conclusions on the basis of a few photographs. In posed photographs I am never smiling. I do not know how to without looking like Mr Carker in *Dombey and Son* and future generations may conclude that I was a right miserable bugger. Only contemporaries could tell them what a little ray of sunshine I actually was, brightening up the lives of all who were lucky enough to swim into my ken.

Of the two grandfathers, I feel more connected with Grandpa Tate somehow. There are no photographs that I know of featuring Grandfather Addison and me, and of course he died so soon after I was born he had no chance to get to know me better. And in any case, I was but one of many grandchildren. I'm not sure which number exactly, but enough down the rankings to be commonplace: just another grandson.

Grandpa Tate, on the other hand, had only three grandchildren, my cousin Bernard, my sister and me. A few photos of Grandpa Tate and me do exist: one or two in Crovie and some in Yorkshire, him in his shirt sleeves bending over to play with me or watching me playing with my bogie and Dinky car on the road. Was this grandfatherly love and attention, or merely observing me for incipient signs of badness?

Apart from being a womaniser and world traveller, my grandfather was also an alcoholic with a fierce temper. If, as the adage has it, imitation is the sincerest form of flattery, it is surprising that my grandfather took such an instant dislike to me, since I would put my hand up to two, possibly three of these characteristics and the missing one I wouldn't mind having aspired to. But perhaps it all depends upon the tone in which he made his prophecy as to my future character. What if, recognising himself in me, he uttered those words with a tone of pride, rejoicing that his genes, although somewhat diluted, were well and alive in me.

Writing now as a grandfather myself, and looking at my grandchildren for signs of me in them, I am convinced that that is how he must have said it. I suspect he would have been rather disappointed in my performance however; a pale imitation of the original. Fortunately for him he had a safety net in another grandchild, and I don't mean my sister she would hurriedly wish me to add, who though not at all bad like me, I think would have made my grandfather more proud.

There was no doubt in my mother's eyes as to who was at fault in her parents' marriage: she never had a kind word for him, never an excuse for his behaviour and would not be drawn on him. I dismiss the idea that it was too painful a place to go back to. She never talked about the war either, not even the good times she had then. No, she was essentially a very private person, never revealing much about her past. But when she did let slip some nugget and I tried to dig deeper, she would rapidly lose patience and snap: "Oh, you—you always want to know the far end of a fart!" and she would stomp off so there was no possibility of eliciting any more information. She was her father's daughter as far as the shortness of her fuse was concerned, and the anecdote also well illustrates the benefits of a convent education in that she was able to use such colourful and figurative language and with such a fine turn of alliteration too.

Over the years, information leaked out like the last pressings of the bramble wine I was to make many years in the future, drop by slow, agonising drop. Once she caught her father with his hands around her mother's throat, and, just a little girl, jumped up and swung from his arm in order to break his grip. She might have saved her mother's life that day but probably he would have come to his senses on his own, the sudden flare-up of temper at whatever had provoked this attack abating just as suddenly as it had started. Not surprisingly, it left a lasting scar on her relationship with her father and as if in testimony to that event, on her own forearm, my mother bore a two-inch scar.

It was nothing to do with that murderous attack however, but the result of a horrific accident when she fell off her bike, suffering a greenstick fracture, the bone sickeningly piercing the skin. Between them, the doctor and her mother sought to reset the break. While her mother held on to the upper part of the arm, the doctor pulled and twisted the lower part and this entirely without any anaesthetic. If even the thought of the pain she must have endured makes me feel sick, imagine what it must have been like for her. It might have been some consolation if the bone had healed properly, but it did not. It had to be broken again and reset, but once again it was not entirely successful. Whilst this did not handicap her to any great extent, it was responsible for her unique style of knitting, a technique which she passed on to my sister when she taught her how to hold the needles.

Interestingly, the aforementioned cousin Bernard has a different take on the troubled relationship between our grandparents. According to him, information he probably received from my Uncle Tommy, my grandmother was a cold, passionless woman whose frigidity drove my grandfather to seek solace elsewhere. It might be, in that respect, he was more sinned against than sinning, but on balance, I suspect not. For one thing, my mother's caring, compassionate nature must have come from somewhere, and furthermore, if my mother suspected him of having a girl in every port, I am pretty well persuaded that she was probably right. Sailors will be sailors after all.

And if my grandmother did reject him, perhaps that was a quite understandable response to his extramarital affairs. I am also perfectly sure that my grandmother would have frowned upon his drinking, perhaps any wife would, especially if it made him violent, as it

43

appeared to do. He was undoubtedly an alcoholic and if she, on the other hand, eschewed alcohol completely, apart from perhaps a glass of sherry at Christmas, I can very well see how they were incompatible.

My mother never got drunk, only slightly tipsy once a year at Hogmanay. In fact, I don't remember my parents ever drinking at any other time of the year, even at Christmas, no bottle of wine ever gracing our table. But my mother did make rhubarb wine. It only made an appearance, like Halley's comet, on rare occasions when certain friends or relatives called and not on each and every visit either. Moreover, it was served in a sherry glass, hardly enough to get "roarin' fou on" like Tam O'Shanter. She only made a couple of gallons a year, not in the industrial quantities I used to since I couldn't afford to buy the "real" stuff. Perhaps when we were safely tucked up in bed, my sister and I, my parents uncorked a bottle and rollicked royally to bed after a glass of two, as it was said to be potent. But I can't see that happening somehow.

By contrast, when my father met Grandpa Tate off the bus at Macduff to attend Granny Tate's funeral, he was miraculously drunk. I imagine the reason for this was due more to the fortification required for the journey rather than grief. The journey from Yorkshire, a long one by public transport even now, would have been more like an ordeal then and some alcoholic refreshment would have helped pass the time as well as dulling the pain. For good or ill, it is undeniable he was an interesting character and interesting characters should be appreciated and venerated, for they do not cross our paths as often as they used to do. In these days of political correctness, you are less likely than ever to meet one as they hide their forthright remarks and opinions under a bushel lest they are labelled in need of corrective thinking, like dissidents in the days of Stalin or Mao.

Given the age my parents finally got round to tying the matrimonial knot, it is not surprising that I do not remember any of my grandparents at all. The only one I do remember vaguely was Granny Tate and not in very happy circumstances either. It seemed to me she was lying in a darkened room. The imagination, as Keats tells us, is a "deceiving elf" and yet it seems to me, this is what happened.

It was in my parents' bedroom at Crovie, my grandmother was in bed and the room was dark. I seem to remember the house full of people and me skipping gaily around the house unaware and not understanding how serious was the situation, perhaps even excited at the unusual state of affairs. She had had a stroke and probably the doctor was there and the ambulance men had arrived to take her to hospital. "Ambulance" here is to be interpreted in the original and etymological sense of the word since they would have had to park the vehicle at the bottom of the road and then carry her there by stretcher, their progress observed all the while by the twitching of net curtains from the gable end windows.

But how was the ambulance summoned? I can imagine my mother comforting my grandmother as my father went to phone, presumably from the box which now stands about the middle of the village and set back a bit from the shore. But what if it had not been installed yet? Time, as we now know, with stroke victims, is vital. Could she have been saved if she had lived in a less remote location? We will never know.

Anyway, that was the last time I saw my grandmother, and in fact, vague though it is, the only time I remember seeing her at all. It was July 27th 1952 and she was 70 years old.

The only member of the family of that generation whom I do remember was my grandmother's younger brother, Arthur. He was married to Emma Park and had three children: Thomas Arthur (1913), Gertrude Mary (1916) and Edith (1918). He was profoundly deaf due to his eardrums being burst as a result of the constant hammering he was subjected to as an engineer in the shipyards. So my mother said, but the census records show him as a printer. Still, he was only twenty-seven at the time of the 1911 census which is the most recent available for consultation and which leaves plenty of time for him to undergo a career change. Many people do. I did myself.

Poor Arthur had the unfortunate distinction of twice being the baby of the family after his sister, Blanche, died aged only six, in 1892. I have a photograph of her, aged about three, already halfway through her young life. She is an adorable, fair-haired little girl with curls. The family must have been devastated.

As with my grandmother, the only time I remember seeing Arthur was also the last time. It was in the summer of 1957 on our annual tour of my mother's relatives in the Shields area, just before his death in the January of the following year. He was standing on the street outside his house. As we drove away, I can remember my mother sighing and saying presciently and intended mainly for my father's ears I presume,

"Well I suppose that will be the last time we will see him"—a remark which inspired me to turn round so I could look at him through the back window as he stood waving goodbye until we were out of sight.

No doubt he was thinking precisely the same thing, only a bit more sorrowfully. He was seventy-four and therefore past his allotted three score years and ten and I presume that is what my mother had in mind. But there was more to it than that. God knows what was going through his mind as he waved us goodbye, but he committed suicide about six months later, on January 17th 1958. My mother said he never got over his wife's death. Perhaps he longed to be with her.

Chapter Five

The Crows' Tree

Granny Tate, my maternal grandmother, and to whom I am said to bear some resemblance, was born a Crow, to which undeniable truth I attribute, somewhat less reliably, my inability to sing a single note in key as well as my love for the Plains Indians of North America.

The earliest mention of a Crow in the parish registers was Robert from Higham Dykes, Ponteland, Northumberland, born in 1675, and it is a pretty safe bet that his father was also called Robert. It was widespread practice to name the first son after the paternal grandfather but I have another reason for reaching this conclusion. In 1704 he married Sarah Gofton with whom he had two sons—both named Robert. The first only lived from 10th April to 7th September 1711. The second lasted even less long. He only lived only nine days from 19th—28th October 1712. It seems a curious practice to me, to stick with the name like that, as if the name was the thing and outweighed everything else. Even "curiouser", as Alice said, in the course of my researches, I was to find out that this was by no means the only instance of this happening.

But worse was to come for the beleaguered Robert. Sarah died in 1712 also. But happier times were just around the corner and the following year, the luckless father and husband married Catherine Meggison (1680-1769). They had three sons and a daughter,

Catherine, born in 1718, and Robert evidently
thought better of his attachment to the name Robert
or Catherine had put her foot down and said no baby
of hers was going to be given that name, for they were
called Thomas, John and George. That did the trick: the
curse was broken and they all survived. Each of *them*,
however, risked the wrath of the gods and named their
first son Robert.

Robert, the patriarch, my great-great-great-great-
great grandfather, died in 1749 and by this time
had acquired the farm of Boghall near Stannington.
His sons, Thomas and John, had their own farms at
Benridge and Coldcoats. George remained at home
and it was to Higham Dykes that he brought his bride,
Isabel Ainsley in 1750. Their daughter, Elizabeth, was
born in 1754 and was followed by Robert, George and
John.

This John, my great-great-great-grandfather, took
over Boghall and in 1789 married Mary Codling
(1762-1838) with whom he produced eight children.
When he was not working or making babies, John
found time to join the Stannington Association for
Prosecuting Felons. The association had more than
thirty members including the local landowner Sir M.
W. Ridley Bart. and the Rev. T. Myers. I quote the aims
and purpose of the Association verbatim in order to give
a flavour of the times, so please note that any errors you
perceive are not mine. The members agreed to prosecute
*at their joint and equal Expence, all Persons guilty of
stealing, defrauding, or injuring the Person or Property of
any Member thereof; or Servants, as Householders, under
any of the said Members; as also all Persons strolling
as Vagrants in their respective Townships; and also are*

determined to prosecute their Servant or Servants who shall, at any Time, be accused of driving their Horses furiously along the Road, and every Exertion will be made to bring to Justice any such Offender or Offenders.

The date was 1827 and it tickled me to see that even back then they had their equivalent of boy racers. But what they did not have was the equivalent of a police force. It was not until 1829 that the Metropolitan Police Force was set up by the then Home Secretary, Robert Peel, the future Prime Minister. As with other things, the provinces were slow to follow. Ten years passed before the Rural Constabulary Act allowed the counties to set up a police force with one constable per thousand head of population but even then this was not compulsory and it was only with the Police Act of 1856 that counties were obliged to establish a police force.

As I said, John had eight children and it was the last, Thomas, (1805-1887) who had the future distinction of being my great-great-grandfather. In 1821 he was apprenticed to his cousin George (1793-1870), a block and mast maker in North Shields but later set up in business as a grocer and flour dealer. He married Sarah Sproat (1809-1849). So far so good, but then tragedy struck. Their first child, John, who was born in 1836, was the first in a catalogue of tragic infant deaths. He survived until he was five at least but probably not a great deal longer. Isabella, the next child, died in 1840 aged 18 months. Their next child, Isabella Mary, died in 1845 aged four-and-a-half. Finally, their fourth, Sarah, died the following year aged three. That was the year that Thomas the Survivor was born. But the tragedy does not end there, for three years later, his mother died. They were all victims of a cholera epidemic.

Isabella Fisher, Thomas's sister-in-law, helped him look after the infant Thomas but in 1852, Thomas remarried. They did not have any children but my mother remembers my great-grandfather saying of her: "Heaven help those who had a bad one, but I had a good one". Her name was Mary Ann Chapman (1814-1893). If the name sounds familiar to you, as it first did to me, you may be thinking of Jack the Ripper's victim, Annie Chapman, and of course, there is absolutely no connection between them, although they were contemporaries.

Thomas's precarious survival got me thinking about my own. I was seriously ill with gastroenteritis and had it not been for the devoted attention of Sister Garrow at Banff's Chalmers Hospital who sat up all night, for many nights, pouring liberal libations of sherry down my throat, I would have died. You might have thought that this life-saving elixir would be my favourite drink, that I would have shares in the stuff, but the truth is I do not have a fondness for it now.

I confess I once got horribly drunk on it when, as a member of the Students' Representative Council, I attended a sherry reception to launch the new body. I began on the sweet and when that dried up, moved on to the dry, naturally. The first one was so vile it made me shudder but the next wasn't so bad and after that they slid down quite easily. Sometime later I made my way somewhat unsteadily to the toilet and when, after some time, I failed to reappear, my girlfriend and my sister, starting to become alarmed, braved all and entered that denizen of men and found me, not dead or collapsed on the floor as they feared, but pressed against the wall, literally cornered by some bloke who was telling me how utterly desirable I was. His blandishments were wasted. They went completely over my head. I had not the faintest notion that I was such an object of desire.

So if sherry got me into that scrape, it seems it was also responsible for my surviving that encounter with death in my first few days of life. If you are a direct descendant of mine you would probably regard that as a "good thing" in the words of Sellar and Yeatman, the authors of *1066 and All That*. If you are not, you probably could not care less, but my point is this—what if Thomas had not survived? The number of descendants one has increases exponentially with each succeeding generation. I can't say how many people exactly owe their existence to Thomas but I do know how many do to me and you don't need all your fingers to count them—at the moment. But one hundred years from now, who can say how many there will be? Hundreds perhaps. Hopefully. One or two of them may even read this book.

Furthermore, if you have been reading this with a great deal more care and attention than is strictly necessary, you may have noticed that going back as far as four generations, every single one of the Crows from whom I am descended was the last to be born. How scary is that? What if any one of these four great-grandmothers had had a headache that day, and what if one of those baby boys, George, John, Thomas and Thomas had never been conceived?

So I am grateful to them all for my existence, to Thomas the Survivor (1846-1911) who, it seems, inherited the grocer's business and of course his wife, Jane Elizabeth Pyle (1848-1907) who did most of the work. She also happened to be a last child, the fourth to Robert and Margaret Pyle of North Shields and also like Thomas, her life was touched by tragedy. She lost her father when she was only fifteen when, as captain of the brig *Thomas Barker,* he was involved in a collision with the *Edith Mary* on February 13th 1864. Along with seven other members of the crew, he was drowned aged only fifty-one. Her mother died eleven years and one day later. She was only fifty-nine.

They were married in 1875 in North Shields and had six children: Thomas (1877-1939), Mary Ann (1878-1961), Robert Pyle (1879-1907), after whom came my grandmother, Jane Elizabeth (1881-1952)— not the last child at last! Then there were the two we met at the end of the last chapter, Arthur (1883-1958) and poor Blanche (1886-1892).

I am afraid I do not know anything about Robert except that he was my grandmother's favourite brother and like his Grandfather Pyle was drowned at sea. It happened on 23rd May 1907. He was living in Swansea at the time. I have a photograph of him in his uniform, from which I can deduce he was not in the Royal Navy. It was taken in Bombay and he was sporting a rather untidy and lopsided moustache. He was only twenty-seven when he died and this photograph must have been taken not a great deal of time beforehand.

Of the first son, Thomas, I know even less, just that he was a bachelor and died in Morpeth Asylum in 1939. Anyone who could have told me anything about him has long since departed the planet. There is a story there for anyone who wants to look into it. The records will be open for inspection in 2039. Be my guest. I do not expect to be here then to tell you when or why he was committed.

Auntie Mary, as I called her, was a precocious child. She was able to walk at nine months but her parents tied her to a chair to prevent her using her new-found skill. They thought it would make her bandy-legged, walking so early. We now know of course that rickets are to blame for that defect, but such were the quaint beliefs of yesteryear.

When I was very young, my mother used to chase me round the kitchen table to pour cod liver oil down my neck in order to avoid the very same thing. For the same reason I was also given malt extract which I didn't mind at all, even licked the spoon. (No wonder I grew up to love malt whisky.) The malt extract came from a big, fat, brown jar, which prior to administration, was placed in front of the fire to soften it up as it was so thick and treacly it set like concrete when it was cold. There was also an orange-juice concentrate, courtesy of the newly-formed NHS, which was delicious—the best orange juice I have ever tasted. But that might just be nostalgia. Whatever. There was never any chance of me ever developing rickets, that's for sure.

How long Auntie Mary was tied to the chair before she was allowed to resume her tottering steps, history does not record, but she took a big step twenty-six years later when she walked down the aisle to exchange wedding vows with John Daniel Blythe in 1904.

Tragedy continued to stalk this branch of the family too. Their first son, Stanley Crow Blythe, died in 1911, aged six, like Blanche. Their second son, John Crow Blythe, was born in 1916. He was a pharmacist who emigrated to Canada and in July 1952, after her husband died in the December of the preceeding year, Auntie Mary joined John and his wife, Mae Elizabeth

Gummow (1919-1984) of Red Deer, Alberta and their two-year old son, Stanley John. They went on to have three more children, Deborah (Debbie) Mae (1955), Patricia Anne (1956) and David Andrew (1962).

I met them all in Abbotsford, near Vancouver, the year we went to Montana (1978-79) with the exception of Auntie Mary and Stanley who was still in Edmonton where he was born and where the family had been living when Auntie Mary first moved out. It would have been remarkable if I had met her, as she would have been one-hundred-and-one. As it happens, she died in 1961 aged 83. As far as I am aware, I never ever met her, but I might have when I was a babe in arms. My mother always kept in touch with her and she invariably sent presents at Christmas.

One year I got a Davy Crockett hat which was particularly appreciated as one of my pursuits at that time was playing cowboys and Indians in the wood adjacent to Ternemny Schoolhouse where we were living at the time, and *Tom Sawyer,* one of my treasures, as it is inscribed by her, dated 1958. It was the last present I remember getting from her.

Another year she sent my sister a pair of knickers and since she was illiterate at the time, it was my duty to write her thank-you letters as well as my own. (Just one of the many disadvantages of being the first-born.) It made a big impression on me because although I can't remember any other Christmas gifts she received, I do remember this because it presented me with the problem of what to write as I was brought up to consider "knickers" a rude word, one which I would scarcely dare to breathe in the presence of my parents and certainly far too rude to be committed to paper. My mother advised I wrote "panties" instead which satisfied my sensibilities and that is what I did, wondering why I hadn't thought of that for myself and thus saving myself the embarrassment of having to utter the awful word in front of my mother of all people who, I presumed, wore the unmentionables herself, only in a much larger size.

I don't recall my sister's reaction to this gift, but any article of clothing I might have received as a Christmas present (apart from the Davy Crockett hat) would have filled me with the deepest disgust: clothes were necessities that your parents had to provide you with. Presents were for pleasure and clothes could never be that.

After Auntie Mary, two more old Crows I remember well, if I may put it like that, were my mother's cousins, Edie and Kitty. They used to visit us at Ternemny in the Fifties, the same time I was receiving the presents from Auntie Mary, and I'm sure they must have lavished presents upon my sister and me too. They were a couple of antiques who lived together at 13, Marine Approach, South Shields. My choice of the "antiques" is very apposite, as you will see.

When I was in short trousers, we used to visit them on our sojourn to the south to visit my mother's relatives, and on the way back from our honeymoon in Sussex in 1972, my brand-new wife and I stopped off to see them as their health was not good enough to allow them to travel to the wedding—which is when I discovered something I had not realised as a boy—they were living in a Victorian time capsule with hard-as-nails horsehair sofas and chairs, complete with antimacassars and all sorts of other articles Victorian, down to aspidistras in brass pots. It was as if time had stood still since they were girls.

Their parents were Robert Crow (1846) and Catherine Shiell (1852-1934) from Newcastle. My Great-grandfather Thomas the Survivor and he were cousins.

Robert was a draper and married Catherine in 1880. They had Robert (1881), who was a plumber, then ten years later, Edith Mary, who was a milliner and finally Catherine (Kitty) (1895) for whom no occupation was given in the 1911 census. Perhaps she was the housekeeper. There was another brother, Sydney, who died in 1890 aged seven. After him came Elizabeth Mary who was born in 1885 and who died only two years later. This explains the gap between Robert and Edie but sadly also tells us that even at the dawn of this new Georgian age, the 1911 Census felt it necessary to require the following information: the number of children born alive, the number still living, and the number who had died.

Kitty and Edie were as different from each other as chalk and cheese. Edie was tall and thin, or at least she appeared so to me, though actually she was small-framed and the impression I got of height was probably due to my own lack of it and the contrast to Kitty who was short and fat. Edie was gentle and kind; Kitty was bossy and "hard" as I once described her to my mother.

On one of their visits to us at Ternemny they showed us how to make "sticks" as kindling for the fire by twisting the newspaper into a knot. They also introduced my sister and me to the card game Canasta and although I haven't the faintest idea how to play it now, I enjoyed it very much then and took a great delight in counting up the scores if my partner and I had won (my sister and I took it in turns to be with Kitty or Edie), but if we lost, I would just gather up the cards and say it wasn't necessary to add up the scores which annoyed the hell out of Kitty but which didn't seem to bother mild-mannered Edie at all.

They were born in Gosforth, Northumberland, and lived a large part of their lives there, which I presume, explains why both of them were addicted to prefacing any remarks of wonderment or appreciation with "Eee, I say" or "Eee, I never." But in addition, Kitty had her own idiosyncrasy which drove my mother to the point of madness, but which I found rather amusing. When she finished a sentence, and I mean at the end of *every* one, she would say, "I say, I said . . ." and then reiterate her previous statement.

But the funniest thing she ever did and I remember it so clearly I can even remember what she was wearing—a brown dress with a white motif. We were in the kitchen in Ternemny when she let rip a barrage of farts which I thought at first was her slapping her thigh, though why she should have taken it into her head to do that, I don't know. Until then I had no idea ladies farted at all, let alone right royally like that and I just about ended myself when I discovered what the machinegun fire actually was. I was prone to getting a fit of the giggles and once I started, I found it difficult to stop. It was even said that when I was very young, I would literally roll around the floor laughing. I did not go quite that far on this occasion but my hilarity put Kitty out somewhat and she was not so much embarrassed, but offended.

It was also Kitty who disabused me of the notion that it was only men who snored, a confession I vouchsafed to my mother one morning after an endless night in which I endured snoring so loud, the snorer and I may as well have been in the same room. To give you some idea of what it was like, I would compare it to a rutting wildebeest. Oh, all right, I admit I've never actually heard one but I am sure that is what it was like.

It was a severe a blow to discover that the fairer sex could be just as guilty of this antisocial behaviour as men, but I didn't lose any sleep worrying over it, never checked with a young lady before asking her out if she snored or not. My mother would have been proud to learn that I did have *some* social graces.

I was very grateful to Kitty therefore, for the entertainment and education she provided me with, but I was always fonder of Edie because she was not so fussy and bossy, and it was only some time after she was dead that I discovered I had another reason to be grateful to her too. She kept up a correspondence with a certain E. W. Milburn in Edinburgh who was researching the Crows and who drew up a family chart. This was kept in a blanket box in the Victorian time capsule, a time capsule within a time capsule, like a Matryoshka doll. Edie died first and when my mother went down to keep Kitty company, she guarded it as zealously as the dogs in *The Tinderbox* and would not let my mother take it out the house to be photocopied. She did, however, allow it out for an airing so the best my mother could do at the time was make some brief notes.

In their wills, Kitty and Edie, somewhat eccentrically, left their money to women only. Thus my mother and sister inherited but I did not. However, I did manage somehow or other to acquire the chart from the blanket box. My feeling is that it was liberated by another of my mother's cousins, Edie Tate, who you shall meet in the next chapter, and who would have passed it on to my mother who certainly did pass it on to me, as well as half her share of the inheritance, which was very kind of her.

What happened to the blanket box as well as the wall-to-wall antiques (probably worth a fortune), not to mention the house itself, I cannot say for certain, but according to my mother, some obscure male relative crawled out of the woodwork when the end was drawing nigh for poor Kitty and persuaded her to leave the house and contents to him. If you are reading this, you know who you are. Kitty may have been adamant about keeping hold of the family chart when my mother was staying there in 1976, but nearly ten years later, the steel in her character was beginning to suffer from metal fatigue, while her mental faculties were also in decline.

This steel however, stood her in good stead years before, when she was well into her eighties and living alone after Edie had died. One night she was woken up by the sound of breaking glass. She struggled up and made her way, with the aid of her stick, to the top of the landing where she saw a figure lurking in the shadows below.

"Who are you? What are you doing here? Get out of here before I call the police! . . . I say, I said who are you? What are you doing here? . . . Get out before I call the police," she called down to the intruder, shaking her stick at him.

He did.

Chapter Six

The Tates, Master Mariners

The salt water, (in addition to the alcohol) which flowed through my grandfather Tate's veins, has been filtered out in the present and previous generation but long, long ago, the Tates were an illustrious sea-faring family. In the beginning there was William (1599) who begat Philip (1633), who begat Philip (1678), who begat Joshua (1706), who begat Jasper (1734-1800). And there endeth my little homage to Mathew 1 v 2-16 which I find not in the least boring and even rather amusing because of, rather than despite, all those "begats".

Jasper is a name which never fails to conjure up for me the image of a moustachioed villain in a Victorian melodrama and there were a quite a few in the Tate tree but the first, above, with the help of his wife Rachel Wardell (1734), produced three sons and two daughters, including Jasper (1774-1814) who was born in Bedlington, Northumberland.

This Jasper, my great-great-great grandfather, married Ann Short (1775-1840) from King's Lynn, Norfolk. They had four sons beginning in 1799 with James who unfortunately did not see the year out. Next were Jasper and William, born in 1801 and 1803 respectively who were more fortunate in life's lottery: both died in 1881. Then there was a gap of seven years before my Great-great grandfather James was born in 1810, just four years before his father died aged forty in 1814, although his mother lived on until 1840. It is possible there were siblings who were born in the interim—indeed it is more than likely, but they did not survive long enough to be recorded in the census returns. Note, however, that here we have another instance of what I regard as that strange phenomenon of recycling the same Christian name even if, in this instance, more than a decade had elapsed since the decease of the first James. It seems to me that this must be a constant reminder of the dead child for the parents while the child himself may wonder if he was born as some sort of replacement or substitute for the first, rather than wanted in his own right.

I don't know if it would be entirely accurate to say that he ran away to sea, but go to sea Great-great-grandfather James did, aged only seven, as a cabin boy. Was it the pull of the sea that drew him or can we interpret this as the sign of an unhappy life at home? It seems a remarkable thing to have done so young. He must have been incredibly courageous or exceptionally miserable to have undertaken such a step. Some may see it through the rose-tinted glasses of romanticism but there was nothing romantic I would have thought, about ferrying coal across the North Sea from Blyth to France, especially in what John Masefield called the *mad March days* in his celebrated poem *Cargoes*.

James rose through the ranks to become a ship owner and one of the most highly respected captains of his generation. Despite the long hours he spent at sea, he nevertheless found the time to sire eleven children with his wife Margaret Montgomery (1814-1899) whose father originally hailed from Kirkcudbrightshire

where, in a tenuous sort of link, I began my teachi⸗
career.

James and Margaret were staunch members of t
Bridge Street United Presbyterian Church in Blyth,
one may deduce from the choice of some of the name
for their brood. The remarkable thing about this family
(apart from its size), is not that there is a quarter of
century between the first and the last child, nor, with
one exception, that they were all boys—but that all the
boys, bar one, became sea captains. And for the second
time in two generations, there was another child death
in the family. But that, I am sorry to say, was not an
unremarkable occurrence: child deaths in the Victorian
era were frequent. Nor by now, should it surprise you
to find that the unfortunate deceased had his name
recycled—in this case Charles, born 1838, died 1843.

Ironically, the other Charles, Charles Montgomery
Tate (1851-1933), the odd one out, the non-seafarer,
had probably the most interesting life of all of them.
Aged eighteen, he left home to seek his fortune as a
gold miner in British Columbia but as miners began
staggering back to Victoria barely alive, he realised that
there was not a fortune to be made out there after all.
Under the auspices of the Methodist church, he set
up a school for the Indians with as many as 200 in a
class and travelled by horse, steamship and canoe to
reach them. He was more than a bit of a linguist,
translating the Gospel of Mark into Chinook as well as
writing a dictionary of that language. He also mastered
other Indian dialects as well. He could certainly speak
Ankameenum because with a bit of cunning that could
easily have backfired, that was the language he chose to
preach the sermon for his ordination exam. Although

they did not understand a word of it, the three examiners were impressed and he was duly ordained.

In his essay *Fifty Years with the Methodist Church in British Columbia* he relates how he was given the "privilege" of organising the Indian mission at Fort Simpson, the chief trading post of the Hudson's Bay Company near the Alaskan border. There he found "some 800 Indians just emerging from paganism of the most diabolical nature". It fairly resonates off the page, his Presbyterian background.

Within three months, he had established regular Sunday and weeknight services and two day schools—a children's school in the morning and the adults' in the afternoon. He obviously worked tirelessly, must have had a great fondness for the Indians, dedicating his life to saving their immortal souls. I am sure he performed a lot of good works and was of great service to them in other ways besides, and yet, perversely, as far as religion was concerned, a sceptic and non-believer like me may argue that what he was doing was replacing their myths with his. Admittedly there are some pretty good far-fetched tales in the Bible too, in the Old Testament in particular, but for great stories, you just can't whack the Indian myths, as any reader of *Hiawatha* can tell you.

There is a bronze plaque commemorating him in St Andrew's Presbyterian Church in Vancouver. With two totem poles at either side and a shoreline featuring a canoe at the bottom, the text tells us, apart from his dates and other details, that he was "Founder of the Coqualeetza Indian school" and at the bottom it states: "His canoe was his chapel". I saw this plaque for myself

64

when I visited Auntie Mary's son, John Blythe, on my exchange year to Montana.

After her husband, Christopher Watson (1848-1896), head joiner on Sir Mathew Ridley's estate at Blyth, died, Charles's only sister, Margaret Ann (1849), joined him in Canada where she died on New Year's Day 1924. As for Charles, he was married to Caroline Knott who was born in Bloomsbury in 1839. She died in 1930. Charles followed her in 1933 and I can just see, when he rolled up at the Pearly Gates, St Peter just waved him through without him having to say a word.

Thomas Tate (1856-1918), Charles's younger brother, also had a colourful life, if not a very sad one. (Do not look for his family in the chart—Thomas was a busy boy and needs a chart all to himself, so I will record some of them here.) In March 1881, aged twenty-four, he procured his Master's certificate and in January of the following year procured the first of his three wives, Mary Ann Morrison (1858-1899) from Blyth and by whom he had seven children of whom I am only going to mention the first and the last four for a reason that will soon become apparent: Edward Morrison Tate (1882-1971); Lilly Jane Morrison (June 6th 1889-21st Sept 1889); Thomas (15th-24th June 1894); James Thomas (15th Oct 1896-15th Oct 1896) and Albert Thomas (1898-1925).

Like Robert Crow, who was determined to have a Robert, Thomas Tate it seems, was determined to have a little Thomas, even if it was just as a middle name. As you can see, it took him three attempts before he had a Thomas who lived longer than nine days and before that there was little Lily who lasted only three months. One can only speculate what their thoughts were when they found out that Mary was pregnant with Albert Thomas. But they need not have worried. Albert turned out to be a survivor, though he was not destined to see thirty even. It was Mary who was to be the Grim Reaper's next victim. Albert Thomas was barely six months old when she died in 1899.

The second wife was Mary Ellen Bergen (1873-1910) whom Thomas married only three months after the demise of the previous Mary and by whom he had six more children. Some may regard that as somewhat shocking—not the six children, but that he remarried so soon after the demise of Mary the First. If we think that rather hasty today, the Victorians would have thought it scandalous, ever since the Queen had set the gold standard on how to mourn the death of a spouse after her beloved Albert died back in 1861.

Mary Two's children made it to adulthood but the oldest was only ten and the youngest only two months when she too died and left Thomas holding the babies. Thomas showed a lot more decorum after this latest tragedy and it was after three years this time, not months, before he tied the matrimonial knot (as opposed to sailor's) in 1913 with Jessie Smith (1871-1951) fourteen years his junior. But there was life in the old sea dog yet and with her he fathered two more children, Margaret (1914-1983) and Robert Smith Tate (1918-1980). Thereby hangs another sad tale, as you will presently see.

During the Russo-Japanese war of 1904-1905, in January of 1905, the *SS Lethington,* with a cargo of Cardiff coal and Thomas as master, was making its way to Vladivostok when it was stopped and boarded in the

Japanese Sea by a Japanese torpedo boat. The ship and cargo were confiscated. Thomas and the crew were sent home by the German steamer *Bayern* and some four months after his adventure, Thomas found himself back home in South Shields. As for the *Lethington* (built in Port Glasgow in 1901), she was renamed the *Wakamiya Maru* and used to transport troops.

Thomas did not fare so well thirteen years later when the *SS Towneley* under his command and with only ballast as cargo, was torpedoed off Lundy island on 31st January 1918 by the German U-Boat *Leo Hillebrand*. Thomas, along with the chief engineer and three others, managed to get aboard a lifeboat and you can imagine their joy and relief when about midnight on February 1st, they attracted the attention of the Belgian trawler *Ibis VI* which came to their rescue. Then cruelly, the lifeboat capsized as they were attempting to board and all souls were lost. He was only two months past his sixtieth birthday. His newest son, Robert Smith Tate, was born on January 6th. Possibly Thomas never saw his son but hopefully he did at least hear of his birth.

You can imagine that there was no love lost between Thomas and the Japanese, but his nephew Nicholas (1856-1907), son of his brother William (1833-1891), was decorated by them, no less. As captain of the *Rosetta Maru*, he carried Admiral Togo and his troops during the Russo—Japanese war aforesaid. He was decorated with a silver star with an emerald in the middle. It seems to me a rather a generous award for merely driving someone about in a boat, even if Togo was known as the "Nelson of the East".

Nicholas's father, William, was distinguished in his own right, albeit in a less sensational way. As master of the *Archimedes*, he was responsible for laying the first cable from Jutland to Newbiggin, Northumberland in 1868.

I am indebted to Thomas's first son, Edward Morrison Tate, in a newspaper interview, for most of the above information. He too began following in the footsteps of his illustrious forebears. He was learning his trade on the *Begonia,* sailing to South America and South Africa. It was while he was in Port Elizabeth arranging the rigging for the painting of the funnel, he fell twenty-nine feet onto the skids for the lifeboat. He broke his left thigh and in his words, "split" his left arm and which he was not able to use again for three months. He also suffered concussion, was unconscious for six weeks and lost four stones in weight. Strange to tell, the patient in the next bed to him had fallen fifty feet and all he suffered was a dislocated shoulder. But as Edward came to realise, it's not the fall that's the problem—it's the landing. It brought his naval career to a juddering halt anyway and he remained rooted to an office job after that. He married Ann Gregory in 1909 and died in 1971 aged 89.

Returning now to Blyth and Great-great-grandfather and patriarch, James—in his later years, he became a pilot at the harbour there, followed by his sons William (above), Daniel (1859-1937) and Isaac (1847-1927). It looks as if they had pretty-well cornered the market in this area and it is possibly for this reason rather than their prowess as sea-going captains, that the memory of this remarkable sea-faring family is commemorated in their home town by having a street named after them.

Another possibility is that it might be in homage to James alone, the first to bring a steamship into Blyth harbour—or it might possibly be for all three reasons. Why not?

At the corner of Tate Street there is a pub named *The Oddfellows Arms*, whose logo features the prow of a ship. Very apposite, as far as my grandfather is concerned and I am sure he would wholeheartedly approve of it—having a pub at the end of the street, I mean. Even its name seems appropriate. But maybe not. I am sure he regarded himself as normal: it was everyone else who was out of kilter.

His father, my great-great grandfather, was Alexander (1842-1924), the fifth son of James and Margaret Montgomery. His mother was Chicken Ann Lee Laidler (1838-1929). Seriously. I kid you not. Her parents really *did* christen her that while under the influence of God knows what substance, but mercifully she was known as "Annie". They had four children: Ann, who died when she was about six years old, William Laidler (1869), Clara Lillian (1872), known as "Lillian", and my grandfather, Alexander (1879) who was born in South Shields.

As I have already said, my grandfather carried on the sea-faring tradition as a chief engineer, but he was the last mariner of that particular line: his brother William was a rep. for a timber merchant's. He married Sarah Rewcastle (1870-1945) in 1898. They were the parents of Edie Tate (1904-1991) to whom I introduced you in the last chapter, as you may remember. She married John Thomson (1902-1973), her second cousin, by virtue of Edie's mother being a first cousin of Ethel Rewcastle, John's mother. Edie was a twin, but her younger brother was stillborn and never christened. She did later have another brother, Alexander, who married Ruth Worsley (1897), a clergyman's daughter. Alexander became a ship's engineer with the Glen Line.

Poor Edie did not have her own troubles to seek. Her first child, John Alexander Thomson, was born on 27th February 1935 but sadly he only survived until May. And then, cruelly, history repeated itself yet again when her next child, also a boy, was stillborn in October of the following year. Fortunately, she had better fortune with her next two children. Edith Margaret Thomson, (Margaret), was born in 1939 and Gillian Rewcastle Thomson followed in 1941. Now be prepared to suspend your disbelief.

Margaret married Michael Elstob (1941) in 1964 and their second daughter, Kathryn, had a stillborn twin brother—the third time in as many generations that this tragedy had smitten this family. Margaret had no idea she was carrying twins. Kathyrn was ten weeks premature and spent the first eleven weeks of her life in an incubator in Carlisle Maternity Hospital.

Edie's husband John, was a jolly, gentle giant with startlingly blue eyes. He weighed over twenty-two stone. I remember him saying that he couldn't use those weighing machines that used to stand in the doorways of chemists' shops because he would break them. He could only sit on straight, upright hard chairs as he couldn't get out of armchairs, at least not without a great deal of difficulty. I remember once as he was sitting on one such chair at Ternemny, my sister, awestruck by the swell of his stomach, like a galleon in full sail, told him in a very serious tone: "You know, Uncle John, if I stuck a pin in your tummy, you would go pop!" His response was to slap his meaty hands on what was visible of his knees and throw his head back in a great gale of laughter.

He was a commodore with the Eagle Oil and Shipping Company from 1956 until he retired in 1958. Eagle Oil itself did not survive a great deal longer· was absorbed by Shell in 1960. John was a very ' philatelist and I imagine a wealthy man who cc have driven flashy cars if he had wanted to but he stuck with Vauxhalls and when the manufacturers got to hear of this loyalty, they asked if he would care to endorse them. John wrote that he found the vehicles perfectly satisfactory apart from the steering wheel, which was situated too close to his stomach!

On 11th May 1943, he was presented with an OBE by George VI in recognition of the events that took place when he was master of the MV *San Cirilo* in 1942, built by Lithgows in Port Glasgow in 1937. On 21st March, with a cargo of refined oil from Abadan, Iran, and two days out of Colombo, heading for Melbourne and Hobart, the *San Cirilo* was torpedoed by a Japanese submarine. Fortunately the cargo did not ignite and John took the decision to head back to Colombo with the precious cargo, so vital for the war effort. The submarine was later spotted on the surface but it was too dangerous to open fire, while for its part, the sub did not fire another torpedo to finish off the job, either because there were none left, or seeing the *San Cirilo* was severely crippled, it was saving one for another victim. Eventually three Royal Navy destroyers turned up to escort the crippled vessel back to Colombo.

It was only a temporary reprieve. In an attack which brings the infamous Pearl Harbor to mind, just before dawn on Easter Sunday, 5th April 1942, all hell was let loose as seventy-five Japanese bombers took off from carriers in the Bay of Bengal and attacked the docks at Colombo. They were engaged by British fighters and every gun available on land and ship, was turned against them with the result that the enemy lost a third of their planes. They never came back in any sizable force again. The *San Cirilo* survived this second attack also and died of natural causes, so to speak, when she was finally scrapped in 1971.

My grandfather's sister, Lillian, married George Gibb (who happened to be a master mariner) and they had five children. Young George (1900) married Marion Carr. A long, long, time ago, in 1973, on our camping tour of the Benelux countries, the year after we were married, the young bride and I paid them a visit in Rotterdam. I don't remember what George did to earn a *beschuit* exactly, but it was something to do with shipping and I suspect his job was land-based.

Now this is where you may find the elasticity of your credulity being tested yet again, because Marion's brother, Stanley, also married a Marion— Marion Tate (1897). She was the daughter of Jasper Tate (1871-1936) and Gertrude Maria Hartman (1871-1968). Thus the Crows and Tates were connected twice over. Amazingly, or at least it is to me, I can cite six further instances where marriages took place within the family. I'm not going to point them out specifically. You can set yourself a little challenge by trying to spot them.

Here is the first one to get you started. On 13th November 1930, George Gibb's younger brother Alexander (1902-1959) married his cousin Edie's husband's sister. In other (and simpler) words, he married John Thomson's sister Ethel (1905-1989). It was through John that he met her in fact: they were school and boyhood friends. Thus John became his brother-in-law and don't forget that Edie and John were cousins to start with so if you can see another relationship there you are welcome to work it out. You may have noticed that Ethel was thirty years a widow; a lot of people don't stay married that long. Sometimes they can't help it; other times they can. My mother was a widow twenty-six years—longer than she was married.

Alexander (Alec) and Ethel's son, Ian Gibb (1936), was a master mariner who also rose to the rank of commodore, just like his uncle (and cousin) John. Ian was with P&O and was the first captain of the *Oriana* from its launch in 1994 until he retired in 1996. In the Jubilee Honours List of 2012 he received an MBE for his charity work, in particular with Trinity House, an organisation dedicated to the safety and wellbeing of mariners. That made the third person in a generation to be gonged, for John's father, Hugh Thomson, who was a chief engineer, also was an MBE.

And so it came to pass that with my grandfather, my branch of the Tates at least, finally ran out of sail and steam power on the high seas, though as we have just seen, the tradition carried on through the Gibbs thanks to my grandfather's sister, Lillian. The course was altered and set, in the next generation, for education. My grandfather's only son, my kind, mild-mannered and gentle Uncle Tommy (somehow my

randfather's personality traits gave him a bypass), was a
choolmaster. He taught English, just like me, or should
say, I taught English, just like him. Tommy's only
child, my cousin Bernard, a right bright cookie if ever
there was one (a member of Mensa, like Leslie Charteris
was), was a systems analyst way back in the embryonic
days of computers and then after his business failed, he
taught Maths at university level. Lastly, to continue the
education theme, my sister Marjorie became a teacher
of Modern Languages.

Thus we come to the end of the Tates, master
mariners, and we turn now to masters of a different
kind.

Chapter Seven

Letterfourie: masters, murders and *Macbeth*

We are in the last decade of the 17th century. Scotland is a sovereign independent country. The Protestant William and Mary are on the throne. William, better known as William III of Orange, popularly referred to by some as "King Billy", had been invited by the English Parliament to rule jointly with his wife Mary, daughter of the rightful monarch, if you want to put it that way. He, the Catholic James VII, as well as being Mary's father, was also William's uncle (not to be counted as one of the marriages within the family if you are taking up the challenge at the end of the last chapter). The trouble with relations. The trouble with religion . . .

Two years later, James returned with an army, not to England, but Ireland, joining forces with his supporters there, only to be defeated at the battle of the Boyne on July 12th 1690, a date infamous in Irish and British history and one which resonates down the centuries to this very day especially amongst people of a certain religious persuasion in the west of Scotland and Glasgow in particular and who possibly rank that date just below the only other date in Scottish history they have heard of—June 23rd 1314. This glorious victory on the battlefield, seven centuries in the past, nevertheless forms the point of reference for the de facto

Scottish national anthem as the Scots go down to yet another humiliating defeat on the football field. After *his* humiliating defeat at the Boyne, James fled back to France.

In 1694 Mary died of smallpox, leaving William, a Dutchman, as sole ruler of the British Isles. In the same year, another William, William Paterson, a Scotsman born in Tinwald, Dumfriesshire, founded the Bank of England. If that seems slightly ironic, the real irony, especially in these present times of bank, (and indeed whole country) bail-outs, is that just four years later, in 1698, the same William Paterson conceived the disastrous Darien scheme which, no—did not bankrupt the Bank of England, but did something arguably more spectacular—it practically bankrupted the entire Scottish nation. Almost half the population invested in the scheme—and lost their money. If it was a sad day for them, the consequences for their descendants were much more profound. The collapse of the Darien scheme was instrumental in bringing about what generations of battles and wars had failed to do against the "Auld Enemy"—the loss of Scottish Independence and the Union with England in 1707. After that of course, there were the Jacobite uprisings of 1715 and 1745.

Troublesome times, then, these times the Addison ancestors were born into, at least as far back as I have been able to trace them. And if, on the distaff side, the sea was in the blood of my ancestors, then the soil was ingrained into that on my father's side. Alexander Edison [sic] was baptised in Rathven, near Buckie, Banffshire on 17th December 1716. He died on June 4th 1752 which means he lived through both Jacobite rebellions and if he were too young to know anything about the first, his parents certainly would have. They were John Edison and Elspet Macky [sic] about whom I know nothing apart from the fact that they must have been born at the tail-end of the 17th century, during the reign of William and Mary, and there, alas, is where the trail of the past stops as far as the Addisons are concerned, except to say that it appears that John had a sister named Agnes and another called Jean. Agnes married James Horn and they had a daughter, Elspet, in 1718. Jean married James Geddes and had a daughter, Helen, in 1724.

But before going on the follow the trail of the early Addison ancestors, I'd like to put their lives into a narrower context yet by looking for a moment at the Gordons of Letterfourie, the Addisons being a sept of the Gordon clan and with whom the Addisons were necessarily connected since they were their masters and employers. Besides, the lairds of Letterfourie were a pretty interesting lot . . .

The first laird was James, otherwise known as The Honorable James Gordon. He rose to become Admiral of the Fleet of Scotland in 1513, the same year it so happens, that his brother William fell on Flodden Field. Their mother was in all probability Lady Annabella Stewart (1432-1509) youngest daughter of James I (1394-1437) and Joan Beaufort (1404-1437) but there is a possibility they were the sons of Elizabeth Hay, their father's mistress. Without doubt however, the gay Lothario of a father in question (the adjective predates its present connotations obviously) was George Gordon, second Earl of Huntly (c1441-1501), who inherited the title from his father in 1470. On 24th July 1471, after about eleven years of marriage to Annabella, the marriage was dissolved and George lost no time in making an honest woman of Elizabeth by marrying her the following month.

Not a smart move you might conjecture, to trade in a king's daughter for a commoner. Except by that time James I was long dead, murdered by Robert Graham and others, and James II, who had a keen interest in artillery, had been blown up by a cannon which he fired by his own hand. His successor, James III, had been on the throne since 1460. Furthermore, Elizabeth wasn't exactly a commoner either. She was the daughter of the First Earl of Atholl and on her marriage, Enzie, part of the Hays' earldom, passed to her husband and thus Letterfourie (Gaelic for "the slope of the hill where the springs are") became Gordon property. In fact, you may conclude that what George did was actually rather a smart move on his part, but what the Earl of Atholl made of it, I do not know. What I do know however, is that I got off lightly compared to him when my daughter was married. But then I was not a belted earl, only a poor boy from the boondocks—though I was well belted, as you shall find out in due course.

George was married three times in fact, contracted to his first wife, Lady Elizabeth Dunbar, daughter of the 4th Earl of Moray, on May 20th 1445, when he was just a nipper and in order to marry Annabella, George had this marriage annulled on grounds of affinity, that is to say because they were related by marriage. [Note how that did not seem to bother my relatives in the preceding chapter.] The grounds he gave for annulling his marriage to his second wife, Annabella, were similar—consanguinity. This is a very complicated business based upon a formula which can tell you to what degree you are blood-related, but what it amounted to in George's case was that Annabella was descended from the same ancestor as—no, not him—but his ex-wife, Elizabeth Dunbar! I leave you to draw your own conclusions.

How much displeasure, kingly or otherwise, George incurred by this manoeuvre is a matter of speculation but one assumes not too much, for in 1497, yet another monarch, James IV, bestowed upon him the title of Lord Chancellor of Scotland. He died at Stirling Castle on June 8th 1501.

George's other claim to fame, though not a lot of people know this, is that his daughter, Catherine, by his third wife, Elizabeth Hay, became the wife of that chancer (or perhaps not, according to some historians) Perkin Warbeck. And before I finally lay George's bones and amorous affairs to rest, I will just mention in the passing, that his brother William aforesaid, the one who died at Flodden, married Janet Ogilvie and they became the progenitors of the Gordons of Gight, Aberdeenshire. It is through them that the Romantic poet, loyal lover of the Greeks and disloyal lover of several ladies, including his half-sister, that George Gordon Byron, a.k.a. 6th Baron Byron, was descended. Not a lot of people know that either.

We will skip the second laird, Patrick (died 1606), but will mention, because he is more interesting, the unhappy third laird, James, who was imprisoned in Edinburgh in 1636 for his part, along with the Marquis of Huntly, in a plot against the Crichtons of Frendraught whose territories lay on the other side of the Deveron. Crichton was married to Lady Elizabeth

Gordon, eldest daughter of the Earl of Sutherland, but that family link did nothing to assuage the bitterness between the feuding families. Quite the reverse in fact. Briefly, here is the story, the reason why Letterfourie and Huntly found themselves in trouble with the law.

In 1630, Crichton had shot and killed Gordon of Rothiemay over a border dispute and had been ordered by the Marquis of Huntly, who was of course, a Gordon, to pay Rothiemay's son a huge amount of blood money as compensation, which Crichton did. Later that year however, Crichton was in trouble again, this time charged with shooting Leslie of Pitcaple in the arm with an arrow and was ordered to appear before the Marquis once again.

Somewhat surprisingly, since the Leslies were enemies of the Crichtons, as well as being allies of the Gordons, this time the Marquis found in favour of Crichton. Not surprisingly at all, Leslie rode off vowing vengeance and justice and Crichton thought it politic to have a bodyguard to escort him back to Frendraught. Now this is where it begins to get even more interesting. Somewhat bizarrely you may think, who did Crichton choose as his bodyguards but the son of the Marquis, John Gordon—and this is the really astonishing bit, but also Gordon of Rothiemay, also named John Gordon! It does seem a strange choice, unless . . .

It was October and the light was failing when the party arrived at Frendraught and you can imagine how Lady Crichton, happy to see hubby home and exonerated, deemed a celebration was in order and ever the perfect hostess, despite the enmity between the families and Rothiemay especially, persuaded the Gordons to stay the night. She gave them bedchambers in the tower, which just so happened to have wooden stairs, which, in the night, mysteriously caught fire. If her plan had been to kill the Gordons, she was successful in that, as well as causing the deaths of their retainers, and not forgetting of course, the collateral damage to the fabric of the building. Although there was no proof against her, she was widely believed to have been responsible and is immortalised in a ballad which puts the blame solely and squarely on her shoulders.

If similarities with Shakespeare's Scottish play spring to mind, believe it or not, there was another Lady Elizabeth Gordon who came along about a century later and what she did you will find out in Chapter Thirty-four but it seems she also finished her education at the Lady Macbeth School of Matrimony. But if you cannot contain your impatience, and strong and domineering women are to your taste, another, lesser protégé of that institution will be appearing in the chapter after next.

In the meantime, for want of evidence, and on the orders of the King, the third laird of Letterfourie was absolved of complicity in seeking revenge for these deaths, as was Huntly, who had not to suffer the indignity of being transported to Edinburgh for trial, but had been kept under house arrest. Both, however, were compelled to pay an indemnity against any future predations against the Crichtons.

A little over a decade later however, James was back in the jug. His "crime" this time (1647) was that while defending the Bog of Gight along with his brother, Thomas Gordon of Glastirum, and some others, he fell into the clutches of the commander of the Covenanter's army, General Sir David Leslie. They later renamed the Bog, Gordon Castle. I am at a loss to think why.

In 1653, the estate of Letterfourie was forfeited and granted, by the Keepers of the Great Seal, to Alexander Farquhar of Aberdeen. To add insult to injury, James also lost his estates in Rossshire. The worst of times for him. He died in custody sometime before 1656, having sired two daughters, Beatrix and Lillias, in happier times, presumably. Happily however, Thomas, his brother (who was the physician in Huntly's household), somehow, perhaps through that connection, managed to regain Letterfourie which he passed on to his son, John, the 4th laird.

Born in 1627, he was the laird during John and Elspet Edison's time. He married twice, producing James by his first wife, followed by Alexander and Marie from his second. Alexander went into service with the Grand Duke of Tuscany.

John had a long life, even by today's standards, only giving up the ghost in 1715. His son, James, the (also) hapless 5th laird, born in 1660, defended Edinburgh Castle against William of Orange in 1689 and in 1695 married Glicerie, or, according to another source, Grizel, daughter of Sir William of Durn. Dire names in any case. And I thought it was only in the late 20th century that the cruel practice of parents giving their children weird and pretentious names began.

I will come back to the exploits of the unfortunate 5th laird and his arguably even more unfortunate descendants later. In the meantime, spare a thought for the aristocracy. Don't feel envy; feel sympathy. As you will see, the Gordons are good adverts for the adage that money can't buy you love or happiness and one of them didn't even have any of that left by the end of his days.

But now the Gordons have caught up with us happy breed of Addisons, it is time to pick up their story again. Only being a pauper is not a barrel of laughs either, as the other adage has it.

Chapter Eight

Rathven: the origins of the species

Before the Norman Conquest, surnames were not common in England and this new-fangled Norman innovation, like a slow-spreading stain, only reached Scotland in the 12th Century. Normally surnames were based on the occupation of the person originally given the name, or a place name, or a nickname, or, as in the case of "Addison", the first name of the father was grafted on to the offspring, hence Addison means "son of Addy", a familiar form of Adam. The first recorded Addison in Scotland is William Adison [sic] the rector of Luss in 1379. It is a name found most commonly in the east, from Berwick to Aberdeenshire, which of course now scandalously includes the lost county of Banffshire.

You may be wondering, gentle reader, if by any chance, your present humble narrator has any connection with those famous Addisons, namely the man of letters and founder of the *Spectator,* Joseph (1672-1719), and Thomas (1793-1860), who discovered more diseases than you can shake a stick at and who could speak fluent Latin. [But who would know if he could tell his ablatives from his datives?] Poor Thomas suffered from depression and alas, committed suicide aged 72 and no doubt before taking this ultimate and extreme measure, had been heard repeatedly going about the place declaiming, *O me miserum!* Anyway, if those questions have happened to cross your mind, the answer is no, not to either of these, do we appear to be connected. Nor are we related to that American luminary, Thomas Alva Edison (1847-1931) who claims Dutch descent.

I begin the tale of the Addison ancestors with a confession and I may as well admit it right from the start. You may remember that in the previous chapter I referred to Alexander Edison, son of John and Elspet, who would have been born at the end of the 17th century. Alas I have been unable to establish a definite link between Alexander and the next generation to my first unquestionable ancestor, John Edison, my Great-great-great-great grandfather who married Isobel Paterson on 17th August 1758 at Clochan, Rathven. Having said that however, I am perfectly satisfied in my own mind that in a place as tiny as Clochan, they must certainly have been related and most probably were father and son.

John was a crofter at Townhead, a mere six acres in size and in all likelihood supplemented his income as coachman to the 5th laird, James Gordon. Alas Townhead no longer exists. Another croft exists on that site now but what a visit there does reveal is a splendid view in one direction down to Buckie and the coast, and in the other, to the tree-clad and hilly hinterland of what used to be Banffshire but is now Moray as you look west, and Aberdeenshire as you look east. Regrettably, Banffshire, the county of my birth, no longer exists and when I read in the newspapers and elsewhere, "Banff, Aberdeenshire" it irritates me beyond measure and the above is the only time you will ever see me write it. In Stalinist Russia, (amongst other places, unfortunately) it is well known that people were wiped from the face of the earth as if they had never existed, their names disappearing with their bodies. But a whole county? How did we allow that to happen? It's a small protest I know, but I still persist in clinging on to "Banffshire" when I address my Christmas cards to my relatives in the area.

An asterisk next to the entry for Alexander's death (1752) in the old parish register of burials marks him out as a "papist". The asterisked "p" word carries connotations of disapproval at best, the sort of bigotry and prejudice that notoriously still persists in certain parts of Scotland today, though not at all in Banffshire now, but during Alexander's lifetime, such anti-Catholic feelings were raw and rife throughout the entire country in the aftermath of the '45.

Alexander's salad days were also the days when people were fined and publically humiliated for working on the Sabbath Day by Presbyterian zealots who made the proverbial scorned woman's fury seem almost like a benediction, a flavour of which we get from the following extract from the Old Parish Records:

14 July 1724 Alex. Machatty, being asked if he had his wool drying and a tent set up to keep it, on the Lord's day, answered, his wool was sett out to dry on Friday and on Saturday's night it was rapped together, in order to ly that way till Munday's morning, the wool being laid out in leeces. The session judged him guilty, and being a papist, he was sharply rebuked for his sin, and was appointed to pay the clerk, fourty sh. Scots.

At this time, a Scots pound was worth only a twelfth of an English one and translated into present day values would be somewhere in the region of £25.

But the real point I'm making becomes apparent when you compare it with this similar case seven years later:

2 Aug 1730 They confessed they gathered dilse, but no partens, on the Lords day, upon which they were rebuked for this and their customary swearing, and appointed to make their compearance next Lord's day before the congregation, and pay 20s each as a penalty. Delation also given in against Partick Cuy, George Hepburn and John Young, servants in Glastirum, as having gathered dilse Sunday last in the sea craigs thereto adjacent. Having confessed, they were sharply rebuked, and appointed to compear before the congregation next Lord's day, and Geo, Hepburn to pay 40s Sc., he having been guilty of Sabbath breach last year, and the other two 20 sh. each of them.

From this we can deduce that the fine was normally 20 shillings for the first offence, yet since the poor MacHattie was fined double that, one is inclined to conclude the reason for his excessive fine was because he was "a papist". There have been several times in the history of these islands when the living was not easy and the dying even harder, when you think of the Black Death and the First World War to name but two some seven centuries apart, but to be a Catholic in Alexander Edison's time, while admittedly not as bad a time as those two examples, was not exactly "the best of times" either, as Dickens put it in *A Tale of Two Cities*.

Naturally no-one can choose the period of their birth but I consider myself to have had the most amazing luck to have been born in the best of times, post Second World War hardship and rationing notwithstanding. My generation was the first to benefit from the NHS; we did not have to fight any wars unless we voluntarily joined the Armed Services; we received free tertiary education; housing was affordable and our endowment policies not only paid off our mortgages but provided a tidy sum besides; employment was readily available (especially for teachers as it was so poorly paid); we were not held to ransom by nurseries since friends minded our children as a favour (and for a small fee); and we have been able to avail ourselves of cheap air travel all over the globe, even if it is just Ryanair who might just cost you an arm and a leg at the end of the day. But you can take comfort in the fact that there is always the NHS to fall back on and which will provide you with a wheelchair which you can trust completely to get you to your destination and back without any problems (unlike Ryanair).

As I mentioned earlier, it came as a bit of a surprise to me, brought up as I was (reluctantly) in the Church of Scotland, to discover that my ancestors were Catholics. But of course you only have to go back as little as 150 years or so from the births of John and Elspeth before you come to John Knox and the birth of the Protestant Reformation. Before that, we would *all* have been Catholics.

My confirmed ancestor, John, (the one who married Isobel Paterson in 1758), had a brother, James, followed by two sisters, Elizabeth and Helen, and an interesting parallel emerges between the two brothers. Both wives were named Isobel, Isobel Duncan being James's wife. From 1763 to 1765, both Isobels took it in turn to keep the Edison [sic] line going. John begat John in 1763 who subsequently married Ann McClelland and who, in the fullness of time, (nearly two hundred years later) were responsible for bringing me into the world. Thank you both. Well done. You knew not what you did.

Meanwhile, brother James, who was rather slower in entering the marriage stakes than John, only tying the knot in 1763, produced another John Addison in 1764. The following year, (1765), John sired Alexander. The year after that, James begat James and then—and this is the remarkable thing—both Isobels produced twins in 1769—George and Ann to John in January, and Margaret and Elspet (named after her great-grandmother?) to James in March. Can you imagine what it must have been like when the twins were two and the families got together for Christmas?

I confess that I have not explored every branch and twig of the family tree since then searching for twins. Like the playing of snooker, that would be the sign of a wasted life, but as far as I know, these were the last twins in the extended family until my Auntie Daisy produced Helen and Jessie Chalmers in 1938. I'll spare you the arithmetic. That's 169 years. Twins, you may say, tend not to run in our family, though there were others after Helen and Jessie. For the purposes of emphasising just how long ago this was, (as well as putting it into the historical context), it just so happens that both sets of twins share the same birth year as those arch enemies, the Duke of Wellington and Napoleon—which is not to imply of course that the original Edison twins were at loggerheads even after a fraught Christmas Day.

John and James's sisters, Elizabeth and Helen, also did their bit to preserve the Addison genes and although the name died out, the genes marched on. Elizabeth married James Farquhar in 1762 and they had two children, Helen (1763) and James (1767). Helen married George Davidson in 1769 and like her sister, wasted no time in producing her own James in 1770.

But to return to the main line, my Great-great-great-grandfather, John Adison [sic], baptised in 1763 at Upper Clochan, first child of John and Isobel Paterson, was a coachman to James, the sixth laird, a position he no doubt inherited from his father. He married Ann McClelland in 1797. The spellings of her name are various and that is the form I have decided on. They had nine children, all born in Rathven. The second, Joseph (1803), was to become my ancestor and for the moment I will only refer to one other—James (1810), to show the close affinity the Addisons had with the two estates of the laird and the Church, for the witnesses at his baptism were James Gordon, the 8th laird and Mr Carruthers, the parish priest.

In Scotland, registration of births, marriages and deaths was not compulsory until 1855. Prior to that, these were made, if at all, in the Old Parish Registers. The responsibility for keeping these was the responsibility of the Session Clerk who brought to the task varying degrees of enthusiasm, not to mention legibility of handwriting. The problem for genealogists today was compounded in 1783, when the government, in its wisdom, saw fit to impose a 3d tax on every entry.

Did John not care a thrupenny bit for his daughters, to coin a phrase? Was this the reason why, although he did register his sons' births, he did not register those of his daughters? Fortunately I discovered their existence in another source, but having found their dates of baptism, that is all I know about them. They have disappeared without trace, or at least off my radar. But genealogy is a never-ending quest and who's to say that they might turn up yet, if not found by me, perhaps by some future family researcher?

John's brother, Alexander, (named after his grandfather?) and two years younger than him, died at a croft called Scraphard. His occupation is given as an agricultural labourer. It makes me think of him desperately wresting a living from the soil, but as the propaganda would have us believe, hard work never killed anyone and perhaps it did him no harm after all, since he died aged 88 on 22nd February 1853. I hope he still wasn't working at that age, but as I have come to realise, none of my rustic, haggis-fed cousins know how to retire and haven't given up working though they are past (some long past) retirement age and their allotted three score years and ten. It wouldn't therefore surprise me in the least if Alexander was still working right up to the end, at least as much as his aged bones would allow. He also seems to have come down in the world from when he was a crofter at Dykehead of Clochan.

But there had been harder times. According to the Enzie census of 1841, Alexander is 77, as is his wife, Ann Pirie (who appears to have been a Protestant by the way). That year the census was taken on the 6th of June. Now, here's the thing. Ann died on the 4th yet Alexander registered her as residing there on that date. The instructions were, as they are today, to record the names of those who had *spent the night* in the house on the night of the census. It doesn't say anything about *living* there. It conjures up an image of Ann, two days dead, not yet laid in earth, like Purcell's Dido lamented, but laid out, probably in the same room as the grieving husband as he filled in the form.

Alexander is to be commended for the diligence and seriousness with which he applied himself to this tiresome task, especially if he was not very good at his letters, which he may have been, to give him the benefit of the doubt when a great many were illiterate, but certainly he had to fill in this tiresome form under very trying circumstances. As you will see in a later chapter, not everyone followed his example of exemplary devotion to form filling . . .

According to the same census, Alexander and Isobel had two daughters, Isobel (35) and Margaret (25). Margaret's birth, however, is recorded as being the 20th October 1805, the day before the battle of Trafalgar and so she could rightly claim to be a contemporary of Nelson—just, for he died the following day. This would make *her* 35 on the day of the census, not Isobel, and would seem to suggest that Alexander had got his daughters mixed up. But that is understandable. He was grieving and perhaps still in shock.

But ten years later, in the next census of 1851, he still appears rather confused. There are only now six years between the girls. Margaret is 45 (which would be correct) and described as a "housemaid" while poor Isobel has aged an astonishing sixteen years for she is now 51 and even worse than that, she is described as an "imbecile". There are three reasons which might go some way to explaining this discrepancy: Alexander's lack of arithmetical skills, or his failing memory. What the other one is, I will tell you later.

One of the new questions in the 1871 census required the respondents to state if anyone in the household was an "imbecile, idiot or lunatic". (No such thing as political correctness then.) It amuses me to think of the head of the household in those days scratching his head and pondering over the shades of meaning before finally plumping on the one he considered the most fitting. Maybe the form came with handy Guidance Notes. But Alexander, it seems, was ahead of his time in this respect and apparently had no such difficulty *twenty* years prior to this requirement in volunteering this description of the unfortunate Isobel, just as he was equally unabashed about describing himself as a "pauper". The impecuniousness of farmers, it seems, goes back a long way, though in Alexander's case I am sure it was true.

Also recorded in the 1851 census is a granddaughter, Marjorie McIntosh aged 13, a scholar, Margaret being her mother. While it is possible that the girl's father was merely absent on the day of the census, I think it is more logical than cynical to suspect that she was born out of wedlock.

According to the records of Preshome RC Church, Alexander's resting place is in St Ninian's, Tynet, near Buckie. As well as poor (in both senses of the word) Alexander's bones, the lair also contains the remains of Margaret Millen [sic] who died in December 1851 and Ann Wilson who died in August 1867. Who these ladies are I am afraid I have no idea. Neither would be a second wife I would have thought, for in 1841 Alexander, as you may remember, was 77 and I would have thought unlikely to embark on a second marriage at that age. Surely he must have learned *something* by that age.

St Ninian's also contains the remains of Alexander's daughter, Margaret, who died in February 1865 and sadly, also her daughter, Marjorie, who died the following month, probably carried off by the same deadly disease. However there is no mention of Margaret's "husband", the elusive Mr McIntosh, nor her sister, poor Isobel the Imbecile, nor their mother, Ann Pirie. But not being a Catholic, Ann would not have been eligible for interment in St Ninian's anyway and I did not therefore expect to find her there. But I scoured St Ninian's cemetery in vain for the graves of Alexander and the ladies with whom he is sleeping the Good Sleep.

It's not the easiest of places to visit. You approach it along a narrow grassy track with a barbed wire fence on either side like the perimeter fence at Auschwitz, only greener, and a couple of gates which you need to open and close behind you. On our visit, a stirk had somehow breached the fence and was trapped in this narrow passage and his panic grew the nearer we approached. We managed to squeeze past each other without damage to either him or our car, and finally arrived at the cemetery where it stands surrounded by fields and where the dead can sleep without any fear of their slumbers being interrupted except by the most determined of visitors.

It's not a large place so it's impossible that my trusty assistant, the faithful Fiona, and I could have missed my ancestors as we trod softly on the dreams of the dead as up and down the aisles of headstones we searched in vain.

There can only be one reason. Alexander was buried in a pauper's grave and if ever there was a marker of some sort, it has long since rotted away. Very possibly the ladies he shares the graves with were paupers too and he had no choice but to sleep throughout eternity with them. In fact, since Margaret Millen predeceased

Alexander by more than a year, it was *she* who had to move over for *him*, just as he had to fourteen years later, to make room for Ann Wilson. I suppose there are worse things than sleeping through eternity between two ladies you don't know. Could be quite an interesting way of passing the time in fact, but on the other hand, it could be hell, not heaven, in which you find yourself. What if they were the equivalent of Margaret Thatcher and Ann Widdecombe and the latter was on top?

I imagine Margaret, who was only a housemaid and an unmarried mother, was also buried in a pauper's grave along with poor Marjorie who would only have been twenty-nine. No memorial exists for them either.

This will have to be it.

Chapter Nine

The Gordons: religion, romance, and ruin

Let us leave Alexander and the other Addisons sleeping the Big Sleep in the middle of the 19th century and go back for a moment to their lairds, the Gordons, where we abandoned them in the middle of the 17th century.

We pick up the tale with the 5th laird of Letterfourie whom I described in Chapter Seven as "hapless". This is because just two years before his death at the age of 86, the poor old man was obliged to pay "cess and levie" to the Jacobites, that is to say a levy towards the support of the Jacobite army amounting to nearly £18,000 in today's money. He had been in default for more than six months so whilst it is plain to see he was hardly an enthusiastic supporter of the Cause, it might be going a bit far to go to the other extreme and conclude he was a crypto supporter of the Government as I have read in one source. I suppose one is always allowed to change one's mind, especially as one becomes older and wiser, but he had fought at Sheriffmuir in 1715 and before that was, as I said, helping to defend Edinburgh Castle in 1689 against William of Orange. Besides, he came from a long line of staunch Catholics.

No, I can't believe that James, at his age, changed his beliefs. Overwhelmingly, this looks like a case of tax avoidance or the avoidance of contributing to Lost

Causes. Whatever the case, James's perspicacity and prevarication almost worked. Only 27 days later, on the 16th April, the Jacobites were routed at Culloden, with Prince Charles Edward Stuart in command of that raggle-taggle band of men, exhausted and hungry from the abortive twenty-four mile march to Nairn and back the day before the battle. Had that attack gone ahead, had the Battle of Nairn rather than Culloden been the last battle fought on British soil, with the advantage of surprise and the Duke of Cumberland's men celebrating their leader's 25th birthday with rations of brandy, who knows if the result (and history) might not have been completely different?

Two years later to the day when James had to dig deep into his pockets to pay his fine, his relatives were digging his grave. He was buried on March 20th 1748 in Rathven, a poorer man certainly, and how often he told his family or anyone who would listen "I told you so" one can only speculate. One thing is certain: he must have died broken-hearted, for in his lifetime he suffered more losses than mere money. His third son, William, was robbed and murdered in the Alps in 1740. Three years before this tragedy, his first son, Patrick (also known as Peter), died in 1737. His second son, James, became a successful wine merchant in Madeira but that of course was like another death, being so far away and communication being so much poorer than today. And as for the fourth son, Alexander, born in 1715—he was a fervent Jacobite, a volunteer in one of Bonnie Prince Charlie's Life Guards, who after Culloden, somehow escaped to join his brother James in Madeira.

That other escape, eventually to France, of his less than illustrious leader, is well documented—Flora

MacDonald and all that—a romantic tale, but what happened after that is less salubrious and less well known or glossed over. He died in Rome in 1788, the place of his birth—*persona non grata* in France, drunkard, wife-beater and philanderer. Admittedly some of his problems undoubtedly stemmed from his incompetence at Culloden, and he had only himself to blame for that, but this is not the place to delve into military tactics and mistakes. Having said that, the troops at his disposal were massively outnumbered and much less well trained. Just as well the supporters who laid their lives down for him were at least spared the knowledge of the manner of his decline, but if they ever thought, had he been victorious at Culloden (or Nairn), he would have ruled Scotland (and Britain) from Edinburgh, then their illusions may well have been dispelled long before that.

After the Act of Proscription of 1746, Letterfourie was known as a "safe house", identified by a white rose in the garden which, it is believed, also indicated the location of an escape passage, the other end of which is supposed to be near the Category A listed two-tier Craigmin Bridge over the Findlater Gorge. The lower tier incorporates what is known as "Bonnie Prince Charlie's cell"—evidence surely that the fifth laird was as good a Catholic as the rest and best of them, but who was perspicacious enough (it would be unkind to say "mean") to realise that his money was better in *his* pockets than squandered by Bonnie Prince Charlie's men.

Returning to Scotland in 1778 after an amnesty was signed, and as 6th laird of Letterfourie, James, the son of the previous James, commissioned the celebrated Robert

Adam to design a new mansion, and according to John Connachan-Holmes in his *Country Houses of Scotland,* Adam's first commission in Scotland after his return from his Grand Tour. I find this somewhat puzzling since Adam returned in 1758 and the new mansion was not built until 1772. But I suppose the operative word is *designed.* It was quite a modest pile really, with Adam fireplaces, naturally, and the doors in the main rooms made of Spanish mahogany, imported from Madeira.

But building a mansion was only one of James's building projects. Along with his brother, Alexander, they provided funds for the building of a church at Preshome. The foundation stone was laid in 1788, the same year as Charles Edward Stuart died. In 1790, St. Gregory's was complete, having the distinction of being the first Roman Catholic church erected in Scotland after the Reformation that actually *looked* like a church and if this doesn't tell you what a hotbed of Catholicism the parish of Rathven was, then I don't know what else will.

As well as being the first, St Gregory's was the biggest Catholic chapel in Britain outside London. Alas James died before the church was opened. He could have inscribed his coat of arms over the door to remind the parish of his generosity but he did not—instead a simple dedication reads "DEO 1788".

Not only modest, but someone who enjoyed a laugh at his own expense. Blundell's *Ancient Catholic Homes of Scotland* relates that he liked to tell the story about, how arriving late at the previous chapel, he was rebuked by the priest: "Good morning, Letterfourie! Last in and first oot!"

From this we can deduce that the laird and the priest were on very good terms. And for those of you who don't know, farmers (or lairds) were normally addressed by the name of their farm rather than their surname, and still are in the North-East. So James Gordon could consider himself blessed for being a Catholic and having a priest with a sense of humour unlike those Calvinists on the other side of the religious divide who saw (and still see) life as being far too serious for any levity, none more in the perennial problem of the sin of fornication. Compare these two examples from the Kirk Session Minutes of Rathven Parish, about 100 years apart:

7 Sep 1746 Compeared John Galt and Margaret Knight in Findochty and confessed guilt of Antenuptial fornication and being rebuked were appointed to Compear before the pulpit when called upon from their Seats and to be publickly rebuked and pay three Pounds Scots which they promised to do.

16 May? 1841 Alex. Smith and his wife Jane Garden confessed guilt of antenuptial fornication, the Moderator after a suitable rebuke and serious admonition ordered them to wait on him at the Manse on Wednesday and Friday that he may have an opportunity of private conversation with him . . ."

By the mid 19th century a more enlightened attitude seems to have prevailed, yet how intensely humiliating that still would have been! Just imagine! And did they, in the congregation, have the grace to blush when they heard this public rebuke and think: *There, but for the grace of God, go I?* Lovers of Burns will, of course, be familiar with *Holy Willie's Prayer,* his brilliant satire on the hypocrisy behind this whole vexed issue of premarital sex, Burns himself being no stranger to being ritually humiliated in front of the congregation as a fornicator.

Did the thought of this public humiliation, not to mention the fine, ever deter anyone, especially when passion was at its peak? It may have done as far as I was concerned at least. There was the awful spectre of what my parents would have done to me if ever I had ever got a young lady "into trouble" as the saying went in those days. Chance would have been a fine thing of course but as I remarked earlier, the internal combustion engine was a great facilitator, and once on my return in the wee small hours after having borrowed my mother's car (my father had died by this time) to take a young lady out, my mother demanded to know, like a lawyer for the prosecution: "How many times have you been married?" But the question was rhetorical. She didn't really want to know the number and I certainly didn't want to admit anything.

James Gordon may have been "married" in my mother's understanding of the word, many, many times or maybe never at all, but he died a bachelor in 1790, aged 83, without issue, or at least legitimate issue, and so Letterfourie passed to his brother Alexander, who, as well as laying out the grounds, later added the wings, since which time the house has more or less remained unchanged, externally. The west wing had a chapel, above which was accommodation for a resident priest. At the time of writing, this grade A listed building and extremely desirable residence is on the market for offers in the region of £980,000. A snip. Given my family's connections with it I would snap it up, snip snap, if I could.

In 1778, Alexander, (who had fought with Bonnie Prince Charlie remember) married Helen Russell, daughter of Mr Russell of Moncoffer, Banff. They had three children: James (1779), Alexander (1781-1810) and Charles Edward in 1785. Where did they get that name from you may wonder? Well, you may just wonder wrong: he was named after Charles Hay, late of Rannes and Colonel Charles Gordon of Shilagreen, so the registration of his birth affirms. The poor soul died in Venice in 1805 aged only 21. Alexander himself died in 1797 aged 82. As we have already seen, the unfortunate Gordon family were no strangers to their children predeceasing them, surely the worst torment that a merciful God can dole out to test the faith of the faithful whatever side of the religious divide you are on.

James the younger survived to become the 8th laird, rich enough to buy the nearby Buckpool estate in 1810, but his life was not a happy one either, despite his wealth. The problem was his wife, whom he had married in 1801—Mary Lucy Elizabeth Glendonwyn, daughter of William Glendonwyn of Parton, Kirkcudbrightshire, not as you may have supposed, somewhere in Wales. She was such a disaster her own father disinherited her and she led her husband a merry dance as he struggled to pay off her numerous creditors.

In an illuminating manuscript, James defended an action brought against him by Alexander Buie, a vintner in Fochabers for £183 16s 10p. Like something out of *Bleak House*, the case was first lodged in May 1821 but did not reach its conclusion until 1831. In his defence, James claimed that at the time of his marriage he was worth £3000 a year. He had been forced to sell more than half of his estate to keep his wife going and was struggling to keep his head above water. Submitting his finances to the scrutiny of the court, after all expenses, it showed that his income was the grand sum of £87 9s 4d. And although they were separated, the grand lady lived on in Letterfourie in the style to which she had accustomed herself. Well, can you imagine trying to get her to leave? And being a Catholic, divorce was out of the question of course.

Nevertheless, despite these marital difficulties, they managed to produce seven children, of whom the first, William (1803) subsequently became the 9th laird in 1843, and since he was unmarried, was succeeded by his brother, Robert Glendonwyn Gordon in 1861. Robert was actually the fourth son: his two elder brothers, James and John, died in 1822 and 1825 respectively and here's the astonishing thing—both died aged seventeen. And as if that was not quite enough to contend with, Lady Gordon fell out with their eldest daughter, threw her out of the house and the poor Sir James actually sent her to France as it was apparently more economical to bring her up there.

Meanwhile, his attempts to steer William into gainful employment by adopting a profession were thwarted at every turn by his mother who exerted a great deal of influence over him. Nevertheless, he came good in the end, became a soldier in the Royal Scots and saw action in Canada during the rebellions of 1837. He eventually retired with the rank of lieutenant colonel in the 3rd West Indian Regiment.

His impoverished father died on Christmas Eve 1843. The poor sod never did have much luck—he would have already gone to the expense of buying the Christmas presents though whether he had bought one for his wife, we can only guess he did not. But for the love of a good woman he might have lived a longer, happier life and would certainly have died a lot richer. He didn't even have the satisfaction of being a merry widower. His good lady died in 1845. I hope for his sake they are not reunited in heaven.

But I am getting ahead of myself here. I won't trouble you with any more of the Gordons' story since the connection between them and my branch of the Addisons ended with the eighth laird. By the time the 9th laird had succeeded to the title, my branch of the family had moved out of Rathven to Portnockie.

And that is where we shall meet them in the next chapter, if you will.

Chapter Ten

Dates, deaths and disasters

One of my favourite authors, Mark Twain, gave the world at least two immortal sayings. The first, and possibly the most entertaining, is: "The reports of my death are greatly exaggerated". The second is: "There are lies, damned lies and statistics".

You will certainly find statistics in this chapter because much of the content depends on my sources— the census returns whose purpose was to collect information for statistical purposes, though what the number crunchers made of the returns need not concern us. There are no deliberate lies told here by me but I have found plenty by my ancestors. Whether they could be described as "damned" lies, I suppose, depends upon your interpretation of the word and the degree of deliberate obfuscation you assume on the part of the respondent who completed the census.

To be fair, they probably did not mean to tell untruths, so let's tip a nod in the direction of Winston Churchill instead and call them numerical inexactitudes. There are certainly a large number of them in the returns and what's more, as you will see, you can't even trust the words (or numbers) they left on their loved ones' tombstones either. Just because it is written in stone doesn't necessarily mean it is hard fact, but it is likely that readers will assume it is. Just some of the pitfalls that the ancestors, either wittingly or unwittingly, have strewn in the path of the genealogist as he follows the trail of the past. And so, warily, we enter the minefield.

The Rathven census of 1851, which is more detailed than that of 1841, reveals that my Great-great grandfather Joseph, (son of John and Anne McClelland) born in Townhead, Rathven, is living in Portknockie. He says he is 50, gives his occupation as "farmer and fish curer" and is married to Janet Coull who he says is 43. They have a daughter, Mary Ann, aged 19, whose birth is given as Findochty (pronounced Finichty, with the stress on the middle syllable) so they must have left Rathven somewhere in the late 1820s and certainly by 1832 at the latest.

There are seven other children in the household at that time as well as his brother George (36), and since his occupation is given as "farm servant" this would seem to suggest that farming rather than the fishing business was in the ascendant, assuming that he was working for Joseph of course. Also in the house on that day, 31st March 1851 are Elizabeth Donaldson aged 13 whose occupation is given, rather quaintly, as a "shepherdess" and finally, Margaret Jamieson, aged 24, a domestic servant.

For some curious reason best known to those who devised the 1841 census, respondents were required to round down to the nearest five years, the ages of those over fifteen, hence Isobel the Imbecile's impressive spurt of years between the 1841 and 1851 censuses and the third mysterious reason I alluded to as the reason for the discrepancy in Alexander's daughters' ages. Why they should have thought up this hare-brained idea I have no idea, but it is not in the least helpful for genealogists.

Thus Joseph, baptised in 1804, (more of this later) in 1841 must have been 36 or 37, and should have written down 35 but he put down 30 for both him and his wife. Perhaps he did not fully understand this bizarre rule, or could it just be that Joseph, and possibly other people like him, these peasants from the boondocks of Banffshire, far from the seat of government, resented what they saw as this prying into their private affairs and deliberately got their sums wrong? His occupation then was a cooper and he lists his five children, not according to age, but to sex, with the boys coming first, naturally.

By the census of 1861, the family has moved, upwardly mobile you may care to put it, to a farm of 100 acres called Hillhead near Cullen, employing two men and two boys. Times were getting better. According to this census, Joseph is more accurately described as being 57, while Janet is only 50. By 1871 however, she has made up the lost years and is 62, while Joseph has only put on another seven years, making him 64. You see what I mean about the ages on the census returns. They just don't add up and are not to be trusted any further than a one-armed man could toss a caber.

And they have moved again, this time to Summertown, near Fordyce. It was to be Joseph's last move and he did not survive to complete another census, for in 1881 Janet is a widow and an annuitant aged 75. It is good to see that in the days before we all become recipients of a stately income once we attain a certain age (as long as we are spared), that Joseph made provision for his and Janet's old age. But maybe she was the one filling in the census returns all along, for that age is incorrect too. Her name on the tombstone in the old kirkyard of Fordyce is the worst preserved, being pretty pockmarked and it is difficult to distinguish between a 3 and an 8 or a 6 but it seems she died on Feb 1st 1888 aged 78. The death certificate records her death as "Disease of Heart (Time unknown). Apoplexy. Paralysis of right side—5 days". And so, before the real death, the living death. She must have known, you would have thought, that the end was nigh and I for one, can imagine her hoping the sooner the better.

If you trust the tombstone, that would have made Janet's birth year either 1810 or 1811, depending on whether she had had her birthday yet or not. Whatever the census returns say, it is written in stone that Joseph died on 29th June 1877 aged 74. While that date may appear to be conclusive, unfortunately his baptismal record of 16th February 1804 comes in the midst of entries for 1805 with a few erratics thrown in from 1800, 1801 and 1803. Was his a late registration, or a slip of the quill? If the age on the tombstone is to be believed, he would have to have been born in 1803. Furthermore, at this time it is likely the Addisons were still adherents of the Old Religion whose practice it normally is to baptise infants as soon as conveniently possible after birth, so 1803 seems the more likely suspect. In any event, it seems we can say with certainty that Joseph was seven years Janet's senior.

Joseph's death was rather unpleasant. He died of diarrhoea followed by ulceration of the bowels, not to mention weakness of the heart and fatty degeneration. If his dying was hard, his living was not easy either, at least in a couple of respects, for his headstone sadly records the death of an infant daughter, Anne, as well as a son, Alexander, Student of Divinity and Missionary at

Wishaw who died in the manse there on 4ᵗʰ May 1876, aged 29, so the stone says, but look closely, for it is easy to mistake the nine for a zero. He died of heart failure and had been ill for five days previously.

It is a solemn reminder of how the lives of the Addisons and the lairds of Letterfourie were connected and touched by tragedy—poor Joseph living long enough to see not just one, but two of his children predecease him, just as we have seen, was not uncommon with the Gordon family.

There are a couple of curious things about this headstone. Firstly no dates are given for Anne, though I know she was born on the 4ᵗʰ August 1842 and was baptised on 14ᵗʰ November so she must have lived that long at least. It also tells us perhaps that she was healthy enough when she was born as there was no rush to have her baptised. Why her dates were not included is a mystery. And there is a mystery too about Alexander's age, for if the date of death is correct (and we would assume it is) then his age is wrong. He would have been 31 for he was born on 8ᵗʰ July 1844. I suppose when you have as many children as Joseph and Janet, it must be easy to forget who was born when, and as we have seen, Joseph was never quite sure of his own age, never mind his children.

They had ten children in all, all born in Portknockie apart from Mary Ann and John who were born in Findochty, which means from the age of twenty-two to forty-one, Janet was practically perpetually pregnant. When you think there were no automatic washing machines then to wash the children's clothes or microwaves to cut down on the time spent preparing meals or even a TV to plonk them in front of so you had a minute to yourself—that woman deserves a medal. Or perhaps someone should have done her a favour and told her what was causing all those babies.

We will come to the children later, but in the meantime, moving laterally so to speak, to John, Joseph's brother and his wife, while I know next to nothing about their lives, the manner of their deaths was interesting. Eight years younger than Joseph, John became a miller and practised his trade at Earlsmill, Keith. He was found dead by the side of his bed in a lunatic asylum in Aberdeen, on February 12th 1856, having been admitted on 19th November the previous year. His wife had an even more tragic end, as you shall presently find out.

But it was a happy day twenty years prior to that, the 16th April 1837 when she, Mary (Marjorie) McPherson, was married to John Addison at St Thomas's in Keith by the Rev. James MacLachlan. On the 6th of January the following year, along came the patter of tiny feet in the form of little Alexander although it would be some time yet before he would be able to walk. Draw your own conclusions. A honeymoon baby is mine.

Alexander had a sister, Ann, but she did not appear until February 1845 and whatever the reason for that long interval, I can imagine Alexander was not best pleased by this cuckoo in the nest, where, to mix my metaphors, he had ruled the roost for so long. I hope he loved his baby sister, but if he did not, he did not have to tolerate her for long. She died of TB in January 1855 and we can imagine her dying by degrees, hacking herself to death on a couch like Emily Brontë, rather than dying suddenly which would have been more shocking at the time but arguably more merciful in the end.

I have unfortunately, witnessed both of these ghastly scenarios in my own lifetime and in my own family—to my Uncle Jack and Aunt Gina whose daughter, Frances, had Down's syndrome and whose life expectancy they knew was going to be limited. She died aged about 30. Then there was my Uncle Eddie and Aunt Daisy whose son Graham was killed in a freak road accident on 28th September 1968 when he was only 20. Lightning, you would think, would not strike twice in this fashion but my cousin Roy's son, Martin, was killed in a similar fashion on 9th July 2002 when he was 27. In neither of these cases were they to blame.

God forbid that I should survive my children or possibly even worse, that I should lose one of my grandchildren, but if I did, especially as cruelly and senselessly as in the two road accidents above, I do not know precisely how I would react, but when you stare into the abyss of despair it is easy to see how you may become deeply depressed, and back in the pre-Prozac days of the middle of the nineteenth century, managing to cope must have been that much harder.

That's what happened to poor John Addison anyway. He was admitted to Aberdeen lunatic asylum ten months after Ann's death suffering from despondency and paroxysms of rage, blaming himself for Ann's death and believing that if it had not been for his neglect, she would have been alive still. Worse still, in my view, was his delusion that his immortal soul was incapable of salvation.

Prior to his admittance, he had attempted suicide by hanging and strangulation and was considered a danger to his wife. The doctor in charge of his case also notes there was a history of insanity in the family, one sister and several cousins (steady on, doctor, that's my relatives you are talking about) and that some thirty years previously, John had shown similar tendencies himself. He was a poor wee soul when he was admitted, thin and stooping and losing his hair. He did not respond well to treatment, becoming weaker and weaker and more and more emaciated. On the morning of the 12th February 1856, he was found dead by the side of his bed by the watchman on his rounds. His body and his bed were still warm. Cause of death was syncope (fainting) from debility and exhaustion. He was forty-four.

Marjorie died just a year after John on 11th March 1857 at home in bed. I suppose that is the place that most of us expect and hope to die, yet we are not afraid to go to bed at night like Peggotty explained to the eponymous David Copperfield when he expressed astonishment that so many of Peggotty's family were not afraid to go to sea where so many had perished or "drown dead" as Peggotty put it better. This is how her death was recorded in the *Elgin Courant* on 20th March 1857. I quote it in full and verbatim so you can get a flavour of how it was reported.

AWFUL WARNING.—On the afternoon of Tuesday last, the inhabitants of Keith were startled by the cry that the dwelling-house at Earlsmill, occupied by the widow of the late John Addison, miller, was on fire, and that she herself had fallen victim to the flames. A crowd of people was speedily gathered to the spot, but the fire had gained such mastery that nothing could be done to check it or save the unfortunate woman, whose charred remains were, with the exception of an arm entirely burnt off, ultimately found among the ruins. It would seem that she had of late been but too much addicted to drink; and on this occasion, having been the worse of it, and taken to bed with her a tobacco pipe, she had herself kindled her own funeral pile.

I should really say nothing at this point and leave you, dear reader, with your own thoughts to draw your own conclusions, but I have an itch that I must scratch. My point is that it is remarkable that the poor woman is not mentioned by name. Rather her very unfortunate and unpleasant death is treated as a little homily on the evils of drink (though I would cite tobacco as the main culprit). In her defence, I would say that it would be reasonable to suppose that she was still grieving for her dear departed husband, whose removal to the lunatic asylum before that was another sort of death, which itself followed hard on the heels of Ann's.

It's hard to imagine anything more painful for a parent than the death of a young child unless perhaps it is the death of an older child, like Ann, its personality already evident, its hopes, dreams, aspirations snuffed out . . . I for one, would not blame Marjorie if she did turn to the bottle in search of some comfort and solace.

She, (or rather what was left of her) and John, her husband, along with poor Ann, are buried in the same cemetery as John's Uncle Alexander, that is to say, St Ninian's in Tynet and like him, there is nothing there to say they ever existed. This too will have to be their memorial. They came to sad ends but hopefully they had some happiness in their lives such as the birth of their children, not knowing what the future held for them.

It is just as well none of us can see too far ahead into the future but it is hoped we can do so with rather less trepidation than Burns did in *To a Mouse* which famously ends with:

> *An' forward, tho' I canna see*
> *I guess—and fear.*

Chapter Eleven

Portknockie: the provost's tale

The sad, even tragic fates of Anne and Alexander, children of my Great-great-grandparents Joseph and Janet Coull, were the first I came across in my researches, beginning as I did by seeking out the stones that marked the ending of the ancestors' lives. Their siblings, including my Great-grandfather William, will be appearing later, but for the moment we are going to focus our attention on Joseph and Janet's oldest son, John, born in 1833.

He married Elizabeth Bruce (1833), known as "Betsy", in 1859. In 1871, they are living at 45, Lower Castle Street, Cullen. John describes himself as a "feuar and carter". [A feuar is the owner of a small piece of land, as I expect you know.] They have two sons and two daughters: Elizabeth (Bessie) aged 9; Joseph (8), who somehow contrived to be born in Grange; Mary Jane (2) and George Bruce (4 months).

Ten years later, and now living in Seafield Street, John gives his occupation as a "farm servant" (downwardly mobile, though he was to rise again to become a farmer at Mount Tabor near Buckie) whilst his son, Joseph, is an apprentice ironmonger, working for J.F. Grant, the Square, Cullen. Mary Jane is still there but Bessie is not. Probably she had left home, no doubt employed as a domestic servant somewhere but there is no mention of George, who, poor soul, seems to have perished in the interim. On a brighter note, however, the birth of another daughter is recorded, that of Jessie Ann, aged 5.

John died suddenly at Mount Tabor on 27th April 1904 aged 71. His wife Elizabeth died at Summerton, the home of their son Joseph in March 1910 aged 77. After serving his apprenticeship with J.F. Grant, an ironmonger, young Joseph moved to Portknockie where he worked as an assistant to Alex Pirie for four years before starting up his own business as a general merchant.

He immersed himself in village affairs and was popularly known as the "Provost of Portknockie" before any such office existed. He was instrumental in improving the harbour at Portknockie after which he thought it befitting that Portknockie should be elevated from the status of village to burgh and therefore it was only fitting that he should officially and unanimously be elected as its first provost in 1912.

As well as serving on the Parish Council, he also served on the School Board and became a JP in 1897 when he was thirty-five. He was a self-educated man who possessed a set of the *Encyclopaedia Britannica* and read the *British Weekly* every Sunday. He was a regular attender at Seafield Parish Church, where he was a regular attender and an elder, without being evangelical about it.

Away from local politics, he was a Liberal whose skills as an orator, it is said, would have equipped him for the higher office of M.P. had he been so inclined. But he preferred to be parochial, a Portknockie partisan, though in 1920, he did become President of the Banffshire Liberal Association. In any spare time he had, he could be seen on the golf links at Cullen or the more prestigious course at Spey Bay where he played with Ramsay MacDonald who was born just along the coast at Lossiemouth.

Joseph was three years his senior and unfortunately had been dead for the same number of years before his pal became Prime Minister and so never knew what really exalted company he kept. Maybe just as well or it might have put him off his stroke and he might have lost the hole. Somehow I am reminded of the tale of Louis XIV, the Sun King, who, on being operated on for an anal fistula is said to have advised the surgeon to treat him like those patients (and probably peasants) on whom this radical surgery had been practiced beforehand (or should that be behind?). It seems, initially, to be an astonishing remark from the megalomaniac monarch who didn't give tuppence for the peasants though he could well afford it. But there was method in his madness: it was so the surgeon's hand did not tremble as it probed the depths of the regal (and divine) posterior.

Joseph married Louisa Sutherland and they produced three sons: Alexander (Alecky) (1891), George (1893) and Joseph (Joffy) (1895). There were also three daughters: Bessie, Louisa and Mary Louisa. The latter was the baby of the family, born in 1903 and never married, dying aged 54 on 14th January 1957. And if you think that is young, I have news for you: she lived to a good age compared to her sisters and one of her brothers.

Poor Bessie, the first of the family to be born, in January 1889, died only eleven months old on December 7th the same year. Can you imagine what it must have been like, burying your first child on that wet and windy hillside? It must surely have been wet. Heaven itself must have wept at such a sight, especially on the Moray Firth coast in December. But surely, as the parents and mourners huddled around that tiny grave with their umbrellas, no-one would have believed that they would be back in a little over four years in almost precisely the same circumstances.

On the 14th February 1894, Louisa, their second daughter and fourth child, died aged ten months. No-one, you would have thought, deserves such bad luck as that. I don't know if Joseph's faith went a bit wobbly at these trying times, this hard blow coming so soon after the first, nor do I know how religious Louisa, his wife, was, but it would have been enough to shake my faith to the core, had I had any in the first place. Yet, ironically and to me, inexplicably, tragic events such as these seem to induce not just a paroxysm of grief but also of prayer and actually increase, rather than decrease, the faith of the faithful and from which they seem to derive some comfort. I am happy for them that it does.

It may not have seemed so at the time, but times did get better—for the next twenty-four years. It must have seemed the bad times were all behind and the good times were beginning to roll as, over time, Joseph's business expanded and the sons stepped into ready-made employment. Alecky was the baker (the bakery was erected in 1913), George was the grocer, while young Joseph worked alongside his father in the draper's shop. Above it there were as many as twenty tailors employed at one time. All they needed was the butcher and the candlestick maker and the Addisons would have had the town sewn up good and proper, so to speak.

Then embarrassment for the town's leading citizen and pillar of the community. On 19th November 1913, the Provost was fined £1 at Banff Sheriff Court for employing Joseph Wilson "under the age of 16 for more than 13 work days without a doctor's certificate" and failing to have lime washing of bakehouse renewed.

But much worse times were just around the corner. The First World War came along and ruined this nice little set-up, just as it affected the life of practically every family in the country from the most densely populated city to the remotest cottage in the country. You only have to look at the list of names on the ubiquitous war memorials scattered about the country to see how widespread and numerous the carnage.

Joffy, the youngest brother, who had been in the Territorials, joined the 4th Gordon Highlanders (No. 202,807). He saw a good deal of action, was wounded, suffered trench "frostbite" and was promoted to sergeant before being killed at Roeux, near Arras, on 23rd April 1917 aged only 23.

George, his brother, was in the war too, but fortunately survived, having been given a discharge after experiencing heart trouble after being wounded in the knee. That wound very probably saved his life or at least preserved him for another thirty-four years, nearly, but it was still a short life for all that, for he died on 21st January 1951 aged only 58. But think what enormous changes George lived to see in that period between Joffy's death and his own! Not quite as amazing as the changes during my father's lifespan of fifty-nine years though. He was born just five years after Man's first faltering flight at Kitty Hawk and died the same year as Apollo 11 landed on the moon. A giant step for

Mankind indeed. Orville and Wilbur would have been impressed.

Oldest brother Alecky died younger still, on 19th March 1945 aged only 54, the same age, note, as his sister Mary Louisa. They were not blessed with long lives, this family.

Joseph, their father, died suddenly at his home, which he named Summerton after the family seat of Summertown, at midnight on 11th February 1921, aged only 58. He had been unwell for a few days but on the day of his death had been in the garden and even had done some work in the afternoon. The cause of death was heart failure and chronic nephritis, inflammation of the kidneys, in non-medical language.

A large cortege followed him to his last resting place in the cemetery of the beloved burgh that he had established. Sometime later, quite a lot later by the look of the houses, they named a street after him, or perhaps it was in recognition of the service rendered to the community, commercially and otherwise by this prominent family. Like their father, George and Alecky both became JPs. If you go to Portknockie, you will find it easily enough: just head down towards the sea and follow the signs for the Fiddle Bow Rock.

Louisa, his wife, survived him for more than twenty-six years: she did not die until August 30th 1947 aged 84. That's a long time to be a widow, and if you live as long as she, you can expect a little rain to fall into your life as the poet (Longfellow) pointed out. To have had two sons and two daughters predecease you seems unbearably hard, but there is more. Alecky's wife, her daughter-in-law, Mary Bruce Mair, died on 9th March 1934 aged only 40. And just over a year before, her sister, Jessie Sutherland, died at Summerton on 17th February 1933 aged 68. A long life can be something of a missed blessing.

After this catalogue of death, it would be fitting at this time to insert a humorous anecdote, by way of light relief, concerning the two brothers, George and Alecky. They were out playing golf at Cullen one day and you can imagine how the exercise and fresh sea air would have honed the appetites of two young, fit and healthy lads. Ravenous with hunger, they reconnoitred the pantry and could not believe their luck when, under a covered dish, they discovered a meat loaf. They made short work of that, but on reflection, some instinct told them they had committed a crime and the crime must be covered up. Accordingly, they replaced the meat loaf with a brick of peat.

What they did not know was that their crime was of a greater magnitude than they had supposed. The meatloaf aforesaid was destined for the stomachs of the future Prime Minister of these islands and their father who had similarly been engaged in knocking hell out of a little white ball with a stick at Spey Bay and whose appetites, one imagines, were no less whetted. It is a great pity (or peety, I should more appositely say, to give the word its Doric pronunciation) that one could not have been there to have witnessed the look on the faces of the prospective diners as the lid was lifted off the dish, but one can imagine it very well. George and Alecky had taken the precaution of taking to the hills but the music would have to be faced sometime . . .

George inherited the political genes from his father and was an able orator but unlike him, was a Labour man. George's wife, Margaret (Maggie) was the classmate and friend of William Duthie, later Sir William, and Conservative MP for Banffshire from 1945 until 1960 when he retired. He enjoyed twenty years of retirement before he went to the big debating chamber in the sky. He is reputedly said to have remarked to George that if he had stood against him (as the Labour candidate) then he, Sir William, would have lost.

It was kind and flattering of Sir William to have said that, (as he might, to a friend) but rather fulsome. It should be taken with a dose of salt. Pin a Conservative tag on a sheep in Banffshire in those days (and up to not so long ago either) and the good, loyal, faithful voters would have elected it to Parliament. It would indeed have been a testament to his powers of oratory had George swung that seat to depose Sir William, who was highly regarded as a good constituency MP.

I met him on September 24th 1959. It's not that the date is etched on my memory; it was not that memorable an occasion, especially for Sir William who had come to address a meeting at Ternemny. There was only a handful of people in attendance and amongst them, I am sure, not a single heckler, nor even an awkward question, so an eminently forgettable experience for him. I only remember it because I had just embarked on a new hobby, that of collecting autographs, and Sir William was my first. I remember how everyone laughed when I asked him for it and someone joked that was one vote he could count on in the future anyway.

Ten years later to the day I was very far from laughing. That was the day my father dropped dead.

Chapter Twelve

The Summertown Mysteries

Fifty-nine years before that dreadful day, on November 16th 1909, my father was born at Summertown, Fordyce, a small croft of 84 arable acres in the parish of Fordyce, which had been in the hands of the Addison family since 1871 at least. When you look at it now, you can't help but marvel at how tiny it is and reflect on how many people were living and sleeping under its roof and wonder how they managed to cope. Of course large families were much more common then than now, and like the Old Woman who Lived in a Shoe, children just kept coming, regardless of the size or suitability of the accommodation. By 1901, Summertown had seven windowed rooms and was bulging at the seams even before my father's three sisters came along after him, and was even more cramped in 1871 when it consisted of "two rooms with one or more windows".

Living there then, in addition to Great-great-grandparents Joseph and Janet, there were their sons Joseph (31) and William (23), my future great grandfather. There was also Ann Ewing (27), Joseph's wife, and her daughter, Jane Spalding, aged seven. They also had a daughter of their own, Ann, who was three and here we come to the intriguing mystery of Joseph Addison (7), described as a "boarder" and born in Heligoland, Germany. We will come back to him presently but in the meantime I would like to add there were also two servants, Charles Veitch (13) from Fordyce and William Chapman (11) from Deskford. Imagine that, eleven years old and already out in the world earning your living. Even thirteen seems to be a tender enough age to be doing that. And, almost as amazing to my mind, is that in those already cramped conditions, they still found room to take in a lodger, George Gordon (64), a mason's labourer from Deskford. If this tells *you* anything, what it tells *me* is that times must have been hard and money in short supply.

If I was surprised by all that, you can imagine how intrigued I was by this boy Joseph who had been born in Heligoland in 1864. How? Who was his father? Who was his mother? Presumably he was some sort of a relation of Joseph's and no mere ordinary boarder, but in what way? And how come he was born in such an out of the way place like Heligoland?

That's the joy of genealogy: the pursuit and hopefully the unravelling of such mysteries. But the untangling of your family roots can present you with some knotty problems, satisfying when you are able to untease them, frustrating when you can't. Like a maze, you often take wrong turnings and follow false leads. And, as I have so often discovered, the more you find out, the more mysteries you uncover. Fortunately I was able, eventually, to pick up Joseph's trail, as well as that of his children, and I was very glad I did as it led in directions I never expected. Furthermore, on this journey of discovery, I came across some fascinating stories and tragic tales. But you will have to be patient, dear reader, I am not going to tell you them just yet.

Heligoland itself did not pose any mystery for me as I had already heard of it thanks to the few specimens from those airts I had in my stamp collection. I never regarded myself as a philatelist, but I do believe stamp collecting is an underrated hobby, considered by some fit only for cissies, whereas I saw it as a painless way of absorbing knowledge along with the instant gratification it provided whenever I acquired new additions. Then there was the competitive spirit it fostered amongst my contemporaries and me, and not least the practice in arithmetic it gave me as I counted my collection, well over a thousand stamps. I confess I once measured out my life in foreign stamps to misquote J. Alfred Prufrock, but never once thought of it as wasting my time or my life. In fact, I would say it inspired in me a desire to travel, to visit the places from whence these items of miniature art originated.

It is a pastime that has probably all but died out now, too passive for the shoot-em-up video game generation and I admit I haven't looked at my collection for years. God knows what treasures, what rarities I might have amongst them and which I could use as a get-out-of-jail card if the going got really tough financially. And you may be amazed to hear it, but this innocent-seeming hobby got me into trouble on more than one occasion, and which will be told later in its proper place.

Meanwhile, for you non-philatelists and geographers, may I inform you that Heligoland is a tiny, long, slim island off the north German coast, well two islands actually, but the other island of Düne is, as its name suggests, little more than a sandbank and uninhabited. The islands were ceded to Britain by Denmark in 1814 though the British had occupied them seven years prior to that, during the Napoleonic

Wars. It remained in British hands until 1890 when it was given back to Germany as part of the wheeling and dealing that went on during the carving up of Africa in the latter part of the nineteenth century.

But the circumstances surrounding Joseph's origin were not the only mysteries that the 1871 census threw up. The three-year old Ann Addison was born in Summertown in 1868 but her half-sister Jane had been born in Fordyce four years previously in April 1864. Obviously Jane was the result of her mother's former dalliance with a certain Mr Spalding. But who was he?

Jane's birth was registered by her mother who appended her "mark" to the certificate. You may have said that X stood for the father too, for it was not until four months after Jane's birth, on August 20th, that by a court decision, the father was deemed to be James Spalding, a farm servant from Rhynie. No DNA testing in those days that would have proved it conclusively.

One wonders too what the neighbours thought of young Joseph marrying a "fallen" woman but plainly it didn't bother him and it would seem her father-in-law had no such qualms either, or if he had, had got over them or learned to live with them, literally. But I like to think that both Josephs were ahead of their time and more tolerant of mistakes being made, running counter to the prevailing morality of the time.

Anyway, by 1881, Joseph, Jnr. now aged 41, has moved back to his roots, to a farm of 33 acres called Hill Park near Buckie in the parish of Enzie (pronounced Ingy). In addition to Ann, he now has two sons, William (8) and George (5). His stepdaughter, Jane, is now recorded as Ewing, her mother's maiden name.

The census of 1891 shows Jane has changed her name again, this time to Jamieson. Women tend to do that when they get married and Jane's husband was George (1858-1931). They produced three sons and a daughter, Bella, who died on 13th November 1899. She could have been no older than four, possibly less. Jane, her mother, died at 22, Seafield Road Buckpool on 12th August 1937 aged 73. All are buried in Buckie cemetery, for anyone who wants to look them up, or down at their graves, I could say.

But now we come to another intriguing little mystery. Joseph and Ann's 1891 census reveals the existence of a certain Joseph A. Ewing, aged three. Unfortunately no parentage or relationship is given, but if we turn to the next census, that of 1901, we find a Joseph Addison (not Ewing) aged thirteen, described as a "grandson" and a "scholar".

It seems a reasonable supposition that the two Josephs are one and the same. So who were his parents? The finger of suspicion has to point to Ann as being the one who presented Joseph and Ann with a grandson despite the fact there is no sign of her being married, at least not by 1901 when she was thirty-three, still at home and apparently left on the shelf. But as my mother would have pointed out, you don't need to be married to "be married". So if we assume she was the mother, who was the father? A clue may be in Joseph's name as recorded in the 1891 census, but what a strange coincidence that it should happen to be the same as his grandmother's. Perhaps the absent father was more of a kissing cousin than a first cousin.

I hope you don't mind gentle reader, but I am going to leave you with the mystery of Joseph's parentage unsolved. Some things are better left a mystery, like a magician's trick which always disappoints you once the secret is revealed, leaving you feeling a bit cheated and wishing you had been left with the wonderment. I may get round to investigating it myself sometime, but if one of you readers out there gets there before me, I'd be delighted to hear from you.

Whoever Joseph's natural father was, it seems as if Joseph, his grandfather, regarded him as his son anyway, for the Banffshire Advertiser of the 9th November 1911, under the heading ENZIE MAN KILLED ABROAD has the "sad intelligence" received via cable that *Joseph Addison, the youngest son of the late Mr Joseph Addison of Hill Park, Enzie had been accidentally killed in Vancouver, British Columbia.* The article goes on to say he had emigrated in the summer of 1910 and first got a job on the railways but not long before his death had started working in a coal merchant's business, which is where the fatal accident occurred. He was only twenty-four.

Joseph himself died suddenly at Aberdeen Royal Infirmary on the 21st October 1904 a week and a month short of his 64th birthday. Ann died at Wellheads, Enzie on 28th February 1923, aged 79. That's a reasonable innings I suppose and at least she went before her sons, William and George, even if it was not by much. Both died in 1925, William in February aged 49 and George in December aged 52.

William's son, Joseph George, fared rather better in the longevity lottery. He died at Gray's hospital, Elgin on January 10th 1985 aged eighty-four. His wife was Elizabeth Coull (1901-1945) and I would not put any money against her being some sort of relative of his since his great-grandmother was Janet of that ilk. In a reversal of the usual state of affairs, he was forty years a widower and just as well he got used to sleeping without her since they did not bury him with her. She sleeps throughout eternity in the old cemetery in Buckie; he is in the new.

As you traipse about the serried rows of headstones in Hillhead Cemetery you will not find a great deal of Coulls, or Addisons for that matter, but you cannot help but notice and be amazed at how many Fletts, Mairs, Woods and Slaters there are which tells you what a close-knit community Portknockie is and where John Donne's immortal words: *send not to know/ For whom the bell tolls,/ It tolls for thee* were never truer as it is very likely to be for a relation of some sort. Furthermore, it is sobering as you read the inscriptions in your quest to find your lost relatives, to discover just how many headstones bear the legend "Lost at Sea". That is not an uncommon event in the North-East of Scotland where so many families dice with death on the high seas, sometimes the very high seas, as they pursue their quest to put fish on the table, rather than bread, so to speak.

And whilst it may go some way to explaining why these communities have such strong religious convictions, ardently praying that they and theirs will be spared from the wrath of the North Sea—it baffles me since it plainly did not prevent so many of their ancestors from sleeping with the fishes.

Chapter Thirteen

Grave Matters

Just as close-knit as the fishing community was the farming community. In the last chapter we followed the trail of Joseph Addison (1840-1904) and we turn our attention now to his brother William, my great-grandfather. He was born in Rathven in 1847 and at the time of his death was farming at Auchip, near Fordyce. His wife was Jane Wright, a domestic servant. In those days, what else is a woman to do, as anyone who is reasonably familiar with the Brontë novels is aware. She came from Muttonbrae, a little croft of 20 acres of which 17 were arable. It is the next croft but one after Summertown, up the hill to the north (you can see it from the front door) while Auchip lies just a little further over the hill, no more than three miles away as the crow flies.

Jane's father was John Wright; her mother Margaret Lobban. They were married in the manse of Fordyce by the Rev. James Grant on December 27th 1874. He was 26; she was 24. They were a modern couple in the sense that they put the cart before the horse so to speak, since by that time they already had a baby—my grandfather, Charles, who was one year and three months old.

All that stands of Muttonbrae today are a few steadings and even they are late 20th century. It's a base for a heavy plant contractor. The Wrights would weep to see it now, their humble dwelling razed to the ground to make room for a shed for a JCB, to their eyes a sight as outlandish as a species of dinosaur.

Jane and William had five children: my grandfather Charles (1873), Maggie Ann (1876), William (1882), James (1888) and Alexander John (1894). There will be more details on these later, but suffice it to say at this juncture that farming was in the blood. All the boys became farmers while Maggie Ann married Peter Clark, a farmer at Birkenbog Home Farm near Cullen. It was they who brought up Netta, her brother William's daughter, who was only two when her mother died.

The youngest son, Alexander John, was the most adventurous, seeking his fortune in Ceylon, as it was then, to become a tea planter. Which is a type of farming after all, is it not? When I was much younger, about the same age as Alexander John, I was a tree planter. "Tree" not "tea", note. You can see them still if you know where to look, to your right as you head south down the M74 though it is a bit harder to spot them now since they upgraded the road and moved it away from the plantation. I always give them a fatherly glance as I pass by. Someone once said, variously attributed to the Chinese and the Talmud amongst more modern contenders: *Every man should plant a tree, have a child and write a book to ensure a measure of immortality.* I feel quite smug about that, having planted more trees than you can shake a spade at, written several books, but sired only two children, which, I suppose is the right way you should go about things.

Great-grandfather William's bones lie next to his father and mother's in Fordyce. Judging by the headstone, he was not doing too badly. One of the most eye-catching memorials in the cemetery, it is a dark-grey marble affair with a couple of pillars on each side and with some tasteful decoration in white including some strands of ivy, and at the base, in bold, black, block capitals which stand out a mile: ADDISON. It must have cost a pretty penny or two, yet money well spent if you want to achieve a sort of immortality if you have never written a book, for age has not weathered it and it looks good for the next few centuries too.

Imposing, but not in the least pretentious, it has a pointed top and records the death of his wife, Jane Wright on 4th March 1915, aged 66 years. She died at Auchip of heart disease and pneumonia. At the same time that these words were inscribed upon the stone, William saw fit to pay tribute to his daughter-in-law, Christina Horn, [sic] who died aged 20 at Boggierow, Portsoy on the 27th May 1899. She was the first wife of my grandfather, Charles, and third child to Alexander and Mary Horne of Boggierow.

Poor Christina, what a terrible time she had of it. The cause of death was given as: *failure of heart's action (fainting), pregnancy with persistent vomiting. 8 months.* In other words she was so sick her heart just gave up under the strain. I empathise with this enormously. I hate, loathe and abominate being sick and suppress it as long as I can, so the thought of poor Christina being sick every day for eight months, perhaps many times a day, fills me with horror. It would not surprise me in the least if she prayed for death. And all she did was to get pregnant.

Nowadays I suppose they could have treated her and saved her life. According to Government statistics, in 1900 the number of infant mortalities was 140 per thousand births. A century later, this figure had been reduced to 5.8 per thousand births. Some difference! Complications such as breech births now regarded as "simple" were life-threatening then. If my wife, Fiona, had been born half-a-century earlier than she was, not only she, but her mother, might have died—for she was a breech baby. And, you may remember, I also was very nearly an infant casualty. So to our children and our grandchildren, I say this: get down on your knees and thank—no, not God, but the advances in medical science.

The next to be recorded on the headstone is that of William himself and there is something subtly different about the text on the stone. To my eye it seems to be not quite parallel with the rest of the writing, being somewhat on the slant. Anyhow, it tells us that he died on the 16th December 1921, aged 74 years, the same age as his father, coincidentally. The death certificate tells us that he died of bronchitis, not on the 16th but the 14th, yet another example of how just inadequate the idiom "written in stone" is to convey the idea of something true and immovable.

Below William's name someone has added, almost certainly his daughter-in-law and the deceased's wife, Lilian: "Also his youngest son, Alex. John, tea planter, Ceylon, who died at Colombo on 5th April 1936 aged 43 years". That too is inaccurate, as you shall see.

And that was all I knew about him until 2005 when Netta (youngest daughter of William Addison 1882, [see below]) spotted an article in the *Press and Journal* about my first book and as a result of which I was contacted by his son, Sandy, who was able to give me more details. That and other stories, along with the coincidences to which I referred in the last chapter will be told later, but for now I will just say this, and you will soon see why—he died of a burst appendix. By the time he got from his plantation to the nearest hospital in Colombo, it was too late: he had developed peritonitis.

His uncle William above, farmed at Cruats, just outside Portknockie—look for it on the right just before you enter the village from Cullen. He was married twice. His first wife, Jessie Ann (Janet) Fraser (1888), died suddenly in 1923 aged only thirty-five in a nursing home in Aberdeen but not before she had presented him with three daughters: Jean (1916), Margaret (1918) and Jessie Ann (Netta) in 1921. Netta died on 31st March 2007 aged 86, unmarried. She lies in the same grave as her father and her husband's second wife. I won't say "stepmother" since, you may remember, she was brought up by her aunt, Maggie Ann.

William's second wife was his former housekeeper, also called Jessie Ann. (Was there something about the name that appealed to him?) She also happened to be a second cousin of his which we won't go into. Her surname was Reid and she was known as "Shan" (a linguistic glide of Jessie Ann). She died on August 2nd 1960 aged 78. William had gone long before to prepare a place for her. He died on 27th October 1949 aged 67.

In 1901, when my Great-grandfather William and family moved to pastures new in Auchip, as eldest son, my grandfather succeeded to Summertown and that was where my father was born, just as his siblings were before him. His mother was Helen Ledingham Munro and she and his father were married on the last day of 1902. That must have been a Hogmanay to remember.

But maybe not. Why not you will find out in the next chapter.

They quickly produced William (Bill) (1903), then Charles (Carl) (1905), James (Jimmy) (1907) and then George, my father, in 1909, every two years as regular as clockwork. It was not the end of the line however: perhaps they desperately wanted a daughter or perhaps they wanted a large family or perhaps they didn't— babies just were a fact of life and you certainly couldn't blame Catholicism by this time. There were three more children to come, all girls—Georgina (Gina) (1911), Margaret (Daisy) (1913) and Helen (Trixie) in 1915. Then the clock stopped. Four boys then three girls— quite a tidy arrangement, though another daughter would have been more pleasing in terms of symmetry.

The family stayed at Summertown until May 1918, when despite its unprepossessing name of Clayfolds, my Grandfather Charles took up a tenancy there on the Duke of Fife's estate. During his tenure at Summertown, my grandfather had religiously kept a farming diary. The road to hell is paved with good intentions, so the aphorism has it, and he continued the journal on the new farm. Here is what he wrote: *May 7: Planted potatoes. May 18: Started to sew turnips. May 22: [Only the date—the rest is blank]. 1919. Began to sew corn Apr 8. Finished sewing April 22. Sewed grass seed, planted potatoes April 24. Began to sew turnips May 17. Began harvest Aug 28*[th]. And that is it. The entire farming journal for Clayfolds. Verbatim.

But then at 138 acres, Clayfolds was half as big again as Summertown and he would have been far too busy. Having said that, in the 1897 sixteen-year lease for Summertown, the rental is recorded as £59 of which

£9 is for part of Muttonbrae. My grandfather therefore (along with his father), would have been accustomed to farming a few extra acres, especially I imagine, after his maternal grandfather died on February 9th 1892—if he was not already doing so. But there always was a pretty close relationship between the two neighbouring crofts. On the 4th April 1881 (census day) my grandfather then aged 7, was spending the night at Muttonbrae with his grandparents. Twenty years later, the situation is reversed and his 82 year-old widowed granny, Margaret Wright, is living at Summertown along with his parents and siblings.

Moving house is one of the most stressful things you ever do in your life. The experience was so bad for us that it has been a quarter of a century since we last moved and have no plans to do so ever again, especially since we have accumulated a great deal more stuff over those years, not least fallen heir to that white elephant, my mother-in-law's piano and which weighs just as much. But all that is nothing compared to moving farms. Goods and chattels would have been removed by horse-drawn cart, a journey that would have taken the best part of a day despite the relatively small distance involved, but that was child's play compared to moving the cattle which were herded all the way o'er hill and dale from Summertown.

By then all the children except Trixie were of school age and none old enough to leave. Whilst it must have a been a great relief for my grandmother to have been able to pack them off to school, it makes me think about Jaques' speech about the Seven Ages of Man in *As You Like It* about the "whining" schoolboy who crept "unwillingly" to school. Their local school was

Bogmuchals. It was a modest two-roomed, two-teacher school, in the middle of nowhere. It is still standing today, but now transformed into some sort of lumber storage shed.

It was a long, long way, especially for the tiny legs of the little ones and in all weathers, rain or shine and in the winter, snow—and snow is something that that part of the country does better than anywhere else in Scotland. The school leaving age was fourteen at that time and so we can imagine all the Addison children from Bill to Gina as they made their two-mile trek together to swell the numbers of Bogmuchals. That would make anyone unwilling to go to school I would have thought, but in addition, I imagine my father's brothers, as embryonic farmers, were especially unwilling at this imposition of academic learning when they could be out enjoying the freedom of the fields the livelong day, learning their trade, even if it was hard work. But this is only mere speculation and it is also speculation that my father was the least unwilling as I do not know when precisely he decided the farming life was not for him.

My grandfather had been suffering from high blood pressure and died suddenly of a cerebral haemorrhage on January 29th 1948, aged 74. I was only seven months old and although my grandmother was to live for almost two more years before shuffling off the mortal coil on 30th November 1949, not surprisingly, I have no recollection of ever meeting her either. Her death was precipitated when she fell and broke her leg but it was myocarditis and pneumonia that actually carried her off. She was 79.

And thus, when my mother's mother, Granny Tate, died in 1952, I became to all intents and purposes, a grandparent orphan. As far as I know, after he came to her funeral, my grandfather Tate was never seen again. He died in January of 1954, wintertime, and not a time conducive to easy travelling from the North-East of Scotland to the North-East of England which, when the wind comes from an easterly direction, can get the benefit of snow-dumping blasts straight from Siberia.

I was only six-and-a-half and my sister was still some way short of her third birthday, which would be a further disincentive to my mother making the journey. I am sure I would have remembered it if I had been there so I am sure I was not. Nor do I remember missing my mummy and daddy while someone, such as my Aunt Janet (the most likely suspect), looked after my sister and me.

So I can't be sure and I could be completely wrong, but what I suspect is that my parents, not even my mother, attended his funeral. I never thought of asking and alas there is no-one alive now who can tell me if she did. As I said in Chapter Four, I don't even know where his grave is.

That is a very serious matter if you crave some degree of immortality and haven't written a book (as he didn't). I couldn't say if he planted a tree or not. Poor Grandpa Tate. I remember you. But that, I'm afraid, is just about your lot.

Chapter Fourteen

Sex and the Munros

Lucky or lazy? When my grandfather, Charles Addison, cast his eye around for a second wife, he found her in Berryleys, only about half a mile away from Muttonbrae, (where his mother came from and where he was born) which, in its turn, is scarcely another half-mile away from Summertown. If it hadn't been for the brow of the hill, they would have been able to send messages by semaphore. How lucky (or lazy) was that, to find the perfect mate so close at hand! Having said that, you may remember my Uncle Tommy married the girl next door, although it has to be said she was born in Aberdeen and he was born in North Shields.

My grandmother was Helen Ledingham Munro and I remember my Aunt Gina telling me that the Munros came from the Black Isle. Like so many family stories which are passed down in the verbal tradition, whilst they may contain a broad truth, they may not be absolutely accurate in the particular. The earliest Munro to settle in the Fordyce area was my Great-great-grandfather David who was born in Tain in 1801 to Andrew and Margaret or Marrion [sic] McKenzie and who married Elspet Gibb from Rathven in 1826.

Tain is not quite in the Black Isle but it *is* a stronghold of the Munro clan and home to the famous early 17th century dissenter, the Reverend John Munro who opposed (to put it mildly) James VI's attempts to unite the Presbyterian Church of Scotland with the Episcopalian Church of England. He was imprisoned, escaped (twice) and thereafter preached in Tain without a stipend for the next twenty years or so until he died in 1630. That's dedication.

I was also told that the Munro ancestors were "Wee Frees" and mainly for the benefit of overseas readers who have been lucky enough to escape the delights of disputes ecclesiastical on Scotia's shores, I will explain that after the union of the Free Church with the United Presbyterian Church in 1900, the dissenters remained outwith the union, regarding themselves as the true Free Church. "Wee" is what others called them, not they, themselves, and whilst that may accurately reflect their numbers, it is in fact an oxymoron, for there is nothing "free" about their enormous narrow-minded conservatism with a small C. Whilst the Free Church today is strongest in the predominantly Gaelic speaking areas of Scotland, there still is, to this day, a Free Church in Tain and it would not surprise me in the slightest if the posteriors of my Munro forebears had not warmed an unforgiving pew in that congregation.

David and Elspet's first son, Andrew, was married in the Free Church and his first two children baptised there in 1849 and 1851. Furthermore, if I were a betting man (which I am not) I would not mind putting my pension on my grandmother, Helen, also having been baptised into the Free Church as her two youngest siblings certainly were. Having said that, I have to point out, in the interests of balance and not least, factual accuracy, that her parents, John Munro and Georgina Ledingham, were married in the United Presbyterian Church, and she herself was married in the newly formed United Free Church in 1902, just two years after its foundation.

It is therefore semantically accurate to state that my grandmother was not a "Wee Free", nor were her siblings, nor her parents, contrary to what I had been led to believe, but, and it is a big BUT, they *were* members of the Free Church and don't forget that the "Wees" were just the dissenting rump after the union with the Established Church, the real hardliners but the Unionists were pretty strict too. I was told my grandmother was staunchly religious and I can well believe it, something she would have inherited from her parents and her grandparents, in whose veins a great deal of Calvinism still coursed and which I doubt had been watered down very much by the time she married my grandfather. That is why there may not have been a great deal of alcoholic refreshment at Summertown on Hogmanay 1902 despite it also being their wedding day.

But back to the past. David Munro married Elspet Gibb (1801) in Rathven on 5th January 1826. Both were living there at the time and this is of particular interest to me as it shows that Rathven can truly be said to be where my roots are since both the Addisons and Munros came from there, though the Munros came along a couple of hundred years later it has to be said.

The registrar recorded David's name as "Munroe" and if I had been him I would have adopted that variant spelling of the name. I know of two brothers with different surnames due to a slip by the registrar who recorded the birth of one as "MacDonald" and the other as "McDonald". I think "Munroe" has a certain cachet, though not as much as "Monroe", like the

141

President and the film star. But plain Munro is what I am and let me be the first to say it, suits me better.

David and Elspet wasted no time in producing Andrew (1826) followed by six others including my Great-great grandfather John in 1831. I would call that a large family, though for the times it might have been considered quite modest. In those days before television or even steam radio and the electric light, the evenings must have seemed interminable even if you did have a good book and a guttering candle to read it by. There was little else to do, especially in the long winter nights, than go to bed and where the adage early to bed and early to rise did not just apply to the morrow's day, apparently. The Munros liked to "put it about a bit" as the saying goes, as you shall see.

Despite sharing the same name, I am not named after Great-great-grandfather David Munro. I doubt if my mother had ever heard of him. She just liked the name "David" and perhaps the "Munro", which I got as a middle name, came as a piece of flattery and a peace offering after the way my parents just upped sticks and ran away to get married. I don't know. Anyway, my namesake lies in a rather dark and gloomy corner of the old cemetery at Fordyce. I wouldn't have picked it for myself. The headstone tells us: "David Munro, farmer Standingman, died on 16th October 1860 aged 66". It also tells us that Elspet followed him nearly ten years later, on 7th February 1870 aged 69 years.

But wait a moment. Clearly there is something wrong here, another instance of how, if we take for gospel what is written on a headstone, then we do so at our peril. The discrepancy between David's date of birth and his age, according to the headstone, is easily explained however. The stonemason had six on the brain it seems and should have carved a zero rather than a six when he came to recording David's age.

But this stone raises another problem. I have not been able to find Standingman on any Ordnance and Survey maps, nor have my resident local experts been able to enlighten me as to where it was either. However, the 1866 OS map (Sheet IX) shows on Standingmanhill, and just slightly to the west and across the road from Berryleys, an unnamed building. Since we know that the Munros were in Berryleys in 1880, it seems not unreasonable to suppose that that building was Standingman and once they moved to Berryleys, it was allowed to fall into disrepair.

Anyway, after David died, the 29 year-old John Munro (my great-grandfather) found himself promoted to head of the household at the 23-acres Standingman. And just as my Uncle Jimmy, who although he was the third son, inherited the family seat of Clayfolds, his older brothers having married and moved into farms of their own, so John's elder brother, Andrew, had married and moved out by the time of his father's death. He also left the family profession of farming behind, becoming a shoemaker in Portsoy. He married Margaret Watson on May 6th 1848, the daughter of John Watson, a blacksmith, and Janet Laurence.

Andrew was married twice and by his first wife, Margaret, had four children. Margaret died in 1870 and sometime between 1851 and 1861, their second child and first daughter, Elspet, also died. In 1884, Andrew himself perished under tragic and mysterious circumstances. He went missing from his home in Pork Lane, Aberdeen on the 9th December. Two months later, his body was pulled out of the Victoria Dock at Aberdeen harbour. It was presumed that he had tripped and fallen in. Did he slip on ice? Had he been drowning his sorrows and then decided to drown himself as he had not drunk deeply enough (or too much), or was it purely an accident? Could it possibly even have been murder? Who can tell?

Reporting his demise, the local paper described Andrew as being of "eccentric habits". I would have liked to have known him if that is the case. I have a soft spot for eccentrics. I think they are interesting people who bring a vicarious sort of pleasure to those of us who live more ordinary and humdrum lives, though I am prepared to concede they might not be the easiest of people to live with. I would be flattered if people thought of me as being slightly eccentric, but my wife, who knows me best I suppose, says I am merely hard to live with. I think that is a slur on my character. I may have been slightly difficult once, I grant you that, but these days I am a pretty mellow fellow who does what she tells me without question or hesitation.

Anyway, going back thirty-six years prior to this tragedy, Andrew, having married and left the croft to set up shop as a shoemaker in Portsoy, is the reason why Great-grandfather John, not Andrew, succeeded his father to Standingman. John was born on Christmas Day 1831 at Muir of Glassaugh, in the parish of Fordyce. Now *that's* what I call a present to give your wife! And you may call me an incurable romantic if you like, but five years after we were married, I sort of took a leaf out of David's book and gave my wife the best (and only) Valentine Day's present ever—a son. For his part, he must have thought that his old man had done *something* right, because he too copied the idea and gave *his* wife, not a son, but a daughter, on Valentine's Day 2012. [This is called family planning by the way, not coincidence, despite what you may be thinking.]

John's family remained at Glassaugh until 1837, then after a short time at Clashendamer, moved on in 1841 to Slogmahole (winner of the Worst-named Croft of the Year Competiton and after which the organisers saw no point in continuing with the contest). In 1851 they are at Hillhead of Clashendamer, in 1860 at Standingman, and about twenty years later in Berryleys which must lay claim to being the Munro family seat since they stayed there for the best part of forty years before they moved on to North Bodiechell in Aberdeenshire in the 1920s.

Farming folk tend to put down deep roots and the Munros were unusual in their mobility. The modern phrase "upwardly mobile" here more literally describes their movements on Standingmanhill. They were a hard-working family who were constantly improving the land by clearing, draining and cultivating it. An 1826 map by John Thomson of Edinburgh shows just how little of the land around Fordyce was cultivated then. Their last move however, was also unusual as it was well outwith the area, moving far, far, away (for those times) into the neighbouring and mightier county of Aberdeenshire. Why they moved so far away remains a bit of a mystery but I believe the reason for their migration had something to do with the Seafield Estate putting the farm up for sale and the Munros either not wanting to buy it, or in a more likely scenario, not being able to afford it, or being outbid.

That may be a slight mystery but the census of 1861 presents us with a more intriguing one, for as well as

John and his 61 year-old widowed mother, the record shows that John has an 11 months-old son, Alexander, who was born in Boyndie. So who was his mother? And where was she? She is not mentioned as being part of the household. Whilst we have to remember that the census is essentially just a snapshot, one would have thought that if the mother had been absent from the family home for some reason, with Alexander being so young, she would have taken him with her.

I am indebted to Iain Gray, one of John's distant descendants, for supplying me with her identity. All we know about her is that her name was Jane Harper and John seems to have had custody of Alexander since birth. Unusual now and even more so then when girls who got themselves "into trouble" were left holding the baby, literally, and had to fend for themselves as best they could, and as often as not, shunned by society or, incredible as it may seem now, were committed to an institution for the insane. It is to his credit that John faced up to his responsibilities, let Jane get on with her life unencumbered with an illegitimate child. Unless she died in childbirth of course.

The 1861 census also threw up a surprise though it was not until later that I discovered it. Also under the elastic roof of Standingman that night, amongst several others, were John's nephew, James, born in February 1859 at Rathven, and Ann Munro, born in Turriff in 1840. Naturally I assumed that James was her son, but further delving revealed that this was not the case. It turned out that James was his brother's illegitimate son by Margaret Massie, a domestic servant. The last trace I have of James is in 1881 when he was working as a farm servant for the Riach family in Urquhart, Morayshire but up to that time he was brought up as a member of Munro family.

Ann Munro, née Lawrance [sic] was the wife of John's brother George (1834-1908). Whether Ann was a relation of half-brother-in-law Andrew's mother-in-law (she was a Lawrence) I will leave someone else to find out, but considering how tightly-knit communities were then, I would not in the least be surprised to find out they were. George had a 6-acre croft at Burnmouth, Gollachy, near Buckie and supplemented his income as a salmon fisher, or the other way about.

Ann and George were prolific, providing James with no less than eleven step-siblings, but don't worry, I don't propose to go down that line except to say that after they had exhausted all the usual names you would expect to see in the Munro menagerie: George, David, Elspet, Alexander and so on, they ran out of names and called their last child, born in 1884, "Christian" though they called her "Chrissie". Thank God for that. But it might just suggest they followed a religious bent, like their ancestors. That wouldn't surprise me either.

James was just the first of the illegitimate Munros. Little Alexander we met earlier, but hang on to your hat, there was a third. Little Isabella Munro was born in Cullen in 1860 to Isabella McKenzie. Ah, but which Munro was the father? Well, it can't be Andrew, he was happily married; John and George have already put their hands up, as we have seen. So who does that leave? Well, you have a choice between Archibald and Alexander. I will explain later why the latter is ruled out, so by process of elimination, we arrive at Archibald, and like his brothers, he does not seem to have shirked his responsibilities either.

Pending Archibald getting a wife, Isabella seems to have been brought up by his sister, Margaret. What's one more when you have had six already and go on to have three more, not forgetting the one your husband had before you met him?

Margaret (1829), was married to Thomas Burns (1818), an agricultural labourer from Rathven, originally from County Meath in Ireland. He had a daughter, Judith, also born there about 1840. It would appear that he was a widower and it would not be stretching credulity too far to imagine that his wife probably died of cholera or typhus in the years following the failure of the potato crop that began in 1845 and poor Thomas and Eddith [sic] (or Julia as she later appears in the census records—could "Eddith possibly be a misreading of "Judith"?) fled to Scotland—just two of the estimated two million who abandoned Ireland for Britain, Canada and the United States. Thomas, who was eleven years older than Margaret, died somewhere between 1881 and 1891. She died in 1897 aged sixty-seven.

On Dec 21st 1872 at Enzie, their eldest son, John, married Elizabeth Stuart (1851-1920) from Rathven. They are worthy of mention because they went on to create a football team of their own and whose names and details I shall spare you except to say that the last shall come first, for the second-last child and youngest son, George, was killed at Gallipoli in 1916. He was only twenty-four. The only other member of the family I will mention is William, George's nearest brother in the dynasty and who died in Vancouver in 1963 aged seventy-four. Not for the first time, this made me pause and reflect on the randomness and unfairness of the way life's cards are dealt out, especially when we only get one chance of life on this planet—as far as we know.

In 1861, John's brother Archibald (1836-1913), the father of Isabella above, was working as a ploughman for my Grandfather John's future father-in-law, William Ledingham, at Breach, near Fordyce. He later became a distilleryman before becoming a "flesher" and finally a crofter in Rathven. He was married twice: firstly to Penelope Craik in December 1869 and secondly to Annie Neish. He was a man whose life was filled with a great deal of sadness. His first-born legitimate son, George, was born in 1871 and died just five weeks later. And in an amazing parallel with the death of his Uncle Andrew eleven years and ten days previously, on December 19th 1895 to be precise, James, another son with Penelope, was found drowned in Cluny harbour, Buckie. What caused him to trip and fall into the icy water we do not know, but it does seem as if this was just a tragic accident.

As for poor Archibald himself, he died a widower in a lunatic asylum in Elgin in 1913. We must remember of course, that it was much easier, back in the late nineteenth and early twentieth centuries, to be certified and admitted to an institution for the insane, just as nowadays it is much easier to get into an institution of higher learning and become certificated. The cause of death was anasarca which sent me scurrying for the medical dictionary and which entailed looking up practically every other word of the explanation. Simply put, it is a severe type of oedema, or swelling, often brought about by heart, liver or renal failure. One can't help but speculate that lonely and alone, he turned to the bottle for comfort . . .

I can find no trace of David and Elspet's youngest son, Alexander (1838) or the last child, Helen, who was born in 1844. I rather fear that Alexander did not mature to manhood. My Munro mentor, Iain Gray, has found a burial receipt dated 9th September 1848 for "the burial of a son of David Munro, Clashendamer". Since we know what happened to the other brothers, and unless Elspet produced another son after Helen, when she was already in her mid-forties, it does not seem to be too much of a speculative leap to conclude that this was in fact, payment for young Alexander. And that is why, dear reader, he could not have been the third brother out of four to have produced an illegitimate child. He did not get the chance.

One day Iain, or I, or someone else, may be able to prove conclusively that Alexander did die aged ten but there is little hope of finding out more about Helen, however. As I remarked before, girls have a habit of marrying and changing their name and vanishing without trace, with complete disregard for any genealogist who might happen to come along more than a century later. It's hard enough sometimes, the further you go back, to find information about the males. With females it is often impossible.

So, regretfully we must leave Helen to her relative obscurity (see a pun in that if you like) and now let us turn to the Munros I *do* know more about, to the next generation—my Great-grandfather John and his descendants.

Chapter Fifteen

More about the Munros

Great-grandfather John Munro (1831) married Georgina Ledingham (1845) in Banff on November 24th 1863. Her father was William Ledingham (1802) who came from Chapel of Garioch, (pronounced Geerie) Aberdeenshire. His wife was Hellen [sic] Wood (1808).

Before we proceed with the Munro story I would just like to say a few words about the Ledinghams. William's life was touched with tragedy, if I may be allowed for once, to employ litotes, that underused figure of speech to convey understatement. In an event that foreshadows the next generation, as you shall shortly see, their second child and first son, Alexander, died on 3rd March 1851 aged about eleven. But he was not the first to die: the second son, John, died on 11th November 1850, aged about four. Nor, I am sorry to say, does this tale of woe end there.

The third and last son, William, died in 1867. By his brothers' standards he had a long life, reaching the ripe old age of eighteen but it was very far from being a happy life. He was what the Victorians called a "sickly child". His death certificate gives the cause of death as "scrofulous sores since infancy and dropsical effusions for four months". Dropsy is a build up of fluid in a body cavity, while scrofula is an infection and unsightly swelling of the lymph glands in the neck, sometimes known as "tuberculosis of the neck". In medieval times it was known as the "King's Evil" and could be cured, it was said, by the touch of the monarch. Poor William.

But hold on. I am not finished yet. William's wife, Helen, died in 1851, on August the 5th to be precise, just a matter of months after young William's birth and five months after they had buried Alexander. And if that is not litotes to say that William senior's life was "touched by tragedy" then I don't know what is.

There were three survivors: my Great-grandmother Georgina, and her two older sisters, Helen (1838) and Margaret (1843). Georgina was only six when she lost her mother. Poor William never knew her at all. How on earth did his father cope? Farming and looking after a young family seem like impossible odds.

Baby William, it seems, might have been brought up during his short life by his uncle and aunt, George and Helen Ledingham, at Castleton of Inchdrewer, Banff. Then there were the domestic servants of course, a ready source of employment for women in the countryside at a time when so little else was available for their sex. While Helen was still alive, there was the twenty-six-year old Ann Leslie from Rothiemay and the twenty-five-year old Jannet [sic] Calder from Rathven who no doubt stayed on at Breach after Helen's death though their workload had increased. Ten years later they are gone but by that time the girls were well able to fend for themselves.

Despite these terrible tragedies William did not rest on his laurels. Perhaps he even threw himself into his work. He had been in Breach since 1841 at least and in 1851, the year that Helen died, it was 100 acres, five times the size of Standingman. Ten years later, it had expanded to 120 acres.

It was to Standingman that Great-grandfather John brought his bride, Georgina Ledingham, in 1863, and it was not until 1881 that the family, which now consisted of five children, moved from Standingman to Berryleys, which at fifty acres, was nearly twice the size. It was there that they were soon joined by the short-lived Georgina (1882-1917). And if her premature death is a sad story, there is a sadder.

There was another Georgina, her sister, the first-born of the family, who was even more unfortunate. She was born on 13th March 1865 and died just seventeen days later, on the 30th March, of ulceration of the mouth and bowels. The pain and grief of her parents must have been almost too much to bear, must have made the next pregnancy, especially, a much more anxious time than it might otherwise have been. Seventeen years later, the pain had obviously dulled enough for them to give their last daughter the same as their first. To me, it seems a curious thing to do, yet as we have seen, it is not the first instance of this happening, nor will it be the last.

I am fortunate to possess a photograph of the family which was given me by my Aunt Gina. Unfortunately Alexander is not included in this family portrait. It is inconceivable that he would have been excluded on the grounds that he was not a full member of the family but considering that he was eight years older than his first step-sibling, it should come as no surprise to us at all that he had his own family by then.

He married in 1888 as a matter of fact, and in 1891 is living in Bogroy cottages, Fordyce, over the hill and not far away, a mere two-and-a-half miles from Berryleys, as the crow flies. His occupation was a farm servant. His wife's name was Catherine Oswald, three years older than him, from Buckie, and she came with a ready-made family in the form of a daughter, Maggie Strachan, born in Deskford in 1887. He also has a daughter by his own hand, so to speak, Catherine, born in Rathven in 1890 and that is why, probably, he could not attend the formal family portrait—far too busy looking after the kids. He had three more children and died in 1930. Catherine lived for another eight years.

Unfortunately there is no date on the family photograph but the youngest, Georgina, looks as if she is about eight or nine so I estimate the photograph would have taken about 1891. Naturally they are wearing their very best for this special occasion. How uncomfortable (and formidable) my great-grandmother looks in her stiff bombazine with the upright collar and the brooch at the throat! Helen scarcely looks any less uncomfortable though her collar looks slightly more forgiving. Her dress looks as if it might be velvet and has puffed sleeves with so many buttons up the front that it must have been taken an absolute age to get dressed in the morning, especially in winter with her fingers numb with cold in those days before central heating. Georgina looks a lot more free and easy in a white sailor-type dress with broad stripes on the arms. But then she was still only a girl and had not yet embarked upon the burden of being a woman. Great-grandfather, looking whiskery, is wearing a three-piece thick woollen suit like his sons, and all with their pocket watch chains proudly on display.

How young they all look, even the great-grandparents! It is a curious feeling to look at them, frozen in time, more than a hundred years later, they not knowing what life held in store for them, and

I knowing everything, at least what really matters: what became of them; what they did for a living; whom they married; how many children they had and what they would least like to know I imagine—when they died, especially in the case of Georgina. But before I go on to tell you all that (briefly), this for me, is what is especially interesting about that photograph.

My grandmother, Helen, looks incredibly like my Aunt Gina at the same age—remarkably so. It's almost enough to make you believe in pre-reincarnation, to coin a word. And talking of family resemblances, John senior, likewise, could not deny being John's father without being called the biggest liar in Christendom. Young John stands behind his father, who is seated and so it easy to compare them. They have exactly the same close-set eyes. I couldn't put it better than Thomas Hardy did in his poem *Weathers* where he reiterates the line *And so do I.* Now I know who is to blame for binoculars being no use to me other than as a telescope, as when fully closed, they are still too wide apart for me to look through with both eyes at the same time. It took a while before this unattractive feature re-emerged in me, though of course it may well have done in young John's children and grandchildren, but since I have no photographs of them it is impossible to say.

Whilst this is a comforting thought—to think that when one is dead and gone, one's genes might continue to pop up when you may have expected them to have been watered down out of existence long ago, there is a downside in that they might cause much dismay to the recipient. And so, if any of my great-grandchildren or great-great-grandchildren even, are reading this with their close-set, shifty eyes, I am very, very sorry. But cheer up. You'll probably still find someone to marry you. After all I did, and so did John Munro, and one day you too may get your revenge and pass on this affliction to the next generation, though you may never live to see it.

Out of the entire family, George was the one who made good, if by that you take material to be the yardstick of success. At fourteen he became a draper's apprentice and somehow ended up as a buyer for a wholesale clothing manufacturer in Manchester. He married Gladys Kersley and they had three daughters, Gina (another one), Brenda and Sheilagh. His baby sister, Georgina, was his housekeeper and she never married. She died of a burst appendix on May 8th 1917 when she was only 35. Now you will see why I mentioned the cause of death of Alexander John, the tea planter in a previous chapter. Another case of lightning striking twice. Incredible to think that there should be two burst appendix deaths in the family, the second less than twenty years after the first. But then everyone has to die of something, as my mother philosophically and bravely remarked when she was handed her own death sentence of non-Hodgkins lymphoma.

Georgina lies with her parents in that dark corner of the old churchyard in Fordyce, next to her grandparents and not far from the memorial to Alexander John which does see the sun, although he is not there. The gold lettering on the stone is very much faded on each side so that it is only the middle part that can be read easily but apart from her own details, Georgina's headstone also records that her father predeceased her on January 12th 1906, aged 74, though according to my figures, he died eighteen days after his 75th birthday. Her mother died at Clayfolds on 29ᵗʰ December 1926. She was 83, so the stone says, (believe that if you like but I don't think she was quite as old as that) and the first of the many relatives who were to end their days there.

My granny's older brother, John (1868), was a farmer at North Bodiechell near Fyvie, Aberdeenshire. He died there on 12ᵗʰ June 1943 aged 74. In 1901, he married Elizabeth (Lizzie) Brown, who was a nurse until she became a farmer's wife and who probably never worked so hard in her life after that. She died on 8ᵗʰ August 1938 aged 66. Interesting to pause and contemplate at this point that here we have two contemporaries, one of whom never even knew about the Second World War and the other who never knew how it ended. Extraordinary. What a difference a few years make! If it were me, I'd rather go before, not knowing, rather than mid-conflict not knowing the outcome, like dying when you are in the middle of an Agatha Christie novel. They had seven children.

Their first, poor William John, died on 4ᵗʰ November 1923, aged only 19, of scarlet fever. He is buried with his parents in Fordyce new cemetery. The long, tall headstone reads: "Erected by John and Elizabeth Munro, Berryleys, in memory of their beloved son". It was the following year that the family moved to Bodiechell. It is touching and good that they always intended to come back to keep their boy company and no doubt they are sleeping more peacefully knowing they are back amongst their roots, little knowing, (how could they?) that Banffshire would be abandoned one day, long after their days were spent and Aberdeenshire would come to Berryleys like the mountain coming to Mohammed.

157

My grandmother's brother, William (1873-1937), was the academic of the family, as may have been guessed from the 1891 census where, at seventeen, he is described as a "scholar". Remember his younger brother, George, had already embarked upon his career in the clothing industry, having left school at fourteen. After leaving Fordyce Academy, William went to Aberdeen University, graduating in 1896. He began his teaching career in Stoneywood, Aberdeen before moving on to Paisley and Montrose before securing a job up as a geography teacher at the prestigious Hamilton Academy. He finally became the headmaster of Hamilton Technical School. In 1902, he married Elizabeth Clark, herself a teacher, and they produced three children: Elizabeth Eleanor, Marion Georgina and William Ledingham. The two girls became teachers and neither married. Will became a heart surgeon. Whether he ever lost his heart to anyone and married I am afraid I cannot tell you.

The youngest brother, Archibald (Archie) Dunbar (1879-1948), became a stationmaster at Keith which was an important junction in those days with the main line coming in from Aberdeen and linking westward with the Highland Railway to Inverness and beyond. He married Jessie Gauld in 1910 and they produced four children. The youngest, George Gauld Munro (1924), took a BSc (Eng) from Aberdeen University in 1945, then somehow took a wrong turning when he began working as a teacher before coming to his senses to work in a field for which his degree had better equipped him—the United Kingdom Atomic Energy Authority which had been set up in 1954.

Their first-born, in 1912, Georgina Helen (Ella), not to my ears, the most pleasant-sounding of names, (like Archibald), married Bill Shand. Just as well he was not called Sam. Imagine your wife telling you, "We're having Sam 'n' Ella for tea." They emigrated to Australia and Ella's younger brother, Archie (1914), followed them out there, no doubt lured by tales of sunshine and the good life.

I vaguely remember him and Nan, his wife, and their son, Keith, who was slightly older than me. It seems to me that we were at their house one day and Keith and I went on hunger strike, or at least refused to eat our tea. I don't remember what the fare on offer was. I was probably just following Keith's lead. (Other boys were always leading me astray and getting me into trouble as you will find out later.) My parents were horribly embarrassed but no amount of threats from my father would induce me to lose face in front of Keith and eat the stuff. Then his father picked up the phone which was conveniently to hand on the sideboard.

"If you don't eat that up in the next minute, I'm going to phone the bogeyman."

I didn't know him well enough to know if he would really do it or not. I didn't *think* my father would resort to such desperate measures but Keith's father looked as if he meant it and I couldn't afford to take any chances. I didn't stop to see what Keith was doing. I had that food down my neck quicker than the voice at the other end of the line could say, "This is the Bogeyman speaking."

Archie was a barber in Banff, cutting his customers' pates down to hedgehog prickles at the back and the sides, then larding Brylcreem on the thatch at the top until it formed such a hard carapace that not even if you

159

heard that your house had been burned down with all its contents, including your mother-in-law, would your hair be able to stand up in horror. I can remember once resting my head on my Latin book (there was no better soporific) and when I woke up I noticed that it was covered in greasy marks as if a candle had been dripping wax on it all night.

It was a bad time for gents' and boys' hairstyles, (akin to women's clothes in the 20s or men's in the 70s) and which has only been surpassed in our own times by the follically challenged, who choose to go for the *coup de grâce* of utter baldness rather than the loss of their crowning glory by a thousand diminishing cuts.

Lastly, Archie's brother, John (1918), drew the short straw. During WWII, he served in the Air Force in the Far East and was taken prisoner. His father, Archie (the stationmaster) tried desperately to find out what happened to him but died broken-hearted without success. In all probability he was one of the 61,000 POWs who died in the construction of what was known as the "Death Railway". There are some things it is better not to know . . .

But now it is time for *you* to know the solutions to the mysteries I left you with in Chapter Twelve.

Chapter Sixteen

"Heligoland" Joseph

So, just *who* was the father of "Heligoland" Joseph?

"To begin at the beginning," as Dylan Thomas famously began *Under Milkwood*. It is not always the best place to begin a story but on this occasion it is. The answer is George Addison, born on 23rd January 1839 in Portknockie, the older brother of my Great-great-grandfather Joseph. In other words, Joseph could just as easily have put Joseph down as his nephew rather than a boarder on his census return of 1871 at Summertown but I'm sure when he filled in that form on April 2nd after a hard day's toiling in the fields, the last thing he had on his mind was future genealogists who would come along more than a century later and who would wonder who the heck this Joseph was. By a process of elimination (which includes being eliminated by death) I narrowed Joseph's father down to three possibilities and in the end George emerged as the one.

But what on earth George was doing in Heligoland and how he came to meet Catharina, the daughter of Paul Rickmer Denker (1813-1851) and Catharina Jasper Dreyer (1813-1890) I do not know, but I suspect there was something fishy about it in the literal sense of the word, despite the fact that when we last met George in Chapter Ten, he was a farm labourer and living with, if not working for, his brother Joseph. Anyway, meet her he did and marry her on 22nd May 1861. She was born on 26th January 1837 in Niendorf, Lubeck,

Schleswig-Holstein. She had a younger brother, Jasper
Paul Denker (1841-1911).

How long they lived in Heligoland I cannot say
either but they were certainly living there in 1864 as
that was where Joseph was born. Their next child,
however, George, was born in Cullen in 1866 so they
must have returned to Scotland by then at the latest.
Approximately two years later they had a daughter, Tina
Denker, who was born in Lossiemouth, but by 1871
they are in Cullen again, living in Seafield Street.

By the time of the next census, in 1881, they have
moved again, this time to 21, Baltic Street, Aberdeen.
As we have seen so often before, their ages, as recorded
in the census returns, are about as reliable as a bus
timetable (where I live anyway), but it tells us George
is a cooper aged forty-two, Catharina is forty-three,
"Heligoland" Joseph is seventeen, George fifteen and
Tina, who was only thirteen or fourteen, is already
working as a milliner. Both boys were employed in the
family business as coopers.

In the next twenty years they moved twice more—
firstly to 9, Victoria Road, Nigg then later up the
street to 198. And they have had two more children:
Catherina and Joseph. George is now a fish curer and
Tina is a "mother's help". The shock of having a baby
at forty-eight, I would have thought, would have been
mostly a cause of dismay, so it's no surprise that Tina
had to give up the day job to help her mother cope.
Meanwhile, young Catharina was now a dressmaker,
but amazingly, had only aged five years during the
decade. It may not be the holy grail of eternal youth,
but it certainly is a remarkable achievement.

I have to say however, that George and Catharina show a terrible lack of imagination in naming their third son the same as the first, even if the first one had left home by this time and so there was no danger when their mother called, "Joseph, your tea is on the table!" that both would ignore her, each pretending he thought she meant the other. And I won't even bother to point out that "Catherina" is just a Sunday name for "Tina".

But I have been teasing you, dear reader. Of course the real explanation for this eccentricity is that Joseph and Catharina were grandchildren, not their own. Personally, I think it would be just grand if, when it came to filling in the census form, people put *that* in front of "son" and "daughter" where applicable, instead of teasing poor family researchers and sending some barking mad as well as up the wrong family tree. I think teasing is a cruel thing, especially when it is done to children. I remember my revered Uncle Tommy saying so and I have never forgotten it, as I was the one being teased. Thus I never teased my children, not that I remember anyway, and I certainly have never sought personal pleasure by watching my grandchildren squirm by teasing them.

But having put that mystery to bed, like the Hydra of Lerna, you get two back in return, as Hercules found out long, long before me. Who were their parents? Reader, I will not tease you any more. Happily, I can supply the answer. In 1888, "Heligoland" Joseph married Agnes Freeland (1868) the oldest daughter of John and Jane Freeland, a white fisher from Nigg, and that's where they are living at the time of the 1891 census with baby George who had just been born. They went on to produce Tina (1893) and Joseph or

"Dovey". I do not have an actual date of birth for him but it seems to me there is a pattern there, like my father's siblings who came along every two years, like clockwork. To my mind it is well within the bounds of possibility that Dovey was born in 1895 and therefore could well have been the six-year-old Joseph living with George and Catharina on the night of the 1901 census.

We will come back to George and Tina later, but just let me say at this point that George's story is a remarkable and extremely sad one—tragic may have been the word for it but for one happy event which makes it fall just short of that and provides some sort of happy ending. It is an extraordinary tale as you will see, but before that, let me tell you about his Uncle George who lived just down the street and who has a very important part to play in this narrative indeed, radically changing the lives of many of his nieces and nephews, not to mention countless others, whose lives would have been completely different if it had not been for good old Uncle George.

Like his brother Joseph, George also married an Agnes (surname at present unknown) and in 1891 he is living with her in Seaton House, Sinclair Road, Nigg, along with baby Jemima aged three. By 1901, they had moved to 36, Victoria Road, but there is no mention of Jemima. Hopefully she was sleeping somewhere else that night and not the Big Sleep but I rather fear the worst as I have not been able to find any subsequent trace of her, nor have I have any record of any further children they might have had so, sadly, it looks if George and Agnes's genes died out. Even worse, it also looks as if Agnes, herself, might not have survived very much longer.

On 9th March 1914, George arrived in Saint John, New Brunswick, Canada, on the *Letitia* out of Glasgow. He appears to have been travelling alone. Did he leave a life full of sadness behind him and go to seek a new life abroad as so many Scots, especially, had done before him? Or had he gone to prepare a place for Agnes?

Five months later, we find him sailing back again, this time from Montreal on board the *Cassandra*, arriving in Glasgow on 24th August 1914. The significance of the date will not have escaped you. Britain had intervened in the little local difficulty between Serbia and the Austro-Hungarian Empire just twenty days previously, yet it is probably of no relevance to our tale. Even if George had, in a fervour of patriotism, caught the first available ship back home to do his bit, if they didn't laugh in his face, he would have been told that they had no use for an old man like him. He was forty-seven, after all. Besides, it was all going to be over by Christmas. We know now of course it wasn't and it wasn't until October 3rd that Canada sent a convoy of troopships to the trenches. No, it's much more likely that George's return had nothing to do with that global conflict at all and was much more to do with domestic matters.

Whatever the reason, there we are going to leave him on the quay at Glasgow for the moment and complete the story of "Heligoland" Joseph.

He died at 18 Menzies Road, Torry, Aberdeen on August 19, 1919. Nineteen was not a lucky number for him it seems. But I suppose someone had to die on that day and millions did when you remember that the Spanish Flu epidemic was only halfway through its course, still had a year and four months left to run in fact—not that that had anything to do with polishing poor Joseph off.

Poor Joseph right enough. Apart from his unlucky number of nineteen, he was unlucky in love too in the sense that he had two wives predecease him. On June 30th 1900 he was married for the second time to Helen Cormack Wood (1874-1917), the last of six children to Robert and Mary Wood, a fisherman from Cove, Kincardineshire. He was hitched to her not a moment too soon—their daughter, Mary Agnes (Aggie), was born in July. That's what I would call timing, though under Scots law, as long as the parents did get around to marrying later, the child was deemed legitimate. Thus my grandfather, Charles Addison, was not, or should not have been labelled illegitimate, if ever he was.

Aggie was presented with a sister, Jane Freeland Addison in 1902. (How accommodating of the new wife to allow this hark-back to the previous incumbent!) There were to be four others. You will meet them later but let me now briefly introduce you to the last, Charles (1915) who seems to have been a bit of an afterthought, coming seven years after his sister Nellie. Better late than never, I imagine is what Charles had as a motto.

I only mention him at this juncture because his father was fifty-one when he was born. Like teaching and the police, fatherhood should be a young person's game. You couldn't say that the shock killed him because it didn't, but "Heligoland" Joseph did have a weak heart and died of angina pectoris four years later, thus rendering poor Charles an orphan when he was only four, the poor soul having already lost his mother when he was two, a time before memory and yet I cannot subscribe in this instance to the philosophy "what you've never had you never miss".

Try to imagine it (I hope you haven't had to experience it): not even five and parentless. Life deals out some pretty tough cards to some people and there is absolutely nothing you can do about it. There are choices you make later in your life that you can, should, and must take some responsibility for, but as I said in the foreword, to be born is such an amazing lottery, the consequences of which are so scary, I'm not sure if I'd like to take the risk to be born again, in the non-religious sense of the expression, naturally. As it happens, it did turn out all right for me the first time (if it was) but how it turned out for Charles, despite his unpromising start, you will find out later.

It's a sad moment, for me at least, but the time has finally come to say goodbye to "Heligoland" Joseph, who, ever since he first swam into my ken when he was but a lad of seven at Summertown, had intrigued me immensely, in no small measure due to his exotic origins. He had a short life, which was not without its sadness, but fortunately he left a legacy in the form of his descendants and it is with them that we pick up the next part of the Addison story, including the nearly tragic tale of his son George.

Chapter Seventeen

Joe's Kids: The Canadian Cousins

Less than a year after their father, "Heligoland" Joseph died, on July 18th 1920 to be precise, that parentless pair, Aggie and Jane, set sail from Glasgow on board the *Sicilian* bound for Canada and arrived in Quebec on July 27th. Aggie had just turned twenty; Jane was still two weeks short of her eighteenth birthday. It is at this point that Uncle George re-enters this narrative. They were going to stay with him, at least initially, at 44, Pelham Avenue, Toronto. Just when George left that quay in Glasgow where we stranded him in the last chapter and returned to Canada I cannot say for certain, but it was certainly before 1920 obviously and probably some time before that.

The sisters intended to find work in domestic service. It was all they knew. But not too long after their arrival, the two bonnie lasses from Scotland, to twist Jane Austen's immortal words, being in want of a good husband, found themselves in possession of precisely that. However, their being in possession of a good fortune was alas, lacking, being immigrants themselves.

Aggie's husband was a labourer and therefore hardly rolling in cash. His name was Fred Cikul, born in Romania in 1896 to Nick Cikul and Catherine Harvatuk. Although he was brought up in the Greek Orthodox Church, he was married on 31st May 1924, at St David's Church, Toronto.

It was not uncommon for immigrants to anglicise their surnames. You can see the point with those seemingly unpronounceable names which seem to have an affinity with the last four letters of the alphabet to the exclusion of all others, but you would not have thought that Fred's name would have offered the least challenge that way or orthographically either. But Fred preferred to be known as "Cycle" and that's what he changed his name to. It seems an unfortunate decision to me, given the tendency we all have towards the diminutive, but he could never have foreseen the connotations in a different land, thousands of miles away and long before a time when Norman Tebbit proudly boasted of his father who "got on his bike" and long before the term "village bike" was not so much a form of communal transport but more a pejorative term to describe a young lady in the community with loose morals.

Aggie died on 6th September 1947 and lies in Prospect Cemetery, Toronto. It was not a long life; only as old as the century. I don't know when Fred died. It's a surreal idea I know, but somehow I can't dismiss the image of him pedalling his way as furiously as Bradley Wiggins to catch up with her in heaven.

Jane was quicker off the mark in the marriage stakes, marrying William John Whitford, on 10th October 1923 and emigrating for the second time when she joined him in Detroit, Michigan, the following month. William was also an immigrant, born in Hayle, Cornwall, on 13th December 1893. He arrived in New York on 7th September 1913 and by July of 1922, aged 28, had settled in Detroit where he was a machinist in the automotive industry.

Jane gave birth to Muriel on the last day of 1924 followed by three more girls and finally, after a gap of eight years, the son they had perhaps been hoping and waiting for, Joseph John Whitford, was born in 1941. Jane died on 19th April 1967 aged 64 and is buried in Cadillac Memorial Gardens, Clinton Township, Michigan. William had predeceased her on August 18th 1965.

Aggie and Jane's brother, John Wood Addison, was born on 1st October 1903 in Torry, Aberdeen. He arrived in Canada on the good ship *Saturnia* in July 1923 with $10 in his pocket, as he was required to do by law, destination his sister Jane's who had paid his fare and, declaring himself neither mentally or physically defective, and being able to read and write, was allowed to join her at 10, Cluny Drive, Toronto.

He arrived in time for her wedding but there was barely time to do anything else before she left for the USA four months later. Five years later, John is twenty-four, working as a landscape architect and living with Uncle George at Pelham Street. He married Irene Thomasina Beatrice Tyrell (how's that for a handle?) who was born on January 27th 1909 in Argentina of all places. Her father was Irish and had a bit of a handle himself—Thomas Richard Grattan Tyrell. Hence her being saddled with Thomasina one supposes.

Irene arrived in New York from Liverpool aboard the *Caronia* on 8th April 1909, aged three months. It's hard to imagine anyone being better travelled at such young age than her, especially before the invention of the jet engine and the De Havilland Comet which shrank the world. It was not too much longer however before she went on the longest journey of all—to the *undiscover'd country from whose bourn/No traveller returns,* or so Hamlet unreliably informs us since he had seen his father's ghost not so long before he uttered the immortal lines. She died on 24th October 1931 and is buried at Mt Pleasant Cemetery, Toronto, which sounds a pretty nice place to be dead in, only not when you are 22. John married again and had a daughter, but that is all I know about them. He died aged 81 on March 19th 1985 and was laid to rest in Prospect Cemetery, Toronto.

In 1928, he and Irene had a son, John Tyrell Addison, who died in Verona, Ontario on 10th May 1992 aged 63. I've never been there but I have been to its more famous namesake in Italy and I think that is a pretty good city to be dead in since the stampede of tourists on their way to see Juliet's balcony (built in 1936) would not bother you any longer. But congratulations to the Verona tourist board for capitalising on the Bard's play, something which neighbouring Vicenza failed to do with much more justification since that is the birthplace of Luigi Da Porto (1485-1530) from whom Shakespeare pinched his plot and most of his characters.

John's younger brother, Andrew (Andy) Leiper Addison, together with his sister, Helen Wood Addison (Nellie), had arrived in Canada three years before him, disembarking in Quebec on 3rd November 1920 from the *Empress of Britain,* out of Liverpool. This was just a little over three months after the first tranche of Addisons, Aggie and Jane, had set foot in Canada. He was fifteen; she was twelve. He was born at 8 Ferry Road, Torry on February 11th 1905, she at 23 Walker Road, Torry on 31st January 1908 which shows you that their parents were not unaccustomed to changing addresses themselves, though nothing like as radically as their children. And if it seems an incredible responsibility to heap upon the narrow shoulders of a mere boy of fifteen, the looking after such a young sister on such a long voyage, the truth is he was not left solely in charge of her. Just who that person was will be revealed shortly.

Aggie and Jane had evidently gone ahead in the knowledge that Andy and Nellie would follow. Andy, for his part, did not prepare a place for anyone if we are thinking of the phrase in the way Jesus used it. He lived the longest of all "Heligoland" Joseph's children, not handing in his dinner pail until 19th April 1990. He was 85. That is an achievement for an Addison male, especially, with their perennial heart disease.

In 1930, aged 22, Nellie married John (Jack) Blackhall Stephen. They had two sons, Thomas (Tommy) (1931) and George who sadly lived for only two years, from 1934-1936. Two years later, Nellie followed him to the grave. She died on 7th September 1938 aged only 30. She sleeps the Big Sleep in Prospect Cemetery Toronto where, as we have seen, she would be joined later by her siblings, including Andy, above, and her husband, Jack.

He was born in "The Shop", Portlethen, which at that time was in Kincardineshire but has since been swallowed up by the insatiable maw of Aberdeenshire. It's curious, is it not, that Nellie and Jack were born so near each other yet had to travel halfway across the globe to meet? One wonders if their ancestors had stayed put whether they would have met anyway. I, for one, would not put any money against it. As you know, my ancestors were not much addicted to travel when it came to finding an incubator for their genes.

And so we come to the last son of Joe's kids by his second wife. Charles was born on 1st February 1915 in Nigg. Being orphaned so young, he must have been brought up by a relative in Scotland, Tina, his twenty-six year-old half-sister, being the most likely candidate.

On June 22nd 1942, he married a local lass, at least compared to his siblings, but not nearly so close as his Portknockie cousins or his Fordyce forbears. She was Helen Stella Marriot from Kemnay, Aberdeenshire, born on 9th October 1913. Interestingly, Helen's father, James Albert Marriot, was born on 26th September 1882 in Dalbeattie, Kirkcudbrightshire and married Catherine Leslie Andrew on 14th April 1909. He died in Turriff on 19th January 1947.

Interesting to no-one apart from me and I only mention it because Dalbeattie is where my wife and I began married life, not in a house like most people, but in a non-residential caravan in the municipal caravan site, much to the curiosity of several of our pupils who came to gawk at their new teachers. I expect they imagined a bit of slap and tickle would be going on, maybe hoping to catch us at, we being newly married and all that, but they could never have imagined what we were really up to. Behind the closed caravan door and discreetly drawn curtains, it was the palms of my hands that the new wife was tickling with the belt or tawse as it is sometimes known. Dismiss any thoughts of BDSM you may be entertaining: she was merely practising giving me the belt in order to improve the aim and power with which she could administer corporal punishment to her badly behaved, teacher-baiting pupils.

But I digress. Charles became a pharmacist and emigrated to Australia, New South Wales to be precise. They had two sons: Joseph (1943) and Boris (1945). Josephs abound in the Addison clan, but this is the first recorded instance of a Boris. Charles died in 1976 aged only sixty-one.

And that concludes the story of "Heligoland" Joseph's children by his second marriage—remarkable in that every single one of them emigrated and with the exception of Charles, probably would not have done had it not been for good old Uncle George. We will turn to Joseph's children from his first marriage shortly, but before we do that, let us complete Uncle George's tale. There is not much left to tell.

Aged sixty-seven, and travelling alone, he set sail on the *Letitia* from St John, bound for Belfast, Liverpool and Glasgow. He gives his occupation as a cooper so that at least tells us he pursued the old family profession in the new country. He disembarked in Glasgow on 21st December 1931, his final destination being 422, Stonegate Road, Meanwood, Leeds. Who lived there? And why disembark in Glasgow when it would have been nearer his destination to have disembarked in Liverpool? Had he come home to die in the homeland, or was it for just one last visit? For the moment I am sorry to say that these questions will have to remain a mystery and we turn now to George, Tina and Dovey, "Heligoland" Joseph's first three kids.

If Tina did look after her half-brother Charles, her duties were short-lived since in October 1920, a year after her father's death, she emigrated along with Andy and Helen and like them, all she had was £5 in her pocket and the clothes she stood up in. All their fares were paid by generous Uncle George.

She died just less than nine years later on 18th September 1929. She was only 36. She had been suffering from TB for a year but it was the Addison heart that let her down in the end. She died at 1866, St Clair Street, Toronto, where she was working as a housekeeper for George. They had moved there from Pelham Avenue seven years previously. She was the first of the clan to be buried in Prospect Cemetery. It hardly seems the happiest of lives, but it is eclipsed by what happened to her brother George. It is an incredible tale.

He began work as a cooper with the rest of the family but when the First World War broke out he joined the Royal Navy and saw action in the Mediterranean. His ship was torpedoed and the family was told that he had "died on active service". In actual fact he had somehow survived, and half-drowned, was washed up on a beach in Italy and taken to hospital. He had nothing on him that identified him and to compound matters, was suffering from total amnesia. And there he remained until the war ended. It was only after then, when he heard English being spoken, that he regained some of his memory.

Some months later he was shipped back to a hospital in England and eventually he made a full recovery. But every silver lining has a cloud and it is a pity that that is not how the tale ends—happily—but alas it does not.

You can imagine his shock when, once the family had got over theirs at his return from the dead, and after throwing themselves on his neck and after much renting of raiment and weeping of joy, George was at the receiving end of some news as devastating as his own was joyful. Not only was his father dead, (perhaps just as well or the shock of seeing his son alive and well after all these years might have killed *him* considering his weak heart) but the family with whom he had just become reunited were just about to flee the country lock, stock and barrel. Well practically.

By the end of that fateful year, 1920, they had all left Aberdeen with the exception of John, who you may remember, joined them in 1923. I have reason to believe that Charles might have been living in Turriff, not that far away, but he was only five and whose very existence might have come as a complete shock to George, depending on when precisely he had been torpedoed. And when Charles grew up, he too moved away just about as far as it is possible to go without leaving the planet. As for Dovey, he was in London, training as an architect. (Could it possibly be it was he who Uncle George was heading for in Leeds in 1931?)

I am not sure precisely when it was that George presented himself on the doorstep at 18, Menzies Road, but it must have been sometime after his father died in August 1919 and before July 1920, for Aggie and Jane, on their immigration forms, put him down as next of kin, residing at that address. If he had ever imagined that having once lost their brother and him being miraculously restored to them, that they would never again let him out of their sight, then poor George would have been severely disappointed. To him it must have seemed that no sooner had he been welcomed to the bosom of the family again than they were turning their back on him and deserting him in their droves.

On the other hand, with the exception of John, their passages and fares would have been arranged and paid for some time before the sailings and presumably some time before George's resurrection, perhaps not long after their father's death. And yet poor George could be forgiven for feeling as if he were the carrier of some sort of foul contagion that the rest of the family wanted to distance themselves from as far as possible.

As a matter of fact, he *did* feel abandoned and never did renew ties with his family again after they went to Canada. He always said that he had no family and it would appear that he did fall out with John before his departure, for on his immigration form, John gives as his next of kin, not George, but an aunt, Mrs Annie Main, one of his mother's sisters evidently, residing at 22, Bank Street, Aberdeen. An embittered man, George died in 1966 aged 75.

I am glad to report however, that there is a happy ending to this sorry tale after all. His girlfriend, Agnes Banks Murison, had not married anyone else during George's absence and supposed death, and they married in 1920. (What a year that was for George!) They had two sons, George Murison Addison (1921-1995) and Rodney Murison Addison (1922-1998).

Rodney married Mary Isobel Kean in 1947. Rodney, who was Vice-Chairman of the National Savings Committee for Scotland, was awarded the OBE in the New Year's Honours List of 1976. His wife and children, Marjorie Helen (1955) and David Gordon Murison (1958), saw him receive it at Buckingham Palace. Welcome, David. To the best of my knowledge, you are the only other David Addison in the family. And here's another curious thing. Both our sisters are called Marjorie. There was one other Marjorie Addison, you may recall, the one who burnt herself to death in 1857 in Keith. For my sister's sake, I hope the similarity stops there. I have warned her not to take her pipe to bed with her, just in case.

And so we have come from Heligoland to Canada via Torry and Nigg. There are still some unanswered questions of course, not least what was a wee cooper from Banffshire doing in Heligoland and mixing with the local girls? Maybe he had been in the army for a short time but more likely it was something to do with the fishing industry. There is a close affinity between the fishers of the North-East of Scotland and the Danes of Jutland. I have even heard it said that if both speak in their local patois, they can pretty well understand each other. One thing is for sure: "Heligoland" Joseph and his descendants will be mightily glad his father did chat up the local girls, or one in particular, even poor George. Nor will they forget their debt to Uncle George of course, though that was another thing poor George's descendants missed out on—being born in Canada.

But Joe's kids are not the only Addisons who were born at the other side of the Pond. There is another branch of the Addisons who colonised Ontario even earlier. Just who they were and who they were descended from, together with some intriguing tales of adultery, rape and murder, you will find out in another chapter, but before we come to that, for neatness' sake, I must tell you a little about the last three of Great-great-grandparents Joseph Addison and Janet Coull's brood—Jessie, Charles and Louisa.

Chapter Eighteen

Of fish an' folk and the Broch

As I pointed out earlier, females are a bit harder to trace since they have a habit of getting married and losing their maiden name, to name just one thing. I have therefore and unfortunately, no information about Mary Ann, the first of the family, other than she was born in 1832 in Findochty but I can tell you that Jessie or "Janet" as she was called, the third child, married John Forbes who was born in Cullen in 1838. She was born on 21st November 1836 in Portknockie. They were married on 19th December 1857 when Janet was barely a month past her twenty-first birthday. Their first daughter, Janet, known as "Jessie", (just to make things confusing) was born on 9th March 1858. I am sure you are more capable than I am of doing the arithmetic.

John was a brick and tile maker. For a year and a half before he died on September 18th 1896, in Cullen, he had been suffering from inflammation of the kidneys. Unable to work, and with all savings, if any, gone, he died a pauper. Jessie died in Aberdeen in 1900.

Elizabeth Bruce Forbes was their second child, born in 1859 and who died twenty-seven years later in 1886. Alexander, the third child, had an even shorter life: he was two months short of his second birthday when he died in 1865. After him there were four others but unfortunately another son, John Thom Forbes, died in 1894 aged about twenty, thus they experienced the sadness of burying three children, not an infrequent occurrence in this narrative, as you cannot have failed to notice.

Elizabeth, unsurprisingly, was a domestic servant, though she did not serve very long. In 1881, the last year she would appear in the census records (though thankfully she did not know that), she was staying with her seventy-eight year old widowed grandfather, John Forbes, a cooper at the Inchgower distillery near Buckie. It's good to see the in-laws were also in the cooperage business, only the golden nectar their barrels were designed to contain is much more to my taste than the silver darlings of my ancestors'. John died of chronic bronchitis in April 1885, aged eighty-two. His wife, Jessie Sutherland (1814), had predeceased him in 1870, and unlike the Addisons who found wives on their doorstep, more or less, John Forbes, the elder, went all the way to Latheron in Caithness to find a bride.

Well, the real story probably is that *she* came from the boondocks of Caithness to the comparatively more cosmopolitan coast of Banffshire possibly by taking the much shorter sea crossing across the Moray Firth. She was twenty-five when she married; dead by fifty-four. It was a short life but it was not wasted. She gave birth to seven children but it is only her first-born, John, above, for the purposes of this narrative that we are interested in, as that is how the Addison line marched on into the next century as it was he who "had to marry" as my mother would have put it, Jessie Addison. You wouldn't make the connection by the surname, but that doesn't matter in the slightest. It's the genes that matter at the end of our days. By our genes we live on in, albeit in a diluted sort of a way and, in my opinion, the best we can hope for after we have turned up our toes.

John and Jessie's first child, the Janet aforesaid, married John Parr (1855), a blacksmith from somewhere in England. It is a name commonly found in Devon or Somerset and that is another long way to come in search of a bride. They were married about 1880 and began their married life in Rathven though they later moved to Inverurie. There were six children from that marriage but I will only mention the second last, Jeannie Frances Mann Parr who just managed to make an appearance in 1897 on the 28th December. She married John Mitchell who was born the same year. The reason I mention her is because she was the ancestor of John Mitchell whom I met in 1969, in what I call the "Summer of Content".

I remember sitting up late that year with my cousin Margaret watching the grainy, live television pictures from the moon and hearing Neil Armstrong fluff his lines as he uttered his immortal lines: "That's one big step for man, one giant leap for Mankind". John was a prison officer in Retford, about thirty miles from where I was staying with Aunt Gina and Uncle Jack in Nottingham. My uncle was a salesman with a timber firm and had got me a job there as a tally boy for the summer. It was not purely nepotism: I had done the same job the year before and so I had "previous" as they say in the criminal world. In an entrepreneurial spirit that would warm the cockles of Norman Tebbit's heart, I took a train to London, bought a newspaper, found a flat, took a bus to an industrial estate in the East End and went round each firm asking for a job until I found one. What's more, I even got one for the Best Beloved of whom much more later.

Anyway, it was thanks to meeting John Mitchell that summer that I was made aware of the existence of the Parr and Forbes families, following their line of descent from Janet Addison. Not as momentous I grant you, as a moon landing, but without that meeting I would not have been able to take that small step towards completing that branch of the family tree.

Before we take our leave of them, I would just add this. Like his father, William Forbes was a tile maker who appears in the 1881 census aged fourteen but does not reappear again. Perhaps he emigrated. I have not sought assiduously to trace him, but I fear the worst. In 1901 however, we find his thirty-one year old brother James, a shoemaker, living at 69, Kelvin Street, Glasgow with his sister Mary Ann and his one-year old daughter Catherine Murphy. Since there is no mention of the baby's mother, one cannot help but conclude that Mary Ann had been drafted in to look after her while he went to work.

Thus we come to the last two of Joseph and Janet's brood: Louisa and Charles. With your indulgence, I will begin with the last first (though for logistical reasons I had to put him first in the chart).

Like the others, Charles was born in Portknockie. In the 1861 census, he is living at his father's 100-acre croft of Hillhead, Rathven along with his siblings, John, Joseph, Alexander, William and Louisa. Sometime between then and the next census, he had flown the nest and is a boarder at 50, Back Street, Fraserburgh, the home of Susan Trail and her family. You will be not surprised to learn that he is a cooper to trade and there was plenty of need for barrels in the Broch (from the Gaelic *A' Bhruaich*) as Fraserburgh is popularly known, since it was a major fishing harbour then and still is today, while others have dwindled away to a minnow of their former selves. Amazingly, it has no fewer than thirteen churches, most of them evangelical—that's one per 1,000 head of population. You remember what I said about the faith of fishers. The funny thing is they are also the catch and they don't realise it.

On December 19th 1874, Charles married Mary Angus, a blacksmith's daughter from Fraserburgh. They went on to have nine children. In 1891, they were living at 63 Charlotte Street. Charles has now changed his occupation to "fish curer" but in 1901 he is back to making barrels as well.

Being a cooper was an extremely skilled job. The barrels had to be made to specific specifications: 32 gallons in capacity, (to contain about 1,000 fish, known as a "cran") and the staves had to be half an inch thick, precisely. Above all, the joints had to be watertight, for if not, the brine would leak out, air would get in and the contents ruined.

Curing was a lot more complicated than it sounds, much more than just a simple matter of packing the barrels with salt. For a start, the curer actually *bought* the fish. Normally he would have an agreement with specific vessels and then he had to make sure that he had enough barrels of course, as well as salt standing by when the catch was landed. Five or six tons of salt were required for every hundred crans. He would also have to employ his own gutting and packing team which consisted of three women, two to gut and one to pack.

The gutters were also highly skilled. With one slit of the knife, they could rip out the guts and the gills and could process as many as forty fish a *minute*. Some could do even more! The packer had to be equally speedy. She would pack one row with the heads facing the centre of the barrel, cover them completely with salt, then put the next layer on top with the tails towards the centre. And then of course, the curer had to sell the fish—and make a profit.

Clearly being a fish curer was a much more responsible and risky occupation than being a cooper on whom he relied very heavily. The adage "If you want a thing done properly, do it yourself" springs to mind when you think of Charles's two jobs, or maybe he was just minimising his risks—or cutting out the middleman.

His children were becoming independent, so shortage of cash was probably not the reason for his double-barrelled job, if you forgive the pun. By 1901, Jessie is a domestic servant; Margaret a shop assistant in a baker's; Lottie is working in a draper's and Alexander, aged sixteen, is learning the cooper's trade. Nine years later he is dead. William and George are still both at school, while Nellie and Charles appear to have flown the nest. They were twenty-two and twenty after all. There is no mention of another son, John. Hopefully he was just out of the house that night and not in heaven.

And that brings to a conclusion all I know about the Broch Addisons. I do not even know when Charles and Mary died. After all, both were on right side of fifty at the 1901 census and hopefully the next census would see them still alive and well. Plenty there for others to follow up should they wish, but we are going back to the last of the family, baby sister Louisa.

She married William Seivewright in Fordyce on 6th August 1870 and after a brief period in which there was just the two of them enjoying each other's company—they would never know such peace again—Louisa started her baby factory, producing one every year or every second year for the next two decades, enough for the Seivewrights to form their own football team or hold a Last Supper if they had had a room big enough to contain a table that they could all sit around—which is very doubtful in the tenement flat at 110, Byres Road, Partick, Glasgow where we find them in 1901.

William, the author of all these children, was an undertaker's clerk. He was fifty-five by this time. In the midst of death, there was life, if he had anything to do with it. His son, Alexander, was a commercial traveller and if he was away at least some of the time, that must have eased the pressure on space just a little bit. Young William was a chemist's assistant; George a carpenter; James a cabinet-maker; Ann a clerkess; Charles a clerk, while the others were still at school. There is no occupation recorded for Joseph, nor for Louisa, neither daughter nor wife—not that they would have been short of something to do. Washing day must have been a weekly nightmare; the making of meals a daily ordeal.

The eldest child, Jessie Ann, became a nurse and worked in the fever hospital at 68, North Oswald Street, Glasgow. On census day, the night of 31st March/1st April 1901, there were 97 people sleeping under that roof of whom only sixteen were patients, most of them aged between three and seven, along with a one-year old and his twenty-six year old mother.

In those days before he took up the hobby of making babies, and even longer before he entered the dead body business, back in 1861, the fifteen-year old William Seivewright was living with the Watt family

185

in Ordiquill learning the shoemaking trade from his mentor, James Watt from Cairnie, Aberdeenshire.

In due course William became a teacher himself. In 1881 he had taken on a couple of apprentices, the eighteen-year old William Cowie and the sixteen-year old James Cooper. There was also the fifteen-year old Jane Barclay from King Edward who was helping Louisa with the household chores. Little did she know how much her workload was to increase . . .

As well as making shoes, William was supplementing his income by crofting seven acres at Kirktown, Ordiquhill. Since the one-year old George was born at Ordiquill, while his older siblings were are born at Fordyce, we can deduce that the Seivewrights must have moved there by 1789 if not before. But when and why William gave up the shoemaking and crofting and moved into the burial business in the big city to I do not know, but the rest you do.

And that, dear reader, brings us to the end of the trail, at least as far as I have it, of the Banffshire Addisons. It is time now to cross the seas to Canada again and find out about that other lot of Canadian Addisons I mentioned earlier.

I warn you it is somewhat "sensational", as Lady Bracknell said of her diary. You may want to keep it to read on the train. Or the plane. They weren't around in her day.

Chapter Nineteen

The other Canadian Connection

In Boyndie, near Banff, a baby boy was born on 5th January 1840 to George Addison (1814) and Elizabeth Steinson. They were married on 25th August 1838 in Banff. Elizabeth's parents were the exotically named John Steinson and Margaret Aviens. If the latter sounds French, Steinson, which sounds German, is not. It is in fact a corruption of "Stevenson" probably coming from the bad handwriting on the part of the person who recorded John's grandfather's birth, or even before.

In another foreign linguistic connection, George died at Little Toux on October 2nd 1878. It sounds as if he died in France somewhere, but in actual fact it is just three crofts away from Summertown. Translated from the French, it means "cough" and if you think that's a weird name for a farm, then you should see some of the rest. Clashendamer you have already come across, but how about Badenvouchers, for example? And all three just within a couple of miles radius of each other!

George (1814) and Elizabeth, without the least consideration for the confusion they might create for future genealogists, decided to call their baby George. When he grew up, he married Jane Webster on 10th December 1862. She was the daughter of Isobel Brown and James Webster, a shoemaker and sometime crofter who was born in Marnoch. Some ten years later, George and Jane set sail for Canada, never to return. Why they left I have not yet been able to find out, apart from the universal reason of the grass being greener at the other side of the Atlantic and having suffered some twenty years or more of Banffshire winters—and that's only counting the ones he could remember. And there was another incentive, as you shall see presently.

George and Jane were the pioneers, the first Addison settlers in Ontario. It was not for another forty years that the other George Addison set foot in Canada and nearly another ten before the rest of the contingent arrived. Their common ancestors were John Addison and Ann McClelland. They may have been closely related but it would not surprise me at all if neither set of Addison descendants knew of the other's existence, though geographically speaking they were not far apart at all, only a matter of a mere 130 miles or so, which is nothing in North American terms. Ontario is so vast it takes the best part of a day to get from one end to the other. You begin to think it will never cease.

George and Jane settled in Bandon where he found work as a miller, which might, or might not have been, his trade when he left Scotia's shores. At some stage in his career, the dam which he (and others) relied on for their daily bread, burst. Since it was never rebuilt, that spelled the death of Bandon. The inhabitants of this tiny community of a dozen or so homes drifted away and you can't help but feel with a name like that, its demise was in its genes.

George was forced to seek alternative employment as an agricultural labourer. Later his son William (Billy) who was a teamster, managed to buy up the whole of Bandon. At that time the Government was encouraging people to settle so he probably got the land at a knockdown price. It still remains in the ownership of the family even to this day, with William's granddaughter, Betty Hulley, even if nothing of Bandon itself remains apart from an abandoned threshing machine and the dust of the dead in the cemetery who, of course, had already departed, destination unknown, before its demise.

George, the pioneer, died on July 26th 1909. Jane, born in 1836, died on 14th December 1921. Along with her husband and her brothers, (more of them later) they are all buried in Hullett township, Huron County, Ontario. By that time, the other Addisons were beginning to arrive in Toronto.

Hullett was named after ("for" as the transcontinentals prefer to put it) John Hullett, one of the directors of the Canada Company. The Company was founded by John Galt, no less, the Scottish novelist of *Annals of the Parish* fame. Not a lot of people know that. I certainly didn't before researching this book, and why should anyone, not even students of literature? It has absolutely nothing to do with *that* book.

The purpose of the Company was to promote the colonisation of Upper Canada (present-day Ontario) by assisting emigrants with low fares and cheap land as well as cheap tools and implements—the incentive I was talking about. The first wave of settlers came from England, followed by the Scots and then the Irish. One of the earliest settlers of Hullett township ("township" just means the area round Hullett) was Thomas Walker who took up land near Clinton in 1833. Most of those early settlements were eventually absorbed into it.

George and Jane had seven children spanning three decades and since George (1867-1878) was born in Scotland and Louisa (1872-1947) was born in Ontario, we can conclude that their pioneering parents must have left Scotland sometime between 1867 and 1872. And indeed the Passenger and Immigration records do show a George Addison aged 31 who arrived in Ontario in 1871. But that is all the records tell us.

Jane Webster was one of eight children and at least three of her brothers emigrated to Ontario the same year as she did. (Marry me, marry my brothers.) Two are buried in Hullett while the other is in Wingham, which, even today, is a tiny community of less than three thousand souls and would have been even smaller then. Despite its diminutive size, it has nevertheless, produced the famous Man Booker prizewinning writer, Alice Munro, who has immortalised Wingham in her books.

But Wingham has another, more dubious, claim to fame. It is so small that the entire place is served by the same postcode: NOG 2WO which some wag has translated as "No-one goes to Wingham Ontario". There is probably a great deal of truth in that.

It would appear that Jane's four remaining siblings also emigrated, leaving their parents who were in their sixties, behind them. Imagine how devastating it must have been for them to have said goodbye to all their children like that, knowing that when they set sail it would most likely be the last time they would ever see them again. I can understand a little how they must have felt.

In 2000 we flew out to New Zealand to visit our daughter who was taking a year out after university. Her going there was not a problem since we knew she would be back, but when, during our visit, she dropped the bombshell that she had applied for permanent residency, I remember during the entire day of our departure I felt physically ill and when it came to the actual moment of parting, and afterwards, it felt like a bereavement. If only it were Canada, I remember thinking, it wouldn't be half so bad.

As it turned out, she had put her application in too late and we were mightily relieved when it was rejected, but of course we did not know that at the time. One of her Kiwi friends offered to marry her, purely as a means of her gaining citizenship but she chose not to go down that route. As it happened, he died before the year was out in a light aircraft crash. She could have been a widow in New Zealand at twenty-five.

So, knowing that his entire family was about to desert him, was that why James Webster, aged 61, had another child, Susan, born in Marnoch on October 9th 1869? I hope you like mystery stories, dear reader, because I am going to tell you one. You might say that George Addison's father-in-law's story has little to do with us, but I do not apologise for including it here because of the intriguing mysteries it threw up.

For one thing, what an amazing thing it would be if Isobel Webster were Susan's mother! The 1851 and 1861 censuses show the difference between James and Isobel's ages vary between six and two years, with Isobel being the senior. We will put the incredible twenty-seven years difference in 1871 down to an even bigger clerical error and if we take Isobel's birth as being 1808 at the latest, you can see she would still have been the medical miracle of her day. Susan *must* have been a granddaughter, unless of course James was telling no less than the truth and she *was* his daughter. After all, Charlie Chaplin became a father again at 73, to name but one ancient father. On the other hand, if she was his granddaughter, what kind of a parent is it that leaves a two-year old child (or younger) behind and takes ship halfway round the world?

This of course also begs the question: who was Susan's mother? And the mystery deepens still because also in the 1871 census, as well as Susan, there is a fourteen-year-old Jane L Dunn, born in Alvah and whom James is particular to describe as "daughter of wife". Since Jane was born in 1857, it would have been pushing it a bit for Isobel to have been her mother, yet possible. And if she wasn't, who was? And why was James so keen to stipulate that she was nothing to do with him?

Neither Isobel nor Jane are recorded in the census returns for 1881. Only the seventy-one year old James and the eleven-year old Susan remain. Sometime later she too moved to Canada, probably on the old man's death, and on 14th December 1898, married Thomas Henry Eades of Wingham. She died a little over a year later on March 28th 1900. She was only thirty.

But back to the Addisons. You may be relieved to know I do not intend to go through a list of George and Jane's descendants' marriages, children and deaths, as you may begin to feel you were reading something akin to a telephone directory, only not so interesting. Instead I will only mention those who took my interest.

Take Dora Jemima Ruddell (1885-1959) for instance. (One wonders if she got the Jemima from good old Uncle George's daughter.) She married late in life, to the Mayor of Clinton no less, William Walker, almost certainly a descendant of the original settler. Poor William had a very unfortunate end. They were tearing down a house when a brick wall fell on them.

Dora was injured but William was killed, thus putting paid to the aphorism "as safe as houses".

Apart from being the home of the aforementioned Alice Munro, Clinton, only a little larger than Wingham, has another claim to fame, or rather notoriety. In 1959, this small community was rocked by the murder of a twelve-year old girl, Lynne Harper. A local fourteen year-old boy was arrested and sentenced to death. He was finally acquitted by the Ontario Court of Appeal, wait for it—in 2007, forty-eight years later.

John Cartwright Addison, (JC), Dora's younger brother, and the sixth out of seven children, was born on 26th September 1880 in Bandon. He was married twice, firstly to Annie Grace Maud on 9th October 1902 in Wingham. She was born on 5th March 1881 in Toronto and died on 25th September 1908 in Orillia but went home to be buried in Prospect Cemetery, Toronto, the same, note, as those other Addisons, thus ironically, they were closer in death than in life. The following year JC married his second wife, Beatrice Maude Ego (1884-1958), born, bred and dead in Orillia.

Orillia is a big metropolis by Clinton and Wingham standards and indeed it was given city status in 1969. It has a population today of some 30,000 and rejoices under the sobriquet of "Sunshine City" after Stephen Leacock's *Sunshine Sketches of a Little Town* though Orillia's claim to be the little town of Mariposa in the book owes more to wishful thinking than fact, as Leacock himself said his fictional town was a composite. However Leacock's house, now a museum, *is* situated there, that no-one can deny.

One wonders if, when he was courting wife number one, John Cartwright's chat-up line, albeit a tad formal, was: "Will you come into the garden, Miss Maud?" But perhaps it hit exactly the right note, so to speak, in the first decade of the 20th century. It seems a bit of a coincidence that his second wife was also a Maude, albeit it was not her first name, as in my experience Mauds aren't exactly thick on the ground. In fact, I've never met a single one, ever. But that is not the reason why I am telling you about JC, nor is it because he married two young wives who preceded him to heaven, nor is it because he built a car in the back kitchen. I will tell you the reason in a moment.

With the first Miss Maud, JC had three children whose names I must mention because they are so wonderful. Firstly there was Emory, the only Emory Addison I think it is safe to say there has ever been, and ever likely to be. He was born on 7th September 1903 in St Thomas and died in 1959 in California. Incidentally, St Thomas was an important railway junction in the heyday of the iron horse and so it was perhaps fitting in a way that it was there, in 1885, that P.T. Barnham's Jumbo, the celebrated giant elephant, the one who gave his name to all things large, was struck by a locomotive and later died of his wounds.

Emory's brother, Thomas Carlyle Addison, was born on 22nd July 1906 in Orillia and died on 21st December 1972 in Hunstville. He married Myrtle Elizabeth Lamb (or Bobbie as she preferred to be known—I can't imagine why) on January 30th 1930 in Toronto. She was the daughter of Joseph Lamb and Mary McDonald, thus when their first child, Betty, was born on 2nd March 1932, Joseph was able to go around Hunstville (another tiny town in the Canadian Shield) proudly boasting: "Mary's had a little Lamb." They had two other children, the alliteratively named Bob and Barb and that's all I propose to say about *them.*

Why they named Thomas after, (I suppose I should say "for" since we are in North America) the great 19th century Scottish satirical essayist, I can't imagine, unless they thought some of the greatness may have rubbed off on him, the antithesis of giving a dog a bad name. What I *can* tell you is that the original was born in Ecclefechan, Dumfriesshire. Never was there a name more Scottish, yet I remember reading in that celebrated French magazine, Paris Match, that he was "né à Ecclefechan en Angleterre".

I visited his house once upon a time and there in a bedroom, maybe the very room where he was born, was a chair and on that chair was a large felt hat—his hat, according to the notice. I couldn't resist it. After a quick check that no cameras were watching, I slipped it on. It flopped down over my ears. I like to have contact with greatness whenever I can, touch what they have touched, but I will not incriminate myself by admitting to other close encounters I have had with objects belonging to the dead and famous, apart from the time in Roskilde Cathedral when I couldn't resist touching the coffin of Queen Anne of Denmark (1575-1612), first wife of Christian IV (1577-1648), and was given a hell of a rollicking by a guard. But they shouldn't have put her in a velvet coffin, should they? That's just *asking* to be touched, like some sculptures are. Isn't it?

Romeo had a question too: he wanted to know *what's in name*? Well I'll tell him: it's the difference between getting into this book and not. By his second wife, JC had eleven children. I am only going to mention those I deem to have unusual names and I apologise to those with the more common, or garden variety for omitting them. I am in the autumn of my years and well-travelled besides, yet I have never met such a bizarre choice of names with which to lumber your children, ever, as these.

There's Annie (1912-1997). Not in the least unusual, but her full handle was Annie Grace Maude Beatrice, the only one of the eleven to have been victimised in this way when it came to the accursed problem of trying to fit a long name on a passport. There's Claude (1913-1998). There's Velma Irene born on 23rd November 1914 and who was dead by the end of the year, poor thing. There's Aubrey (1920-2002). There's Oswald (1921-1995) and there's poor little Edith Cavell, born 13th February 1919 and who died just four months later on 21st June 1919. You could never conceive of these names in Scotland, at least certainly not in those days, but I wouldn't put any money on there not being little Addisons coming along in the future with even more extraordinary names.

All these Addisons with memorable names died in Orillia and apart from that not so curious fact, what it demonstrates to me once again is the fragility and the randomness of life. Edith might have been a victim of the Spanish flu; Velma was too young for that epidemic, yet died; Annie and Claude were potential victims yet lived to what I would call a ripe old age and Aubrey and Oswald, born too late for the Spanish flu, also lived to a good old age.

JC seems to be the most prolific of all the Addisons when it comes to producing children and that is one of the reasons he makes the book. His score is fourteen, though some of his ancestors run him rather close. But the main reason he makes this book is because of his descendants.

Amongst his ordinary-named progeny, JC had a son called George Edward, born in Orillia on 13th August 1908 and who died in Paris on 9th December 1995. Not as exotic as it sounds. That's Paris, Ontario, not *the* other place, tiny in comparison with nearly everywhere else and named for the nearby deposits of gypsum which is used in the making of plaster of Paris, hence the name. He married Isobel Ann Pond in the less exotic Paris (especially for Canadians) on the 15th September 1935.

Isobel's father was, to my ears at least, the stern and portentous-sounding Samuel Algernon Pond. Her mother was Mary Isobelle Lillie, and when she married Samuel, she may have, had she so chosen, and is common practice on the other side of that other Pond we call the Atlantic Ocean, retained her maiden name and placed it before her husband's. Had she so done, then she could have signed her cheques "Mary Lillie Pond" had she wanted to. And I bet, for any amount of money, she didn't.

George and Isobel's headstone in Paris is quite romantic and unusual. It is shaped like a pillow, with their names on it, his on the left, hers on the right, possibly just like they slept together in life and in the middle is written: *Together Forever.* They were not separated long. Isobel went to heaven on March 1st 1996. Unfortunately for them 1996 was a leap year so they had to wait an extra day before they were reunited—just 102 days in all.

They had three children, still all with us: Peter George born on 5th September 1939 in Paris, Ontario (naturally); Mary Elizabeth, born 22nd April 1943 in

Brantford, Ontario and Margaret Anne born in the same place on 2nd December 1944.

Brantford, a.k.a. Telephone City, was where Alexander Graham Bell invented what he called the "harmonic telegraph" in 1874. Well actually it was at the family farmhouse on Tutela Heights which was later absorbed into Brantford, and it was really in Boston that he built his first working model of the telephone, but despite these slight inattentions to detail, so massively proud of its association with the great Scottish inventor is Brantford, that in 1917 it erected the massive Bell Telephone Memorial in the gardens named after the great man claiming that's where it all began. As indeed it did.

When you stop to think of what he achieved and then add to that the invention of television by another Scot, John Logie Baird, we should never forget, in the field of human communication, how so much is owed by so many to these two Scots.

If JC produced the most children, his grandson Peter takes the prize for being the most married. Third time lucky and happily married to Patricia (Pat) Ellen Malane on 26th of October 1979 in Calgary, she was preceded in marriage firstly by Bente Clara Nielsen in Grimsby, Ontario in June 1964. Bente was born on May 30th 1943 in Copenhagen to Werner and Else Nielsen.

The second marriage was in Paris in June 1973 to Ann Laura Henderson who was born in May 1950 in Toronto. They divorced five years later in Calgary. There were no children from that marriage but from the first there were Rebecca (Becky) Elizabeth on 14th October 1965 in Deep River, Ontario followed just over a year later by Timothy (Tim) George on 23rd October 1966.

The third marriage produced Andrew Arthur Malane on 7th January 1981 in Calgary and finally, Julia Mary Isobel was also born there on 14th April 1983.

In the next chapter, as we pick up the story of Peter and the first of his three marriages, prepare yourself for those tales of adultery, rape and murder I promised you a while back.

Chapter Twenty

A Canadian Affair

When abroad, it is always an interesting exercise to read the war memorials. For a start, you discover wars you have never heard of. The others that you have, that everyone has, can knock you off balance a bit, especially if you are in the North American continent. The dates of the World Wars which you had learned so assiduously in primary school no longer apply here: the Americans arrived years late for both, but thank God they did turn up in the end.

The Canadians too were late for WW II but only by a matter of days. That was because they were waiting for Peter George Addison to be born so he could claim he was a pre-war baby and appear to be even more ancient and venerable than he already is. He made it by one day when he made his appearance at the Willett Hospital, Paris, on 5th September 1939.

His father was George Edward Addison and his mother Isobel Anne Pond. You may remember in the last chapter we left them sleeping peacefully together, sharing the same pillow in the cemetery in Paris.

George was born and grew up in Orillia but left home aged fifteen and lived for a while with his brother Carl in Weston, a suburb of Toronto, before moving to Paris when his brother, the aforementioned Thomas Carlyle, told him about an advertisement placed by Mr Wilson who was expanding his barber's business there. Carl himself was an undertaker, eventually owning his own funeral home in Huntsville. The family home was above the shop and his son Bob, who had lived with bodies all his life, did not have to go far to find employment when he followed his father into the business. It was no dead end job: he expanded the business, absorbing two funeral homes before selling out to an American corporation. In 1972 he personally took care of his father's funeral arrangements, which must have been an interesting experience to say the least.

It has often been a matter of idle speculation for me to wonder how people ever become undertakers. It's hardly the sort of thing that boys come up with when they are asked what they would like to be when they grow up—like an engine driver. (Do they still say that, now the age of steam has gone?) In Bob's case we know the answer, but how did Carl get into the business of burying bodies? Fortunately I can tell you.

One day, aged about fourteen, Carl was passing the GM dealership in Orillia when he overheard a middle-aged gent complaining to the mechanic that his big swanky car wasn't running properly. The mechanic was at a loss, but nothing daunted, Carl intervened and proffered a suggestion. You can imagine what the mechanic suggested this know-all brat did with his advice but the well-to-do gent said, "Let's give the kid's idea a go." So they did and the car went perfectly. Impressed, the man gave Carl his card and said if he ever needed a job, to give him a call. Since Carl wasn't getting on too well at home, that's precisely what he did. The rich geyser turned out to be A.W. Miles who, in 1911, owned the first motorised ambulance in Toronto and in 1914, could proudly boast the first motorised hearse in the whole of Canada.

In the same year, Miles conducted the mass burial in Mount Pleasant Cemetery of the Toronto victims of the *Empress of Ireland*, Canada's largest peacetime maritime disaster. The *Empress* was struck in thick fog by the Norwegian collier *SS Storstad* on the St Lawrence River near Pointe-au-Pierre, Quebec. Over a thousand people perished with only 465 survivors. Of the 138 children on board, only four survived. Also amongst the passengers were 175 members of the Canadian Staff Band of the Salvation Army of whom only eight survived while 167 were "promoted to glory" as their memorial puts it.

One survivor of the disaster, for the very good reason that she was not on board, was Emmy, the ship's cat, a veteran of every voyage but this and who could not be coaxed onboard on what turned out to be the *Empress's* last sailing. It is also said that she watched the departure from Pier 27 where most of the recovered bodies were brought back.

Maybe Carl thought he was going to maintain, or coax into life, the vehicles that take us on our last journey, as well as those which transport us to the nearest hospital though it may well be futile in the end, especially if it's a blue light job. While his mechanical skills may well have come in handy from time to time, performing a Lazarus on apparently dead internal combustion engines, as an assistant in the funeral parlour, Carl's remit was the apparently much easier task of laying out stiffs who, once rigor mortis had worn off, were not expected to spring into life and leap off the table.

A.W. Miles was also something of a philanthropist. In 1912 he opened Miles Park, a two-acre amusement park and zoo which contained an elephant, two camels and two giraffes, as well as monkeys, donkeys and exotic birds such as ostriches. Admission was completely free. In 1936, Mr Miles moved the park to a 200 hundred-acre site at Erindale, where, as well as there still being no admission charge, he also provided free transportation, lunches and ice cream for Sunday school parties.

George, who had learned the barbering trade in Orillia, responded to Mr Wilson's advert and so that was how he found himself in Toronto in the early 1920s across the street from the funeral parlour. Carl would occasionally call on George for his assistance in the transportation of bodies, both the living and the dead. One day George got a most unusual call from his brother. One of the dromedaries had escaped—could he help him track it down and capture it? George didn't hesitate. They found and recaptured the fugitive on Lakeshore Boulevard and took him home. Grumpy at the best of times, you can imagine what the camel thought of that after his brief taste of freedom.

Before she married George, Peter's mother, Isobel Pond, was working for the largest employers in Paris, Penman's Textile Mill, but she gave it up after her marriage. They met at St James Anglican Church where George was a bass in the choir. It was about this time George set up his own business and since he was such a talented singer and musician, I hope he also set up his own barbershop quartet.

Peter and his two adopted sisters, Mary Elizabeth and Margaret Ann, who came along later, lived in what North Americans call a "duplex". When we went to Montana in 1978 and showed our new friends a photo of our house and tried to explain to them that we only owned (or rather owed) and lived in half of it, they had a terrible time grasping the concept of "semi-detached", then a light would seemingly go on and they would exclaim, "Oh, you mean it's a duplex!" and Fiona and I, who had never heard of that word before, would look at each other, shrug our shoulders helplessly and say, "Yes, I suppose we do."

Their neighbours and landlords were the principal of the high school, C. Ward Butcher and his wife. Peter had not yet reached his first year towards heaven when, but for the grace of God, he might have been dispatched right there and then by the aforementioned Butcher. Peter's mum (or mom) had taken him out of his pram (or baby carriage) to change his nappy (or diaper) or to feed him (or make him sit up and take nourishment). In the meantime, the Butcher had reversed his almost new Dodge (how about that for an irony), over the perambulator recently vacated by baby Addison. Far from being overcome with remorse at the mangling of the baby vehicle (without as much as a scratch to his own) and relief that the contents had escaped injury, he blamed Peter's mother for leaving it in the drive. For her part, she blamed *him* for failing to see the baby buggy and rendering it into scrap metal. But how *could* he have seen it since his method of reversing was to look forward so he could see where he had been? Sounds reasonable to me. That's why we have history. We only truly appreciate who we are and where we are in the grand scheme of things by knowing who and what came before us.

The families never saw eye to eye after this incident and relations remained cool between them until the family moved to 30, West Broadway where George set up a barber shop in the house instead of renting premises in the downtown area, while Isobel went back to work to help pay the mortgage.

At the tender age of five, Peter underwent another near-death experience, or so it seemed to him at the time, when he was taken from his mother, strapped to a narrow bed on wheels, someone covered his face with a cloth and proceeded to smother him. He passed out and when he came round again, he had a raging sore throat which nevertheless did not prevent him from yelling the place down—which reached an even greater pitch and fervour when he was told that he would be staying in the accursed place of torture for another night. Nothing would pacify him until his father, borrowing a car, took him home where he was plied with copious amounts of ice cream—which is supposed to soothe the raw and aching throat after a tonsillectomy.

I can empathise with this experience as I had my tonsils removed at about the same age and found it equally traumatising. Another similarity between Peter's early life and mine is we also seem to have shared an idyllic boyhood spent roaming the woods, biking everywhere and reading voraciously when we weren't exploring the great outdoors. But we will skip over those happy days and move on swiftly to more trying times, to Peter's first marriage, adultery, rape and to the boy who was to grow up to be one of Canada's most notorious murderers.

After graduating from McMaster University, Hamilton, and in order to earn the cash to put himself through medical school, and since teaching jobs were plentiful, Peter found a job teaching Science and Math (as the North Americans quaintly call it, as if they can't say their esses) to 9th and 10th graders (our third and fourth years) at Grimsby High School, a mere twenty minutes' drive from his alma mater and his old friends.

One of Peter's colleagues, Fred, bet him $5 that the glamorous Danish 13th grade student called Bente would not go out with him, or date him, as they say. There were only four years between them, yet if I had tried to pull that sort of stunt over here, it would have been "the speak of the place" as we in the North-East say, and indeed that is exactly what happened when one of my teachers did the same thing at approximately the same time.

Fred reckoned he was on to a sure thing as she already had a boyfriend with whom she was madly in love. But perhaps he had not reckoned on Peter's charm or had not considered the kudos to be gained by her from dating a teacher, even if she was not under his tutelage, so to speak, for Fred lost the bet. He never stumped up the money and never will now. Two years after Peter left Grimsby, Fred was struck by lightning while watching a football game at the school. [Readers on this side of the Atlantic should not confuse this with real football.]

Bente went to teachers' college and after they were married, she and Peter moved to Wawa, a gold and iron ore mining town up north, just the year after the Trans-Canada highway reached the town. It sounds like the sort of noise that a child in its pram would make if you snatched its lollipop but, in fact, the town's name comes from the Ojibwe word *wewe* meaning "wild goose" and as you approach the small community on Highway 17 (the Trans-Canada's alter ego in those parts) you will be greeted by an impressive 28 foot high metal statue of a Canada goose with neck outstretched and wings half-unfurled.

After a year in Wawa they made a crucial decision to move to the appropriately named Deep River, the river in question being the Ottawa which reaches an incredible depth of over 400 feet near that point. It was, and I suppose is, a new town, founded in 1944, to house the scientists engaged in the construction of the ZEEP (Zero Energy Experimental Pile) reactor at the nearby Chalk River Nuclear Research Laboratories.

The celebrated Canadian journalist Peter C. Newman wrote a famous article printed in MacLean's Magazine in 1958 with the very apt title *Deep River: Almost the Perfect Place to Live* in which he refers to the majority of the population as being young, male, highly educated and bored. That might partly explain what happened next.

Peter and Bente made friends with Chris and David Williams. David was one of the world's top metallurgists at the time and Peter would occasionally crew for him on his International 14—a two-man racing dinghy, for the benefit of landlubbers. By this time, Peter and Bente had had Becky and Tim, aged three and two, while David and Chris had Russell and Harvey aged about five and four. David and Bente were members of the local drama group where they got to know each other a bit better.

About a year later, David and Chris split up after she found out he had been "screwing around" as the North Americans put it so pithily. One (note the word) of David's extra marital conquests was the wife of one his colleagues and a fellow member at the yacht club.

She also happened to be a colleague of Peter's, but that is incidental to our tale. Chris, meanwhile, was having an affair with the wife's husband, whom she later married. I suppose they could just have agreed to wife swapping but doing it on the sly like that perhaps added an extra buzz. How would I know?

Peter and Bente meanwhile were living in a log cabin on the site where Peter was building a house. He was not able to complete the house during the summer, and when the chilly days of autumn came, David altruistically suggested that Peter and family move in with him. There was plenty of room to spare since Chris had left with the kids. I am sure you are ahead of me here. Whilst Peter grabbed a sandwich and dyspeptically rushed off to complete his labours on the family home, David and Bente were getting to know each other even better and this time I *am* using the term in its Biblical sense.

When David was offered a one year's posting to a German nuclear facility, Bente took the chance and ran away with him, despite having claimed earlier that the affair was over. Four months later it really was. After Germany, David was recruited by the Americans and never returned to Deep River. Bente went back to Denmark, met someone else there but that soon ended too and she returned alone to Ottawa where Becky and Tim would join her during the summer holidays.

One year they decided to stay and that is where they went through High School. Bente, like a butterfly from its chrysalis, emerged from her hippy stage, went back to university and eventually ended as Vice President of Angus Reid, Canada's premier polling company. When she retired, she moved back to Deep River. Despite all the marital discord and the ensuing divorces, the place still holds happy memories for her. That's nostalgia through rose-tinted glasses.

After Chris left with her kids, Peter never saw them again so his time with David and Chris's oldest son, Russell Williams, was limited to not more than a year or so but to Peter he seemed a perfectly ordinary and normal five-and-six year-old. It was a lot later that Russell became notorious but before that he was the pilot in whose hands were placed the lives of Very Important People such as the Queen and Prince Phillip, the Governor General, and the Premier of Canada.

He was a twice-decorated military pilot and ended his glittering career as a colonel and commander of CFB Trenton, the busiest air force base in Canada, the place where troops leave for Afghanistan and the dead come back for burial. He also helped plan the security for the G-20 Economic Summit in Toronto in June 2010. He might have gone on to even greater things, who knows, as he was only forty-seven when it came to an end when he was arrested on two accounts of first-degree murder, two counts of enforced confinement and two counts of breaking and entering and sexual assault. Later on, no less than eighty-two counts of breaking and entering were added. Your money and jewellery were perfectly safe: all he wanted was women's underwear. He had more knickers than Marks & Spencer, all neatly laid out and catalogued, like a lepidopterist lays out his specimens. He had so many knickers in his collection in fact, that he had to burn some to make room for the new ones. Disturbingly, some of them belonged to girls as young as nine.

It began in 2007 with a spate of mysterious thefts of women's underwear in the little town of Tweed (named after the Scottish river) and where the unknown thief came to be dubbed the "Tweed Creeper". By 2009 he had progressed to assaulting women, tying them up and taking degrading photos of them in an ordeal that lasted for hours and during which the victims feared that they would be raped and murdered. They weren't. That was to come later. As it is with any addiction, Russell needed bigger and bigger fixes.

He was caught after his second murder, that of Jessica Lloyd (27) who went missing on January 28th 2010. Apart from his BMW, he had a Nissan Pathfinder with unusual tyre treads. These were matched to tracks in the snow in a field near Jessica's home after police set up a roadblock in the area. They also found a print of his boot in the frozen ground.

After his arrest and after five hours of interrogation, after being confronted with the evidence of the tyre tracks and the boot imprint, Russell asked for a map in order to show police where he had hidden Jessica's body. He also confessed to the murder of Marie-France Comeau, a 38 year-old military flight attendant whose body was found at her home in November 2009. He had beaten her and tied her up in the basement before taking her upstairs to the bedroom where he raped her and hours later, suffocated her. He had videotaped and photographed the whole thing from all sorts of angles, as he had done with the two women he had previously sexually assaulted but not raped. He also confessed to the break-ins. Small beer after that. The "Tweed Creeper" had finally been caught.

He pleaded guilty. There was no point in denying anything, as apart from the photographic evidence, he had logged all his crimes, as well as keeping newspaper reports of his exploits. He was given two life-sentences for each of the murders, ten years for each of the rapes, ten years for the forcible confinements and one year for each of the burglaries. He will not be available for parole until he has served twenty-five years, in 2035. He will be 72.

Bizarrely, although he was stripped of his rank and booted out of the air force and his uniform burnt, they could not stop his pension of $60,000 per annum. That equates into £38,000—not bad for sitting on your butt in Kingston Penitentiary in solitary confinement twenty-three hours a day. A lot of people don't make anything like that working their butts off.

But what use of money has he, unless it is to recompense his victims or reimburse the state for his board and lodgings? Having said that, he may prefer death. In fact I am sure he would. He did try to commit suicide by sticking a toilet roll tube down his throat soon after he was charged with his crimes of which he felt deeply ashamed and in his own words described as "despicable".

Despite this amazing catalogue of crimes, more might yet come to light. His arrest sparked off fresh investigations into unsolved murders around the country where he had been stationed . . .

Of course it is difficult to sympathise with Russell. Timothy Appleby interviewed Peter for his book *A New Kind of Monster* and I think that title hits the nail on the head. He *was* a monster and he *was* different. If you were to put him in an Agatha Christie novel, (except the murders in her books are much "nicer") he would be the one whodunit as he was the least likely of suspects and after reading it, you would toss it aside as just being just too preposterous and far-fetched for words. The commander of the local air base, the biggest in the country, a decorated military pilot, a secret knicker raider! Don't be ridiculous!

No-one, in their right mind, would *choose* to do what he did, given the heights he had risen to in his career, the heights he might yet scale and where being caught for the theft of even one pair of panties would have brought an end to all that, as he must have known full well. Yet he felt some compulsion, some demon, some inner drive compelling him to commit these crimes. Such a waste of talent. Such a waste of life. Not just his, but his victims of course.

In mitigation it was pointed out that he was from a broken home. Very true. But not every product of a broken home goes about doing what David Russell Williams did. His brother didn't for a start. Who *can* explain what was going on inside his twisted mind? Probably he himself is the least able to explain the reason why he perpetrated these awful crimes but if the break-up of his parents' marriage was a factor in some sort of obscure way, it is true that Mrs Bente Addison was a bit player in that break-up, not to mention the much bigger part she played in the dissolution of her own marriage.

You, dear reader, may see all this as a bit of a digression, which I don't deny, but too interesting I hope you agree, to omit from this memorial epic. In fact, you could say that since Chapter Two, this book has been a bit like those *deviations* you get in France which take you miles and miles out of your way before you get to where you want to be, because we are going back now to my story. The rest of this book is nearly all about me, me, me.

But don't let that put you off. It's confession time. I was a pretty bad boy too. (You can put a comma between the adjectives if you like. I wouldn't presume to.)

Chapter Twenty-one

Early Lessons

Naturally, after the flood in Crovie, our cottage, along with many others, was uninhabitable. In fact, the flood marked the start of the demise of Crovie as a fishing community though how thriving it ever was would be difficult to say. With the illustrious Gardenstown just around the bay, I have a feeling it was, and would always would have been, the poor relation.

It only sprang into existence in the first place as that was about all the land left for people after that infamous period in Scottish history known as the Highland Clearances where the much more profitable sheep could safely graze on the best land while the peasants were all but driven into the sea, forced to wrest a living from this new element by rapacious landlords of whom the Duke of Sutherland was only the most notorious. After all, when you think about it, no-one would deliberately *choose* to live in a place like Crovie, on a strip of land with the sea in your face and rocky cliffs at your back, would they? It would certainly have declined anyway in the fullness of time but the flood certainly acted as a catalyst in its demise.

Now, all these years later, many of the cottages have been transformed into charming little holiday homes by people who see Crovie as a romantic retreat, a place of escape from the hurly-burly of modern life in the city. And not all by white settlers from south of the border either: ours came into the possession of our dentist in Banff, less than ten miles away, though who owns it now I could not say. It has undergone extensive remodelling as you would expect: two windows in the gable end where there was only one before, and a dormer window in a roof with bright new orange tiles which make it look years younger than the tired old grey slates. It is of course, just as near the sea as ever, one of the closest, right on the bend before a little inlet which affords some cottages the luxury of being set back a few more yards from the sea.

I do not know where the residents of the other flooded houses went in the aftermath of the Great Storm but we—the poor, homeless relations—went to live at Clayfolds in Alvah, near Banff, with Uncle Jimmy, Aunt Janet and their three children, Jessie, George and Beth, all just a bit older than me. Jimmy inherited the farm because his two elder brothers had already married and needed not so much a place of their own, but a farm of their own.

As with my great-grandfather on the distaff side, James Tate, whose sons followed his seafaring ways—so all my Grandfather Charles's sons, my uncles in other words, became farmers—apart from my father. Gina was a nurse (as you may recall from Chapter Two) and married Jack Ingram, a salesman for a wooden flooring company in Nottingham (as I told you not so long ago); Daisy married a local farmer, Eddie Chalmers; and the baby of the family, Trixie, a hairdresser, married Lachlan McCallum, a joiner from Lochgilphead in Argyllshire. She got this unusual name from the postman who said she was a "tricky little thing" apparently on account of all the mischief she used to get up to.

From Clayfolds we moved to 1, Fountain Street, Banff, a mile or not much more, from my birthplace in Chalmers Hospital. It cost £100. It is an end-terraced, stone-built property with the quoins picked out in paint as is the tradition in the North-East. Our neighbours were the Lemons. He was an ambulance driver who, when he was off duty, parked his ambulance in the waste ground across from our house as if it were some sort of private vehicle.

The question I often ask myself is would my grandmother have survived a few more years if had she been living with us in Banff at the time of her stroke instead of Crovie? She would have undoubtedly got to Chalmers hospital much, much earlier, driven at the clappers by Mr Lemon (assuming he was off duty at the time), his bell ringing furiously and in a town to this day which has so little traffic that only relatively recently it acquired its first set of traffic lights. And they do say the sooner you get a stroke victim to the hospital, the better the chances of a full recovery. But of course that was sixty years ago and it may not have been so crucial then as now, medical science having come on in leaps and bounds in the interim.

And talking of death, the second of my encounters with death occurred soon after we moved into Fountain Street. By this time I am beginning to have clearer memories of events and I remember well my first pet, a long-haired black and white cat called Fluffy, for the very good reason that that is exactly what she was. And in my mind's eye, I can see the gate on the street which led into a narrow passageway to the "back" door, though it was actually at the side of the house. It was into this narrow passage that someone threw some poisoned food that poor Fluffy ate and died of, murdered by some unknown, cowardly, cat hater.

Apart from the ambulance, the waste ground was home to a forest of nettles. Higher than us (but remember we were only knee high to a grasshopper), and with the aid of a scrap sheet of corrugated iron, my friends and I constructed a maze of twisting paths through this dense jungle by jumping on the roofing until the nettles were squashed flat. Stings of course, were inevitable, but as we all knew in those days, the juice from the stem of a docken leaf was the tried and tested antidote.

But one cannot play among the nettles forever; apart from death, life has other stings. I had to go to school. Banff was not my first educational institution. That was Bracoden. I must have walked there with my dad and it must have been unwillingly, for, apart from the long, steep climb, I have only two memories of it, both so excruciatingly embarrassing that I hesitate to set them down here for posterity. But reader, you will remember that we were very young at the time, not even nearly six, to paraphrase the titles of A.A. Milne's books—for I started school at the tender age of four.

The first incident was running out of the classroom to find my daddy. After my bolt for freedom I remember thinking: *what do I do now?* I knew he was in the building somewhere, but where? It seems to me that the doors had glass panes and I managed to track him down, running into his classroom. But now, on reflection, I suspect that this is not what really happened at all. For a start, the glass must have been very low indeed for me to be able to see into the classroom and secondly, could I really have opened the door—it would certainly have been the kind with a handle that you had to turn and with my diminutive hand, a time-consuming process—and plenty of time for my teacher to have recaptured me I would have thought.

A more likely scenario was I made it only as far as the door and then screamed the place down and my dad had to come and calm me down. But that was not the way I remember it: in my version I embarrassed him horribly in front of all his pupils by running into his classroom. It just goes to show you the disadvantage of having a father as a teacher in the same school: had he not been there, I would have accepted this enforced separation from parental protection like all the others, or so I would like to think, and not made a fool of myself in this way.

And if it were a disadvantage on that occasion, then on the other shameful occasion I considered it a positive advantage. It was sports day and the gods, for once, had provided a boiling hot day instead of the usual one just good enough to allow these latter-day Roman games to proceed, but bad enough so that they could have a jolly good laugh at us mortals as we competed against each other and the elements. The ice cream van was doing a roaring trade and everyone, but everyone, was indulging in what was then much more of a treat than it is now, for although the guns of war had long been silenced, rationing was still in force. What my friends were having I must also have. The desire to be accepted, to be part of the group, not to be left out, not to be different, was by far the greater motivator than the desire for the ice cream itself. Or so it seems to me now, distorted as my memory may be through the prism of time.

"I'm afraid you've not got enough money there, sonny," said the ice cream man, when I had at last made my way to the front of the queue, thus confirming my worst fears as I reached up on my tippy-toes to spill out the contents of my trousers' pocket onto the counter at his window.

I don't remember whether or not he had a pricelist of his wares on display but if he did, it would not have made the slightest difference to me anyway. I could scarcely count, the number of fingers on one hand probably being the apogee of my arithmetical skills—an affliction which has persisted to this day, but as I stood in the queue, I could see that my peers appeared to have more money than me. But farthings and ha'pennies made a big fistful in a tiny hand and I hoped that I might yet have enough, though some instinct, some foresight, must have made me keep my money out of sight, burning a hole in my pocket, instead of clutched in a sweaty little fist like the other children.

What happened next was even more embarrassing, but not for me. I can't remember if I scooped up the insufficient coppers or not before I fled in tears. I hope I did at least have the presence of mind to do that before I fled, probably with a great deal of sound to where my father was standing with a colleague. Sad to relate, my father did not have enough money either, which must have meant that he had no money at all, for I remember his shame-faced look as he turned to his colleague and asked him if he could borrow whatever was needed to silence this sobbing brat.

That was Bracoden, a period in my life I would rather forget. I do not think I could have been there very long before I went to Banff Primary. Unfortunately my memory of it is almost as hazy as it is of Bracoden. I do remember, however, that my teacher was Miss Bourne and it seemed to me she was glamorous, though I have only the vaguest idea of what she looked like. There is a photograph of her, slim and dark-haired, standing at the back of the classroom, her face not much bigger than a pinkie fingernail, while right at the front, dominating the foreground is a cute little boy.

I imagine that the class had been specially arranged for the photographer's visit, the better-looking children being put at the front, the cross-eyed, the buck-toothed, the plain and the plain ugly ones being relegated to the back for the duration of the photographer's visit. Surely, even in those days, being top of the class and furthest from the teacher did not apply to the baby, intake class? Surely it was too soon to tell that I had been placed at the bottom of the class through merit, or rather the lack of it? It must surely have been my good looks that had earned me this prime position on the starting grid of education.

Perhaps Miss Bourne's glamour came from being from Australia when that really was at the ends of the Earth and not a mere fatiguing 24 hours flight away. I must have written her a letter for there exists somewhere a postcard which she sent me from the *Canberra* on her voyage home in which she thanked me for my letter. Was it love and devotion that inspired this or was it written under protest under parental orders? Not only under parental orders, but *by* my parents, since at that age I was surely incapable of stringing enough letters together by myself to compose a word, let alone a letter. Alas, I cannot say, but that was the end of our correspondence and the end of our relationship.

And so Miss Bourne passed in and out of my life, streaking across the path of my years as ephemeral as a comet and yet searing a trail in the memory. She is pretty sure to be in heaven by now. I remember her with fondness and regard her as my first teacher though she was not. Nor can I remember any of my subsequent teachers until Miss Dingwall whom I did not get until Primary Four in Ternemny when I was seven or eight, some three or four years later. These are gaps in the memory that are lost forever and probably of no significance, yet are these not supposed to be the formative years? So, since I can remember absolutely nothing of those classroom experiences, where was I, what was I doing whilst my mind was supposed to have been forming and I was learning some essential life skills?

"It's a poor sort of memory that only works backwards," the White Queen remarked to Alice in *Through the Looking Glass*. I'm afraid that is the only kind of memory I have and it doesn't appear to be working that well these days either.

The one thing that I do clearly remember was that I had to learn spelling and I only remember that because of one traumatic occasion. I had difficulty with the word "build" I remember. For the life of me, I could not see what the silent "u" had to do with anything and I tended to leave it out, and although it didn't look right, I couldn't think for the life of me what the missing letter was. But I was green and cabbage looking about practically everything in those days and the mysteries of English orthography were mine not to wonder why but to simply learn by rote. I do not think there was a punishment other than shame and humiliation for getting these words wrong, unlike my sister-in-law who got the belt at school more or less every Friday morning for failing her spelling test, although she could do it perfectly well for her mother the night before. Fear of the belt had cast an evil spell on her apparently.

My mother, too, helped me with my spelling and this was the traumatic time I was referring to. The word I was having difficulty with was "altogether". Time and time I tried it, trying every possible combination of letters yet none of them seemed to be right and I dare say my attempts became wilder and wilder and further and further wider of the mark. Tears began to flow as I became more and more exasperated, as was my mother who could not believe I could possibly be so thick and who, somewhat ironically reached the conclusion that I was deliberately getting it wrong in order to torment *her*.

"Right," she said at last, slamming the open book face down somewhere above my head. "I'm off for the stick and if you haven't got it right by the time I get back, you're going to get it!"

I knew she would and I knew I couldn't, so I set up a wailing even louder than before until it began to percolate through my tiny mind that she was away much longer than I would have thought and I began to cease my wailing as my eye espied the spelling book lying there and I believed I could see a way out of my difficulty. I could not weep and wail and get a stool and climb up and learn the word and commit it to memory all at the same time, so I stopped the crying whilst I concentrated on the means of my salvation. Then, after I had committed the beastly word to memory and in what I imagined was a genius stroke of subterfuge, I began the blubbering again. It must have been the signal my mother had been waiting for, for at this point she appeared bearing the rod.

"Well?" she said.

Suppressing sobs, I spelt it out, not pat as if I had just memorised it, but slowly as if I was thinking about it very carefully indeed, hesitantly suggesting a letter, looking for signs of approval in my mother's face. I thought I was so, so cunning.

"There you are," my mother said, uttering a sigh of relief and casting aside the learning implement. "I knew it just needed that to make you do it. And don't you be so thrawn the next time!"

I did not argue, I just let my shuddering shoulders gradually subside and I was let out to play.

Play, in those days before paedophiles were ever heard of and parents became paranoid, consisted of being set loose to roam the livelong day at weekends and the freedom to go where we liked and do as we liked. The nettle park I have already mentioned, but at the bottom of the street there was a path that led down to the beach and I imagine I spent many a happy hour there, but there was one incident one day so horrible that it stems from the world of nightmares.

There were just the two of us and we were far away from our usual territory, land unfamiliar and quite new to us. There was a building and we approached it, curious to see what it was. Then I watched in horror as I saw a man grab a sheep, roughly throw it onto its back and what I remember most were its desperate bleating and the sparks from a gun as he repeatedly fired into its head. I seem to remember there were other animals awaiting execution too and there were channels running with blood. We must, of course, have stumbled upon the abbatoir, though it was not a name I had ever heard of, nor had it ever occurred to me to wonder how the meat on my plate made the transition there from the likes of my Uncle Jimmy's farm. Now, in an instant, I knew. One kind of innocence erased in a couple of seconds.

Having finished his bloody execution, the man looked up, saw us, shouted at us and began to run in our direction. We fled. I wonder to this day what the killer would have done if he had caught us. It makes me think of the young Pip when Magwitch caught him in the cemetery in *Great Expectations*. I can imagine him shaking us with his bloody hands until our teeth rattled and telling us if we told a soul of what we had seen, he would do the very same thing to us, then he would rip out our guts and eat our livers.

Perhaps that is just a nightmarish fantasy. He was but a man going about his grizzly job, but I have always had the uneasy feeling that even then, in the early 1950s, animals would, and certainly should, have been dispatched a lot more humanely than the way I had just witnessed. I should have reported what I had seen to my parents but I did not. I wanted to put it out of my mind, but I was scared more of what my parents would do and say. The world of adults was the law then and children were scarcely listened to. I doubt if I would have been believed in the first place and more likely got a scolding *and* a skelped behind for straying too far from home.

All my other memories of those early years in Banff also concern incidents outwith school. I think I must have been in the habit of coming home for lunch—or perhaps this memorable day was an exception.

"I think you'd better take a raincoat back with you, David," my mother remarked, for the sky was ominously dark.

"Why is everyone outside looking up at the sky?" I asked casually, for before I had entered the house, I had noticed that strangely, our neighbours were all outside staring at the heavens instead of remaining indoors like sensible people when a deluge is expected imminently. I was so innocent I had not thought this odd spectacle worthy of mention up till now.

At this point my mother remembered that there was to be an eclipse of the sun. I had never heard of such a thing and so it was that I saw my first, looking at it through a couple of film negatives, a practice which would certainly be frowned upon today, if such things were still readily available. In ancient times, so the experts tell us, those early humans must have been terrified to see the sun being gobbled up by an invisible monster mouth and the light growing dimmer and dimmer, assuming reasonably enough, that when the light went totally out, that would be THE END.

But speaking from a similar perspective, that of being barely much more of a primitive myself, knowing next to nothing about anything, let alone the movement of the heavenly bodies, I was not in the least terrified, merely curious and fascinated. Perhaps in those ancient days those primitives were filling their furry pants in fear, but not if my reaction counts for anything. But then not everyone around them was keeping their heads like my neighbours and my mother, still less having a name for the phenomenon, so in all probability they *did* think they were about to die—and soon—for the rate at which that life-giving sun was disappearing before their (unprotected) eyes must have seemed inexorably and relentlessly fast. And then, at totality, while they no doubt marvelled that they were still alive, slowly, out of the darkness, there came forth light. No wonder religion came about to protect them from what they could not understand and to which they gave thanks for their preservation.

We now know of course that total eclipses of the sun occur twice a year somewhere on the planet, and partial eclipses twice as often as that, so you would not have expected the gods to have got off with pulling that same stunt year after year, putting the fear of death into the earliest inhabitants of the planet. But the old ones are the best ones, so they say, and so it goes on—the oldest joke in our solar system, even if does give fewer and fewer people the willies these days.

Whilst the eclipse did not scare me, my friends and I were sufficiently primitive not to tempt fate by walking under a ladder and sometimes we would avoid the cracks on the pavements. Most of the time we didn't bother with the latter—it was too time-consuming and besides, we didn't really believe that something terrible would happen to us. It wasn't that we were too sophisticated to be superstitious. No, our feeling of security was based on empirical evidence—we would often deliberately knock each other off balance and a foot would inevitably land on a crack but not one of us dropped dead on the spot, or even later in the day, or even later in the year.

But it is beginning to catch up with some of us now.

Chapter Twenty-two

My Bad Banff Days

There were two shops on the street at the top of Fountain Street and to which I was often dispatched on errands. I don't know what the difference between them was but my mother had a definite preference for one, while I had just as definite a preference for the other, and not just because it indulged my natural talent for laziness as it was nearer either. The simple truth is that the shopkeeper used to give us kids a sweetie of some description to send us happily on our way. It had probably less to do with his natural fondness for children and more to do with encouraging us to patronise his shop rather than that of his rival, but I couldn't have cared less.

On this memorable day, my mother gave me strict instructions *not* to go to the nearer shop. I have no recollection of what I was being sent to buy, but I do remember thinking: *how will she ever know, especially if I finish my sweetie before I get back?* I gave into temptation and of course my mother knew right away what I had done. That staggered me. How could she tell? Like a magician who never explains his tricks, she never did tell, but to me it seemed some sort of alchemy and I looked at my mother with a new respect. Were her eyes everywhere? Of course, like magician's tricks, when the answer is explained, the answer is so prosaic that you would prefer the mystery a million times over. I expect that the other shopkeeper sold whatever it was a farthing or something cheaper and when my mother saw the change she KNEW. Once again I had failed the test and let her down. And not for the last time, as you shall see. She thought *she* held the rod, my mother, but another way to look at it was that it was *I* who was the rod, not the rod that broke her back, but the one that broke her heart.

Yes, I was a very bad boy and we have not even got to the teenage years yet. (That's a treat in store for you.) I expect I was the terriblest two there has ever been, but I don't remember.

Another bad thing I did was on Sundays, of all days. I don't remember my parents going to church in those days—in fact I am sure they did not because I don't recall ever attending the house of God with them, or my sister and I being looked after while they did, but I suppose it *could* have happened. But to my severe disappointment, not to say disgust, on my day of rest from slaving over a slate, I was made to go to Sunday school.

Yes, I really did have a slate. It had a wooden border with lines etched on one side and what would have been called graph paper on the other side, had it been made of paper. You had a slate pencil too and if you made a mistake—simple—you licked your finger and rubbed it out. Much more efficient than a rubber on paper (eraser for the benefit of my North American readers) which could leave a black, smudgy mark, or if you rubbed hard enough, tore, or left a hole in the paper. And when the teacher told you to wipe your slate clean, you spat on it and rubbed your hard-wrought efforts out with your sleeve, though she would have preferred if you had used the damp cloth provided.

The slate. How economic! How environmentally friendly! How 21st Century! And how hypocritical of my parents to send me to Sunday school and not go to church themselves!

Anyway, every Sunday in life, I was given thruppence for the collection and sent on my way to be made a better person. Ironically, it was making me worse by leading me once again into temptation. I used to hope that I was given three pennies rather than a three-penny bit as there was a café opposite St Mary's and I could spend a penny on a sweetie there after attending the dastardly Sunday school by keeping one back from the collection. I had no crisis of conscience over this. I thought it was no less than my due, my wages for working on a Sunday. I was so naive, so young in crime, it never occurred to me that I could have had the penny sweetie every Sunday regardless of the type of money I set out with, until one of my fellow sufferers, some junior Napoleon of crime, pointed out that if I spent a penny, (so to speak) *before* the religious instruction, I would still have two to put in the collection.

Grandpa Tate's prophecy that I would turn out to be a "bad bugger" seemed to be well on the way to being fulfilled by the time I was six at least and looking up at me from hell, I am sure he would have been well pleased to see his prediction coming to pass. In my defence however, I would submit that I was just a weak personality with a sweet tooth in a time of austerity and the temptation was huge.

Robbing the church was one thing, but violence *in* it is another thing entirely and yes, I did that too, though not to the same extent as the assassins of

David M. Addison

Thomas à Becket or Robert the Bruce who "done in" the Red Comyn in Greyfriars Church in Dumfries and which is now a chemist's shop. Not a lot of people know that.

This bad deed I was guilty of came about because, another thing my parents made me do, something I resented very much, was to wear a kilt to school and Sunday school. It was a Royal Stewart I remember, not even in my clan's colours. I don't suppose I wore it on every occasion but I had to some of the time, and what's more, I was the only one who did. It was particularly embarrassing when I had to go to the outside urinal as it was so much harder to do what the other boys did. All they had to do was unbutton and point Percy at the porcelain, whereas I had to hitch up my skirt (as I thought of it) keep it pressed to my stomach with one hand, fish out Percy from my underpants with the other (I was not a true Scotsman, being half English), point him, shake him and/or squeeze him to get out the last drop and pop him back again.

The fairer of the species will not be able to fully understand what a challenge this presented to a boy of six, having to manage these manoeuvres with one hand only, and because of the bumpfle of my "skirt", I could not even *see* Percy, he not having grown to his present prodigious proportions (though far be it for me to boast). Yes, all of that was bad, but what was worst of all—the other boys called me a "cissy".

I tolerated those jibes for a long time. I suppose "tolerated" understates how I felt, and truth to tell, I do not remember how deeply these insults upset me, but I can imagine they did quite a bit—as they would anyone. *Nicholas Nickleby* (1838-39) and *Tom Bown's*

Schooldays, published twenty years later but set in the same period, notoriously featured schools in which bullying was institutionalised. This was not the case in Banff Primary but was very much the case in one of my secondary schools, as you will see, and sad to say, bullying is still endemic in many schools today, even worse than it was in my day as the bullies no longer need to see you face to face. They can do it now by what they euphemistically call "social networking sites".

The advice given to people who are being bullied, probably by people who have never been bullied, is to stand up to them. Easy to say, harder to do if you are small and slight of build, like me, and lacking any confidence in your skills as a pugilist, scared of pain and scared of ending up with a face that looked like something the cat had sicked up, so I just put up with it. Until on one particular Sunday, in Sunday school, I did what one small, skinny boy gotta do.

A boy behind me insulted me in the usual manner and I turned round and let him have it, right on the nose, with all my strength. There were copious amounts of blood and of course, confusion and alarm. I was the aggressor, the bad boy, and told so in no uncertain manner, that we didn't do that sort of thing in church. I don't know if they brought Jesus into it, turning the other cheek and all that. But I hadn't suddenly snapped in a moment of uncontrolled fury. I remember very clearly thinking that this was the very place to pick a fight, for the adults would certainly break it up if the boy retaliated and began rearranging my face. I had not thought it all the way through though. What if my tormentor "got me" on the way home, or at school the next day? And what if I were meted out a punishment by my Sunday school teacher as well—such as being banned? Now there's a thought on which I would have acted earlier! But what would my parents have had to say to that?

If their response to my crime astonished me, it must have bowled over my Sunday school teacher. She marched me home afterwards so she could inform my parents of my nefarious misdeed, sure, I am certain, that my parents would be horrified and probably hopeful that she would witness my backside getting a good leathering. Far from being a witness to castigation however, she saw a moment of celebration as my parents told her they were glad that I had at last started sticking up for myself. For the first time I remember, my parents were actually proud of me!

It would be nice to be able to report that that put an end to the bullying and it may have done, and it would be nice to report that from henceforth I was indeed banned from the Sunday school, but I was not—probably given homilies on how blessed are the meek instead. But there is one thing which could have been done which would have prevented that bloody Sunday—if only my parents had seen fit to dress me like the others and not make me stand out. And the funny thing is my father was a teacher and he should have known that!

If the bullying was an unpleasant memory, then another unpleasant, not to say traumatic experience I had to endure in my days in Banff was the extraction of my tonsils. I was six and it was very fashionable then to whip them out at the first sign of tonsillitis. Thus I was admitted to Chalmers Hospital for the operation. I don't remember all the details, as mercifully, time has drawn a curtain over the worst of the affair, but I was petrified by the whole experience, missing my mummy, fearing the morrow and which the promise of ice cream after the operation did nothing to assuage.

I was right to be sceptical. The pain in my throat was excruciating and the ice cream was a hard brick of Wall's, never the best of ice cream at the best of times and these were the worst of times. I was not tempted by it but persuaded by my mother to try it as it would help my throat, so she said. But it was too sore to swallow so I preferred to wallow in misery.

I don't know how long I stayed there but certainly a minimum of two nights—the night before and after the operation. I know about the latter as I roared all night with the pain which scarcely would have helped. I was in a ward of men. They seemed to me to be old, but they may well have been quite young. I do remember one of them shouting down the length of the ward, "For God's sake, shut up you little shit and give us some peace!" Actually, I made that up. His language was probably a lot more colourful than that. Whether or not that had the desired effect or inspired me to a further outburst only with increased decibels I don't remember.

Somehow I survived the night: my roommates did not strangle me although I would have understood if they had dispatched me at some stage during that longest of nights. Maybe they would have but were incapable of getting out of bed and that was what saved me. They must have been heartily glad to see me go, just as I was to leave. The best part was going home in the ambulance which I thought conferred on me the status of a wounded hero returning from the Front and I hoped the neighbours were watching to see how brave

I was, coming home all alone in an ambulance and me only six.

I also remember one particular visit to the dentist. There must have been others I suppose, but I only remember this one. It was in a big house, the surgery, down a narrow lane and coincidentally next to the doctor's though I never remember going there. Perhaps I was healthy though I did contract chickenpox about this time—a very bad dose of it, on my tongue and down my throat. I resisted the itch to scratch apart from one spot on my stomach and I devoted all my attention to that, picking off the brown crust to let the puss ooze out. Not surprisingly, I still bear the scar today, a large white mound like an albino volcano.

The dentist's waiting room was very large (maybe everything is very large when you are six) and what I remember particularly about it was the large white mantelpiece which had rows of parallel lines carved into it so that the effect was to create a pattern of rectangular blocks. I remember studying them and thinking how like teeth they were. In fact I was sure they were the dentist's trophies and wondered how he got them in there and marvelled at how even they were and all so alike, like dentures.

It hardly increased my confidence, as accompanied by my mother, I made my way up to the surgery. I'm not sure exactly why at that tender age I needed an extraction, but I did. Perhaps it was something to do with having too many teeth. I still have too many, my lower jaw being so crowded that some teeth at the bottom overlap.

Sitting in the dentist's chair I could not but help but focus my attention on the contraption sitting in the corner. It seemed a monstrous thing with that big metal cylinder and the black mask, but most scary of all was that looping coil of sinister, corrugated black rubber hose. When the man in white began wheeling it towards me I thought I was going to die. It looked every inch like a killing machine to me and when he tried to put that hard, black mask with its horrid smell over my face, I struggled and writhed and kicked and screamed the place down because I literally thought I was fighting for my life. No amount of soothing platitudes from my mother would pacify me. She would say that, wouldn't she, to make my snuffing out easier for her. And it was no good now saying sorry for being such a bad boy, that I would try to be better in future if she would only give me another chance, as she had plainly decided that this was the final and only solution to my multitude of misdeeds.

By some sort of trickery and sleight of hand, the clinical killer finally succeeded in placing the mask over my nose and mouth, and seconds later, the deed was done. It wasn't so bad being dead after all. It was just nothing. Not even blackness. Why had I made all that fuss? There was nothing to fear. Nothing at all. But what's this? A flock of snowy white geese in a farmyard passing in front of me in single file. It seems extraordinarily vivid, the colours heightened, the details so distinct and I am so close to them I could have put my hand out and touched them if I dared. But how very strange! A woman in a red costume with matching hat, sitting in a chair at the other side of the geese. And then the face comes into focus and the face is smiling and the face is saying something. "It's all right, David. It's all right." And when I looked, I saw that the killing machine was back in the corner. I had survived. My death was but a dream.

It was not all bad, those early days in Banff. There was a happier occasion. While the event itself was momentous, I am afraid it made so little impression on me that I can scarcely remember it at all. We were all crowded into the Town Hall—there seemed to be masses of us, and we were all given some treat to eat and a mug to take away as a souvenir, long since lost or broken in my case and maybe worth quite a bit of money today even if there were millions of them once. I dare say there were balloons and bunting and speeches and perhaps some music too, like a brass band or at least some wifie at the piano leading us in patriotic songs and the national anthem, but I remember none of that.

It was the celebration of the accession of Her Majesty Queen Elizabeth II to the throne and I should have remembered it better and I am sorry now, for she has turned out to be one of our better monarchs, bless her, not to mention one of the longest reigning. Like my parents, she has not had her troubles to seek when you think of what her children have put her through. Families are trouble, and that includes the Commonwealth family, when you think of some of the buffoons she's had to pretend to be nice to and "buffoon" is one of the nicest words I can use to describe some of the megalomaniacs that have come and gone and are still here (unfortunately), on her watch.

I also recall attending another celebration, though not nearly so prestigious. But unlike her Majesty's party where, for once, I seemed not to have blotted my copybook, I did disgrace myself at this—spectacularly.

I was to be going directly to the party after school and before I left that day my mother gave me strict instructions: firstly I was to knock on the door and wait to be admitted and secondly, I was to eat everything that was put on my plate.

I am ashamed to say that I failed miserably on both accounts, but not perhaps for the reason you may imagine, particularly in the case of the latter. I was on my way to Granny Maxton's, I recall. Presumably it was her grandson or granddaughter in whose honour the party was being held, though it is curious that I should remember her name rather than the birthday boy or girl. What I do remember was that on the way there, I fell in with some bad company, some other guest, who challenged me to a race to our destination. We arrived at more or less the same time, but my challenger alas, did not stop short at the door but opened it and ran in without knocking and although I remembered well my mother's instruction, in the heat of the moment, I followed suit and I tumbled in breathlessly on his heels.

I do not recall our reception by our hosts and no doubt they kept their thoughts to themselves about the ill-mannered way that George and Jane Addison were bringing up their son—and him a teacher too. I would have been good, tried to be good, but I was easily led astray.

But even when I was good and obeyed my mother, it still worked out wrong. Was it the fear of her long arm with a rod at the end of it, or her all-seeing eyes that knew when I was doing something wrong even when I was well out of her sight, or was it just idiocy on my part—but remembering that I was told to eat everything on my plate, and although I did not like it in the slightest, and thought it tasted rather funny, I dutifully began to gnaw my way through the birthday candle that the kind mother of the birthday boy or girl had put on our plates as a memento.

Just another occasion when I was an embarrassment to my parents. No doubt the story was passed around and around and grew in the telling as these things tend to do and I probably was the laughing stock of the whole of Banff. But I wasn't aware of that and I didn't care because I walked away with something much better than a half-gnawed candle—a present, which I thought was odd, as surely it should have been the other way about! It was a big Standard Vanguard car, obsolete now, with the distinctive long curved "beetle-back", very reminiscent of cars you see in black-and-white movies set in 1940s New York or Chicago and usually involving gangsters. I seem to recall it was purple and I bore it home as proudly as any Roman emperor on a triumph.

That was the best party I had ever been to. The one for the Queen and her present of a mug couldn't hold a candle to that.

Chapter Twenty-three

Ternemny: Oh Happy Days

Looking back now, they were the halcyon days, a golden age, the days in Ternemny. Darker days were just around the corner which were to include the death of two children, one in suspicious circumstances, and it's just as well that no-one could see what lay ahead, especially those who were to die and the dispatchers of those young lives.

The trouble about living in a golden age is you don't realise you are in it at the time. The Fifties are often thought of such a period, a simpler, less complicated time, a time when mother stayed at home and devoted herself to rearing the children while father went out to work and brought home the bacon which was cooked and served up to him by the devoted wife when he came home.

It is often said that it is a time to which we would do well to return. There might be some merit in that argument, yet I am not so sure. Apart from the advances in technology which I would hate to do without now, a lot of dark things went on in the Fifties. There was capital punishment for example and while they were not chained to the kitchen sink exactly, the status of women would be enough to make a feminist born in the 21st century choke on her cornflakes, much like we, in the first half of the 20th century read in our school history books about slavery in the 19th and were appalled. And not least there was the attitude to sex and illegitimacy, the shame of having a child "out of wedlock". This will occupy some space later on but for the moment let us just say that matters had hardly moved on since Burns's time. While we no longer made the fornicators appear before the congregation to be ritually humiliated, there was a culture of shame and humiliation all the same, which in the case I am going to tell you about later, resulted in tragedy.

But I knew none of that. It was 1954 and I was just a boy in my seventh year towards heaven, not even realising I was already there. There was a wood a minute away from my front door with a burn running through it and a dam at the top. I rarely ventured as far as the dam and think I only dared once to venture further than that into the Wild Wood, like Mole in *Wind in the Willows*. Some explorer me, too cowardly to explore this territory that seemed so far from home and yet there was absolutely no risk of ever getting lost. It was not a very wide or thick wood: you could practically see from one side to the other and all I had to do to get home was follow the burn.

The truth is I was banned by my mother from going anywhere near the dam—you know how mothers worry about their children and water. They think that they don't mix very well, whereas for a child, there is nothing more attractive than the lure of water. To go beyond the dam therefore, would be a step far too far for a timid boy who thought he had already o'er stepped the mark by a mile, and who, from his Banff days, suspected his mother of having supernatural powers to detect what he was up to. Where she imagined he got the jam jars full of tadpoles I could not say, but jam jars by the score I got of the glutinous slimy mixture which half poured, half squidged from my hands as I lay on my stomach and pulled out the jelly with the black dots much more easily I imagine than Jack Horner pulled out a plum with only the aid of his thumb.

The great hunter then bore his catch home to the garden where he tipped the contents of the jar into a disused porcelain sink already filled with water and weeds. Where the sink came from I have no idea but it was perfect for watching the development of the frog, from the appearance of the back legs, then the front and the gradual disappearance of the tail until the final metamorphosis was complete with myriads of tiny black frogs no bigger than the size of my pinkie fingernail. If it was fascinating for me, it was also fascinating for Korky, the family cat, who would perch on the rim of the sink and with curved paw, scoop the tadpoles out of the water. Despite this satanic black paw, our garden was so hopping with frogs that you had to be careful where you were walking, but I understand that frogs are beneficial to a garden and as a keen gardener, I imagine my father was delighted with the results of my nature study.

This may seem ironic but another thing that made Ternemny seem heavenly to me and the first thing that I looked for when we arrived and did not see (much to my delight), was a church. I could scarcely contain my glee at the thought of there being no more Sunday school. At long last I would be on a five-day week though at that time very few occupations could boast this luxury. I remember thinking that teaching might be a possible career for me when I grew up, and if not that, whatever it might turn out to be, I told myself that I must, without fail, check how many working days there were in the week before I embarked on this vocation.

The exception to this, the other profession I dallied with, was dentistry. That was because our dentist seemed a very rich man because he lived in a very big house and not only did he have car, but he had a caravan too! We only got our first car, a Vauxhall Wyvern (SE 6820) when we moved to Ternemny. It was second-hand of course and was later replaced by SE 9771, an Austin A40, which had previously been owned by Mr Wilson, the manager of the garage in Banff. I think he was a friend of my father's, or maybe they just knew each other from school.

Although I was pretty interested in cars, it never occurred to me to pursue a career which involved them in some way or other, but believe it or not, I did toy with becoming a minister, because as I saw it, they only worked for *one* day a week and even then for not much longer than an hour. That seemed a very attractive proposition indeed, but it was not, I knew, a very highly-paid profession and I did not seriously consider it for long. I thought I could tolerate the extra hours of work for the financial remuneration they brought.

It was not long before my illusions on there being no more Sunday school were shattered. The minister from Rothiemay, a young man called Dickie, with a prominent Adam's apple, aided and abetted by a young lady from the nearby farm of Ternemny, took Sunday school in the school. We had an attendance card which was duly filled in by the teacher. Her name was Helen Adam and her initials in the box, week after week, seemed to mock the escape I thought I had had.

If that was a disappointment, there was something else that was very far from that. From the perspective of a young boy who thinks he is so sophisticated that a much younger sister is worse than useless, he had to admit that she did have one use—at Christmas. When my credulity was stretched too far to believe in Santa Claus any more and I told my mother of my suspicions, she admitted the truth. "But don't tell Marjorie," she cautioned. No threats of skinning me alive were necessary if I did. The longer before she reached the age of disbelief the better as far as I was concerned.

There was one Christmas in particular I remember, perhaps it was the last of my sister's belief. She and I got up at the crack of dawn (excitement made sleep impossible) to find—and I could scarcely believe my eyes—the two armchairs at either side of the living room fire piled high with mysterious parcels. The one on the left was my sister's; the one on the right, mine. There was a bagatelle board, I remember, and a bulldozer that made a horrendous noise on its rubber tracks when you switched it on by means of a switch next to the exhaust pipe on the top. I don't know who gave it to me and I don't remember a single thing my sister got, but I do remember it as the most productive of Christmases ever. Why would I kill a golden goose like that?

In our dressing gowns, my sister and I opened all those tantalising presents before a fire that had been banked up for the night and which, despite a good poke from my mother, sluggishly failed to send its feeble warmth out more than a foot into the bone-chittering room. But we cared not a whit for that as we unwrapped parcel after parcel. Our mother went back to bed but probably not to sleep with that bulldozer relentlessly pushing the silence through the closed door and up the stairs. But there was one thing she could be sure of on this day—my sister and I would not fight, not with all those presents to distract us.

We had a tree of course, a real one naturally. As far as I am aware, those pathetic imitation ones had not yet been devised, and I remember my father making decorations for the ceilings. He used the sewing machine to sew two lengths of different-coloured crepe paper together then he snipped the edges with scissors to create a fringe. One end was attached to a corner, then given a twist before the other end was anchored to the other, then a second streamer was added to the other two corners and hey presto, you had a room transformed and looking very festive! There were also some very fragile paper decorations which I imagine came from my mother's girlhood home, antiques now, even if I am wrong about that and they were actually bought in Banff in the days before my memory began.

Ternemny. Most people have never heard of it and you will not find it on a map either. So just where is this Scottish Shangri-La?

Close your eyes and you'll miss it. It used to be in Banffshire and although it hasn't moved anywhere, it is now in Moray. And just to make matters more confusing, our postal address was Aberdeenshire. Ternemny Schoolhouse, Knock, by Huntly, Aberdeenshire. That was what I used to write at the top of my Christmas thank you letters which my parents assiduously made me write—the one drawback to Christmas.

The address tells you that it is near Knock, which won't help you much without the help of a large-scale map, so imagine you are proceeding (as we believe PC Plod says when giving evidence in court) in a

terly direction along the A95 from Banff,
ı do not deviate, you will eventually arrive in
.ı. ̇ ̇ ut should you branch off at Glenbarry (look
ror the pub) and take the left fork along the B 9002
you will arrive in Ternemny in just a couple of miles.
Be alert or you may miss it. There is no sign. Just the
schoolhouse and the school (now converted into some
sort of workshop) and a few houses strung along the
side of the road. Should you come to a sign off to the
right pointing to Knock, you have come too far. And
if, perchance you should miss *that*, you will end up in
Huntly.

Ternemny then, in my boyhood, consisted only
of the school and schoolhouse adjoined, as well as a
handful of prefabs, eight in all, or at least, that's how
many I think there were. Over the wall from our garden,
and if I thought *that* was big, that of Mr Campbell's
next door was immense by anyone's standards. He was,
in fact, a retired primary headmaster or dominie, maybe
even of Ternemny, once upon a time. He came from
Ayrshire and was at one time secretary of the prestigious
Burns Club in Alloway where, being Burns's birthplace,
you can imagine they take their Burns very seriously
indeed. He wrote a book, published in 1953 by James
Blair, Aberdeen, entitled *A Burns' Companion (being
Everybody's Key to Burns' Poems)* in which he explains
every reference in every poem and song Burns ever
wrote.

There was a big black furnace kept caged in the
senior room and it was part of my father's duties to
stoke it and keep it supplied with coal, while in the
junior room, it was also part of his duties to run the
local library (or at least issue the books and receive the

returns), the custodian of the literary treasures which were held under lock and key, concealed behind great plywood boards. It was from these shelves that I cut my teeth on such literary jewels as the Nancy Drew Mysteries and Angus MacVicar and, of course, Enid Blyton, who is unquestionably to blame for my being addicted to reading, though she is sneered at by some academics nowadays. I did not need to borrow the Classics such as those works by R. L. Stevenson, Jules Verne and R.M. Ballantyne, to name only a few of my favourites: they were part of the furbishment at home.

One book which I did *not* read, however, was Mr W. B. Campbell's academic work. I wish I had had it when I was teaching Burns to my Higher classes but it was a bit too much over the head of even a short primary school pupil, poetry not really being to my taste in those days of innocence and ignorance. Despite that, I won the Burns Federation Prize three years in a row for Scots recitation. I still have the copy of *Poems and Songs of Robert Burns* that I won in 1957. I know the date precisely because it has a bookplate in it, signed by my father, as headmaster. Another of my treasures. And before you go thinking "nepotism", don't, because you would be wrong. I imagine Mr Campbell was the judge; it certainly wouldn't have been my father lest that very accusation was levelled against him. Similarly, when it came to the SSPCA essay, the entries were judged by my father's friend, Norman Emmanuel Faid (may his name be praised), who was well qualified to undertake this task since he was an English teacher. He was later to become my English teacher at both Fordyce and Banff Academies. You will meet him again later.

I know what you're thinking. Uh! Huh! My father's friend, eh? And you may think me a trifle boastful for mentioning winning these prizes, but you won't when I tell you there were seven in my Primary Five class (a bulge year, you see), three in the top class and I don't know how many in the middle, Primary Six. But let us say four or five, which would be a reasonable guess. So you see, I was competing against no more than fifteen. That's not too bad odds, even if they did increase somewhat as the exceptionally small class of three pupils disappeared and we moved up the room to make room for the fresh intake: Primary Five on the left, Six in the middle and Seven on the right.

I was also lucky that no budding genius was around in my time and fortunately there was such a difference between the ages of my sister and me that internecine rivalry between us was avoided as she was in the "baby" room. I passed on my crown to her when I left.

My father taught us all, though how he juggled three classes at once I am not sure, though he seemed to do it effortlessly enough. But he had a MA degree from Aberdeen University, followed by a year at Teachers' Training College. Amazingly, and it seems quite incredible today, some of my father's fellow dominies never went to college, let alone university. More than ten years later, when I was undergoing my own teacher training, I was surprised one day to see a number of strange faces in our Education lecture. It turned out that these were the uncertificated teachers doing their training. One lecture, one hour, no exam. Nice work if you can get it, and they had been doing the job for years. Did the Government really think they could pull the wool over our eyes when they could now proudly boast that they had a fully trained and qualified professional teaching force? Maybe they could to some, but it certainly aroused a great deal of anger and resentment amongst us students.

I suppose one of my father's methods (and it seems elementary) was to give us things to write while he taught lessons to the others and if I were ever distracted, I don't remember ever being so. What I do remember was the geography lessons where we stood in a semicircle under a map of the world which had a lot of pink in it to denote the British Empire. Why pink was chosen by the cartographer I can't say, but red might have looked too bloody. My father asked us questions and if you got it right you stayed where you were but if someone could not answer, or got the answer wrong, then the question was offered to the next person and if you got that right, as a reward, you were allowed to move up to take that person's place in the semicircle. And so it went on and you could move down as well as up of course. It added a competitive edge, at least as far as I was concerned, to the lesson. Well, not really a lesson really, more a test of what we had learned, or were supposed to have.

I usually ended up at the top but at the next meeting under the map, I always found myself, like Sisyphus, at the bottom again. And of course, there was no such thing as shouting out. If you knew the answer, you put your hand up and sometimes you were so desperate to answer but knew you had to remain silent, that you literally danced on the spot with your hand in the air and any visitor happening to step into the room at that point would have wondered why my father did not let the child out to relieve its bladder before it burst.

Meanwhile, Mr Campbell, our neighbour, having retired from the chalk face, turned his hand to market gardening, supplying the school kitchens with some of his produce. I could see my father doing something like that, if he had been spared. Well, maybe not, but he did love gardening, producing both flowers and vegetables. I can remember my mother and father on Great Slug Hunting Expeditions among the lettuces. Armed with a darning needle, they would skewer the unfortunate creatures and drop them into a jam jar filled with brine. Not a pleasant death but that's what you get for being a slug. The very name seems loaded with disgust.

Although I don't know where the rest of Mr Campbell's produce went, I do know what happened to the strawberries, or some of them. There were rows and rows of them, masses and masses of them and a great many went into the bellies of my sister and me. We did not nip over the wall and help ourselves if that is what you are thinking. No, we were "volunteered" by our parents who were always willing to offer our services to the community long before community service was ever dreamt of, and not for any ill we had done either. But picking the strawberries was its own reward as we were allowed to eat as we picked and our backs being nearer the ground, I don't remember suffering any backache either, but I do think they were the best strawberries I ever tasted and ever expect to taste again. And if you have ever seen the acres of them growing under polythene in the south of Spain before they make their appearance in our supermarkets, you will not wonder why they are so insipid.

If Mr Campbell was ever married, I couldn't say for sure. He might have been a widower as I have a vague notion there might have been a daughter somewhere. At any rate he lived alone. Perhaps my sister thought he was lonely because one day she and her friend knocked on his door and asked if he was "coming out to play". He must have been eighty something; they would have been about eight. Unfortunately he was washing what was left of his hair and could not oblige.

A real man o' pairts was Mr Campbell. He also kept bees. That was where I got Tiger the cat. He was just a kitten then, little more than a mewling, his poor parched throat too dry to make any sound. He was crouched, terrified under a hive. I don't know if he had been stung but that's what I risked, not to mention being bitten and scratched as I lay flat out on my stomach, inserted my arm in the narrow space under the hive and hauled him out. I took him home and gave him a saucer of milk. He had beautiful markings, hence his name, and I loved playing with him when he was a kitten. He stayed with us for a good number of years until he went to the cattery in the sky.

His arrival however did not please Korky the Tadpole Cat. He took the huff, went out one day and never came back. But then he always was a law unto himself, half feral. He was often in fights, either protecting his territory or fighting over the ladies. I remember him limping back one day with his coal-black fur completely stripped from his side and bearing ghastly head injuries besides. If he was the winner, I would not have liked to see the loser. My mother attended to his injuries which he submitted to with uncharacteristic meekness and once recovered, undaunted, he went out again attending to his harem. So one day when he never came back, we feared the worst, either death by mortal combat or less gloriously, under the wheels of a car.

Then one day my Sunday school teacher reported that he was alive and well and living on her farm with his girlfriend. Korky was in love. For him to have settled down with one lady was a bit out of character but I suppose he wasn't getting any younger and had sowed plenty of wild oats by this time anyway. I never saw him again and never really missed him because of Tiger. I hope he had a long and happy life with the wife.

I was always accustomed to having animals in the house. There was Rex, the collie, with his white mane and brown eyes and like all collies, extremely intelligent. I don't remember when we got him; I just remember him always being there so probably he was with us in Fountain Street at least. I wanted him to be like William Brown's dog Jumble who followed him about everywhere, but Rex, like his successor, Jimmy, half Dandie Dinmont and God knows what else (which was to his benefit, as it gave him much needed longer legs), showed an unswerving loyalty to my father, possibly in the mistaken belief that he was head of the household.

I still remember Rex's last days. He had pneumonia and my mother had made a jacket for him to try and keep him warm. He was so weak he had to be carried outside to do his business and then there was one evening that my parents took him out and after a while my mother came back alone, sobbing. My father was digging the grave in the school playing field. It was late and dark and I was in my pyjamas so I did not attend the ceremony. In any case I did not want to be there but the next day my mother showed me where the grave was and I made a cross and planted it there. It never occurred to me that Rex may not have been a Christian.

Fortunately, for my sake, when it came the time for Jimmy to go to the kennels in the sky, I was not there, nor was my sister. It was a long time later and we were both students and our father had long since gone to heaven himself so it fell to my poor mother, alone, to call the vet out and she held Jimmy in her arms as he administered the fatal dose.

Losing a pet, as I don't have to tell those who have gone through this ordeal, is just as harrowing as losing a human member of the family, but there was one occasion when I wept buckets over the loss of a living pet. His name was Charlie and he was a Cocker Spaniel. We only had him for a short time before he was taken away. I am not sure why this was. I think it might have been because we were fostering him for some reason and the owner wanted him back. Anyhow, when the SSPCA man came and shut him in his van I was inconsolable. He had been shaping up nicely as a Jumble. He was removed at playtime. I don't know which would have been worse—to have come home from school to find him gone or to see it happen before my horrified eyes. I pleaded and pleaded but it was to no avail.

Playtime was not nearly long enough for me to get my grief under control and though I did manage to stop blubbing, I could not hide the signs of it.

"What's wrong?" my colleagues wanted to know.

"My d . . . d . . . dad b . . . b . . . bashed me."

It was all I could think of and fortunately no-one asked for details.

Then there was Billy the white rabbit who had to have his name changed to Biddy after he produced a litter of four. She must have already been pregnant when I got her and it came as a great shock to us. The question was, what was I going to do with her children? Give them away was the answer—but to whom? Who would give them the best homes was what my mother said, and who was the nicest to me was what I thought. I suddenly became very popular: people started being very nice to me indeed. I had never known such power or popularity.

Finally, there was Billy the brown-and-white guinea pig who once did the toilet on me but that is about all I remember about him. I was daft about animals as you can see, but I confess I did neglect poor Billy and should have taken him out of his run and stroked him more. Perhaps I might have done if he had not used me as a pabby (my childhood word for the toilet).

There was another animal with which I also had too close an encounter—Charlie, the horse that bit me. He was a massive Clydesdale with beautiful feathered feet and a mighty bite, as I was to find out. He was the dray horse for the distillery and had the additional job of transporting tables and chairs from there to the school for the annual whist drive in aid of school funds. One day I decided to reward him with a lump of sugar. After all, it was his day off and he deserved something for his enforced labour. Accordingly, cupping the sugar cube in my outstretched palm, I proffered the titbit towards his muzzle. Charlie lowered his mighty head and the next minute I was in dancing in pain, in shock at the sight of blood streaming from my fingers. It was only then my mother showed me how you *should* give a horse a lump of sugar, with your palm perfectly flat. Thanks mum.

Pity you hadn't shown me that beforehand. You were there when I did it.

As you can see, my early life in Ternemny was closely associated with animals and Charlie brings the catalogue to an end, except for one other creature that I was rather scared of. He was a Muscovy duck who was scared of nothing and nobody. He would follow you about, ruffling his feathers and tell you in no uncertain language (I'm not certain if it was Russian or merely duck) that you had better mind your manners as he was watching you. His name was Khruschev and he belonged to the village blacksmith, Mr MacDonald.

Dismiss all thoughts of the village blacksmith in Longfellow's poem of the same name. He was not of mighty build—modest would be more like the word; the tree in his yard was a massive beech, not a chestnut; his face was not tanned, but black as befitted his trade. And if he went to church (which would have been in Rothiemay), he would not have wept at the sound of his daughter's sweet singing which reminded him of his wife in Paradise, for regardless if ever had a daughter in the first place, his wife was alive and well. Any children would have flown the nest years long before we came to Ternemny. I wouldn't say the MacDonalds were ancient, but they were certainly born in the century before mine.

They were mortal enemies of Mr Campbell, keeping alive the infamous massacre of Glencoe which took place in 1692 and during the lifetime of my earliest known ancestors, John Edison [sic] and his wife Elspet Macky [sic]. But it was more good-natured banter than actual animosity, unlike two former pupils of mine who took it into their heads, or at least one of them did, to revive this centuries-old feud, attacking the other, merely on the grounds of the name he bore and long after they had left school.

Presumably that was where this modern MacDonald had heard of the Glencoe massacre but when I attempted to teach them in the same class, they showed no such animosity, united as it were, against the common enemy—me. During one lesson, one of them, the Campbell one it was, shouted across the room at me: "You're a bastard! Ma faither tellt me you wis." Yes, I had been in the teaching game so long by then I was now teaching the second generation.

But I am getting far, far ahead of myself, to a time far beyond when this book is intended to finish. I mention it merely to make a point, the point with which I began this chapter—that you can see why some people see the Fifties as a time we would do well to return. Pupils would never have dared to address their teacher like that then.

Still, I should be grateful I suppose. No-one ever actually physically assaulted me—though I did come pretty close to it on a couple of occasions.

Chapter Twenty-four

The Trouble with The Dingle

When we moved to Ternemny in 1954 I moved into Primary Three in the junior room. My teacher was Miss Dingwall. I'm guessing she was forty-something but maybe she just seemed a lot older than she actually was. She wore a flowery overall, her hair braided in coils over her ears making her look as if she were perpetually wearing headphones. Not a good hairstyle, but worse was the ring on her finger. It was a nice enough ring I suppose but I didn't like it because when she clapped me round the ears, it made my empty head ding like a bell. It looked like an engagement ring but it wasn't because it was on the wrong hand. Maybe she had had a love affair that ended in tears but more likely it had once belonged to her mother. I thought her surname should have been "Dingwell" but we called her "The Dingle" because she made our ears tingle, which is nearly as good.

I am not sure why I got this treatment. I am sure I was not a bad boy. I had *been* bad as you have already read, and will be much worse later as you shall see, but I was not bad then, not in her class, with my father just through the wall. What kind of idiot (or coward) do you take me for? It was probably because I got a sum wrong or had not put the hat on my number five exactly along the line, or the curves on my Sammy the Snakes were too fat or too thin. She used to patrol our serried rows, armed with a ruler, on the lookout for errors as we laboured over our work and like a guillotine, brought it down on our offending fingers not with the flat side, but the narrow edge. Ouch! That was sore.

If this makes her sound like a tyrant and a bully, she wasn't really. I wasn't scared of her, well just enough to do what she told me without question, just as she was not scared to clout the dominie's son because she knew my father would take her side of the story—if I had ever thought, in a moment of madness, of complaining of unfair treatment, which of course I never did. No, all she was doing was her job and probably very well and efficiently too. It was normal practice to administer punishments like that "to encourage us" in Voltaire's sense of the expression. After all, how could we ever be expected to learn anything unless it was knocked into us, since it is a well-known fact that children are innately resistant to learning?

And another thing she made us do: when we were being told something especially important, we had to sit on our hands so we would not fiddle and thus we could devote our entire concentration to the matter in hand, so to speak. And the windows too, being large, let in the light, physically, and also metaphorically, as being so far above our heads, there was not the remotest chance of our tiny (and formative) minds ever being distracted, unless it was by the occasional sparrow on a flypast.

And if I have also given the impression that Miss Dingwall was a staid old maid then that is a misrepresentation too. She did get married to a retired farmer later, a widower I believe, a Mr Leslie, at some time when I was in the senior room. For how long this latter-day romance had been going on I do not know, as for some reason, she did not take me into her confidence. But another thing that shows she was far from staid was she went on foreign holidays long before package holidays became commonplace despite Mr Thomas Cook's company having been inaugurated more than one hundred years earlier.

I know one year she went to Capri and why that should have stuck in the mind especially I haven't a clue. But what I do know is she went to even more exotic places and brought back coins (or at least one) with a hole in the middle. Most commonly, a coin like this is the currency in places like Japan, India and China so I think she must have visited at least one of those. This would have been a real adventure in those days: commercial air travel was in its infancy and in all probability she travelled alone. Staid old maid, by no means. And some of us were the beneficiaries of her travels too. With the addition of a pink ribbon, the coin became transformed into a medal awarded to the pupil who was top of the class.

The rationale was, in a spirit of competitiveness, we would be encouraged to work even harder to achieve this accolade. The flaw in the thinking was there were some people who could never have won the medal no matter how hard they tried or how long their grey beard grew. Disheartened, demoralised, they gave up competing, and before very long did not give a fig for a Chinese fen, even if it did have a pink ribbon attached.

I remember the first time I won it, instead of examining its provenance, as I wish I now had, it never occurring me to, since I thought it was merely a medal, I immediately pocketed it instead of hanging it round my neck. This was not an altruistic gesture designed to spare the feelings of my classmates but because I was so overcome with confusion and embarrassment that to wear it in front of them, ironically, I thought would make me look like a prize idiot. However, out of their sight, at the back door, I proudly put it round my neck so my mother could see my achievement and praise me the minute I stepped over the threshold. Of course she would, I now realise, in all probability, have been alerted to this momentous event during the morning break in our house where the Dingle and my father habitually repaired for coffee. The display of apparent modesty which I appeared to show in the classroom would have been better placed at home as it would have shown my mother that I had at least one admirable trait, for she and I were often at loggerheads, if not outright war.

I don't even know what I did to achieve this pinnacle of success, whether it was the result of a test or just showing a general excellence over the others by answering more questions correctly in class. I presume I did win it again, but don't remember ever wearing it again. Maybe I became blasé, maybe I never did, although four years later in Primary Seven, I did become dux of the school. I got a medal for that too, a proper medal—a little metal shield in two colours with DUX written on it and which is another of my treasures. I never openly strived to achieve this honour. It just happened, and let me remind you, lest you think my head too inflated, there was not a great deal of competition, at least in terms of numbers and there cannot be a scintilla of suspicion of any favouritism on the part of my father either, as I was the only one in my class after the 11-plus to pass into an A stream for two languages, to that non-icon of academe, Keith Grammar School, of which more in due course.

There were a couple of other things I remember about Miss Dingwall. We were given a third of a pint of milk a day by a generous and well-meaning Government to make our young and growing bones nice and strong. That was for our elevenses. The bottles had silver-foil tops, which, unless the bluetits had got to them first, Miss Dingwall helpfully pierced with the use of her trusty nail file so that we could insert our straws through the slit. It never occurred to me to question the hygene implications of this operation, just as I am sure it didn't to her. It never put me off the milk, which I remember, had a thick layer of cream on the top. I could never drink it today, not because of the microscopic pieces of Miss Dingwall's nails which might, or might not, have sprinkled the top of the cream like caster sugar, but because I am so used to the healthier, virtually fat-free, red-topped milk. The very sight of all that cream would turn my stomach now.

In the winter however, this procedure was unnecessary as the milk was frozen so solid that it actually lifted the foil off the top and it sat perched jauntily on the cream like the helmet on a medieval knight. If the foil didn't give, the bottle actually cracked. We *must* have had colder winters then and it's not the memory playing tricks and exaggerating through the veil of time.

And if the milk was frozen, then we could be assured that the water in the outside lavatories would be frozen too. Not much of an inconvenience to we boys who could just make yellow snow, and of course I could just pop home if I needed to do a number two, but what the girls did I do not know, unless in these emergency conditions, they were allowed to use the one and only indoor toilet in the school, intended for staff use only.

One child did use it on one memorable occasion (and please excuse me for mentioning this) but this person, after having spent tuppence rather than a penny, had the misfortune to drop her dinner money into the pan just as she was going to flush her deposit away. The poor child came to my father in tears. What was he to do? To flush or not to flush? That was the question. Would flushing remove the money too? What is a dominie to do when he knew that that child's parents could ill-afford to see money literally go down the drain like that? In fact that financial scenario could, and probably did, apply to practically every child who attended Ternemny, for money in those days was a lot tighter for most families than now, only one breadwinner being the norm.

There was one rich kid though. Well, I thought he was rich anyway and I was probably right, for after all, did not his father own the village shop and therefore all the goods therein, including the sweeties? There was something of Little Lord Fauntleroy about him with his bow tie and wavy blonde hair. Being in my sister's class and thus four years younger than me, he was not worthy of my condescending attention even if he was a boy and not a girl, yet I used to go down to his place to play now and again, with my habitual playmates, David and Richard, at his mother's invitation. Or perhaps it was one of the public services that my mother regularly volunteered me for as Sammy was an only child.

Such a sacrifice wasn't as bad as it sounded. We were given sweets as wages and on one occasion I remember being given a sugar mouse which was bounty indeed.

David M. Addison

They came in two varieties, white and pink, and it seems to me that the pink was the sweeter. To make them last longer, you held them by their tails (a piece of string sticking out their bottoms), and like a mouse, gnawed your way down the body beginning with the head. God knows how many calories there were in one of those but we ran round the countryside like deer and would have run them off in next to no time.

One day, being at a bit of a loose end, or more likely, suffering from sugar withdrawal symptoms, one of us suggested that we went down to play with Sammy. It may even have been me. I have no idea what we played at but at the back of the shop there was a big yard cluttered with all sorts of things, and our imaginations were even bigger. When it came time to go home, and this *was* my idea, we politely informed Sammy's mother that we had had a lovely time playing with him but regrettably, we had to go home now for our tea. I had hoped for a mouse, but anything less would have been acceptable. Our chins must have hit the floor as equally politely, she thanked us for coming and sent us away with nothing, not even one of those little tins of tiny chopped up pieces of liquorice which we bought for the sake of the tins as they had pictures of racing cars on them. Collectors' items. That was the last time I ever remembering us coming out of our natural habitat, the wood, to make the four-mile round trip to play something with poor Sammy.

That was a mercenary act and bad thing to do I suppose. My lust for sugar was always leading me astray, but I was just about to do something much, much worse and which was to land me in the biggest trouble I had ever got into in my life up to that point. And sugar was

262

not to blame this time. No, believe it or not, it was all Miss Dingwall's fault.

She must have been pretty musical, Miss Dingwall. She could play the piano and she put on concerts. And one other thing she did, which I hated, and which was responsible for my shame—she taught us Scottish country dancing.

It was an extracurricular activity and attendance was voluntary except for me and my sister. It didn't bother her, but it bothered me a lot. It was bad enough having to dance with *girls* but what was especially painful about it was I knew my two comrades in arms, Richard and David, were free and at large outdoors, roaming the wood. Had I not been the dominie's son, I reasoned, I too could have been outside enjoying myself like them, free as Nature intended, not going through this torture.

I sulked and bemoaned the cruel hand of fate that had dealt me this card, subjecting my parents to endless moaning before and after each session. What use was cissy dancing to anybody, I protested. To me it was worse than Sunday school and that was saying something. I don't remember what we did there precisely, except I had to get dressed up for it in my uncomfortable best clothes. God was watching and you had to show some respect. I am sure there was no fun in it but at least I didn't have to do much, passively listening to stories about Jesus and other good blokes from the Bible and muttering a few words of prayer, but this stupid dancing required me to be active and under the watchful gaze of my parents (for my mother came too), I was forced to ask girls to dance which was bad enough in itself but the subsequent teasing was worse as they mentally kept note of my choices and remarked on them later, like this was a sign that I was madly in love with them or something. Maybe that was how the whole Bobina thing came about.

Bobina was deemed to be my first love by my fond parents but I never kissed her or even held hands with her outwith this extramural Scottish Country Dancing activity. So innocent was this "romance" that I could not even pronounce her name properly. I can only assume that I asked her to be my partner more frequently than the other poor unfortunates and my parents were guilty of outrageously bad arithmetic when they concluded that one plus one on the dance floor equalled an item off it. Probably Bobina just happened to be standing in the wrong place at the wrong time—the nearest victim.

What need did I have of girls? My alter ego was Davy Crockett. I was a frontiersman and woodsman, like him. Davy never had anything to do with girls. When he was only three, he "killed him a b'ar" according to the song that was regularly played by Uncle Mac on *Childrens' Favourites*. This fantasy was aided and abetted by the Davy Crockett hat that Auntie Mary sent from Canada which readers with a good memory may remember in the chapter about the Tates.

My pleas fell on deaf ears. My bad moods failed to move them. Slamming doors and stomping feet only served to result in warnings that if I repeated that behaviour I would not be able to sit down for a week. Very well then, if I could not avoid having to dance, then at least I could do it very badly, shuffling rather than skipping the steps and asking the poor partner up with as much bad grace as I could muster, to make it perfectly clear that I did so under sufferance. And then came the memorable day, the day of shame.

It was a lovely summer's late afternoon I recall, and that day is seared into my memory. I knew that Richard and David were engaged in much more worthy and boyish pursuits such as climbing trees and building our hut. One thing they definitely were not doing was playing cowboys and Indians as all the squaws were otherwise engaged in doing the Gay Gordons and the Bluebell Polka, many of them taking it in turns to be braves since so few of us boys were there—another thing that rankled with me. Why me? But I knew it was because my dad was the dominie and he thought he knew what was good for me.

This shortage of braves explains why, when it came to the ladies' choice, there was never any escape for me. On this day, seething with pent-up resentment at weeks of enforced dancing and the sight of the cloudless blue sky framed in the classroom windows, when Ann, Richard's sister, asked me to dance, I refused. Anyone who had asked me would have received the same treatment as I was in a murderous mood, though it definitely did not help that Ann unwittingly reminded me that her brother was not here, as I had to be. You'll just have to take it on trust that I had the grace to refuse reasonably kindly. Unfortunately, poor Ann had a very large and unsightly birthmark that covered half her face. I state absolutely and categorically that that had nothing to do with my refusal. All I wanted was to do one hated dance less—but that was not the way she saw it, nor did anybody else.

In tears, Ann fled to the other side of the room to be comforted by Miss Dingwall. A moment later, when my father was informed about this appalling breach of etiquette, it was not a pretty sight as he wiped the floor with me. Time stood suspended as everyone stared at this awesome spectacle. He would have done the same with anyone but he had to show one and all that no favours were being granted, no quarter was being spared just because of who I was. I needed to be made an example of.

But this public humiliation was not the end of it. Far from it. I was, of course, made to apologise to Ann and dance with her, and when I got home my parents tore into me again. And that, I thought miserably, was another price I had to pay for being the dominie's son. Had I been any other boy who had done this awful thing, I would not have had to endure this second shaming, though with the benefit of hindsight, in a place as small as Ternemny, such a transgression would have been the speak of the place, regardless of who had done it.

Shaming and humiliating it certainly was, but for me it had a happy outcome in the end. Somehow I persuaded my parents that the real reason for my refusal was my hatred of the dance and reluctantly my parents permitted me to stop attending the classes. If the other parents assumed that I had been banned and that I was miserably moping away as a result, then nothing could have been further than the truth. But if it helped calm the savage breasts of outraged parents, well and good, as justice could be seen to have been well and truly done.

"You'll live to regret it," my parents warned, shrugging their shoulders in helpless resignation, their last-ditch attempt to make me see sense.

There were moments during this incident when I thought my life would be severely curtailed, so I was happy to hear that I did seem to have a future, but I was happier still to think there would be no more accursed dancing. And I never ever regretted not being able to do these dances. I have never liked dancing of any type, though I quite like to see some tap dancing and regard Gene Kelly's dance in *Singin' in the Rain* as one of the most iconic moments ever in the entire history of film, while at the other end of the spectrum, I consider ballet to be the absolute pits. I admit there has been some pretty good music written for it, but I think that's like saying what Mark Twain said about golf: "a good walk spoiled".

But despite this revulsion to dance, I have occasionally been seen to "dance" at weddings, after a few libations, naturally. *Strip the Willow* is my favourite. There is always someone there to point you in the right direction and nobody cares if you are doing the right steps or not, or keeping in time to the music, so I never regretted my abandonment of the Scottish Country Dancing class. But why grown-up and consenting adults ever voluntarily join such clubs leaves me at a loss unless you are single in search of a mate. I know of several instances where romance has flourished at such places—which is par for the course, for is it not at the dancing that most people meet their fate? Like the balls Jane Austen's heroines were always going to and in the days of my youth where the Saturday night dances at Cullen or Portsoy or Macduff were a sort of cattle market where the opposite sexes could eye each other up and if you were lucky, pair off.

Now, I have heard, bizarrely, supermarkets form the same function nowadays. I wholeheartedly approve. It's free to get in for a start and there's no music to drown out your carefully crafted chat-up lines. As you traipse up the aisle scanning the shelves for something you fancy, it might just be a prelude to walking up that other aisle that ends in front of the altar. It could be a life-altering event indeed, bringing a whole new dimension to the concept of shopping, where you might come back not just with a microwave meal for one but a mate—even if it is just up to Christmas.

Chapter Twenty-five

The Trouble with Harry

I had no interest in girls then, despite the alleged affinity with Bobina, but if I had been, I wouldn't have needed to go anywhere to meet them. I was a bit like a cockerel with his brood of hens, the only boy in a class of seven. I am not sure how long this state of affairs persisted, me ruling the roost like this but then, one day, along came Harry and I was no longer the undisputed most handsome boy in the class. I can't remember what it was about, but one day we had a monumental fight. I do know however that it had nothing to do with him usurping me as the alpha male of the class because he came at some stage in Primary Four and this titanic battle took place during Primary Seven.

It was at the end of interval and we were lined up waiting to go into the classrooms for the bell had rung, a hand bell that would have been rung by my father but for some reason neither he nor Miss Dingwall appeared. If we had been left at large in the playground I doubt if this battle would have happened: it was being confined in a small space with expanding time and with nothing to fill it that ignited the spark.

It took me only a moment to discover Harry was a better fighter than me, for a smashing blow to my nose right at the start shocked me with the pain and not least, surprise, and I never recovered from it. I don't know what injuries I inflicted on Harry, if any, but I know my nose was bleeding copiously and my face felt sore all over. I knew I was losing badly and my only form of salvation would be when my father arrived. I also knew I could not sustain this beating for much longer without suffering the additional humiliation of having to admit defeat and I prayed that Harry would stop before my face became so pulpy that even my own mother would not recognise me. I was also longing to cry out in pain, never mind with the shame.

The beating went on and on and still my father did not come.

Why he did not and why he did not hear the baying of the spectators for more blood as they cheered us on, I do not know. Perhaps the phone had rung just after he had rung the bell to summon us to lessons and he and Miss Dingwall had gone back into the house, as bizarrely, there was not a phone in the school, or perhaps some visitor had arrived in a masterpiece of bad timing. Little did my father know, or anyone, that the ringing of that bell signalled the start of round one in what felt like fifteen before my father finally arrived to stop the carnage.

Presumably Harry and I were the last to notice, me preoccupied with trying to protect my face, he concentrating on transforming it into something more like a baboon's bottom. It would have been the silence from the spectators that arrested Harry's battering fists as he firstly became subliminally conscious that there was a change in the atmosphere, then, catching sight of my father, slinking back into line as if he had not been beating his son and heir into a state of unconsciousness, if only he had been given a few more moments. We all stood straight and quiet with our hands by our sides as if nothing had been happening, even me, as if we were good little Victorian children and had been patiently waiting to be admitted to our classrooms, like we had hardly exchanged as much as a whisper in the interim. How pathetic and laughable to think that we could pull the wool over his eyes like that with me dripping blood like a pig with its throat cut.

My father took one look at me. "Go to your mother," was all he said.

How humiliating! But I needed no second bidding. On the cusp of tears, I fled the scene of battle, and the second I was out of sight and sound of the others, gave vent to the pain that I had been longing to express for ages, as well as letting go the dam of my tears. This was a shocking revelation to me. If I had fondly imagined that I *was* the alpha male around here, then from that moment on I knew I was not. Harry and I never fought again. I knew my place.

It was when we were in Primary Four when the other story concerning Harry happened. In my father's room we were ranked according to the results of weekly tests and please pardon the lack of modesty, but I have to say, I invariably sat at the top of the class. Our desks were two-seaters, great heavy things with an inkwell in the middle and which it was the occasional duty of the senior pupils to fill up. Sometimes it was filled too full and sometimes, when you sat on your desk rather than behind it, as you do, you could give your trousers a nice black circular stain which your mother failed to see the funny side of.

I do not think that the same ranking system operated in Miss Dingwall's room because when this incident happened, I was sitting about the middle of the class. Alternatively, the seating could have been arranged according to the results of an arithmetic test or maybe I was just a late developer.

On this other memorable day, someone tapped me on the shoulder and I turned round to see the girls giggling and Harry grinning. To my utter disbelief, there was Harry with his spaver unbuttoned, proudly displaying his erect boyhood. I looked away instantly, deeply shocked. I really was.

I did not tell Miss Dingwall there and then. Perhaps it was out of embarrassment but I think it was more the case that I was too stunned to say anything. However, I did tell my mum and dad later that day. In other words I clyped, the worst sin that a child can do to another. But if it hadn't been me, I'm sure that at least one of my harem could not have resisted blurting out the details about this unexpected lesson in human biology and the story would have got to my father sooner rather than later. And if it *had* happened like that, I too would have found myself in hot water, interrogated as to why I had not reported the incident right away, never mind not at all. Which is why, when I did tell as soon as I could, at lunch time, I did so in tones commensurate with the enormity of the deed: "Harry took his *thing* out!"

And after lunch Harry paid the price. We watched in silence as my father meted out the punishment. He had two belts: a black, thin one with three prongs which many years later I donated to a French *assistant* so he could show his sophisticated colleagues back home the barbarous methods of discipline beloved by the Scots. I now wish I hadn't for sentimental reasons but I still do have in my possession somewhere, a thicker one, made by Dick's of Lochgelly, which had two prongs. It is a collector's item now and I am certain that was the one that Harry got and which I was once on the receiving end of too, though I haven't the faintest idea why. All I remember was that I ran home crying to my mother after school, not so much because of the stinging hand but because of the injustice of it. Whatever it was I was supposed to have done, but hadn't, my mother took my side and when my father got home, she told him off for belting me. It seems to me however that my father already knew this and did not put all his strength into it but he was at pains to show everyone that he showed me no favours.

But there was no doubt that Harry was guilty and we watched, mesmerised, as he received his dues. We watched awestruck, for we had never seen anyone belted before. Like my fight with Harry three years in the future, it seemed as if it would never stop. Hand and hand about. Four . . . Five . . . Six. Six of the best. It was over at last.

It seems harsh now. Two, you may have thought, would have been sufficient to make the point. If it was meant to deter others and speaking as the only boy in the class, I needed no such encouragement not to expose my private parts to public ridicule while the younger ones must have wondered what Harry had done. Having said that, I do not blame my father for what he did. It was part and parcel of the culture of the times. Harry had committed the worst of crimes and paid the price of the ultimate form of corporal punishment.

If ever there was an aftermath, I never heard of it but I would be amazed if Harry's parents ever remonstrated with my father, claiming that his punishment was a bit excessive. That was the way it was then, in the Fifties. Compare that incident with this.

Remember the boy in the last chapter who called me a "bastard". There was another boy in the same class who once stood on a desk, took down his trousers and waved his willy about. That makes it sound as long as a scarf (and I couldn't possibly comment as mercifully it was not during one of my lessons) and he may have been inordinately proud of it which is possibly why it came into his tiny mind that he thought it should be put on public display for the delectation of the girls and the jealousy of the boys. I'm no anthropologist but I expect he would tell you that it was some primeval urge to advertise his suitability as a mate.

What was his punishment? Well, the parents were called into the school and "concerns were expressed" about his behaviour and assurances were given by the parents that the family jewels would be kept in the family vault in future. That was it.

Times have certainly changed. Like the advances in manned flight I referred to earlier, in the classroom, things had changed no less radically in just about the same time span, though I would hardly call them an "advancement". From the time when I first became a consumer of education in the Fifties to when I finally ceased to be a provider of it in the first years of the twenty-first century, you could scarcely conceive of two more different worlds.

Chapter Twenty-six

The Macs, the mad bull and other misdemeanours

At Number One, The Prefabs, lived our nearest neighbour, Mary McLeod, the district nurse. She had a special relationship with my parents, firstly because she was a fellow professional and secondly because she was a nurse like my mother. She came originally from Lewis or Harris and could speak English like a native though it was not her native tongue. That was Gaelic.

Like Miss Dingwall, she too married later in life, and also like Miss Dingwall, married a farmer. Although he had a Scottish name, her husband came from the deep south of England, or so I would judge from his vowels. When she moved away to take up her new situation as a farmer's wife in Grange, near Keith, (where Joseph Addison, the provost of Portknockie was born), my parents kept in touch with her which turned out to be very bad news for me, but perhaps it was even worse for them. You can judge.

It is one of my enduring memories seeing my parents, like in a latter-day Vermeer painting, sitting at either side of the fireplace, ankle-deep in feathers, a big, fat, snow-white goose between them. It was a present from Mary Mac as we called her, for our Christmas Day dinner. Being a farmer's son, I suppose this gift was received by my father with gratitude, and no less by my mother I presume. It certainly looked like a goose and when alive I am sure it honked and hissed like a goose, but to me it looked like a big white elephant if you remember my feather phobia. It is just as well that it was not me who Ebenezer Scrooge commandeered to buy the goose in the butcher's window for the Cratchits as I could never have touched it. I don't remember eating ours or what it tasted like and would never have remembered it at all had it not been for that plucking scene which, all these years later, I can still see in my mind's eye as if it were yesterday.

Before that unforgettable day, when Mary Mac still lived in the prefabs, I did a bad thing. One day she took me and my cousin Graham (the one who was killed in a car crash aged 20) with her on her rounds. I expect Graham was staying for the Easter holidays or something like that and Mary Mac made the offer to get us out of my mother's hair. I remember nothing of the visits and as far as I know we did not blot our copybook—until we got home. All would have been well had Mary Mac not gone into her prefab, leaving us in the back of the van to our own devices. I don't know why she did that and I don't know why we just didn't get out: perhaps we couldn't. Maybe she just forgot about us and we were locked in.

We wouldn't have starved anyway for there was a bag of dog biscuits in the back. Actually, I seem to remember it was more like a sack. I think she might have had a Spaniel but I can't be sure.

"Have you ever eaten a dog biscuit?" Graham asked after a while. I assured him I hadn't. In fact the idea rather appalled me but Graham assured me they were quite edible.

I'm not too sure what followed next and I don't remember what the dog biscuit tasted like either. Maybe I had a bellyful of them or more likely I spat the first one out and then the notion dawned upon us that they would be much more fun not as foodstuffs, but as missiles. What I do know is that when Mary Mac appeared a long time later, she was appalled at the scene of devastation that met her eyes. There were broken dog biscuits and crumbs everywhere. We must have had a dog biscuit fight and then proceeded to have a wrestling match on top of them. She could have wept, was near to tears, a mixture of anger and despair rising in her gorge at the thought of the massive clear-up operation ahead of her. We were given a good scolding and sent home with our tails between our legs while she went to get the vacuum cleaner. When my mother got to hear of it you can imagine her reaction and we were sent over to apologise. I have a nasty feeling that embarrassment and shame made us not as contrite as we should have been, merely blurting out our apology before fleeing. I was never invited out on her rounds again.

The next bad thing I did was quite a lot later, after she was married, though I am sure she would not have forgotten, even if she might perhaps have forgiven, the dog biscuits. We were invited to her house for the evening and in the course of conversation, it came out that I was a keen stamp collector. It so happened that Mary Mac's husband was a collector too and he produced his album for me to look at. Only I thought that he had *given* it to me. It was if I had stumbled into Aladdin's cave and the lust of finding these riches was upon me. Page by page, my eyes shining, I began extracting some specimens and transferring them into the breast pocket of my shirt. They were the ones I didn't have and they were many, two or three on every page and I was looking forward to spending many happy hours transferring them into my own album when I got home. This was turning out to be the best evening I had ever spent. And to think that I thought it was going to be boring!

How long this philatelic frenzy lasted I cannot say. Naturally my eyes were fixed on the stamps but I can imagine Mr Mac watching in horror as his treasured collection was desecrated before his very eyes. Initially struck dumb in horror, he overcame his embarrassment, finally found his voice and pointed out my vandalism to my parents. How great was my embarrassment when my error was pointed out, how great the shame at being unmasked as a fool!

But I was not as foolish as I looked or felt, for after all the fuss had died down, after it had been patiently explained to me that when people gave you something, you were not to assume that it was yours to keep, only to look, and although I remembered them perfectly well, I pretended to have forgotten about the stamps in my pocket. I am sure Mr Mac had not forgotten them either but was too polite or too embarrassed to say anything, waiting for me to make the first move, if not now, when I got home when surely the "mistake" would come to light, hopefully before my mother put the shirt in the washing machine. But I never did, never confessed and that was the *really* bad thing I did, not ripping the stamps out.

Readers will be glad to hear that Mr. Mac did get his revenge in the end although he had to wait a long time. One year my parents volunteered my services at their dairy farm. What's more, the Macs did not come to collect me for this enforced labour, nor did my parents take me. No, I had to get there under my own steam. That meant on my trusty bicycle with my suitcase strapped to the back mudguard. It must have been twelve miles at least, possibly as many as fifteen.

It was an offer I could not have refused and it was just as well that I did not know what was ahead of me as every push of the pedals brought me nearer my rendezvous with toil and trouble. I was not to know that I was about to work the hardest I ever had in my young life, even worse than the tattie howking, and backbreaking though that was, what made me drag my broken back out of bed at the crack of dawn the next day and go to the next farm was, I confess without an iota of shame, the money. I was never so rich in my life as during the tattie holidays. My pocket money in those days was 3d a week. It won't mean anything to the decimal generation but that was worth just over one new penny a week. You could buy a packet of Rowntrees' Fruit Gums with it or a packet of Spangles or three Penny Dainties. That was about it.

Ever since that experience on the dairy farm I have never grudged the price of a pint of milk because I know just how much work goes into producing it and if you have never got up with the sun and herded cows from pasture to the milking shed and milked them and taken them back to pasture again and shovelled tons of cow manure into a barrow and transported that to the dung heap and put down clean straw only for their ladyships to immediately open their bowels on top of it, and Niagara is nothing compared to the pee a cow can do, then you probably are one of those *do* moan about the price of milk.

Back then I did not buy the milk but I did silently curse my parents who had subjected me to this unpaid toil. And at the end of the day there was another trial to endure. They were not exactly a fun-loving couple, the Macs. Their idea of a good time was to read the Bible in the evening, aloud, before retiring early to bed, to give us the strength to do the same thing all over again on the morrow. That was bad enough, but then, one evening, Mr Mac handed me the Bible.

"Would you like to read us something, David?"

"Em . . . Er . . . What?" I stammered, appalled.

"Anything you like."

Blushing at being the centre of attention, I let the blessed book fall open in my hands and began to read the first words that met my eyes without scanning ahead first.

"How beautiful are thy feet with shoes, O prince's daughter! the joints of thy thighs are like jewels, the work of the hands of a cunning workman.

"Thy navel is like a round goblet, which wanteth not liquor: thy belly is like an heap of wheat set about with lilies.

"Thy two breasts are like two young roes that are twins."

By this time the words were swimming before my eyes, my throat had become strangely dry as if all the moisture in my body, (apart from my bladder, mercifully), had decided to transfer itself to my palms which were leaking profusely. I was aware of a dreadful silence in the room and my face became hotter and hotter yet I dared not look up to see if I had done enough to put us out of this misery, for I am sure the Macs were just as embarrassed as me. And so I ploughed on.

"*Thy neck is as a tower of ivory; thine eyes like the fishpools in Heshbon, by the gate of Bathrabbim: thy nose is as the tower of Lebanon which looketh toward Damascus.*

"*Thine head upon thee is like Carmel, and the hair of thine head like purple; the king is held in the galleries.*

"*How fair and how pleasant art thou, O love, for delights!*

"*This thy stature is like to a palm tree, and thy breasts to clusters of grapes.*

"*I said, I will go up to the palm tree, I will take hold of the boughs thereof: now also thy breasts shall be as clusters of the vine, and the smell of thy nose like apples . . .*"

And there I came to halt. My voice wouldn't work any more. All those breasts, which I knew were very rude things, had turned my Adam's apple into a stone that had become lodged in my throat. To my enormous relief, they took the Good Book from me and I fled to bed as soon as I decently could. In those days, I was not a disbeliever in God, just not very keen on Him as it was His fault I was subjected to boring old Sunday school week after week. If Sunday was the day of rest, how come was I being subjected to more school? Now, His sense of humour hardly encouraged me to become a fan. Of all the books in that fat book of his, He had to let it fall open at the *Song of Solomon*!

The feeling that I was the biggest fool in Christendom, never mind down here on the farm was reinforced the next day. Not the *Song of Solomon* this time but the bellow of Charlie. He was a Hereford bull and a mighty beast was he. He had a ring at the end of his nose from which slathering foam flew like spume when he snorted his utter contempt for us. As for me, I had nothing but respect for *him*. Well, all right, fear may be another word for it. Not for a price above rubies would I be tempted to go anywhere within a stomping hoof's distance of him. And then, fresh on the heels of my embarrassment and shame of the previous evening, the next day he broke loose from his pen. However, before he was able to make his bolt for freedom, or gore, or trample us to death in the process, somehow Mr Mac managed to grab the ring in his nose.

"Get a graip!" he yelled at me, over his shoulder, as he wrestled with the bull. "In the byre! Hurry!"

I sped off, very happy to leave the scene, as you can imagine. But in the byre I was faced with a dilemma. There were two graips, a good one and another with several of the prongs missing. Which to chose? Realising that speed was of the essence, I plumped for the broken one with some vague notion that Mr Mac was going to defend himself with it or prod the bull into some sort of submission like a bullfighter with his banderillas. In the course of this contest I reckoned that the graip may well come off second best so I plumped for the broken one, my reasoning being, better one really broken graip than two half-broken ones as the proverb nearly has it, and I bore it back, with not a little trepidation, to Mr Mac who was still hanging on to Charlie's nose, who, by the sounds of it, was far from amused at this treatment.

Mr Mac took one look at it. "What's that! What bloody use do you think that is, you bloody idiot! Get me a proper graip!"

Thank God he was a Christian or I may have been called worse. And maybe I was. To be honest, I don't remember what he shouted exactly, but it was obvious he was very, very angry and it was now plain to me that what I had brought was the graip of wrath.

My parents had often been angry with me but I had never experienced anything like this before, but then it would be hard to beat an angry bull and a furious man in a confined space for sheer undiluted, concentrated rage. Feeling more foolish than frightened, I didn't need to be yelled at twice and returned as quickly as I could with the right graip. Resisting any urge to stick it up my backside first, Mr Mac used it to break up a bale of hay. If only he had told me. It seems Charlie was famished and the inner beast inside being satisfied, he was pacified.

But I could not forget the way I had been shouted at. It wasn't that I resented that so much; it was because I had made a complete and utter fool of myself again and so soon after the Bible reading. It was clear to me that I was not cut out to be an orra loon.

Later that day I set in train the move towards my own freedom. I waited till teatime before announcing that I was really missing the scouts and I would be leaving in the morning. It was a good thing that my work was unpaid as it meant I was under no obligation to stay—I could just get on my bike. Besides, I reckoned, I had paid off my debt for the purloined stamps—with interest.

I was let off having to read the Bible that night, unsurprisingly. Later the next day I was back in the bosom of my family in time to hear a telephone conversation between my father and Mr Mac.

"He's never shown much of an interest in the scouts before," I heard my father say.

Thanks, dad for blowing my cover. But it was true. I didn't care for the scouts much. It seemed to me that we did not do a lot apart from stand at ease and fall out and our badges were given out rather than earned, yet I was made to go because my parents thought I should, or maybe they thought the dominie's son should show an example. I don't know, but one thing was for sure: having explained the reason for my premature return was because of the scouts, there was no way I was being let off that.

I have often wondered if Mr Mac had phoned to find out the lie of the land. Was he merely the kind and concerned ex-employer phoning to find out if I had got home safely or was he phoning to find out whether I had run home telling tales of slavery, raging bulls and religious zealotry?

He need not have worried. I have never mentioned these things until now.

Chapter Twenty-seven

Dangerous Liaisons

I think Number Two the Prefabs was occupied by Mrs Stewart and there are only two things I remember about her. The first was that she wore glasses, not because she needed them, or so it was rumoured, but because she found some frames that she thought suited her and so she snapped them up before they were bought by someone else. That shows how far-sighted she was. The second thing was she came over to the house one evening to report that she had heard my sister swearing very bad words indeed, over and over again. My parents' reaction was entirely predictable. Shocked to their foundations, they took down her knickers and skelped her bare bum—several times, I am sure.

It seems draconian now, and even then I thought so and felt not a little sibling sympathy. She must only have been six or seven. She wasn't swearing at anyone or about anything, just saying the words, going through the known repertoire with her pals. All she would have known was they were bad words—that would have been the thrill of the game. She would not have understood anything at all of what they meant. And whatever the limitations of her eyesight (and it looks as if there was nothing wrong with that) there was certainly nothing wrong with Mrs Stewart's hearing. Perhaps she *was* morally outraged, clyped out of a sense of public duty, but it seemed to me there was more satisfaction than regret in the way she delivered this bad news.

I couldn't swear to it, but I think at Number Three lived the Klims, as we called them. That is not their full name and I will not attempt to spell it. They were Polish, or at least the head of the family was, and it was in their back garden that Mrs Stewart overheard my sister commit the crime aforesaid with Ann, whom you have already met, and others.

Her brother, Richard, must have been a year younger than me, as was David who lived next door to him at Number Four. I don't remember David's father, nor his sister, but I do remember his mother because she was lame and because she was given to telling prodigious porky pies, none of which I can remember unfortunately. Probably she did not see herself as a liar; no doubt she had convinced herself that her version of the events was the way it was. Maybe she invented these fantastical events to make her humdrum life more interesting.

At one point she was the school cleaner which I knew worried my father as she did it very inefficiently and the problem duly arose about bringing her deficiencies to her attention and finally having to tell her that her services were no longer required. It is not a task many people would have found easy, especially in such a tiny community where you could not avoid rubbing shoulders on a daily basis, but for my father for whom decision-making did not come easily, it was a particularly horny dilemma. I have no idea what David's father did to earn a crust but the most likely thing was he was a farm labourer or worked at the nearby quarry. In any case, I imagine money was in fairly short supply and "crust" would have been the operative word. And another thing that my father would have had to consider was the difficulty in obtaining a replacement as I think she got the job by default in the first place.

I clearly remember her on one occasion as she stood at the end of the road that led up to the prefabs shouting down to, and at, my father as he delved in his garden. What it was about I don't remember, but probably had something to do with her dismissal and I remember my father interrupting her harangue to say, "That is a damned lie and you know it!"

I also remember her paying me in kind to go to the shops for her because her own David refused to go. When my parents got to hear of it, they said that I was not to go either, but when your pocket money was only threepence a week, a little extra source of the sugary sort was not to be sneezed at. Her son should have run this errand of course; she certainly could not have gone there herself as the nearest shop was more than a mile away. She and I saw no harm in doing us both a good turn, so whenever called upon, and if I could do so without detection, which was pretty often, I did the needful. It didn't take me long on my bike.

My bike and I were inseparable and gave me not just a great deal of pleasure but a sense of independence and freedom that I was not to experience for years later until I passed my driving test and was allowed to borrow the family car. Before that mechanical form of transport, I transformed my beloved bike into a motorbike by the application of two pieces of cardboard to the back fork which made a most pleasing sound as they were struck by the spokes. I also fitted an odometer and if my memory serves me well, it went round the clock. That is to say I did more than a thousand miles. I particularly loved cycling in the snow, making tracks and deliberately skidding.

But back to the Klims. Mr K was one of those people who was gifted with his hands. He always finished first in the annual Hallowe'en neep lantern competition though it was meant to be done by the pupils themselves. Have you ever tried hollowing out a turnip? In the olden days, they could have made the convicts to do that instead of breaking stones. He was also a very talented artist who could just draw something straight off in seconds, such as a donkey that we could pin a tail on at parties, but his *pièce de résistance* for me, and certainly the envy of us all, was his sledge.

Slatted and sleekly curved, it was the very Rolls Royce of sledges and could outpace my sledge (and my sister's) by a mile. Ours was made by our father with hemispherical runners commissioned from Mr MacDonald, and very grateful I was for it too. It could travel like a bullet on ice, but on fresh snow it would sink up to the boards that formed the seat, especially if anyone was sitting on it, leaving a smooth flat trail behind as opposed to the two parallel lines left by Mr K's. Apart from the one used by Richard and Ann, he made one which was raffled in aid of school funds and a disappointing day it was for me when I did not win it.

And whilst we are on the subject of sledges, here is another very bad thing that I did, this anecdote courtesy of my sister whose memory and the veracity of this tale I do not doubt, though I have not the slightest recollection of it. The school entrance lay at the top of a slope that led down to the road. The playground here was slick with snow, compacted hard under the tread of countless feet and the occasional vehicle, such as our car, an ideal runway for our heavy sledge. There is something else you should know and that is that across the gate there were a couple of parallel iron bars whose purpose was to prevent us kids from running straight out onto the road. But they were also very good for swinging on and doing exercises on such as turning head over heels, like gymnasts.

So there we were, pelting down the slope, me in the front, my trusting sister at the back, expressly told not to hold on to me as that would be "cissy" and unable to see anything ahead of her except my back, which suddenly disappeared from view as I rolled off just the moment before we reached the barriers. That denting of the bar with her head may well have saved her life, for had that brake not been there, who's to know that a car might not have come along at that precise moment and printed its tyre track on her forehead instead? Far better a duck egg than that I am sure, just as I am sure I must have explained to her that that that was the plan all along, that I would tell her when to roll off and that the sledge would just have to take its chance—as well as any passing motorist.

But I had not reckoned on the split-second reaction required for such a manoeuvre and that is why she came a cropper. It was not a deliberate attempt at sororicide. If it had been, it failed miserably. With the application of some butter, which was the tried and tested panacea for bumps on the head in those days, my sister was as right as rain again in a few moments and as far as we are able to tell, she suffered no lasting brain damage. Likewise, after a longer passage of time, I was able to sit on my backside again. To be honest, I don't know if I was punished in this way for this latest bad thing, but I would have thought it more likely than not, for just as butter on a bump made that better, what would make this bad boy better (or so my parents believed), was a bloody good belting on the backside with a bamboo cane.

I wouldn't say I had a death wish like the lovers in *Ethan Frome* (which the sledge incident reminded me of) but a crazy thing I did was to go on my bike to the top of the road where the prefabs were, pedal like hell until my legs could not go round any faster, then stop pedalling and crouch as low as I could over the handlebars and without looking to the right to see what might be coming, but hugging the verge as closely as I could, shoot out onto the main road. The aim was to see how far I could freewheel along the road, the same road where my sister might have been run over had it not been for that bar. My distant goal was the road that led up to Ternemny Farm and the quarry but I never quite made it so I had to keep on trying again and again . . .

How many times I attempted suicide by this method I could not say, but here I am to tell the tale, unscathed. It's just as well my parents never knew about this insanity or I am sure they would have impounded my bike which would have been tantamount to cutting off my legs. All I can say is that in those days there were fewer cars about but of course the longest odds do come up once in a while and just at the other side of Glenbarry, about four miles away from where I was doing my death-defying stunts, and about as many years later, another boy, the brother of a schoolmate at Keith Grammar School, was not so lucky when he was hit and killed by Sammy's father when he was making deliveries in his van.

He was not at fault and even if he had been, you can imagine the devastating effect it had on him. I don't know the precise circumstances of that incident but it could just as easily have been me. Not only did I not stop at the bottom of the road but it never occurred to me to stop and think what effect my death would have had on the poor, unsuspecting driver, not to mention my parents, and yea, even my sister to whom I was not the best of brothers, as you will see.

Apart from his sledge contribution, Mr Klim was a good servant to the school in another way. I am not sure where he worked exactly, but he drove a bulldozer and he was able to borrow it in order to level our playing field. I am sure that this contributed substantially to our prowess on the football field and the running track. Every year, in Keith, the Keith and District Inter-school Sports were held, and year after year the Shield was won by Ternemny Primary School. In eight years, there was only one year in which we failed to win it and when there was no more room for any more of the little metal shields on the Shield itself, we were allowed to keep it in perpetuity. Perpetuity in this case only meant a few more years. Ternemny was downgraded to a one-teacher school in 1962 and closed its doors to pupils for the last time only a few years after that.

My last year was the most successful year in the sporting history of the school where we carried all before us. As well as the Shield aforesaid, our gold and green hoops struck terror into the opposition teams as we won the Football Cup and the Football League, while the girls, only to be slightly outdone, won the Rothiemay &

District Netball League. I have to admit that our success on the football park was hardly due to me, where my position at left back usually meant I was left out much of the time, leaving it to others to score the goals while the midfield generally prevented raids on our territory. On the rare occasions when they did break through and I was called into action, it did not matter too much if I failed, for there was always the last line of our defence, our goalkeeper, Archie Mitchell, (or was it Alex Kellas?) who despite his diminutive size, was a goalkeeper par excellence, not afraid to fling himself to the ground in any direction required to keep his goal intact, like you see professionals do today.

On the running track however, I came into my own. I was fleet of foot and fitter than the proverbial fiddle and why should I not be, being outdoors most of the time, running as wild as heather in the woods or riding my bike which, incidentally, I learned to ride by dint of holding onto the playing field wall, then letting go, picking myself up from the unforgiving tarmac, dusting myself down, swabbing the grazed knees with what I am sure was an insanitary handkerchief and starting all over again. There were never any such things as fairy wheels in my day. Even if there had been we would have rejected them as being for cissies.

My knees were often grazed since I wore only short trousers (and was prone to falling over or scraping them on the trees I climbed). I am not sure when I graduated into long trousers but I know I was still wearing shorts when I first went to Keith Grammar. They were really a symbol of boyhood and immaturity, the day I graduated into long trousers being a symbol that I had made some rite of passage, passed into the next stage of growing up.

Sex, is of course one of those rites of passage too and I had my first sexual experience when I was nine or maybe I had just reached the tender age of ten. It was Mrs Klim senior, Richard's granny, who initiated me, and what you are about to read is the world premier of this defining moment in anyone's life, never mind that of a naive young boy.

I remember it well, as I suppose one does, though mercifully a bit of a veil has been drawn over some of the more grizzly details. We were in the kitchen of Richard's prefab and his granny, a big, stout woman, was sitting at the table doing something like shelling peas. Richard and I were fresh from shooting down scores of Indians with our trusty branches of beech and as innocent as strawberries, to borrow Dylan Thomas's simile. Come to think of it, maybe that is what she was doing, husking strawberries, fresh from Mr Campbell's garden of course, just across the road. (There were prefabs on only one side of the road, so extensive was Mr Campbell's garden.)

Richard's parents were out, Ann was possibly playing (or swearing) with my sister and the other squaws out of the sight and sound of Mrs Stewart, though I am sure my sister never did it again, and even to this day, would never dream of uttering a wee sweary word, even if she hit her thumb with a hammer. There is just no substitute for having your knickers pulled down and bad habits knocked out. I never wore them, which no doubt explains why, despite all the bamboo canings, I still grew up bad.

So there were just the three of us in the house. She was one of those jovial people, Richard's granny, the kind whose every sentence is punctuated with gales of laughter at their own wit. But when she suggested that we should take down our trousers and show her our pinklers, I didn't find it in the least amusing. We never mentioned sex in our household. Even when it was "discovered" in the Sixties, it passed our family by as I mentioned earlier. But once again I am getting ahead of myself. There will be more sex later.

"Amusing" would be the understatement of 1957 as far as I was concerned. Too terrified to flee, I was rooted to the spot. Next moment the lady had exposed her not insubstantial breasts to us and while I was still in shock, she grabbed me by the wrist and before I knew it, my hand was being rubbed across the strangely heavy, flabby, pendulous pieces of flesh with the hard knobbly bits at the end, the likes of which I had never seen before and certainly never dreamt I would ever see until I was much, much older—if I were lucky enough to live long enough and could persuade a lady to let me have a peek. I knew they were called "paps" and I knew they were one of the distinguishing features between a man and a woman but I don't think I realised then that apart from their functional purpose, they were also designed to be squeezy toys for big boys and men.

"How's your pinkler now?" Richard's granny laughed, making a grab for my crotch in jest or in earnest and laughing more uproariously still at seeing the stricken look of terror on my face, but making contact only with air as I suddenly regained the power of my limbs and stepped smartly backwards, just in the nick of time.

Naturally I kept a wide berth from my would-be teacher in matters sexual after that and of course never mentioned the incident to my parents. That would have been excruciatingly embarrassing. I didn't even have the vocabulary, only the rude names that I had heard Harry say and which I knew I would get a good hiding for if I ever so much as whispered them in our house.

But Richard's granny was not the only member of his family that I needed to beware of. His Uncle Peter was a serious lunatic. The Wild West was the woods on our doorstep, as I have already said, and although we did not get a set until 1958, I was brought up on a diet of TV Westerns and used to see the *Lone Ranger* and also non-cowboy fare such as *Whirly Birds* and *Circus Boy* at Richard's house and maybe even at David's too.

We regularly had gunfights with our rifle branches and six-shooter sticks but Richard and his Uncle Peter did it for real with real airguns and real pellets. I remember Richard having to have a pellet removed from his forehead just above his nose because he had been stupid enough to stick his head out from behind a tree during one of their duels in the woods. At the same time they took a pellet out of his left palm. That was because Uncle Peter had told him that if you put your hand up really close to the barrel, it was so close that it would miss. And Richard believed him. Maybe Peter believed it himself.

He was big, more bear than man, with a deep growl of a voice and very poor English, unlike Richard's dad whom I don't remember as even having an accent, although I can't visualise his face. I have no idea how long the brothers had been in the country, but I expect they came over during, or just after, the war. Maybe Peter came later after his brother had reconnoitred the place and which may well explain the difference in their ability with the language. He was a regular visitor to

Richard's house on his motorbike and on one occasion he gave Richard and me a lift on his pillion to the scouts.

What were my parents thinking about? No helmets of course, none of us. The "You Know It Makes Sense" campaign to wear crash helmets was still many years in the future. Peter made no concession to speed and hardly any to corners. Thank God there were only two of them as we tilted over to take them without any appreciable loss of speed, I clinging on for dear life to Richard's waist, who in turn, could scarcely have had a secure tenure of his uncle's broad midriff. If he fell off so would I, just had I allowed my sister to put her arms round my waist, she might have been spared the duck's egg on her forehead.

Apart from the scarcity of corners, the only other good thing that could be said in favour of this whirlwind journey was that it didn't last very long. I think we had to walk back, much to my relief because no matter how terrified I was, I still would not have had the guts to admit that I was too scared to do it again. It was not so much death I was scared off—in those days I more or less considered myself immortal—no, it's just that if I fell off the bike at that speed I knew it would be very, very sore. Death was the last thing I feared.

There were, thank God, gentler and less scary moments and pursuits. In the playground, just outside one of the shelters where we could take cover if it was raining (we were banned from the school during playtime), was set a hole with an iron rim about two inches in diameter. This was for a game of "bools". I doubt if young people today have ever heard of such an innocent pastime, so I will briefly explain that the object of the game was to get your big glass bool into the hole, while at the same time trying to hit your opponents' bools. If you struck one, you were allowed to keep it. For this purpose, after you had had your throw, you replaced your big bool with a smaller bool, about half the size. They had coloured centres so you knew whose was whose.

An innocent pastime you may have thought and so it was until Richard arrived one day with a juggernaut of a bool which his father had procured for him at his work. It was a ball bearing, a massive heavy thing, a Leviathan that carried all before it, so heavy that it just rolled over the bumpy surface of playground without deviating from its terrible path, unlike our lightweight glass bools which were prone to strike off at any tangent on the uneven terrain. This made it easy for him to land in the hole, the prize for which was the confiscation of our bools. But that's not all: Richard had another weapon in his armoury. His small bool was a tiny ball bearing which was almost impossible to hit as our big glass one would usually just bounce over it and if perchance we did mange to hit it, he would give us one of his, or rather one of our little glass ones back, not the tiny, silver ball bearing. It was a bit like a battle where one army had swords and the other had rifles. How long we put up with this senseless slaughter I can't remember. Probably we just refused to play with him until we played on a more level playing field, so to speak.

One slightly more risky game we played was called "knifie". We all had penknives in those days. You started off with your feet together and the object of the game was to throw the knife at a point somewhere near your opponent's feet and he had to move his foot to where the knife stuck quivering in the ground. The winner was the one who was left standing and still able to throw the knife. In a variation, you started off with your legs as far apart as you could and the winner of the game was the last to bring the opponent's feet together. Naturally, as the game progressed, it got more and more exciting.

There were a lot of lame boys hobbling about Ternemny in those days. No, not really. There were some close shaves but I don't remember anyone ever being injured. I don't know why the rules did not state that it had to be played barefoot. That would have made it vastly more interesting.

One activity I considered far more risky and daring was climbing what we called the "Slippery Slope". It was on the edge of the wood, a massive beech that had been blown over in a storm sometime before our arrival. Maybe the storm of 1953. It held a greater attraction to us over other trees as it provided a challenge, a challenge I regret to say I never managed to achieve. The trunk was thick, too thick to get your arms or thighs right round and at an angle of 45 degrees, it was not long before you could see how far it was to fall should you slip. I didn't fancy that hard landing where I could hit my head on a stone or be impaled on something spiky, so before I made it to the first branch, I chickened out and slithered down again to terra firma.

I would call it too much imagination. My sister's friend, Mary, probably would have called it cowardice had she seen me, but I made sure there was no-one around to witness my pathetic efforts. I did, however, see her shin up it like a squirrel and once ensconced on the lower branches, she hauled my sister up. After that it was easy. There were branches aplenty. They do grow on trees as a matter of fact.

Naturally pride prevented me from asking for any such assistance and once she had got over that initial hurdle, my sister was able to climb the Slippery Slope unaided. And so it was that she, four years younger than me, achieved greater heights than I did. This and the Slippery Slope turned out to be a metaphor for our lives and life in general, though I failed to realise it at the time.

She was a striking redhead, Mary. They made a formidable pair, the two of them, both redheads and more boyish than some boys at Ternemny I could name, but won't. The friendship lasted until Mary left Ternemny to go to Ordiquhill, then the following year, my sister went to Keith Grammar and so they saw little of each other after that and nothing at all after we moved to Deskford. It was sometime during this period that the great national scandal concerning Mary broke.

But for that you will have to wait until another chapter.

Chapter Twenty-eight

Some Amazing Coincidences

In 1976 when I exchanged the hills and arguably the even lovelier littoral of Bonnie Galloway for the cooling towers and miles upon miles of intestinal-looking pipes of Grangemouth's petrochemical industry in order to take up my post as Principal Teacher of English at Abbotsgrange Middle School, practically the first thing my new colleagues wanted to know was if I was related to a pupil of the same name who was creating havoc in the classrooms. I was able to confidently put my hand on my heart and declare that I had no relatives in these parts.

And so, when I saw in the local paper a certain Gordon Addison appearing almost weekly at Falkirk Sheriff Court, I paused only briefly to wonder if he could be a relation before dismissing the possibility. Let there be no misunderstanding: far from being a serial criminal, Gordon was appearing on behalf of the ungodly, and for all I know, amongst his clients he might well number that other family of Addisons who really were nothing to do with us, your honour. Honest.

As it happens, Gordon *did* turn out to be a relation, a third cousin in fact, and the time has now come to reveal that amazing coincidence I promised you so long ago (Chapter Ten) that you have probably forgotten all about it.

I did not know it then, nor, I am pretty sure, did my father. I certainly never heard him mention it, but approximately ten years before we moved to Ternemny, the schoolhouse had been occupied by another family of Addisons—Lilian and her two sons, Alexander (Sandy) and William (Willie). Lillian was the widow of my grandfather's youngest brother, Alexander John Wright Addison, to give him his full handle. He was apprenticed to a lawyer's in Banff but aged about nineteen, was diverted from pursuing a possibly dusty legal career when he was seduced by a Swiss company into seeking adventure in far-off Ceylon as a tea planter instead.

He was born on the 7th July 1894 at Summertown. That made him twenty years younger than my grandfather, the oldest child. On one of his furloughs back home, and staying at his brother William's farm at Cruats, he met Lilian Mair, a teacher in Portknockie. She was born in Rathven on 21st March 1898. It was then that he made another life-changing decision. Reader, he married her.

But just think what an enormous decision it was for her too, to trust herself to this young man, to leave home and family behind at a time when the world was much bigger than it is today. It must have taken a lot of courage to leave the security of the life she knew and take that giant leap into the unknown. But perhaps that's not how she saw it all. She was a woman in love and perhaps had a romantic sense of adventure, just like her husband. But little did she know that the adventure would be cruelly cut short and she would find herself on the way back home all too soon . . .

Their first son, Sandy, was born on 30th August 1930 at Atchencoil Tea Estate, Kalthuritty, in what was at that time the Kingdom of Travancore in the southern tip of India. An exotic place to be born, for sure. Slavery was not abolished until 1855 (which made it a lot earlier than a lot of other places) though it was notorious throughout India for its rigid adherence to the caste system. Then in 1936, in a landmark ruling, the last Maharajah of Travancore permitted the lowest castes of Hindus to enter temples where only the upper castes had been permitted before. Having said that, in the 1920s, under the reign of Sir Rama Varma (1885-1924), Travancore was considered enlightened compared to most other Indian states in the matters of education, medicine and even the enfranchisement of women. Today it is part of what we call "Kerala".

Atchencoil had originally been a coffee estate but after a severe attack of blight, it was decided to switch to tea, and Alexander was dispatched from Ceylon to oversee the transition. It was situated on a hillside in dense forest—jungle would not be an exaggeration, home to exotic animals such as tigers, leopards and snakes, which some may regard as more repulsive than exotic. With neighbours such as these, being a good shot was a handy accomplishment, a skill which Alexander already possessed and which the new bride soon acquired. Home for them was a bungalow, the last few miles reached either by Shanks's Pony or by horseback, so being able to ride was another skill that Lilian needed to master and the sooner the better, for her sake.

It was in this exotic and remote location that Sandy was born. The doctor in attendance was Dr H. T. Somervell of Mt Everest fame. In May 1922, he and the more famous Mallory reached the height of 8,170 meters—26,804 feet or 2,231 feet from the top—before having to turn back as they realised in their exhausted state and suffering from frostbite, they would not be able to make the summit before nightfall. That remained a world altitude record until Somervell himself broke it in June 1924, accompanied by Edward Norton when they reached a height of 8,570 meters (28,116 feet, a mere 919 feet short of their target), a height not surpassed until the 1952 Expedition, unless of course you believe Mallory and Irvine did reach the summit—still a matter of speculation today.

As a matter of fact, Mallory and Irvine passed Somervell and Norton who were on their way down, and Mallory, having realised by this time that he had forgotten his camera, borrowed Somervell's. It is documented that he and Mallory read Shakespeare to each other in their tent on the 1922 expedition and therefore Somervell must have been very familiar with Polonius' advice to his son Laertes: "Neither a borrower nor a lender be" but he chose to ignore it. And quite rightly too, though he was not to know that that was the last time he was to see his friend, or his camera. Although Mallory's body was found in 1999, unfortunately the camera was not—the camera that might have proved that Mallory and Norton *had* made it to the summit, or had not, for that matter. The chances are small, but who knows, it might turn up one day and settle the question forever.

However, before that incident and after the 1922 expedition, Somervell, in another remarkable expedition, explored the Indian subcontinent from north to south. And there, at the very tip, he came across the medical mission in Neyyoor with one poor surgeon, Dr S.H. Pugh struggling to cope alone, often performing ten to eighteen operations a day, and he vowed to come back after his second expedition to Everest. He was as good as his word and returned in the August of 1924 but the following year returned to England to get married. Bringing his bride back with him to Neyyoor, he stayed there from 1926 till 1949, and that is how it came to pass that his and Sandy's paths crossed.

Sandy's brother, Willie, arrived less than a year later on the 18th July 1931. He was not born at home but at the residence of Judge Byers in Racecourse Road, Coimbatore where, in the event of an emergency, medical facilities were closer to hand. The judge was a friend of Alexander's.

Unfortunately on 11th April 1936 Alexander was just too far away from medical help himself. He was back in Ceylon by this time, managing two estates at Kinellan, Bandarawela and at Clarendon, Nuwara Eliya. It was at the former that he developed appendicitis, the nearest hospital in Colombo was hours and hours away, and he died of peritonitis aged only 41.

And so it was, aged only 38, that Lilian found herself a widow far from home and with two small boys aged five and four to support. She returned to Scotland, to the North-East and to her former profession. It was not long before she became headmistress at Tomnavoulin, Glenlivet, in the heart of whisky country and after a spell there, she moved to Ternemny sometime in the 1940s.

Naturally, they stayed in the schoolhouse, as did we. The headteacher was required to in those days in fact. Sandy and Willie slept in the big room to the right of the stairs (my parents' bedroom), Lilian slept across the corridor on the left (my sister's room) and my bedroom was at the back where the maid slept. Our maid slept with my father, fortunately for me, as it meant I could have a room of my own.

Sandy and Willie, like me after them, went to Keith Grammar, but their experience was totally different from mine. As you will see in the next chapter, I absolutely hated it, whereas Sandy loved it. He was a diligent pupil who ended up as *Proxime Accessit*. As well as devoting time to his studies, Sandy was also keen on sports, also unlike me. He played outside left for the school football team as well as tennis and indulged in some boxing too. So, although I followed in his footsteps chronologically speaking, that is where the similarity between Sandy and me begins and ends.

When Willie left school to become a nautical engineer with Hall's in Aberdeen, it made sense for Lilian to give up her post in Ternemny. She secured a teaching job at Kittybrewster on the outskirts of the city, while Sandy attended Aberdeen Grammar for a year before beginning his medical studies at the University.

I don't suppose she taught him how to dribble, probably that was an innate skill he had had since birth, but one of Lilian's protégés at Kittybrewster was Denis Law, the striker for Scotland and Manchester United (though he also played for other clubs). Non-football fans (such as my wife) may need to have it explained to them that this means that his job was not to throw down his tools for more remuneration, but to score goals, which Denis did with amazing proficiency.

Incidentally, on the subject of Kittybrewster, there is in Blyth, Northumberland, a trading estate, a county council estate, and best of all a pub, all rejoicing under this name, as well as (and I am sure you will not have forgotten), a street named after my illustrious seafaring ancestors, the Tates. As to the origin of the name, a certain inhabitant of Blyth will be disappointed to learn that the name is not derived from one of his ancestors, nor was Kitty a man as he imagines he discovered during his genealogical researches, but in fact the name comes from the Celtic *Cuitan Briste*, meaning "broken fold".

Lilian was succeeded at Ternemny by the Browns who created the vacancy for my father by moving to Rathven. She was the middle of three sisters, Maggie and Cathy, but between Lilian and Cathy, there was the tragic brother, Alex, born in 1900.

He suffered from "sleepy sickness" not sleeping sickness, please note, nothing whatever to do with the tsetse fly and probably would be better known today had it not been for the more famous and devastating Spanish Flu epidemic of 1918 which killed 50 million people, thus relegating the carnage of the First World War into a poor second as the biggest killer of this new century, and it barely begun. This sleeping sickness epidemic raged round the world from 1916 to 1928 when it stopped as suddenly as it started. It is estimated that it carried off more than a million people. But some things are worse than death. If it didn't kill you, you could be left entrapped in your body, unable to respond to stimuli, like a statue. If you were not in a coma, that is.

Onset of the disease was rapid. It began with a sore throat accompanied by a headache then a high fever, bodily tremors, severe muscular pain, stiffness of the neck, double vision, hallucinations and a feeling of incredible lethargy, hence its official name of *encephalitis lethargica.* Some made a partial recovery but were left with physical problems such as impairment to their vision but even worse were the personality changes, some victims becoming permanently psychotic.

Even today it remains a mysterious illness. Although there has never been another epidemic, individual cases have been reported and it is thought that the most likely cause is the body's over-reaction to the bacteria that caused the sore throat, causing the immune system to go into overdrive and attack and destroy the nerve cells of the brain. There is still no effective long-lasting cure, and back in Alex's time, the solution was to commit the victim to a mental institution, which is precisely what happened to him. He was admitted to Ladysbridge Asylum just outside Banff and there he died on 11th June 1963 having spent the majority of his life in that institution. He is buried in Portknockie with his parents: Maggie who died on 14th August 1933 and Alex (Alexis to distinguish him from the great number of other Alexanders in those parts) who died on 25th May 1935.

Their daughter, Maggie, married George Bruce Addison and this is where it gets interesting—and not a little confusing. George was the son of Joseph Addison, the first provost of Portknockie, whom you may recall, along with his brother Alecky, was the one who scoffed Ramsay MacDonald's tea. This marriage meant of course, that George automatically became Sandy and Willie's uncle, but he was already a relation of theirs through the Addison line. You may want to look at the Portknockie chart to help you get your head round it, but what it boils down to is that Joseph the Provost and Alexander the Tea Planter were first cousins and that makes Sandy and his Uncle George second cousins. Simple really.

Everyone knows the adage *Truth is stranger than fiction* but not everyone may be aware that Mark Twain added *because Fiction is obliged to stick to possibilities: Truth isn't*. And here is another of the interesting little facts I promised I would reveal and something that you would never put in a work of fiction, not if you wanted your reader to believe you weren't straying into the realm of fantasy.

Alexander Addison, (Alecky the Baker) like his brother George and their father, Joseph, before them, were all JPs, as you may remember. But that's not it. Like William of Cruats, my grandfather's brother, or to put it another way, his first cousin twice removed (that took some working out, believe me), Alecky married twice. Mary Queen of Scots famously had four Maries [sic] but Alecky was not so greedy, he only had two.

His first Mary, Mary Bruce Mair, died on 9th March 1934 aged only 40. She was three years younger than him. The second Mary, Mary Bruce, was born in 1914 and was *twenty-three years* younger which gave her a head start when it came to the widowhood stakes. And indeed she was widowed for fifty-six years, longer than Alecky himself managed to remain alive in fact. He was 54. She died in Brig O' Dee hospital, Banchory, in 2001 aged 87.

Alecky is buried with his first wife (I wonder what Mary Two thought of that) along with his parents in the family plot. Mary Two lies nearby, next to his brother George and his wife, sleeping the Big Sleep on her own. But then she was used to that anyway, so she probably didn't mind. Mary One had a prior claim after all.

George and Margaret's tombstone bears the legend: *It is not death to die.* I think that is quite good actually but eternity is a hell of a long time to sleep on your own, so I hope Mary Two is not repenting in sorrow at her long, long sleep alone with no-one to talk to.

So there you have it. Alecky's first Mary was a Mair and his second was a Bruce. And let us not forget that brother George's wife was a Mair too, nor that their grandmother was Elizabeth Bruce from whom George received his middle name. Now, wouldn't it be interesting if George's first sister-in-law, Mary Bruce Mair, came from the same line of Bruces and wouldn't it be even more interesting if his second came from them too? In a place like Portknockie, it's a pretty safe punt to put your pension on them being related in some sort of way, but how exactly I leave that to future genealogists or family members to investigate and befuddle their brains. The men may have gone down to the sea in ships, but when it came to choosing a wife, they preferred to pick a girl from the home port. Talk about a tight-knit community! As tight as the knitting I tried at Ternemny which got so tight it was impossible to create another stitch after a row or two.

Cathy, Lilian's sister, (you remember Lilian, don't you, after this diversion down the Addison branch line?) was also a primary school teacher. She taught at Portessie, just to the east of Buckie. It has a nickname, "the Sloch", short for Rottenslough, which was the name of the original fishing village until the new village wisely rebranded itself as Portessie. Cathy never married and lived with her grandmother. She died aged 70 on 31st September 1976.

Nell, her grandmother, was a big, strong woman who in her nineties, could still thraw the neck of a chicken and who, in her younger days, used to give a piggyback to her fisherman husband through the swell to his boat so he could at least start off with dry clothes even if they were wringing later. This was common practice all along the Moray Firth where, in the absence of a harbour, the boats had to set off from the shore.

Lilian died on 20th August 1972 in Buckie hospital as the result of a cerebral thrombosis. She was 73. She had had a previous stroke in 1954 which had left her with paralysis of the left side. She was able to walk but lost all use of her left arm and hand. This forced her to retire early and she moved back to Portknockie where she lived with the help of a housekeeper. This unfortunate event sadly also put an end to her golfing. In her prime, she played for Banffshire. But she remained remarkably active in other ways, flying down to see Sandy and his wife, Joan, in Glasgow and even winning a quiz show on Grampian TV. Obviously although the motor skills were impaired, there was nothing wrong with the brain cells.

She is buried along with many of her relatives in Hillhead cemetery, Portknockie. The headstone also pays tribute to Alexander John, her husband, whose death is correctly recorded as 11th April 1936, aged 41, as opposed to the memorial in Fordyce Old Cemetery which gives the date of death as 5th April and his age as 43.

The stone in Portknockie also records the death of their son William who died in Australia on 29th December 2006 aged 75. Some of his ashes were scattered on Lilian's grave; some were, according to his wishes, scattered in the mighty Brahmaputra which, in its 2,191 mile journey from its origins in Tibet before it disgorges itself into the Bay of Bengal, undergoes many changes of name. But when it flows through Assam, where in some places it is as much as six miles wide, the Brahmaputra is what it is known as, and it's Assam that we are interested in because after qualifying as a marine engineer in 1952, that's where Willie, like his father Alexander before him, became a tea planter. He started off by using his engineering skills in the factory and during the course of his five-year contract he was trained in the art of estate management. When that contract was over, he signed up for another five years and there he remained for the next thirty!

By this time he had married a civil servant, Peggy Cowie, from—you'll never guess—Portknockie. As part of her trousseau, whatever other fripperies it may have contained, Willie, a keen fisherman, was equally keen that she brought with her an outboard motor for his boat, not only to his precise specification but place of provenance also. Failure to comply with this modest proposal and procure the said article, one gets the feeling, would have created a serious setback to the marriage. But Peggy came up with the goods and they went on to produce two children, George and Kerim. Like his Great-uncle George in Portknockie, George is a committed Labour supporter. Until recently he was Advisor at the Office of Senator for Queensland, the Hon Joe Ludwig, Minister for Agriculture, Fisheries and Forestry in the Julia Gillard administration.

After Assam, Willie and family spent a year in Malawi followed by a year in Papua and New Guinea. There were no roads in PNG, never mind any schools, so that is why Willie bailed out of the tea industry, ending up as a railway engineer in Sandgate, a northern suburb of Brisbane, Queensland. Peggy is still alive in a nursing home in Sandgate.

Sandy, I am glad to say, at the time of writing, is still with us too and very far indeed from being in any home except his own. He had a distinguished medical career and was awarded an MBE for services to medicine in the 1996 New Year's Honours List which he received from the Princess Royal at Holyrood the following May. Now, amongst other things, he spends his time golfing and curling but I will say no more about him here. Should you want to find out more, you will find he occupies nearly half a page in *Who's Who in Scotland* published by Carrick Media. Your local library is sure to have a copy.

Chapter Twenty-nine

Keith Grammar: The Bullying and the Bus

The halcyon days were drawing to a close. If I did not realise that I was in heaven during the Ternemny days, I knew by reputation that Keith Grammar School was hell. And when I got there my fears were well founded.

The 11-plus exam which separated sheep from goats, those who were to go to Keith Grammar to pursue an academic course and those who were to follow a technical course at Ordiquhill—that dreaded day was drawing nearer and my father began running coaching classes after school. That was another class which I could, of course, not avoid, nor did I want to, for I knew that a technical course would not suit me. Whatever weaknesses my head had, I knew my hands were even worse. I was, what you may call, "handless". There was nothing I could do about it. I just happened to be at the end of the skills queue when they were being handed out. I was probably still in bed when it started.

I expect the authorities frowned on these classes (I presume my father was not the only one offering this service) lest some goats got mixed up with the sheep, but what's a dominie who wants the best for his pupils to do? The non-academics did not attend anyway; it was more a way of ensuring that the potential academics overcame this hurdle that could determine their entire future.

So there were not many of us in this class, maybe just two. At any rate, only one other in my class (of seven remember) made it to Keith Grammar School. She went into a B class, while clever clogs himself, went into an A class. I was the dux after all. Her older sister had gone before, and so it was that the three of us cycled (I can't imagine that we did it in convoy, but perhaps we did) the two miles or so up to Glenbarry where we left our bikes at Mrs Cheyne's back door and caught the bus to school. This was done by prior arrangement, an agreement between my parents and Mrs Cheyne. The sisters had no such agreement but parked their bikes there too anyway since they saw me do it.

"Bloomin' cheek!" remarked Mrs Cheyne to my parents later. Not that she minded really; it was all the same to her whether there was one bike or three but she would have liked to have been asked, as would anyone. The girls' mother was known as "The Duchess". I'm not entirely sure why exactly, but perhaps the bikes story gives us a clue. I do not remember the girls' father, though I am sure there was one. I think he might have been a van driver. They all lived happily together in their stately mansion at Number Six, the Prefabs.

On my first day at Keith Grammar, however, I made my rendezvous with Mrs Cheyne's back door alone. It was well known that bullying was rife at Keith Grammar, where every new boy was put through the gauntlet. There was an old air-raid shelter in the playground next to a wall, creating a narrow passage. The bullies would line up on each side, the victim would be fed in at the top and punched and kicked as he ran down the line, just as quickly as he possibly could of course. By way of a variation, you might have your back put against a tree, your arms held behind your back by a couple of thugs while a third punched you in the belly, not to mention of course, that old chestnut, your head being flushed down the loo.

The headmaster and staff were well aware of this yet did not even attempt to stop it. Which made Keith Grammar School the equal, if you take bullying as the criterion, of some of the most prestigious Public Schools in England, apart from the fact it didn't cost the parents a penny, apart from what they paid in their taxes.

As the last remaining days of the holiday sped by, my mind was concentrated on how I was ever going to survive the first day at this illustrious establishment. Strange to say, I was not (and still am not) much addicted to physical pain and would rather avoid it if I possibly could. Thus, on the first day you would have seen a look of misery and apprehension on the morning face of this fresh-faced loon as he cycled most unwillingly to his rendezvous with fate. But I had a plan.

The plan was that I would bale out of the bus before it got to Keith at Newmill, a few miles out of Keith. My father had friends there. It was at Newmill that he began his teaching career and his friends were his former landlord and landlady. They happened to have twins and fortuitously, they too were to be joining class IA. It was love at first sight for me, when I saw Kathleen with her lustrous ringlets of auburn locks. That was before school started and it was some small compensation that when it did, I would be in the same class as her and see her every day. So out went Bobina and in came Kathleen. It was the start of a new life, this transition to secondary school and I never saw Bobina again.

And like the relationship with Bobina, my romance with Kathleen was another non-event. I never declared an interest, went out of my way in fact to hide my admiration as my parents would have teased me unmercifully if they had ever found out. They would have teased me about any girl, but their knowing Kathleen and her parents would have made it much, much worse. But an even greater deterrent than that was the fear of rejection. And so, for these reasons, no-one ever knew of this pash in my early days at Keith Grammar—till now.

The Newmill plan had a severe drawback however. Despite my protestations that if there was one thing more calculated to ensure I got a good doing as well as cementing my reputation as a cissy, then it was this: my mother insisted that I take the twins' mother a bunch of flowers freshly-cut from our garden. I set off for school in a foul temper, which did at least suppress the nerves which were gnawing at my guts and turning them to water. Apart from the shame and the ignominy of it, try cycling up a hill holding a bunch of flowers in one hand with the other on the handlebars. Parents just don't understand.

Another thing my mother did not understand was my need to grow my hair longer. This was even before the advent of The Beatles whom my parents considered the nadir of decadence and a sure sign that Armageddon was just around the corner. I had been accustomed to a haircut every Saturday in life, whether I needed it or not, on our weekly visits to Banff. It cost a shilling and a severe waste of money in my view since the back and sides of my head could already have been used as the family nailbrush. Whilst I didn't like it, it didn't bother me that much because I didn't care much about my appearance then. But now I was starting to. For the benefit of any girls in whom I hoped to inspire at least a flicker of interest, I wanted to enhance whatever looks nature had endowed me with and this severe crop, in my opinion, did not cut the mustard.

I must have managed to wriggle out of a couple of visits to Banff and the hair above my ears and collar was just beginning to have a nice comradely feel to it when one day, a Saturday it must have been, my mother and I were with the twins and their mother in Keith when she saw an opportunity to do something about this shameful state of affairs. After an altercation in the street which included death threats if I did not obey, my mother made me enter the barber's shop. I instructed him to be as merciful as he could and a while later, emerged slightly shorn but enormously sulky.

"Not nearly enough," my mother ranted. "Just get back in there and tell him you want it done like Ian's! And take him with you to show him," she added without so much a by-your-leave to his mother, or Ian, for that matter.

I was appalled, as Ian, who had reddish hair like Kathleen, but in a complete contrast to her, wore his in what was then regarded as a fashionable American crewcut which emphasised his sticky-out ears. And if I thought I did not look good with short hair, I thought his hairstyle made him look like a toilet brush on legs.

Dragging my heels, as instructed, we went back to the barber's shop. But this is where I did an incredibly bad and bold thing. I don't remember if Ian stayed to witness what happened next or not, but I took a chair to wait beside the other customers and just before it was my turn, I made my escape. When I was reunited with my mother, I was careful to wear a murderous expression to add authenticity to my subterfuge, but beneath the mask I was terrified she would uncover my duplicity, for all hell would have been let loose and my mother would have been perfectly capable in the heat of the moment of murdering me on the spot in broad daylight in front of witnesses.

"Much better," she pronounced as soon as she saw me. And she was serious. Bad boy that I was, she never dreamed that I was as bad as that.

Another thing we didn't see eye to eye on was the matter of dress. I was made to go to school in a brown corduroy jerkin with fetching corduroy shorts to match. The only boy, not only in my class, but the entire school, to be so attired. Most wore long, grey trousers and those who did not, had at least, the shorter version of the same material and a blazer or jacket of some description. There was no such thing as a uniform, unfortunately, only a school tie. The last thing I wanted to do was stand out from the crowd and I felt I did exactly that, like the plum at the end of little Jack Horner's thumb. I became an instant convert to school uniform and have been a strong supporter of it ever since.

Too late, just before I left, Keith Grammar decided to introduce a uniform. Several possible styles were identified and I was chosen to be one of the models. (Don't ask *me* why.) We were paraded on the school stage in front of a large audience of parents and a vote was taken. I remember my outfit had a double-breasted blazer which distinguished it from the others. I rather liked it but it didn't win. I didn't take it personally. It was no concern of mine.

Anyway, on that first day, I baled out of the bus at the end of the road to Newmill, curiously watched by those about to go to slaughter or to slaughter, and after a walk of a mile or so, arrived at the twins' house, where at last, I was able to divest myself of the hateful, shameful flowers and in due course arrived at school at a time much later and nearer the merciful school bell than I would otherwise have done, but still with plenty of time to run the gauntlet.

"You been through the gauntlet?" one ruffian addressed Ian and me a few moments later, as we stood in the playground together trying to look as inconspicuous as possible. I may have been deceiving myself but it seemed to me that he was addressing his remarks to the Corduroy Kid in particular.

I am not ashamed of the enormous lie I told for both of us, but what does it say about him, this latter-day Neanderthal, that he took my word for it, rather than marching us back for a second doing just to be on the safe side, instead of lurching off in search of new victims, a quest in which I imagine he was spectacularly unsuccessful and never questioned the reason why.

Gentle reader, I am sure *you* ask why, in a Grammar School, how could I fool an 11-plus intellectual so easily? The answer is, he wasn't, or I presume he wasn't, if the way he was dragging his knuckles along the ground was anything to go by. Long before the term was ever invented, Keith Grammar was a comprehensive school. The primary schools in Keith, and that included the Catholic primary, all fed into Keith Grammar. Far removed from the Glasgow area and central belt of

Scotland, we ignoramuses from the boondocks in the North-East had never heard of religious bigotry and therefore failed to dole out extra grievous bodily harm to Catholics as they passed through the gauntlet—they merely got the same duffing-up as everyone else.

Someone did though. I don't know his name or what he had done to merit such treatment but if my memory serves me well, it was outwith the week-long reign of terror meted out to the first years. The word went round that so-and-so was going through the gauntlet, and to a boy, and perhaps to a girl too, everyone flocked to see this spectacle. Like a sheep, I followed the rest (the last thing you wanted to do was draw attention to yourself), and thus saw that the stuff of my nightmares before I went to Keith Grammar was even worse than I imagined, for they were hitting him with bicycle chains, and even worse than that, deemed once was not enough, and put him through a second time.

It is possible that with the distance of time and the memory being a bit unreliable at the best of times, that I have not recorded this event faithfully: it could have been a lot worse than that. I had already seen enough and turned away, utterly sickened. Just like if I were about to undergo an operation, I would never watch that procedure on TV first, so I could not bear to watch this ritual torture before my eyes. Unfortunately I had a high vantage point, like the gods in the theatre, and I could see the whole thing far too clearly. One day, any day, this could be happening to me and I'd prefer not to see it—or the results.

This vantage point was at the back gate of the school which led steeply down to the playground. In winter it was transformed into Super Slide and one day Jim

Leslie, my best and life-long friend (though not at that stage in my life) came a cropper there. He smacked his head on the ice so hard he suffered concussion. He was excused lessons and made to sit in the cloakroom for the rest of the day under the supervision of a senior pupil, who might or might or not have been, delighted to miss his own lessons, and there he waited until it was time for the school bus to take him home. In a concession to health and safety however, the school did phone on ahead and Jim's father was able to meet him off the bus and so he was spared the two-mile bike ride home.

If the school did nothing much for Jim's health and safety, I likewise did nothing for my own, by which I mean it was doing nothing that kept me healthy and safe. One day I was innocently walking along the bottom corridor in line with the rest of the class, when for no reason at all, I was spat upon by a boy going in the opposite direction. I don't think it was meant for the Corduroy Kid personally but because of the outfit, I might have stood out as a target. It was a serious amount of spit, not a bit of slather that you could ignore—this was a real gob. Fortunately it missed my face by inches but splattered like a seagull dropping all over my neck and jacket. Did I run after him and challenge him to a fight for this insult? Of course I didn't. For a start, he was much bigger than me, third year I think. He might even have been the one that the whole school turned out to see go through the gauntlet. I hope so anyway and secondly, I knew that after my drubbing from Harry that I was no "bonnie fighter" (as Alan Breck complimented David Balfour after their much more deadly skirmish with the enemy).

It seems to me that fight with Harry was a blessing in disguise, for had I had any misconceptions of my powers as a pugilist, they would have been well and truly literally kicked out of me that day. Harry and I fought fairly. This orang-utan would have kicked me in the face or an even more painful place without stopping to think about it.

It's another tale I never told till now, not to the teachers nor the rector because I knew they would do nothing about it. Least of all would I inform my parents who, at best, would tell me to stand up for myself, or at worst, complain to the rector, who, if he bothered to reprimand the miscreant, would get me back upon the instant or even worse, conduct a vendetta against me and so I would go through life in Keith Grammar living in fear every day.

Well, as it happened, I did live in fear every day anyway, but not reporting this incident meant that the chances of being turned into something red and black and blue were severely lessened. In the actual event, I was not bullied much, but I was not to know that. I lived daily in the expectation of being beaten up and it was hardly conducive to learning. How I wished that I was big and tall with muscles like Charles Atlas instead of being a little shrimp in a brown corduroy suit.

This bullying was not confined to the playground: it continued on the bus. Our bus, which went via Grange, was exceptionally overcrowded. The bus company would be prosecuted nowadays and it was a mercy that we never had an accident, for if we had, the results could have been very serious indeed. If our little tin on wheels was designed to hold thirty, then there must have been more than twice than number. Three or four to a seat in some cases and standing squashed from back to front. Sardines would have thought their tins roomy by comparison.

After Grange, conditions improved considerably and the bus became a much safer place on two counts. Firstly there was a major exodus and one could let one's ribcage spring back into shape and secondly, since a large number of villains came from there, one could breathe a lot more easily.

The back seat was a lawless sort of place, a rowdy wild frontier, where innocents like me would never dare set foot. For my own protection, I stayed as far away from it as I possibly could by leaving it as late as possible before climbing on board, but even just standing squashed in the aisle did not guarantee safety. Someone would shove and the whole aisle would sway like a pendulum. It was imperative to keep your balance, not to fall, not to be trodden underfoot. Once, just for a bit of harmless fun, someone emptied a tube of sherbet over my head, though the joke was somewhat lost on me. Nor was my mother laughing when I eventually got home looking like the Sugar Plum Fairy. Also not laughing, was the girl who had her knickers ripped off in the back seat. In fact I remember she was rather tearful. It is hoped she has been able to find something to laugh at since and has not been traumatised for life by this experience.

There were no prefects on the bus, or at least none that were charged with trying to keep order, or if they were, they didn't bother. But it would have been mission impossible anyway. Or it could be they were at the thick of it. I remember one day the rector came to see this crush for himself. Presumably a parent had complained.

It could even have been my parents after the Sugar Plum incident, but I'm inclined to think not. They were not the complaining sort. Nor do I think it would have been due to the knickerless one. It would have been just too humiliating for her to have told her parents. It didn't make any difference anyway. As usual, things carried on just as before.

There was another way that safety was compromised. The driver sat in his own cab and there was a sliding glass window connecting with the passenger compartment. It was through this hatch that the driver allowed a boy one day to take the wheel and steer the bus. This was the boy who had lost his brother in that cycling accident with Sammy's dad's van. It is just as well his parents couldn't see what he was up to.

But he was in fifth year, maybe even sixth year, and a big lad with long arms so I reckon it was safe enough really. It certainly didn't scare me as much as the possibility of being beaten up or even worse, having my trousers pulled down, lest my underpants were showing signs of wear and tear.

My mother would have been mortified.

Chapter Thirty

The Trouble with the Teachers

If the bullying coloured my attitude to KGS, the teaching did little to enhance it either, especially in certain subjects, like Maths for instance. The trouble was that apart from me being no good at it, we were given masses and masses of homework. We were shown an example on the board and then given exercises to do in class and complete as homework.

I saw the homework as excessive. For those who could do the blasted sums, it probably took thirty minutes maybe, or perhaps even less. It took me a lot longer and the answers were still wrong. I would often be up as late as ten o'clock cursing them and doing other homework besides. What the Maths department failed to realise was, such was their blinkered view of their subject as being the most important in the curriculum—in fact, the *only* one may be nearer the mark—that they did not stop to think we may be burdened with other subjects, or if they did, they didn't care. Not since I had mucked out the cows at the Macs' byre had I worked so hard, and I especially hated the long summer evenings when I could see from my bedroom window, David and Richard, off to play in the woods whilst I had to remain inside and wrestle with logarithms and Latin conjugations.

As time went on I got further and further behind with my Maths. My teacher never sat down with me and tried to explain the mysteries to me. It was a case of sink and swim and I sank, almost without trace, almost at once. My inaptitude was mistaken for disinterest and even that was misinterpreted: I grew to hate Maths with a passion. Which is not surprising. We like the things we are good at that, those we have no aptitude for, we tend to dislike and because Maths was coming out of my ears faster than I could come up for air, I soon began to sink to the bottom of the class.

In an attempt to keep my head above water, my parents, most unusually for them, resorted to subterfuge. Foreshadowing the spy novels by the likes of Len Deighton and John Le Carré, the butcher's van, which called at the twins' house as well as ours, was called into service as a go-between. As well as chops and joints (and bizarrely, apple pies), his illicit cargo was the maths jotter belonging to one of the twins, whose countless exercises I assiduously copied without understanding into my own, though not nearly so neatly. It seems not to have occurred to Miss Goodall to question how I had miraculously caught up so quickly and so correctly too.

Where was the teaching? I never saw it. I only saw a demonstration. And you had to look closely as it was never repeated. By the time I graduated to the infamous Annie Mac's class, I was already seen as beyond redemption, written off and on the scrap heap. She never made any attempt to teach me, ever. I was not the only one. She had absolutely no interest in those who did not share her passion for Maths and so I was left to rot. And in the meantime, my hatred of maths grew and grew and grew while the subject became increasingly incomprehensible.

By the time our paths crossed, if her shoulder-length, straight, pepper-and-salt hair was anything to go by, generations of scholars must have passed through Annie Mac's hands. Countless others came after me too and it is interesting to speculate in how many pupils, in a lifetime of teaching, that this diminutive figure inspired a hatred of Maths. Which is ironic really, when you think of it, as you would have thought she would have wanted to share her passion with as many as possible. But then she probably didn't need to. It's quite possible that she had her disciples already amongst the mathematically able who probably looked up to her as a goddess, metaphorically. It would certainly never have been literally, unless she were ensconced behind her desk, the duplicate of my father's, a high one with a sloping lid with an ornamental wooden balustrade at the top, the sort of the thing you could imagine Bob Cratchit slaved behind. And thus mounted on her pedestal (the stool), she was mistress of all she surveyed.

So small was she that even I towered over her. Well, not exactly towered: if I were five foot then she was maybe four foot six. But she did not need to draw herself up to her full height to put the fear of death in me. She had a Gorgon stare if she had a mind to and a tongue like a cat o' nine tails, both of which were much more of a deterrent than her belt. I don't remember her having to use it in my class (we were an A class after all) but once someone (a tall boy) was sent up to her by a member of her department, probably Miss Goodall, and after the ritual tongue-lashing, she reached into her desk, took out her belt, and the offender from the room unfortunately, so we were not able to witness the surreal spectacle of her administering corporal punishment to this boy whose waist was at her eye-level.

I am sure I never needed to worry about being belted. As long as I kept a low profile and did nothing wrong (apart from my sums) I knew she would ignore me. I suppose she must have spoken to me sometime, but then since I was not worth wasting breath on, she probably didn't.

My father told the story about the son of his previous incumbent at Ternemny who happened to meet the Formidable One in Keith one day after he had moved on to another school, probably Buckie. He, like me, was one of the lost, the doomed and the damned.

"Well, Ian," said Annie Mac, "I heard you got your Higher Maths."

"Yes, miss," quoth Ian. "You see what a good teacher can do." And with that he passed on.

To be fair to her, Annie Mac was not alone. With some exceptions, the standard of teaching was very poor indeed. Methods, the curriculum and examinations had not changed for generations. Experienced teachers could do the job backwards, standing on their heads, blindfolded. From the day they began their teaching career to the day they retired, nothing changed. If it became a bit stultifying, dull and repetitive, teaching was not a bad job in those days, even if it was not highly paid. When I embarked on my teaching career, if I ever entertained the idea that is what it would be like for me, I would have been seriously mistaken, for the teaching revolution was just about to begin.

For my teachers there were no new courses to get to grips with, or as is the case with English teachers, having to write them even. And by the time I retired, despite more and more pupils becoming increasingly more disruptive, it was not that so much that which made me glad to turn my back on the chalk face but the constant change to the curriculum which began with third and fourth years, then fifth year, then first and second years and then back to fifth year and then fifth year again as they still hadn't got it right, apparently. And since I retired, they have changed it again . . .

He was probably an all-right sort of teacher for those days, my Latin teacher, "Beak" by nickname, but the problem about him was he was very often not teaching us at all. He was the depute rector and whenever the rector was absent, which seemed to be very often, he would fly along the corridor to the rector's office, his gown flapping in response to the telephone ringing. His room was not even terribly close to the phone, the door always open on the qui vive for it to ring and he would often be gone for most of the period.

He had a small, bird-like head, bald, with folds of loose skin beneath what would have been his chin if he had happened to have one. He would hoist his lean, bony frame on top of the radiator next to his tall desk by the window and wrap his gown around him, from which perch he resembled nothing so much as *Coragyps atratus brasiliensis*—otherwise known as the black vulture to those unfamiliar with the dry and dusty and defunct language he tried to drum into us.

Beak's lessons were a big yawn. He addressed us boys by our surnames only and we had to stand when we answered. If Maths was my most hated subject, then Latin was not far behind. All those declensions drove me daft and I just did not see the point of learning a language that no-one had spoken for centuries. Just what was the point? I once threw my Latin primer across my bedroom in frustration and rage at the futility of it.

On Fridays however, we had Roman history and culture which I loved, and many years later bitterly regretted that I did not try harder at the language for then I might have been able to translate the inscriptions on monuments and public buildings that I encountered on my travels. But back then I did not know that I was going to become seriously addicted to Roman culture and that it would form the basis of many of our holidays in the future, not just in Rome itself, but other parts of the Roman empire from Carthage to Jerash.

To me Beak looked at least sixty and therefore it was to our great astonishment that we came back from our summer holidays one year to discover that he had married my English teacher, "Greasy", so called because she had a very sallow skin. She had thick, black glasses and tight, curly black hair. She must have been a bit younger than him, though not exactly in the first flush of youth either, to judge by the striations on her face, so I presume the hair must have been dyed as it was raven black. I used to imagine the newly-weds snogging, or in bed together, but no matter how hard I tried, I just could not picture the scene somehow. It must have been more a meeting of minds than physical attraction. And there's nothing wrong with that. I am glad they found happiness later in life with each other. Well one presumes they did.

From one happy marriage (hopefully) to a not-so-happy one. The school was rocked when the head of the English department abandoned his wife and ran off with the glamorous French *assistante*. For we boys with testosterone coursing round our bodies faster than

Stirling Moss could complete a lap at Brands Hatch, she was an exotic creature, the complete antithesis to our teacher, Miss Allan, otherwise and ironically known as "Horny", the very antidote to desire, though it has to be admitted she looked on the wrong side of sixty though she was possibly a great deal younger than that. I liked her though and her subject. She embarrassed me hugely one day when, as she was giving out the fist-year photographs, as she handed me mine she remarked, "That's a good-looking boy!" for all the class to hear. Despite this faux pas, I did not hold it against her. In fact I would say she was my favourite teacher at KGS. As to her taste and judgement, you can judge for yourself. The photograph in question is the very one that graces the front cover of this book. The Corduroy Kid himself.

The spotting of the photogenic Mademoiselle as she crossed the playground, heading back to school after her lunch somewhere, would send us boys scurrying to the bottom of the stairwell so that we could follow her progress up the stairs, hoping to see a glimpse of something more than stocking. It was always a disappointment, well to me at least, but I remember one of us pointing to the bulge in the front of his trousers and remarking, "Standing room only!"

So all the more incredible when the rotund and much older than her, Head of English, ran away with her. It's hard to see what she saw in him physically, so it had to be something else, on her part at least. He had a French-looking name (although it sounded like an Italian river), so my theory is that his silver tongue flattered her that he was a lover of French culture in general, that it was his genes and not just the contents of her *culottes* that he was passionate about.

There was precious little culture in our English lessons anyway which, as far as I remember, consisted of reading plays with zero literary quality. Greasy insisted on calling me "Archy", because I suppose, someone of that ilk in another class sat in the same seat. I also suppose we must have written the occasional essay, though I have no recollection of ever doing so, and if we ever did, alas those early efforts from the Addison pen have been lost to literature. As I said above, it was easy to be a teacher in those days. There were not even any parents' evenings, just an end-of-year exam and in this way our progress over the academic year was measured and our place in class allocated.

I have to say that the report cards were much more informative than the time-consuming and worthless efforts teachers have to write nowadays in which the accent is on the positive, anything negative is positively discouraged and they have to write screeds about which areas need improvement and how this can be achieved. What a lot of guff! Ours told you (and your parents), your mark, the class average and your place in the class. What more would any parent want to know? No wonder there were no such things as parents' evenings.

If I was not exposed much to the jewels of English literature at Keith Grammar, apart from my first year when I did have a good teacher, Mrs Napiontek, (sp?) who married a Pole and whom we dubbed "Nappies"— with whom we read *Kidnapped* (though there were not enough copies to go round and I had to bring my own, as was the case with *A Midsummer Night's Dream*)— then I learned nothing about art or artists either. Anything I do know about those things is entirely self-taught.

All Art consisted of was drawing something and then colouring it in with paint later. I can remember, for the edification of the class, our teacher going through the paintings we had produced for our exam, explaining what was good or bad about them. He began with the best and began working his way down to the worst in the class. Probably the best belonged to Ian, the twin, who was a very talented artist and who later became an art teacher himself. But such talent, I believe, is a gift (a bit like writing) and I remain to be convinced that you can teach anyone to be even a mediocre artist if they do not have an innate talent.

I doubt if our teacher, Mr Young, intended a secondary effect from this lesson, but whatever it taught us about art (which was precious little), it was certainly a lesson in humiliation as he got further and further down the class and found fewer and fewer good points and more and more bad things to say as the number remaining became less and less . . . At last Mr Young held up a half-finished sort of thing, and from my distance impossible to work out what it was supposed to represent.

"My God, that is really terrible," I remember saying, but only to myself, and giving an involuntary snort of laughter at the pathetic effort, though it was a sobering thought to remember that mine had still not appeared. And then all of a sudden I suddenly sobered up as I realised that this *was* mine! It was supposed to be athletes running round a track but I had not got round to colouring in the people yet and from where I was sitting, all I could see were splodges of green. Despite that, I wasn't even the worst in the class, though how many there were below me I couldn't say for sure but I have the impression there were quite a few.

My music lessons were similarly unenlightening as regards learning anything about music and the great composers, only consisting of singing songs which would never have made it into our hit parade in a month of Sundays. There was a hit parade of another type however. My friend, Jim, recalls that as soon as the lesson began his class would take it in turns to ask to go to the toilet. One day the elastic of Mr Harnden's patience snapped and he belted them as soon as they returned. It was not much of a deterrent as he ended up belting about half the class. Shortly afterwards he had to have an operation for a hernia.

He would lose his temper very easily and when he wasn't belting pestilent pupils, he would hit out at a desk or a chair and give the poor inoffensive piece of furniture a good kick. He belted me once for waving my handkerchief about. Quite right too. We treated him shamefully and anyone reading this and thinking of a teaching career would do well to remember this, for conditions in the classroom have certainly not got any better. Discipline is a matter of kidology and if you don't have that, no matter how well you know your subject, the little darlings, given half a chance, will do their very best to prevent you putting it across. I bet he was probably a brilliant musician, but for his own sake, poor Mr Harnden should never have entered the teaching profession.

Poor was the operative word. One day I remember noticing the worn collar of his shirt and the scuffed cuffs of his jacket with the leather patches on the elbows and feeling immensely sorry for him. From that point

I stopped being a bad boy in his class though there was nothing I could do to convert my classmates and prevent them from mauling him like a Christian cast to the lions.

He had a son who failed the 11-plus yet overcame that early setback to become the dux of the school. Whilst this is an indictment of the examination system, it also shows that in places like Keith where the "failures" did not go to a separate institution, but took what was called a "technical" course alongside the academic courses, it was possible, with hard work and diligence, not to mention some academic ability of course, to climb up through the lower branches as it were, to the very top of the tree.

So, if I experienced little real teaching in Maths, English, Art and Music—Science was certainly no different, a subject in which I also showed little aptitude or interest. When it came time, in third year, to choose between Science and German, I chose German. Since my strengths lay more in language than the more mathematically orientated Science, it was always on the cards that that is what I would have chosen anyway but it was never much of a dilemma for me once I had experienced the quality of the teaching.

There were three teachers I remember in the Science department: Tarzan (I'll leave you to conjure up your own image—apart from to point out that the person concerned was female); Do Less (also female with wispy ginger hair and glasses and who was much addicted to the phrase "You must do more" hence her nickname) and the head of department, Mr Baxter, whose hair looked as if it had been frazzled during some electrical experiment. He had, in fact, been involved in some sort of scientific accident at some time because one side of his neck and face had an ugly red mark like a birthmark but also had the tight, wrinkled skin typical of a serious burn. An oil painting he was not, poor devil.

The very first time he had us, he placed a piece of chalk on his desk, then stepping back a pace, he pulverised it with his belt. The message to us was clear though scarcely necessary for there were no really bad boys or even bad girls in our class, nor even any cheeky ones. Later in his career he repeated the same trick on his first day as rector of Macduff and by all reports put the wee ones into such a state of fear and alarm that they burst into tears and mummies had to be sent for.

Another trick he had was to withdrew his belt from under his jacket where it lay concealed, nestling on his shoulder like a pet snake, then slam it down hard on the top of the nearest desk, just to see the startled pupil leap a foot into the air, a reaction which he found hilarious.

I don't think he ever gave us any of the belt and I would have been the prime candidate if he had. He wasn't a sadist in the sense that he liked to dispense physical punishment, but he liked to dish out written punishments, at least to me: "Addison, write out four lessons for tomorrow." These were notes which we had copied down from the blackboard or which he had dictated and which he considered more educational than lines (with some justification) as eventually I became the nonpareil of anyone in the class when it came to an understanding of how the electric bell worked.

These punishments were extremely time-consuming, time of course that I was not able to spend on other subjects or outside getting fresh air, for I was always falling foul of Mr Baxter and not for any reason that I can remember now. I was not a bad boy: I was far too scared, nor did I need any pulverising of any chalk to encourage me to toe the line. Nor do I remember anyone else getting these punishments but I suppose they must have—occasionally. For some reason I cannot fathom, he did not like me and singled me out as his victim.

So frequent were these punishments that I evolved a strategy to cope. Firstly, I did not hand them in unless he asked for them. He gave them out so casually and for no other reason than I was breathing the wrong way, that it was understandable that he would forget he had issued them. By this method I built up a stockpile against further requirements and secondly I employed the use of carbon paper because it was Mr Baxter's delight to not even give them as much as a glimpse, but rip them up right there and then in front of my face and drop them in the bucket. There was a small risk involved in this strategy, for if he had spared a second, just once, to look at them, then pity my poor stinging hands (as opposed to aching wrist and fingers) and of course, I would never have been able to use this deception a second time.

But his plan was to irritate or even infuriate me by this demonstration of the futility of all my wasted hours. I am sure he had no plan to cure me from whatever I was doing wrong, for I could do no right. The same offence committed by another pupil would only produce a sarcastic rebuke, but not for me.

I was punished in another way too: I was not allowed to watch the so-called "experiments" even if the outcome was totally expected. While the rest of the class watched the demonstration, I was left to my own devices which meant I could get on with some much-needed note-copying and I do not think I felt overly deprived at missing them. Rather, I was glad of the time it would save me at home—the thought of an evening not spent writing out science notes made me feel positively light-headed. However, the ban did provoke a response from my mother.

"You tell him that I said you have to be allowed to watch the experiments," she told me one day.

I chose a quiet moment and approached Mr Baxter with a great deal of fear and trembling, like Oliver Twist did Mr Bumble.

"Please, sir, my mother says I have to be allowed to watch the experiments," I managed to get out, my voice cracking with nervousness.

Like Mr Bumble, he couldn't believe his ears at first.

"Oh, she does, does she, Addison? Class, listen to this! Addison's mother says I am to let him watch the experiments. Did you hear that, class? Now *you* hear this, Addison. I am the teacher here, not *your* mother, and I will run *my* class any way I like. So *you* just tell your mother from *me* that what I do in this classroom is *my* business and none of hers. Have you got that, Addison?"

"Yes, sir."

Burning with shame and embarrassment, I went back to my seat. He probably gave me some notes to write out for my impertinence but I don't remember. Or maybe he thought that would have provoked an irate response from my mother which would be better avoided, though I do not think he would have cared a jot for that. Whatever else it did, I am sure this incident cemented his dislike for me while it did nothing to endear him to me either.

There was one experiment I was involved in however and it was one I would have skipped very gladly. It was a lesson on the eye and Mr Baxter asked if anyone in the class could supply us with some cows' eyes. Not such a strange request, for there was a butcher's daughter in the class and she duly arrived one day with a jam jar full of them. Since there were not enough to supply each group, they were put on a window ledge for the interim and then amazingly, someone else provided another supply of eyes a few days later. Now we were ready for the dissection lesson at last.

I noted that my group was not given one of the fresh eyes but the one of those that had been in the jar, in the full glare of the sun for days, if not a week. We thought it was a joke at first, acting like surgeons as we tied our hankies over our noses in an attempt to cover up the smell. I also remember just how hard it was to pierce the eyeball. No matter how hard we stabbed it, the pricker just bounced off it and the eye slithered across the desk. When we did finally manage to perforate it, the stench was unbelievable, sending us reeling backward as if we had been gassed. We played it up for all it was worth.

Mr Baxter thought our reactions were very amusing, which shows he wasn't all bad, and did have a sense of humour. Further proof of this is when he took us down to the burn which separates Keith from Fife Keith. The purpose of the excursion was to show us how phosphorus burnt in water. It just so happened that he chucked the chemical into the water the precise moment a couple of old ladies were crossing the bridge. How he laughed, along with the rest of us, to see the look of alarm in the old dears' faces as they scampered as best they could across the bridge to safety.

There was one other demonstration of the wonders of science I remember seeing. It was on the properties of mercury (which we now know to be poisonous and contact with the skin should be avoided). It was great fun poking the silver liquid and watching as it shimmered away like liquid silk at the touch of our fingers. Our fingers chased after it as if it were the ball in a game of finger football and we marvelled at how, when we broke it up, the tiny, little, perfect droplets magically swallowed each other up as soon as they came into contact with each other. I can safely say that it was the most fascinating science lesson, absorbing even, that I had ever had—if it was a lesson. Perhaps it was a Machiavellian plot of Mr Baxter's to drive me as mad as a hatter. (Mercury poisoning in that profession was not uncommon, it being used as part of the process in the manufacturing of felt hats.) And if there happened to be some collateral damage in the rest of the class also being affected, well so be it. It was all for the greater good as Jeremy Bentham would say.

If you are reading this in heaven, Mr Baxter, I do not hold any slight inclination I may now have towards insanity against you. I am not the kind to bear a grudge. But you knew that already didn't you? When one day you asked if anyone collected stamps, I don't know why I put my hand up since you made my life such a misery. I expect I thought I might curry some favour with you and bring about an end to the war between us, but it didn't. It was only a truce. You selected a mint set of Edward VIII from my collection for some sort of exhibition you were putting on in a shop window in Mid Street and when you returned them, along with a note of thanks, you also included some stamps as a token of appreciation. I reckon you thought this free gift made us quits and nothing changed between us. If only science notes were stamps, I would have had a collection that any philatelist would have given his eyeteeth for.

Thus science lessons continued until our ways finally parted when I elected to take German in third year. You see why I did, don't you? And you were probably just as relieved to be rid of me as I was of you.

Chapter Thirty-one

Being Under the Weather

Every day at Keith Grammar was a bad day, but some days were worse than others. Everyone hates Monday mornings, but for me the feeling of depression began after tea on Sundays. But there was one day that was even worse than that—it was the day that we had double Maths first two periods, an even greater disincentive to getting up in the morning, particularly in winter. My bedroom was so cold that I would lie abed and send clouds of breath into the air like a Red Indian sending out smoke signals, putting off the evil moment when I must expose the rest of my body to the air, the tip of my nose, I knew, already frozen.

To see what the weather was like outside, I had to breathe on the windowpane and scratch a peephole through the frost that had accumulated thickly on the *inside*. The thought of divesting myself of my pyjamas and standing chittering as I struggled into my clothes was so awful to contemplate that I would lean out of bed and reach for my clothes where I had hung them up on the floor overnight as usual and take them into bed with me to warm up. At other times even that procedure I thought insufficient and got dressed in bed despite the Houdini-like contortions and effort required.

Every cloud has a silver lining, so they say, but when I looked out the window on a school day in winter and saw an overcast sky in a particular shade of grey and with no hint of a silver lining in sight, then amateur weather forecaster that I was, my spirits would soar, for there was always the possibility that there would be no school that day or we would arrive late or be sent home early. These were frequent occurrences and one of the advantages of living in the boondocks. We had some exciting journeys both to and from school in the snow, ploughing through drifts and sliding from one side of the ice-slick roads to the other.

Of course, for most of the year, the weather was hopeless for missing some time off school. But on this particular day there was some hope. The wind was ferocious, the tops of the trees tossing their heads like Charlie the bull. My heart was lifted up. Maybe a tree would be uprooted and block our path or the bus blown over. Anything to avoid the double period of Maths that began the day. Even a delay would be better than nothing. Conditions were so bad that my mother gave me a lift to the rendezvous with the bus. Fighting against the elements like this might mean that I would miss the bus and I would be forced to spend the entire day languishing at home. Fat chance! Rather than endure that calamity, my mother would drive me to school herself, but she could save herself a great deal of time and effort if she made sure that I was on the school bus.

As it happened, I caught it with plenty of time to spare and made it on time to school too, if a bit later than usual. But during the journey I became aware of a cramping pain in my stomach. By the time I got to school, the cramps still persisted, intensified even. They were real, yet I did not worry about incipient appendicitis. Nothing that a day or two resting in bed with a good book would not cure. After all, how could I possibly concentrate on my lessons with these persistent cramps? With Maths being first on the day's timetable, there was no time to lose. I went straight to the rector's office and described my symptoms. No imagination required. My guts were cramping like mad now.

If Mr Chadband in *Bleak House* had the appearance of having a great deal of train oil in his system, the rector, a large man with chubby cheeks, definitely had a great deal of saliva in his. It was always drooling out the side of his mouth and he had to continually suck it back in before it reached his chin. Cursed with such an affliction and given the propensity that the young have to mercilessly mock such unfortunate characteristics amongst their educators, it seems incredible to me that he was known only as "Robin", not for any similarity he may have borne to the popular garden bird that appears on Christmas cards, nor for any unlawful activities he might have indulged in like Mr Hood of Sherwood, but simply because that was his name. Perhaps this mercy in the matter of a nickname was a sign of how popular he was. But popularity, in my book, should not be the Number One prerequisite for a teacher and certainly not for a rector, and I would have liked him a lot more if he had done something to stop the endemic bullying. As far as I am aware, he did not even try, which no doubt was why he was popular with the hoods as they could indulge themselves in their reign of terror without fear of interference.

Robin picked up the phone.

"I've got a young man here complaining of a sore stomach," he said looking at me all the while, which made me feel rather uncomfortable. "He doesn't look that much under the weather," he continued in response to something my mother said, and with a complete lack of irony as to the meteorological conditions. I could feel my face flush which must have made me look less of an invalid than ever. There was silence from his end as he listened to what my mother had to say. Finally he hung up the phone.

"Go to your first period class. Your mother is coming to get you. We'll let you know when she arrives."

So it was as easy that! No third degree. It was amazing how quickly the cramps stopped now that the stress was over. My heart was singing at the thought of missing Maths, or the greater part of it, and I envisaged a day spent languishing in bed being attended to by a solicitous mother as I read *The Topper* which was the only comic I was allowed as it was considered more educational than the others because of the *Illustrated Classic* on the back page. That *was* my favourite part as it happens, and in any case, I swapped it for David and Richard's *Dandy* and *Beano* so I did not mind, though my parents did, as they tried to put a stop to it.

But as soon as my mother liberated me from Maths she had bad news for me.

"I've made an appointment with Dr Lees."

"What!"

I felt my legs go weak. Twenty-four miles round trip to pick me up from Keith and the same again, possibly more, to go to Banff and back, buffeted by this almighty wind. My mother was not an experienced driver, but that was not what terrified me. What did was when the doctor pronounced there was nothing wrong with me. Because, you see, I had made an amazing recovery. I had not had a cramp since Robin had dismissed me. I must get my mother to cancel the appointment before we

345

embarked on that journey at least, for her fury would be truly awful when the doctor pronounced me hale and hearty.

"Oh, there's no need for that," I protested. "I'm sure it's not that serious. I'm sure I'll be all right tomorrow." I had hoped that I would be able to spin it out for two days at least, but now not even one may be possible. I could just picture it, after the doctor's visit, my mother fuming, taking me straight back to school and if I happened to miss my lunch, it would serve me right.

"You're going and that's that."

There was a knot in my stomach which became tighter and tighter the nearer we approached Banff. The cramps were back.

My mother came into the consulting room with me. I lay on a couch while Dr Lees felt my stomach. His hands were as cold as the one clutching my heart.

"Is that sore?"

"Yes." It was true. He was pressing rather hard.

"And that?"

"Yes."

"He's got gastroenteritis," pronounced Dr Lees finally.

Wow! Had I heard right? Could it really be true! He thought he had merely made a diagnosis: he had actually saved a life. The relief made me so light-headed, it was the hardest thing not to float off the couch and touch the ceiling. The next was not to hug myself: something as serious-sounding as this must be worth two days off school, if not more. The third hardest was not to look smug, but to put on an invalid's face.

What my mother made of this diagnosis I can only guess, though she must have been flabbergasted. Since I had not been accused of shamming, no apologies were necessary and I do not remember what was said during the journey back to Ternemny. Probably my mother had been rendered speechless.

It was straight to bed. Now it so happened that my bedroom looked directly on to the window of my father's classroom and I could see Primary Seven at their toil. As Jerome K. Jerome remarked, there is nothing more satisfying than watching other people at work and I stood at my window watching them engaged in the same sort of activity that I would have been doing had it not been for this fortuitous turn of events.

At last someone noticed me and pointed me out to the others and then they were all looking at me and I waved to them. Then my father appeared and I immediately ducked out of sight. A few moments later I risked another peek. They were all back at work but I dared not stop and stare at this agreeable sight.

At lunchtime my father came home as usual and came straight up to see me. But it was not out of concern to see how the invalid was doing.

"Do that again," he said, "and I'll take you in and belt you."

Invalid or no invalid, I knew he would. Whether or not he would have done that to anyone else who was no longer under his authority and who was disrupting his classes I could not say. Probably not, but then of course, the situation was never likely to arise in the first place. I was uniquely placed to commit this offence.

I need scarcely point out that none of this would have been possible if my mother had not been able to drive. She had not held her licence for very long— about three years only. She first got behind the wheel in 1956 during the Suez crisis and during that time learner drivers were allowed to drive unsupervised, which is how my mother came to be driving alone one evening on her way to meet her instructor. It seems she was winding down the window and the cuff of her coat caught in the handle. Next minute she had collided with a van at the other side of the road. I'm not quite sure what the aftermath of that was as far as my mother was concerned, but three years later it had some repercussions for me. It transpired that the van belonged to the uncle of a boy in my class who saw it as his moral duty to bash me for this outrage.

"I'll get you at piece-time," he threatened, when this connection somehow came to light.

He was tall and broad shouldered with fists that could drive in fence posts. I didn't like to think what they could do to my pretty little face. I knew he could pack a mighty punch because he would give me, and others, for fun, a paralyser by hitting us on the upper arm. Depending how long it was into the break when he hit you, the effect might just be beginning to wear off in time to enable you to write in your next class. I knew I could not hope to match him. I doubt if even Harry could. My only hope was to keep out of his way and run faster than him if he came after me.

His threat to "get me" was no idle threat as he did indeed spend the breaks, not to mention lunchtimes, beating people up. The fact is he was rather unsanitary and he spent much of the time wreaking revenge on those who had insulted him either verbally, or, as he passed them in the corridor, by pretending to faint at the smell, or wafting their hands vigorously in front of their noses.

He *was* rather pongy, as I knew all too well. Latin was just after lunch, during the course of which, the righting of wrongs, the honest toil of chasing people and duffing them up for their insults and misdeeds had brought forth a profusion of sweat and it was my misfortune to sit next to him. I was lucky however in that these activities meant he was too busy to bash me for my mother's misdeeds.

Naturally I was wise enough to say nothing about his aroma to him personally but I did lay it on thick to my parents one day at teatime.

"You've got no right to criticise him," my father remarked mildly. "Your clothes would stink too if your mother did not pick them up and wash them and put them out again for you."

That gave me some food for thought all right. I hadn't thought about it like that. But there was still the matter of his personal hygene. He did not need his mother to wash *him*. But I wisely kept my own council on that for I was a hypocrite in that matter too.

I was so bone idle that after a bath I could not be bothered drying myself with a towel and left as much of the tedious process as I could to drip-drying while I read a book. But even that became irksome after a while, so I just sat on the pabby seat. I reckoned two chapters, depending, was just about the right amount of time for a soak and a wash and dry. I could not say for certain how long I got off with this ploy and wicked waste of water before I was rumbled.

And how was that do you think? Not because my parents noticed I was dirty, or noticed I did not smell as fresh as a geranium, nor because I was not a pinkish shade of lobster, nor because the towel was too dry, for

349

I had thought of that and cunningly wet it as well as dampening my hair. I thought I had covered all the bases but I had made one very grave error—I had not thought of the bath. It was far too clean! There was no tidemark and they knew perfectly well that I would never have cleaned the bath after myself.

I was hoist by the petard of my own laziness. (And grubbiness.)

Chapter Thirty-two

Pastimes and Punishments

I don't think that young people do it nowadays or if they do, they certainly don't collect the same things, but in my day collecting was nothing short of an obsession. We all did it, or at least we boys did. At the height of my collecting career, girls were beneath contempt and so I've no idea if they indulged in this particular pastime or not, but for we boys it was an endless source of joy, or jealousy. You could compare collections, make swaps and feel a great sense of satisfaction if yours was the biggest—or envy, if one of your friends had a particularly fine stamp for example, or a badge from a petrol station, such as Fina, that I could never have because my father refused to buy that brand for some reason I could never fathom.

I was a marketer's mug. I needed no incentive to eat my cornflakes, especially for the sugary deposit in the milk at the bottom of the plate and then in came Tony the Tiger and Frosties which must have cut my sugar consumption by half as I was not allowed to put any sugar on them, but there was one incentive to make up for that—the little plastic figures which we used to collect and swap. Whenever you got a new packet, the first thing you did was rake in the bag until you found the figure in its little plastic bag and you were usually disappointed as you already had it so you had to have an even larger helping to speed you on to the next packet.

There were cowboys and Indians which chimed perfectly with my pursuits at the time, as did the collection of Rifles that Won the West. Less exciting were the bandsmen: trumpeters, saxophonists and such like. I did have a go at painting the cowboys and Indians with the little tin of paints from the plastic Airfix kits of aeroplanes. This invariably turned out to be a disaster, both from a painting point of view and construction, as I was in such a hurry to see the completed article, I never bothered reading the instructions first which usually meant I had to try and unglue what I had done, to fit a propeller for example, into the fuselage. Usually it was too late and stuck fast. As far as the painting was concerned, it was far too fiddly for my fingers.

"Why don't they reduce the price of the cereal instead of putting that rubbish in them?" my father complained. Whilst I did not agree with him, I could see that he would have little use for a plastic Winchester Rifle, even if it did win the West. He had a real double-barrelled shotgun of his own which stood propped up in a corner of my parents' bedroom. He used to shoot crows at Clayfolds when he was a young man.

Other collectibles were, as I said, the badges that petrol stations used to dole out, along with Green Shield stamps. I remember when these stamps first came out, I got on my bike and cycled to the shop, the nearest one, not Sammy's father's, but the one on the Huntly road to buy a tin of Cremola Foam. There were three flavours: orange, raspberry, and lemon of which raspberry was the best. It cost one-and-sixpence and I became the proud possessor of my own book into which I was able to stick three stamps. I never stopped to consider how long it would take me on threepence a week pocket money to turn the stamps into a "free" gift, even augmented by the seasonal tattie and birthday money.

I also had a collection of Matchbox cars but since I was dependent on people buying me them as presents, my collection hardly came on in leaps and bounds until many years later, when the Best Beloved and I went to London when we were students. She worked in the Matchbox factory and bought me one a week with her employees' discount. They might have been worth a fortune now, had I not given them to my son to play with and they subsequently became battered to hell.

Another thing I collected was car registration numbers. I had hundreds and hundreds of them which I wrote down in a little notebook. It never occurred to me to augment my collection by making them up, which just goes to show you how honest I was, or naive, or stupid, but in my case at least, I had another reason to be truthful. I was suffering from a surfeit of Enid Blyton books. I imagined that one day my little notebook could be responsible for sending crooks to jail as it would provide incontrovertible evidence that the crooks had been in a certain place at a certain time.

I even began collecting birds' feathers. If you think that bizarre, I don't see it as being so much different from collecting their eggs, which seems to be regarded as a respectable hobby—apart from those who are so addicted to their collection that they steal the eggs of protected species. No, what is odd about it is that I should ever have contemplated such a thing when you consider my phobia. I Sellotaped them into a scrapbook with a note indicating which of our feathered friends

353

I thought had cast off the plumage with the help of *The Observer's Book of Birds.* No-one else had a feather collection to rival mine, but there was little satisfaction in that—I had the only one.

But what I collected above all was stamps. Stamp collecting is generally considered for wimps—a quiet, genteel sort of hobby, but in my hands it was another source of conflict and confrontation between my mother and me.

For some weeks I had been rearranging my collection. I'm not sure what my method was exactly, but to me it made sense at the time and it had the advantage as far as my mother was concerned, of keeping me quiet and out of trouble. I thought I was merely pulling stamps out of the album and stacking them in piles round my room; what I didn't realise was that I was stoking up the bonfire of a conflagration. The problem was that while I pulled hundreds of stamps *out*, I did not put any *back* with the result there were masses of them all over my bedroom: on the bookcase, on the window ledge, on the chest of drawers, on the floor—anywhere where there was a flat surface, apart from my bed because they would be crushed. My bedroom in fact, was a sort of walk-in stamp album and every time my mother entered it, it drove up her blood pressure.

My Aunt Nan and Uncle Tommy were staying at the time and I later heard that Nan, in order to help my mother with the housework, had decided to dust my room. She opened the door, took one look at the chaos within, was not struck dumb exactly, for she managed to gasp "Bloody hell!" then closed the door again smartly as if some indescribable Thing was lurking in there that must not be allowed out.

My mother had warned me well, I will admit that, yet it was still a surprise and shock to me when I came back from school one wet and windy Monday, to find that my loose-leafed stamp album had been thrown out the window and its leaves were even more loose now, having been strewn to the four corners of the garden. The loose stamps, however, mercifully, were spared, which is ironic really as they were the ones causing the irritation. They were gathered up, not too carefully one supposes, into one big heap, hopelessly mixed up. It took me hours and hours to sort them out again—and put them in the album.

It was not the best of mixes, my mother's age and mine. Like two different worlds colliding, it was explosive. She was going through the menopause just as I was hitting puberty and when you add to that her short fuse, inherited from her father, and my short temper, inherited from her, it is little wonder that it was not an uncommon sight to see me running round and round the garden, not in the least like the teddy bear in the child's rhyme, but pursued by my mother intent on tickling my backside with a bamboo cane. Long and slender, it made a horrifying swishing noise when she connected only with fresh air and which lent spurs to my heels. Being so pliable, there was no danger of my poor bones accidentally breaking one of my father's precious raspberry canes, but even if they had, he had plenty more.

"Come back here, you little bleeder!" she could be heard to remark on these occasions. Or, for the sake of variety I suppose, she sometimes called me a "little heller" to which I made the rejoinder over my shoulder once, but only once, "I am not an obsolete Austrian coin!" It's amazing what you learn from collecting stamps, even if you do not learn when it is a good idea to keep your smart aleck remarks to yourself.

Gifted with a natural ability to run pretty fast, I became even fleeter of foot as a result of this improvised athletics training, so fast in fact, that I was the second fastest boy in the whole of Keith and District as measured by the area's School Sports Day. In actual fact, I probably was the fastest, but I slowed up at the tape instead of throwing myself at it as I had never experienced such a thing before and I was pipped at the post by a big boy whose stride being much longer than mine, did not have to make his legs revolve in a blur like helicopter blades in order to cover the same distance.

As far as my mother was concerned, I could easily outpace her, but I could not run forever. My hope was that the fury might spend itself with the effort of the chase and the strong arm might be borne more lightly. Once I took refuge in the bathroom, the only room in the house with a lock. If I could have existed only on water, I could have stayed there for days, certainly longer than the rest of the family could before they felt the need to obey the call of nature. I knew I had a strong negotiating position but did not have the nerve to stick to it. The longer I remained in this self-imposed incarceration, so I reasoned, the rage and revenge would grow in direct proportion to the length of time the family's legs were crossed. So, like a lamb to the slaughter, I reluctantly surrendered my backside and thighs to their stripy rendezvous with the cane.

After that event, I reckoned it was better just to keep running, but that was not always possible. Sometimes I was cornered and when the bamboo cane did come into contact with my flesh, the weals were a sight to behold. They did not go down for hours and though they never produced any blood, I am sure a social worker would be more than mildly interested in them today.

You may be wondering what I did to deserve such a punishment and the truth is I don't know. Just being a teenager I suppose, or as Grandpa Tate presciently foretold, just being a "bad bugger". Anyway, I exasperated my mother beyond endurance. "By the left!" she would say when I had somehow provoked her, and "You make me want to spit feathers!" and when regurgitating even a whole pillowcase of them failed to soothe the angry breast, the cane was ready to hand.

My father never used it, but I did exasperate him enormously too. I know exactly why that was: he could not believe that I could be as thick at Maths as I really appeared to be. He was a polymath. He took Latin and Greek at university, but Maths was what he liked best and he could just not understand why I could not do it or share his enthusiasm for the subject. To him problems in Maths were intriguing—a puzzle which you had to unravel and then you could glow afterwards in the satisfaction you felt after you had worked out the solution.

The problem for me was I could never get anywhere near the right answer and couldn't have cared less what it was anyway. I got all the puzzles I wanted from the detective stories which I read voraciously—the intrigue of the plot, its twists and turns and the pitting of my wits against the author. Could I work out whodunit before the end or would the writer deceive me? How could an algebraic problem compete with that? Words, not numbers, was what interested me—which is why, for all its abstruseness and its utter pointlessness, algebra was the least hated of all the maths disciplines in my view because it did, at least, have some letters in it.

And yet my father should not have been so taken-aback at my lack of mathematical skills, for I remember well on our summer holidays in Worcestershire, at Uncle Tommy and Aunt Nan's Dormy House (they were keen golfers), and nearly a whole year before I sat my 11-plus, I was made to do a daily arithmetical test in preparation for it. I forget how long it took, twenty minutes, thirty at the most, but it absolutely ruined my holiday and everyone else's, as I was dragged under protest to do the test every morning. After it, I sulked and was surly for most of the day, my revenge for the imposition, my hope that this would bring about an end to this regime. It didn't. It was meant for the best and I did pass the Separating-of-Sheep-from-Goats Exam so maybe it worked in the end, but it was hell for us all while it lasted.

But having passed it and "graduated" as the Americans say, to High School, in other words, to that non-icon of academe, Keith Grammar, one day my father was helping me with my Maths, trying to get me to see what was so obvious to him but which I still I could not see and which my father misinterpreted as "would" not see. How could *anyone* not see, let alone a son of his? It had to be perverseness and he would knock that out of me. He picked up the hearthside brush. It was red with stiff black bristles. I'll never forget my mother's reaction.

"No, George, no!"

My heart leapt up at this unlikely source of salvation. My mother cares, I thought. But I was soon disillusioned.

"That'll make his clothes dirty! Here, use the poker."

The funny thing is it was probably even sootier.

It was futile. Utterly hopeless. You just can't make silk purses out of sows' ears. My parents perceived me as thrawn and maybe I was at other times—it is part and parcel of being a teenager after all, but the brawn my father used in attempting to knock Maths into my thick skull were unsuccessful and matched only by my teachers at Keith Grammar, as you know. I needed kindness, words of encouragement, even sympathy for someone as severely afflicted in numeracy skills as I was. I did get that later, as you will see, but not at Keith Grammar School.

It is easy to be wise in hindsight and if I were to be tested now, I would not in the least be surprised to find that I have dyscalculia. I don't know and I don't need to know now, but it would have been useful to have known if that was the case then, and the rod might have been used more sparingly. On the other hand, it might merely be that I was and am, just not very numerate, and bad teaching, or the lack of it, in my early years in secondary school, compounded the problem.

I don't hold the beatings against my parents. They did it out of love. I never doubted that but I would have preferred they had loved less dearly as my thin hide would have appreciated it. You may remember from an earlier chapter, that amongst my reading material, amongst the books I knew and loved, was *Tom Sawyer,* and in that book you may remember, Tom imagined that when he was dead, then *they* would be sorry for the way they had treated him when he was alive. I derived a great deal of comfort from that but was impatient for more immediate results, and besides, a flaw in Tom's plan worried me: how could I be sure that I would ever see my parents' remorse? It was not enough for me to *hope* that they would.

So, one time, when my father had knocked me flying for some reason or other, and my head accidentally came into contact with the sharp edge of the coal scuttle, I was more pleased rather than hurt to see that my ear was bleeding. Good I thought, I would make some pretext to go down and show my parents the extent of my injuries, then they would be sorry, for I am sure that my father never intended to draw blood. Unfortunately the bleeding stopped all too soon. It was not much of a cut. No matter, my paint box was at hand and I painted a nice red rivulet from my ear to my jaw before going downstairs on the pretext that I wanted a drink of water. I was disappointed. If they ever noticed the "blood" then they made no comment.

Chapter Thirty-three

Being a bad brother and other tales

If I felt that I was more sinned against than sinning in those days, there was one thing that I did that was really bad and *did* deserve a good hiding. Sibling rivalry is not uncommon and the methods devised to irritate the other are many and legendary but my sister, I believe, was privileged to be subjected to a treatment out of the ordinary—I told her ghost stories, stories I made up out of my own fertile imagination for her edification and education. I did not realise then the powers I had as a storyteller, but I was just about to find out.

One night she woke up, screaming the place down. My parents pacified her, telling her that there were no such things as ghosts and in any case, no-one or anything could get into the house as the doors were all locked, as were all the windows. They did not know then that I was the author of her dreams. The next night they did.

"You know when Mum and Dad said there were no such things as ghosts," I explained, "well, that's not true. There *are* such things as ghosts and what's more, they can walk *through* solid walls." It was no less than the truth, as I believed it to be. I had read several volumes of the *Pan Book of Horror Stories* and, of course, the ghost stories of M. R. James.

If trumpets could bring down the walls of Jericho, it's a wonder that her screams later that night did not bring down the walls of Ternemny Schoolhouse and thus save the ghosts the bother of expending any spiritual energy they may require in the breaking into and entering of houses, the haunting of poor folk to perform. Maybe my cries for mercy were just as loud when my sister grassed on me.

Nevermore, after that, you would think, would I tell my sister nightmare-inducing bedtime stories—but I did. However, before I tell you about that, there was another time she screamed the house down and it had absolutely nothing to do with me.

The decorators had been in and the windows were wide open to let out the smell of paint. The family *corvidae:* crows, ravens, jackdaws and suchlike, so they say, are curious and intelligent birds, know for example, how to drop pebbles into a beaker of water to bring a juicy and drowned worm to within reach of their beaks.

On this particular night, one rook took advantage of the open window to pop in and have a look around my sister's bedroom. The word "nevermore" above will not be lost upon fans of Edgar Allan Poe and it could easily have been a raven, for it looked enormous in that small room. I saw it, quite at home, hopping around, taking advantage of the hospitality by dipping its beak into a beaker of water by the bedside, grateful, no doubt, not to have to indulge in the tiresome pursuit of having to hunt for pebbles in my sister's room in order to raise the level of the water.

I had seen enough and slammed the door on it. I certainly didn't want that thing flapping about the house, thank you very much, and worst of all, going into my bedroom. That would be the stuff of *my* nightmares. Besides, it would be much easier for my parents to get rid of it if it was trapped in the room and my sister could always take refuge under the covers, couldn't she?

I also claim no culpability for the third time she woke us all up with her screaming—though I got the blame. It took place a number of years later. By this time I had discovered another author—Dennis Wheatley, to whom I referred in the Foreword. I was reading *The Ka of Gifford Hilary* in which the main protagonist, who was murdered, comes back from the dead to bring his killer to justice. It made a huge impression on me and I explained to my sister that according to this book, everyone has a ka and when you go to sleep at night, your ka leaves your body, connected by a silver thread which it needs to find its way back. If that thread gets broken, your ka can't find your body and you die.

Have you ever been having a bad dream and the only way to get out of the situation is to tell yourself you are dreaming and the next minute you waken up with a start? Well, that is caused by your ka having to jump back into your body pretty damn quick instead of just creeping in like you do at an ungodly hour in the morning after a night out with the boys, hoping not to disturb the trouble and strife.

Some people, I also learned, train their ka to go wherever they would like and do whatever they want, enjoying these experiences vicariously in their dreams. Just think—free time-travel for life! If you want to try it for yourselves, this is what you do, but remember it could take years of training before you get a result. Just before you fall asleep, you tell your ka that you would like to visit France at the time of the Revolution, for example, or Mexico at the time of Montezuma and the Conquistadors, or just to see how the Egyptians managed to fit the capstone to the pyramids, if you prefer something a little less scary and gory. You can see why, in certain circumstances, your ka may need to make a sharp exit (and entrance). Of course you wouldn't *have* to choose such interesting times, you could always choose something much more safe and boring. But why would you? I didn't worry about my silver thread snapping. I thought I was far too young to die. I wanted to travel and have adventures. I began my ka's training immediately.

How was I to know that this would give my sister more nightmares? I was only trying to improve her life, thought she may have been interested in starting to train her own ka. How was I to know that she would seize on the snapping of the cord thing?

I was deemed to be beyond bad by my parents, more like evil, but from my perspective, I saw myself as being badly misunderstood. I was even quite good, once, which I must just mention to even things up a little, just in case you think, like she did, that I was the worst brother a sister could have.

One day she was involved in a very bad accident in the playground. She was playing takkie, running hell for leather, looking over her shoulder to see if her pursuers were gaining on her, when she collided with a boy doing precisely the same thing but running in the opposite direction. He got up, dusted himself down and discovered he didn't even have a grazed knee. My sister got up—and promptly fell down again. She had fainted with the pain. It later turned out that she had broken her right leg in two places. Her friend Mary, the one who helped her conquer the Slippery Slope, carried her to the house from where an ambulance was called.

This accident made a deep impression on me. As I said earlier, I feared pain more than death and felt a huge sympathy for my sister, as her pain must have been excruciating. When I came home from school the next day, I came bearing gifts—a colouring book and crayons. It may not sound much, but like the widow woman in the Bible who gave the treasury her last bawbee—it probably cost me all my money too. She was lucky I happened to have some at the time as I never got enough pocket money to save any. It must have been what was left of my tattie money after the rest had been turned into *Saint* books or some improving literature of that sort.

I am sure that act of kindness did me some temporary good, upped my parents' opinion of me, just as it would have sent it plummeting downward again had they known of my scheme to haul my sister upstairs by means of a rope dangled over the banister. There was no danger of her making a similar sudden descent however, for fortunately she was too heavy to lift very far and so the only damage that was done was to the banister. It had a rope burn, a very noticeable mark in the varnish like one of the weals on whatever part of my tender hide the bamboo cane had made contact with— except there were two significant differences. My weals were red and with time would vanish; this was glaringly white and would not.

But a little brown paint from my paint box cleared me of the deed. When we first moved in to that house, it was painted overwhelmingly brown. Just because their name was Brown, that didn't mean they had to paint the house that boring hue did it? It was certainly very gloomy and one of the first things my parents did was to have it removed. Probably there was some sort of allowance given to the new occupants of a schoolhouse when they first moved in to permit a certain amount of redecoration.

Anyway, the professionals were called in and I remember coming in for lunch one day to find an overpowering stench of ammonia which seems to have been the preferred method for burning off paint in those days. How my mother could have stayed in that atmosphere I can't imagine. I suppose the painters got used to it and never noticed it, just like people in the flight paths of planes never hear them as they skim over their roofs—though it's hard to imagine how the painters could ignore something not so much under their noses, but right up them. But never mind the paint—it was enough to strip the hair from your nostrils, and God knows what it did to your lungs after it had done that.

In all likelihood, my sister's visit from the crow coincided with the time the painters dangled me by the ankles from the upstairs landing window. That's why the windows were open wide, to let the smell of paint out, not as a conveniently quick and efficient method of disposing of me. Why they did what they did sounds so outrageous that I can't be sure it really happened or whether they merely threatened to do it. Likewise, I find it hard to imagine what I could have said or done that they found me such an annoying little tick that they felt the need to resort to such desperate measures. Even my mother, who was in contact with me for the majority of the waking hours of the day, stopped short of that, and if there was anyone who deserved to be first in the queue to murder me it was she, so those painters were well out of order (in both senses of the expression). I had no head for heights and landing on it from a great height seemed too permanent a cure for vertigo so I gave the mad painters a very wide berth indeed after that.

I have another memory that involved heights. For some reason I was on the roof of the school. Maybe I had gone to retrieve a ball or something and I began slipping off. I held on for as long as I could, shouting for help, but no-one came. I was so high up I was scared that hitting the ground was not only going to result in broken bones (which would be very sore) but paralysis, which would be worse than death. The cold sweat broke out as I began the inexorable slow slide towards the gutter, the last hope of salvation which I knew if I failed to grasp, would mean the fall to earth. I missed it. I expect I screamed before I hit the ground with an almighty bump. My whole body jerked. But I wasn't dead and nothing was broken. I just woke up. It was such a vivid a dream I still remember it from fifty years ago although I can't remember what I dreamt last night. It wouldn't surprise me if my nightmare had something to do with the would-be murderous painters.

The living room, before and after the brown paint, was where we lived from day to day during the week. I suppose, on reflection, that was why it was called the "living room". But on Sunday afternoons we sat in what was called the "best room" or parlour. Where the living room had tiles on the floor, this had a carpet, apart from the lino round the border. The best furniture was there too, though that is not synonymous with the most comfortable, and in the winter, the living fire was carried through from the living room on a shovel and put in the grate. All the doors betwixt and between were opened wide and we children told to stand well back, as my mother (usually she was the one who did it), with her right arm that had not been set right, carried the loaded shovel with its glowing red coals through to the other room with me in its wake as it shovelled smoke over her shoulder. If something happened I wanted to be there to see it.

Once that was safely installed, then the TV was wheeled ceremoniously through with great care and diligence on its purpose-built trolley. It was a 17" Ekco and it cost 88 guineas, an enormous amount, and in order to pay for it, my parents temporarily "robbed" my piggy bank, so they could get it sooner. We were already the last to get it in Ternemny, apart from Mr Campbell, who I remember coming to see a series of all of Shakespeare's historical plays. My parents did not hold with this new-fangled notion of hire purchase. If you couldn't afford it, you did without: that was their credo. And in those days when sets were not so reliable, their greatest worry was that the tube might go, which is why this journey was considered very hazardous indeed as any bump might break it, not to mention various delicate valves, resulting in a costly repair or even worse, the demise of the set entirely which would result in us being off air for some considerable time.

I think it might have been bought from Leys & Duncan in Low Street, Banff. Certainly Mr Duncan was a friend of my father's and if you can't help your friend, then who can you help? It would have been nice if the boot had been on the other foot and *he* had helped *his* friend by giving him a discount, as Mr Duncan was certainly not in need of any financial support. He had two cars. They were both Vauxhalls, and here's the thing—they both had the same registration number—ASE 100. Banffshire had just recently and belatedly, compared to the rest of the country, moved from two letters (SE) followed by four numbers to the new system of three letters followed by three digits and Mr Duncan's would have been a prestigious one, reflecting his status as Principal Provider of Electrical Goods to the good burghers of Banff and District. He also was a radio ham and I remember once being taken to a room above the shop where I was given the chance to speak to someone in Australia. Unfortunately I was so overcome with nerves that all I could think of to say was: "Hello, Ron."

To me that has all the echoes of Eth's catchphrase of "Oooh, Ron!" in the *Glums* sketch in *Take it From Here*, a radio show in the Fifties, which, before the square-eyed monster appeared in the corner of the living room, I used to be allowed to listen to with my parents before being packed off to bed.

This less than momentous occasion (although in those days to talk to someone on the other side of the globe was quite something) probably occurred one Saturday after we went in to the shop to buy a light bulb, or perhaps it was merely to shed some light on a dispute that had been raging between me and my father, namely that Mr Duncan had *two* cars with the same registration, one blue and one red. "Impossible!" cried my father. Yet I would not be swayed. I knew what I had seen and with Grandpa Tate stubbornness, I insisted I was right.

Mr Duncan settled the argument. I was right, of course. He *did* have two cars and they *did* both share the same registration number. Unfortunately I can't remember why this was so. The only explanation that I can think of is that since I never saw them together, one must have been off the road whilst the other paraded about proudly bearing the unique number plate. If this is the answer to the mystery, imagine having to unscrew and transfer the number plate each time you wanted to use the blue rather than the red. Whatever the case, I think it meant the possibility of my father getting a discount on the TV was a non-starter. If Mr Duncan could afford only to run one car at a time, how could he possibly afford to give his friends discounts? Friends are friends, but business is business.

Anyway, whatever the provenance of the TV, sitting in the sitting room or parlour on a Sunday afternoon, I would be regaled by escapist fare such as Fred Astaire and Ginger Rogers films and in the evenings, *Wells Fargo* or some cowboy show or other and after that there was the 9 o'clock news on BBC. I still remember and was haunted by the sound of the signature "tune". Those staccato notes struck dread into me. It was the sound that announced the end of another week and heralded the start of another at the hated Keith Grammar School.

I headed up to bed filled with the deepest depression.

Chapter Thirty-four

Deskford: The Sister's Tale and the Scandal

The only way for the WWII prisoners of war to get out of Stalag Luft III was to tunnel. That wasn't the way to get out of Keith Grammar but my desire to get out of the place was no less intense and on the face of it, my escape seemed much easier. All I had to do was express the desire, persuade my parents, and once I had attained the school leaving age of fifteen, I was free to go. Simple.

Except it wasn't. Whilst the Great Escapees had meticulously planned and prepared for what they were going to do after they escaped, I had not. I had absolutely no idea what I wanted to be on the outside, in the world of work. The truth is I had no desire to be anything except be free of Keith Grammar School, so when I saw the Youth Employment Officer and he asked me what I would like to do, the only job I could think of was what my older friend from the Ternemny days was doing—a lab assistant. So that's what I said and when the officer asked, "Why do you want to be that?" and when I replied, "That's what my friend is doing" even I knew that was the stupidest reason to be anything ever and I didn't need *him* to tell me that, though he did so in kindly terms, not at all as if he were speaking to a moron.

You can imagine that my parents took a very dim view of my interest in escapology and this latest development must have been yet another severe disappointment to them after my less than glittering school career. My father had warned me well that if I had been counting on a job on one of my uncles' farms, then I could forget it: they would not employ a useless bugger like me. If that remark was designed to make me pull my socks up and stick in at school, it was unnecessary—the experience with the Macs was far too fresh in my mind for me to entertain the slightest desire of pursuing a career in shovelling cow dung.

Even I could see that leaving school with some sort of a qualification would be better than none, so my parents set about making enquiries about me being allowed to sit the Junior Secondary Certificate, probably the only pupil in the entire history of Keith Grammar School to have passed through its portals with a pass to study two languages and left with the qualification that I would have been expected to obtain had I failed the 11-plus and gone to Ordiquill.

And I may well have left school at that stage, but salvation came from a most unlikely source—Robin the Commandant. He wouldn't let me sit it. Said I wouldn't pass it. I have no idea what the exam consisted of, but it was bound to have had some mathematical and linguistic content. With all due modesty, I am pretty sure I would have been able to pass the latter, but as to the former, and speaking as someone who vied for 29th place out of 30 in Maths with the malodorous pugilist aforementioned, there was a fair chance that Robin was right, depending if calculators (fingers) were allowed or not. Furthermore, what if the JSC contained questions of a practical nature like: if you want to unscrew a screw from a piece of wood, should you turn the screwdriver to the left or the right? All right, I admit I would have been able to work that one out (eventually), but what if there were questions on more arcane matters like the use of tools I'd never heard of, such as, well . . . the ones I've never heard of. So maybe Robin had a point: if I had not been trained for the exam, how could I be expected to pass it?

Nowadays you would say he had an eye on his back, on the school league tables—in my view one of the less enlightened educational "advances" in recent years, and God knows there have been plenty of others, but such things were unheard of in those days, so presumably Robin meant it or he had another agenda beyond my ken.

So I was enlisted, against my will, for more years of education at Keith Grammar, but this is a story with a happy ending as far as this part of the memorial epic is concerned. Reader, I did manage to make my escape. This time it came in the form of yet another educational reform. Certain schools were deemed uneconomical to exist at all or in their present form. Accordingly, Ternemny was downgraded to a one-teacher school and my father applied for, and became the dominie at Deskford, which itself was downgraded from a Junior Secondary, to a two-teacher primary school.

This sideways move as far as my father was concerned presented me with an opportunity to make a similarly lateral move. I did not know it then, (how could I?) but this was to have profound and far-reaching consequences on my life. The bus to Keith Grammar passed the door but I pleaded with my father to let me go to Fordyce Academy which lay some five miles away on the other side of the unlikely named Cotton Hill and which I could get to by means of my faithful bike. I suspect this heart-felt request caused my father a great deal of embarrassment, for it was long before the days of parental choice and it must have been difficult for him to have to explain to Robin, who was after all, a sort of colleague, why I wanted to leave his poxy school. I never heard that conversation: perhaps my father handed in my resignation by letter and that was the end of it, but I can certainly remember him phoning Mr Cruickshank, the rector of Fordyce, and explaining the situation, for first of all, he would have to have his agreement to admit me. And admit me he did. Thank you, Mr Cruickshank.

The Fordyce saga will be told in due course in its place, but first of all there were the remains of my sentence to serve at Keith. The move to Deskford however, brought about an immediate improvement. For a start, the bus was nothing like as crowded as the one from Ternemny and had nothing of the bullying. It was, in fact, as civilised as a bunch of forty or so unsupervised school children could be, though of course a bit of carrying-on did go on in the back seat, but naturally I was not a party to any of that.

If moving to Deskford provided an escape route from Keith Grammar for me, it turned out to be a descent into hell for my sister. Fortunately she was only there for a little over a year before she was able to make her escape *to* Keith Grammar. She started Deskford in Primary Six, and at first all seemed well, but almost from the first moment that she moved up to Primary Seven, she was relentlessly bullied by two girls. They were the senior pupils in the school now and ruled the roost. It is a matter of speculation whether they would have instigated this reign of terror against another person, or persons, regardless, but my sister was an easy target. For a start she was the dominie's daughter which laid her open to unfounded accusations of being a "teacher's pet". They also made fun of the "posh" way she spoke and the old-fashioned way she was dressed— just one of the handicaps of being the offspring of older parents, as I already knew—so it is easy to see from their point of view, why they picked on her. This verbal bullying was a daily event, the sort of thing that can make your life a living hell—and they made sure it was.

They also involved the other girls in their campaign and they were too scared of them not to participate. They persuaded them to send her to Coventry and then one day the bullying escalated into the physical sort when they formed a circle in the cloakroom and pushed her from one to the other. You may have thought it was training for Keith Grammar, but in fact, the only bullying she experienced there was in the school bus from the same two who mocked her sensible shoes with their round toes instead of the fashionable points. Fortunately they were classes apart—the bullies in a B class and my sister in an A, so apart from the bus, she was able to avoid them.

The worst incident of all was the night of a whist drive in aid of school funds in the village hall, just behind the school, and as she was making her solitary way there, a cowardly hoodlum punched my sister in the face. He was a friend of one of the girls and a pupil at Cullen Junior Secondary, the school which those who failed the 11-plus went to after Deskford.

The headmaster was my father's friend, Bill McBride, who, with his wife Kath, always came to our house for Hogmanay. They chain-smoked through the evening and sank a bottle of White Horse amongst them, though I suspect my mother's contribution was negligible. As the evening wore on, the spectacle of the McBrides trying to light their fags was rather quite amusing. They came to us as they had no children, but they did have cat substitutes who were allowed to do as they pleased. Thank God they were not kids; they would have been proper little brats.

What the boy did was nothing less than criminal assault of course but Bill McBride persuaded my father to let him deal with it rather than reporting it to the police. He called an assembly and ritually humiliated the attacker in front of the entire school. It was effective, probably more so than anything the police could have done, for the ripples from that chastisement seemed to extend the four or five miles to Deskford, as after that, my sister was not at the receiving end of any more physical abuse and even the name-calling abated somewhat.

It was a desperately unhappy period of her life. She would come home in tears, whilst I by contrast, was lapping up life at Fordyce Academy. My father knew what was going on but his solution was to come down even harder on my sister so that the bullies had no grounds for calling her a "teacher's pet". Unfortunately it did not work, only served to increase my sister's misery as she could see no end in sight of the torment.

But the end did finally come, more or less, as I said, when she went to Keith Grammar. She went to the old, dilapidated and crumbling building that I went to and also even had the dilapidated and crumbling Beak for Latin, not to mention the weak and ineffective, at least as far as discipline was concerned, Robin, as rector. But during her time there, a new school was built on the edge of town. That meant goodbye to the air-raid shelter and the gauntlet, but by then it had more or less died out anyway and in any case, as a girl, she would have been immune from that sort of bullying.

I will just mention in the passing that in her class of sixteen at Keith Grammar (nearly half the number of mine) was Jim Naughtie, allegedly the naughtiest boy in the class, according to Miss Goodall. If the name fits . . . It was a reunion as my sister had met him before in not very happy circumstances for Jim. Before they moved to the "big" school there was a joint outing of the feeder primaries to Elgin's Cooper Park and in retaliation for an insult to the colour of her hair, she dragged Jim around the park by his. She called it auburn; his word for it probably had something to do with carrots.

It's a pity she had not retaliated in a similar fashion to the girls who were bullying her, for she was a tomboy and I am sure she could have battered any girl on a one-to-one basis, not to mention most boys, may have even given Harry a tougher fight than I did if she had been four years older, the same age as him. But she was always faced with two girls ganging up against her at the same time.

For the benefit of overseas readers and those who are not fans of Radio Four, Jim is a well-known presenter of the early morning news and current affairs programme *Today.* Anyone whom he has not interviewed on the political or cultural scene is not worth knowing, or to put it another way, they have not made it yet if he has not.

He was the son of my father's colleague, the dominie in the neighbouring village of Rothiemay. I remember Mr Naughtie had a ginger bristly moustache and a two-tone, green-and-white Ford Zephyr Zodiac which I thought the epitome of sophistication in cars. I was right about that: there were less than 23,000 of them ever built and one of the high specifications that made it so expensive (£850 in 1955) was it had a heater. Very useful in a Banffshire winter.

I don't know if it was any better at starting than any of the others, but in those days cars came equipped with a starting handle for use when the car refused to start by the normal method of pressing the starter button. You fitted it through a slot in the front bumper and "wound up" the engine, to my non-mechanical mind, similar to twisting an elastic band. But you had to be careful how you held the handle as when the engine did catch, it would kick back and could break your fingers and especially your thumb if you did not hold it properly, or let go of it as soon as it caught, or even better, in anticipation of it. I know this because I was the one charged with that task, so that when the engine did start, my father's foot was ready to press on the accelerator to keep the revs going. Aside from all that, it was a very handy implement for bashing people's heads in—a convenient portable murder weapon much beloved of crime writers in the Fifties.

I did not have the honour of knowing Jim personally like my sister but I believe—in fact, I am sure I have the advantage of her, when I say that I have seen him totally naked. That was because when my father called in to see his father for some reason or other, as we remained in the car, I saw the young Jim Naughtie, naked as the day he was born, come bounding to the door. (Don't worry, Jim. No photos will be appearing in any celebrity magazines now, or ever. Even if I had had my Brownie with me, I would never have dreamed of photographing you in flagrante.) He would have been about six.

My sister knew another celebrity although no-one has heard of her today, or so I discovered when I tried to investigate her story. But I have to remember it was at least half a century ago. At the time she had gained a certain notoriety because it was such a shocking event, especially in a microcosm like Ternemny where hardly anything ever happens, as Professor Higgins so fastidiously taught Eliza Doolittle to aspirate her aitches. It was the speak of the place before her story hit the headlines of the national press.

I am talking about Mary. She lived with her granny in one of the prefabs, Number Five would be my guess. When she was about fourteen she "fell pregnant" as the saying goes, which makes it sound like an accident beyond your control, which, come to think about it, is actually quite apposite for those days when methods of birth control had many fewer options than now and more importantly, were a lot less readily available.

One of the most popular sources was the barber's, exclusively a male domain, and it has never occurred to me till now, call it an epiphany if you like—that perhaps there was a connection between the condom and the shorn heads of the men who frequented the scissors snappers, less in need of a haircut but more of "something for the weekend" and who lacked the courage to go into the chemist's where, God forbid, there might be women about, or even worse, you might be served by a young, unmarried woman and have to blushingly pretend that you had come in for something for a dry throat or laryngitis, depending on how deep was your embarrassment.

And if sex was so shameful that even married people pretended they didn't do it, to have an illegitimate baby was la crème de la crime, more shameful than murder. That was why Mary went through her entire pregnancy on her own, and strange to tell, no-one noticed. Some women don't have a big bump and I couldn't say if Mary did or not, or whether she just managed to conceal it very well. In any case she must have been very, very frightened, scared half to death and in the prevailing moral climate, too terrified to tell anyone, or ask for help. Which brings us to the next stage of this tragic tale.

Somehow she managed to deliver the baby herself and then attempted to cover it up by concealing it in a suitcase under the bed. Whether she smothered it in a panic to stop it crying or whether with malice aforethought, she thought if it was dead, her shameful act of fornication would never be discovered, or whether it simply died because she didn't know what to do with it, I am afraid I do not know, but what it *does* show is a terrible childish naivety.

Despite it being a cause célèbre and being reported in all the papers, I have not been able to trace the story for want of a precise date. Without that, the proverbial needle in the haystack comes to mind.

I never heard my parents talk about it, though I am sure they must have. It would have been unnatural if they had not and of course they would have been most particular to keep it out of my shell-like. I never read the papers then and am less inclined than ever to do so now, since the Murdoch Empire took over that medium, lock, stock and practically barrel. Had I done so, I might have remembered more details of the case and especially the aftermath about which, regrettably, I know nothing.

And neither does anyone else now, which Mary, for one, will be enormously glad to hear. So you can stick that up your kilt, Calvin—had you had one. What Mary did may be remembered and held against her in your world and the hereafter, or so you would have us believe, but here in the more forgiving present, her transgressions have been forgotten long ago.

Until now. Until by me. Sorry, Mary. (Not your real name.)

Chapter Thirty-five

Deskford: The Perils and the Annals of the Parish

The Ternemny experience had taught me that just because there was no church in sight that did not mean an end to the dreaded Sunday school. No false dawn presented itself at Deskford: I could see the church from the house, just a few hundred yards or so along the road from the school. I may have escaped from Keith Grammar but I could not escape the tentacles of the Church. In fact I was to become more entangled in it than ever before.

The minister was Alfred J. Armour. Quiet, gentle, silvery-haired, trim-moustached and sporting wire-framed spectacles, he was my idea of Father Brown—apart from his turning his back on the Old Religion, and the moustache. The very epitome of a Church of Scotland minister, at least in its moderate twentieth century form and the very antidote to his 18th century predecessors who would be birling in their graves at his liberal and moderate views. Even without his dog collar, which went wherever he went, you would not have needed anything like as many as twenty questions, even with the cheating Eamonn Andrews in charge, to divine his profession on *What's My Line,* a popular TV show that went out on Sunday evenings in the late Fifties and early Sixties.

"Alfie", as we affectionately called him, started up a youth club and if by that you are imagining games of badminton and fun and laughter, then think again. Maybe that's what the others thought too when they turned up, but they were in for a disappointment. Alfie's idea of a youth club (and a good time) was a meeting in the church where we read bits from the Bible while he explained their significance and endeavoured to provoke a discussion. There was only a handful of us and I've no idea how long it lasted once the truth of what the youth club was really like came out, but probably not very long. I imagine people just drifted away but my new friend Jim was one of the regulars. I am pretty sure he came as a gesture of friendship to support me, whereas I *had* to go as my parents made me, you will be unsurprised to learn, dear reader. It only involved a short walk for me, but for him it involved a four-mile round trip by bike, uphill on the homeward leg. No greater love hath a loon than he attendeth a Bible study for his friend.

I don't remember any of the others but there was a girl who once drove me into fits of uncontrollable laughter when she was asked to read a passage which included the hilarious lines: *and [he] laid it in his own new tomb.* You may rightly ask what is so funny about that, even when I tell you that she pronounced "tomb" as "tom". I can't explain it, but I found it rib-splittingly hilarious; maybe I caught Jim's eye and we set each other off. The truth is I can't remember. But I knew it was wrong to laugh and I tried to suppress it until my belly ached, but the laughter would insist on bursting out in a great spluttering and snorting fits like a geyser and showering the person sitting next to me in spit. The enormity of what I had done would sober me up momentarily and I could feel my face burning with shame but the sound of that word "tom" would insist on welling up in my inner ear again. It was the suppression that made it worse. I would dearly have loved to have released the valve and given vent to gales of laughter, but most of all I wanted to flee the place.

Despite this solecism, Alfie still had high hopes of me. He asked if I had entertained any thoughts of joining the ministry. The mansion of a manse that he rattled around in with his antique of a mother and Molly, his sister, who was so thin that she rattled around in her skin, was very tempting. I wouldn't mind living in a house like that I thought, but it was not enough to base a career on, and in any case I knew it was the very last reason to follow a profession like that. I knew you were supposed to receive some sort of mysterious "call" but nevertheless I feigned interest and asked what becoming a minister involved and when he said I would have to study Hebrew and then proceeded to show me what that was like, that gave me the chance to say I thought that was way beyond my capabilities. I would have to find some other source of employment.

There was one job that I *did* covet and aspire to, however. Molly played the organ. Nice work if you can get it and I could not possibly have done that, but it took two to make the organ work—Molly to play it and someone to pump the air into its lungs. There was a boy who received a small stipend for his services as organ pumper and when he could not attend, that boy was me, though I do not remember getting any remuneration. Since I had to go to church anyway it would have been nice to have killed two birds with one stone and made some cash. I think I might have been on £1 a week by this stage, which was still not nearly enough.

There was a huge library in the manse, both in terms of the size of the room and the number of books. When I first saw it, my eyes lit up, but the rows of volumes turned out to be nearly all dusty theological tomes. Nevertheless, I did come away with *The Screwtape Letters,* the lightest volume in the entire library and I made heavy going of that though it is meant to be rather humorous. Of course I was very young then, too young to appreciate the devilishly wicked jokes.

Perhaps Alfie assumed that because I never missed a Sunday, I was a fan of the kirk. My father was an elder and it was an honour he could scarcely refuse: the minister and the dominie were the twin pillars of a community like Deskford. As his son, I had to go too, though even if he hadn't been an elder or a dominie, I still would have been made to go, like I was in Banff, as my parents thought it would be good for me, or would make me good, or best of all, give them a break from me.

Maybe it was the publication of my short, short story in *Young Scotland,* the Church of Scotland magazine that suggested to Alfie that I had potential literary talent or perhaps what he did next was intended to lure me into the ministry by giving me the chance to hear the sound of my own voice without anyone being able to interrupt me. Anyway, whatever his reason or motivation, one Christmas Alfie handed over the pulpit to me when he rhetorically asked if I'd like to write and conduct the sermon. Well perhaps "sermon" is rather too high-falutin' a word for it, "address" would be nearer the mark, but "hypocritical sentiments" were my mother's verdict on this theological gem. It is lost to the world now but it's not a great loss. The thrust of it was not very original but I was only sixteen and it was all I could think of: the commercialisation of Christmas—how deplorable it was and how Jesus was all but forgotten amongst the jangling of tills' bells and Jingle Bells. So you see, my mother was right.

I don't remember if I kept the congregation rapt or if I lulled them to sleep. Probably not the latter, with all due modesty: there was probably not enough time for that and novelty alone might have kept them alert enough to keep sooking the sermon-sustaining Pandrops. Perhaps my experience in the pulpit had some subliminal effect on my future career, but if I ever imagined I would get such a well-behaved and quiescent audience as the congregation of St John's Parish Church in Deskford, then I would have been in for a rude awakening. But I wasn't quite that stupid, so I wasn't.

Deskford, incredibly small, consists of two parts: Kirkton, where the old kirk is, and the metropolis of Berryhillock (at least a dozen houses on the strip) where the shops are, with the new church in neither, being situated on the Cullen-Keith road. Although the shops were much nearer than they were in Ternemny, being sent on an errand could be rather a time-consuming process.

There were two shops, or rather one shop and the Post Office which carried a limited range of goods. Mrs Finnie, who kept the shop, was what we call a "big wumman" with upper arms like gravel crushers, jowels like a bulldog and a black moustache. But it wasn't her scary appearance that was the problem. She was as deaf as a post which meant that apart from when I called in to collect my *Writers' Magazine* which she would just give me without the need for any verbal communication, trying to make her understand what else I had come for did pose certain difficulties, just as I had difficulty understanding what she was trying to communicate to me. We often had to resort to the written word. It was my introduction to the plight of the deaf. I was not to know that in fifteen years or less, I would become much more intimately associated with that problem when my son was born deaf.

Mrs Duncan had the Post Office. I think her name was Edith. Only the vast differences between our ages prevented us from being on first name terms. It was a dark and gloomy place, her denizen, with a great deal of brown about it. She was a widow. I couldn't say for how long she had been in this state of detachment from her loved one, but she must have been very lonely. Why else would she detain this stripling and keep him talking for half an hour or so before she released him with a cake of Duncan's Hazelnut Chocolate, appropriately enough.

I can't remember what we talked about. Nothing of consequence anyway and I don't remember it as being an ordeal, just something that made inroads into my time, but even when I emerged blinking from the sepia tones of the Post Office into the Technicolored world outside, there was a good chance I would be accosted by Mrs Bremner out in her rainbow-coloured garden. Her house lay just across from the road from the Post Office, so it was impossible to sneak past without her spotting me as she was usually tending her blooms.

In contrast to Mrs Duncan, although she too was a widow, she was full of the joys of life, always grinning and laughing, which meant that I was constantly treated (and intrigued) by the sight of the one and only tooth in her mouth, a long and yellow fang in her upper gum. Like my conversations with Mrs Duncan, I can't remember the first thing about our extended colloquy apart from the fact that in response to anything I said, she would invariably preface her remarks with "Fegs!" I wish I had listened more carefully or been blessed with a better memory, for she claimed to be a relative of mine. If she ever explained the connection, I certainly don't remember it now, but my parents agreed she was right. That said, in all my researches, I have never come across her. But then Bremner was her married name and I've no idea what her first name was, let alone her maiden name.

There were other perils in Deskford too. One of the farms was called Burnheads where I used to go to pick tatties and avoid on all other occasions if I possibly could. When I tell you that there was a billy goat there (if his name was not "Gruff" it should have been) who had the freedom of the farmyard and took a great delight in charging and butting visitors, and if you picture the height of a goat's head and then the stature of a slightly short teenager, you will be able to work out that is why, for the sake of my unborn children, I went there as little as possible.

I was also under attack from the other end, so to speak. At one of the Skeiths, I am pretty sure I know which one, but will not name it here to spare the blushes of his descendants. What happened was the farmer came up behind me and gave me such an almighty kick in the behind that I was sent sprawling to the ground and I suffered from an aching coccyx for weeks later. It was a totally unprovoked attack and was hardly because I was slacking, for my posterior presented the perfect target as I bent at my backbreaking toil. Maybe that was it—maybe he just couldn't resist such an inviting target. I vowed I would never go back, regardless of how short of funds I was and I derived a great deal of satisfaction the following year when the farmer rang my father up, I wouldn't say begging exactly, even pleading may be too strong a word for it, but he was short-handed and needed every picker he could get. But I stuck to my guns. He asked my father the reason for my refusal and I heard my father relay my response, duly modified: "He says someone kicked him" and that was the end of that conversation. Revenge is sweet and best served cold, if I may mix my proverbs.

Another farm, Leitchistown, is responsible for one of Deskford's main claims to fame. It was here in 1816 that the Deskford Carnyx was unearthed in a peat bog. It is a magnificent piece of Iron Age Pictish art, now in the National Museum of Scotland in Edinburgh. Despite its classification, it was actually made of bronze.

Whilst the carnyx was also used for ceremonial purposes, it was primarily a war trumpet that extended some seven feet above the blower's head like a periscope so that its fearful sound could be heard above the vanguard. It would have the double effect of inspiring them as well as cowing the enemy. It had a ribbed palate and a hinged wooden tongue that acted as a sort of clapper. Imagine a whole phalanx of these advancing towards you with its fearful sound (more frightening than bagpipes), a sort of background noise to the advancing Picts. I have never forgotten from my primary school days that "Picts" means "painted people", a name given to them by the Romans and although the notion that they painted themselves with woad is discredited nowadays, they *did* paint themselves and *were* tattooed, so it's no wonder that they put the fear of the gods into the Romans. You have only to go down any High Street in modern Pictland to get an idea of how scary they must have looked. Mind you, as far as I know, they did not have a women's brigade then, as they do now.

It is mere speculation, but scholars think that the very rare Deskford Carnyx was actually for ceremonial use and had been buried in order to conceal and preserve it from the Romans after the Caledonian coalition had been routed at the battle of Mons Graupius in AD 83. The location of this battle is also a matter of scholarly debate with one of the outside contenders being nearby Knock Hill and if that is so, it's easy to imagine how it might have been lost in the heat of battle, or its aftermath. There are some things that will always remain a mystery and we can only hazard a guess at what actually happened, based on the balance of probability.

Deskford's other claim to fame is a very fine example of a Sacrament House or aumbry, a stone cupboard used to house the ceremonial bread and wine. It stands in the north wall of the first Deskford church which, in an act of wanton vandalism, had its roof taken off and was allowed to fall into ruin after the new church was built in 1872. Fortunately the Sacrament House now enjoys some protection from the elements. It has an inscription in English as well as Latin which makes it unusual, but what makes it special is the quality and elaborateness of the carving. Fittingly, one of the Latin inscriptions reads: "Ego sum panis vivus qui de caelo descendi si quis manducaverit ex hoc pane vivet in aeturnum" which just in case you have let your Latin slip a bit or you have not read John 6 verses 51 and 52 recently, means: *I am the living bread which came down from heaven: if any man eat of this bread, he shall live for ever.*

It was dedicated by Alexander Ogilvy in 1551 to celebrate his marriage with Lady Elizabeth Gordon, daughter of Adam, son of the first Earl of Huntly. After she was widowed, Elizabeth married John Gordon, son of the fourth Earl who, in his lifetime, Alexander had made his heir, disinheriting his own son, James, by his first marriage to Lady Jane Abernethy. I may be misjudging her, but can't you just see Elizabeth, like some latter-day Lady Macbeth, pulling the strings behind the scenes here? Naturally James was not best pleased at his disinheritance and a feud began between the Gordons and the Ogilvies.

This is not the place to go into details, except to say that James's appeal against his father's extraordinary decision was to due be heard in Edinburgh in July 1562, when by chance he happened to bump into Gordon in the street. A fight ensued and James was stabbed. Gordon was imprisoned but escaped and after a few more adventures, was hanged at Aberdeen. Ironically, all this resulted in the start of the decline of the fortunes of the Gordons, the very opposite of what Elizabeth's machinations had been about, unless I completely misjudge her.

But that was in the future. Both Alexander and Elizabeth's coats of arms are represented with their mottoes on the aumbry and if you are thinking what a generous chap Alexander was to give this humble little church such a fabulous piece of furniture, then think again. He may have been a very nice chap indeed and may have been under his wife's thumb, but as far as this gift was concerned, Alexander was probably really thinking of himself. In those days, making gifts to the Church during your lifetime was regarded as a sort of insurance policy so that when the time came for you to hand in your dinner pail, you would be guaranteed a seat in heaven somewhere near the top table, close to God, not just in the standing room at the back. Very nice for those who could afford it.

I doubt if my address to the congregation of the other Deskford church is going to count for very much. Memo to self: must remember to be buried with one of those shooting stick things. Eternity is a hell of a long time to spend standing about.

Chapter Thirty-six

Being really bad

It was on the bus from Deskford to Keith Grammar that I met my life-long best friend, Jim Leslie, or more precisely, it was when we were decanted at my father's school. He was in the year below me at Keith and I did not associate with him at school, but after the bus pulled away we would spend ages at the end of the road talking about this, that and everything. Meanwhile, no doubt his mother was cursing me for making Jim late for his tea yet again.

His father was a crofter at Wester Darbreich and weekends and holidays would invariably see me up there helping with the hairst or just doing various jobs about the farm as Jim's father worked it himself and Jim was the orra loon.

When Jim came to our house, we would sometimes play cricket in the adjacent field. The Oval it was not, with a smooth-as-silk wicket and I'm not saying it was rough, but it would have given Miss Muffet a headache deciding on which tuffet to plonk her bum. Occasionally we persuaded my sister and friends to join in just to make the batting and bowling a bit more interesting, but those occasions were as rare as rocking horses' droppings. If only the contributions from the cattle that pockmarked our pitch had been less generous, we might have fielded balls with a bit more gay abandon than we actually did, but the saving of runs came secondary to the need to trip carefully through the tuffets. By now you will possibly be beginning to understand why the girls partook of the cricket only as a last resort. But then one day an incident occurred that put an end to their participation forever.

We had a real cricket ball (and bat) and after a long run up (as I had seen Freddie Truman do) I released a vicious delivery intended to be so fast that the batsman (Jim) had absolutely no chance of defending his wicket (three crooked sticks). Incredibly, instead of hitting the wicket, the ball struck a tuffet and spun off at an acute angle—right into my sister's stomach. She doubled over in pain, clutching the affected part and took a lot of persuading that it was purely a fluke and to remain on the field. Calm having been restored, up tanked Freddie Addison once more—for precisely the same thing to happen again. Once she got her breath back, no amount of silver-tongued oratory from me could persuade her this time that I had not done it deliberately and she hobbled off the field of combat accompanied by her friends, never to return. To this day she maintains that it was a cunning plan to get revenge for some perceived slight or other. What she fails to understand is that this feat would have required bowling of such incredible accuracy that I should have ended up bowling for Scotland, if not England, but somehow, I never received the call.

There was one thing that I bitterly resented at the time which is why perhaps, she imagined I had worked the magic spin with the cricket ball. In Deskford we were able to receive an ITV signal which we were unable to do in Ternemny. I am not sure why exactly, perhaps it was something to do with the adverts, but my parents regarded this channel as somewhat infra dig and were not inclined to watch it much, or ever. Nor did they approve of my sister and me watching it. I don't remember this regime depriving me of very much but there was one programme I desperately wanted to see.

You may remember that I confessed to being a fan, almost to the point of obsession, of *The Saint* books by Leslie Charteris, long before their transfer to the small screen starring Roger Moore, whose subsequent portrayal as James Bond I saw as nothing short of treachery. Unfortunately *The Saint* was aired on ITV, confirming my parents' prejudice on the low quality of that channel's output. Even more unfortunately, at precisely the same time, *Dr Kildare* was on BBC. My sister wanted to see that, whereas I, naturally, wanted to see how successfully the filmmakers had adapted my hero's exploits. My parents' decision was this: I could watch *The Saint* as long as my sister did not want to see *Dr Kildare*. Of course that never happened, and rightly or wrongly, I suspected her motives were more in order to spite me than any desire to drool over Richard Chamberlain. Harbouring resentment at a decision that I saw fell far short of the sort of judgement that Solomon might have made, viz, that we took it in turns to watch our respective programme week and week about, I resorted to hopping on my bike to see *The Saint* at Jim's house.

I always assumed that Jim's family would be watching it anyway but now half a century later, I am beginning to wonder if they switched it on as an act of kindness or sympathy towards me. They were, and are, exceptionally kind people. (Jim's mother is still alive.)

Amongst our activities and influenced by The Beatles, Jim and I used to write and perform our own songs, though Jim always preferred The Rolling Stones. I wrote the words, Jim wrote the music, played guitar and performed the vocals. I, who cannot sing and have no sense of rhythm, "played" the drums (beating the hell out of a biscuit tin with a pencil) and we recorded our efforts on a very primitive tape recorder I had somehow acquired. Although it sounded incredibly tinny, Jim's mum and dad would listen very patiently and pronounce our compositions "very good". They did not fool us: we knew they were only being polite, especially as Jim, who is extremely musical and can play by ear, told me that my "drumming" sounded like someone "chappin' in nails in the background".

But it was very kind of them to take the time to listen to us in the first place. My parents, who regarded all Sixties music as a "bloody racket" (with the possible exception of Judith Durham of The Seekers whom they grudgingly admitted had a "pleasant voice"), would never have been so fulsome in their praise, and only Jim's presence would have tempered their criticism from something less than acerbic.

But one day I took advantage of Jim's parents' kindness to such an unprecedented extent that I put them in a very awkward position indeed, though it was only later that I realised what I had done. Let me explain.

One of my early eccentricities was that I was an admirer of that now obscure Sixties' pop group The Swinging Blue Jeans. I am slightly embarrassed to admit it now but at the time I was proud to be a fan for the very reason that nobody else was and it made me feel a bit different, separated me from the common herd. In fact the only record I ever bought in the entire

Swinging Sixties was their *Hippy Hippy Shake* and that does indeed make me different from millions of my contemporaries. For a start, raising the necessary six shillings and eight pence was a hurdle I could only overcome at tattie-picking time, so any record collection I may have amassed in any given year would have been confined to releases in October, extending possibly into November if I was lucky. Another argument against building a record collection was I could get two-and-a-half *Saint* books for that price and a book could last for days, compared to a 45 which lasted a little over three minutes—if you were lucky. Besides, after I had scrimped and saved my tattie money and borrowed an advance from my parents, one year I was able to buy a transistor radio and thus able to hear all the pop songs anyone would ever want to on Radio Luxembourg. With the aid of the earpiece I could listen into the wee sma' hours—something which did nothing to help my resistance to getting up in the mornings.

But the main deterrent to buying any records was that we did not own a record player. Music did not play a large part in my parents' lives. Any music they listened to would have been on the radio and I do not recall them ever doing that though I suppose they might have once I was in bed. I did ask my mother once, when I was very young, who her favourite composer was and she told me it was Eric Coates which was the first time I had ever heard the name.

As I know now and as I probably don't have to tell you, dear reader, he is probably known best for his *Dam Busters March* but his *By the Sleepy Lagoon* is heard by millions almost every week of the year, though they may not realise who the composer is. It is the theme tune to

Desert Island Discs on Radio 4. The whole piece lasts for just under four minutes. Nice work if you can get it and he did, again and again, his music being used for several radio and TV programmes, most notably, *The Forsyte Saga*.

But to my tale. Great news! The Swinging Blue Jeans were coming to the boondocks! Elgin Town Hall in fact. For a fan like me it was a must and the opportunity of a lifetime. The next day was a school day and predictably, my parents would not let me go and no amount of arguing and complaining would persuade them to change their minds. I imagine they were mightily relieved when I sulkily announced that I was going up to Jim's and the silence after I had slammed the door must have seemed not just golden, but 24 carat.

But all was not as it seemed. I was hatching a cunning and deceitful plot. I proposed to defy orders and boldly go to Elgin regardless. It would have been nice to have had some support for this daring enterprise but I could not persuade Jim to accompany me. He had read most of *The Saint* books and we swapped Dennis Wheatley and Rafael Sabatini novels, amongst others, but to go to Elgin to see The Swinging Blue Jeans any day, never mind a school day, was just pushing the boundaries of friendship too far. I do not remember him saying so, but no doubt he played the "school tomorrow" card rather than offend my feelings by divulging the real reason for refusal—on grounds of musical taste. Thus it was that I set off a lonely and disobedient figure to cycle the seven miles over the Hill of Maud to Buckie where I knew I could catch a bus that would transport me to see my musical heroes.

But that wasn't the really bad thing that I did. I knew that after a certain time my mother would phone ordering me to come home as it was late. So for before I left, I asked Jim's parents to say that I was there and I would be back in a bit. It shows just how naive I was, for that could only have instigated a second phone call instructing me to get on my bike at once, or else, with the unnecessary reminder that I had school the next day. Not for one moment did I consider the impossible position I was putting Jim's parents in, taking it for granted, nay *expecting* them to lie on my behalf without turning a hair. Furthermore, what I failed to realise was that I was making them complicit in the crime, accessories before as well as after the fact, and presenting them with a dilemma—should they do their duty and inform my parents of my nefarious plan, or do the dirty on me and clype to my parents?

I discovered later that their solution was to do neither and they left the phone off the hook to God knows what inconvenience to themselves. I expect they hoped that my parents would assume the line was faulty and I wonder if, as time wore on, they dreaded a knock on the door at midnight, or later, to find my father or mother on the doorstep, anxious that I had not returned, more worried than ever since they had seen no sign of me on their way there. Since I was not at Jim's, was I lying dead in a ditch? Or, however remote the possibility that anyone would want me, had I been kidnapped? Oh, how they would have regretted never having let me see all those *Saint* programmes! Tom Sawyer would have wallowed in self-righteous glee. And so would I.

But at the time of that imaginary scenario, I was enjoying myself enormously in the company of The Swinging Blue Jeans. They were all that I had hoped for. What's more, I met them afterwards and got their autographs. And that's not all. I made some friends and even made a conquest. Her name was Evelyn. She was just my type with short black hair, curled round into two sharp points beneath her exquisite cheekbones. She was sporting a black-and-white mini-dress that showed off her slender and shapely thighs. But it was her eyes that captivated me. You could hardly have missed them, thanks to the mascara and eye shadow. Think Dusty Springfield, if that means anything to you, dear reader. If it doesn't, think of a panda.

When it comes to the fashions of the Sixties, I can't help but be reminded of Wordsworth who waxed lyrical about having the good fortune to have been born at the outbreak of the French Revolution: *Bliss was it in that dawn to be alive, But to be young was very Heaven!* If it was the French Revolution that sent Wordsworth into raptures, it was the mini-skirt that enraptured me. If a glimpse of stocking was considered somewhat shocking in the 1920s, young men then would have fainted plain away at the sight of the yards of denier nylon on display everywhere in the 60s. But being made of sterner stuff than our ancestors, we young men thanked our lucky stars that we were born when we were.

But our pleasures were tempered by something that had not been seen since Shakespeare's day—the dastardly tights, which I don't have to remind you, dear reader, started out as men's garments. Some idiot somewhere, probably some woman, dreamed up the idea that tights would be a jolly good addition to women's wardrobes. All too quickly, stockings and suspenders made the transition from everyday women's wear to men's fantasy garments. You were right Wordsworth. Bliss it was indeed to be young, especially when mini-skirts were fashionable and before tights were resurrected. We will never see their likes again.

I don't think it would be an exaggeration to say that this was the best day I had ever spent in my young life, but as Tam O' Shanter knew only too well, the hour approached when I "maun ride". And waiting for me at home was not Tam O' Shanter's "sulky, sullen dame" but my mother with her notoriously short fuse which had been smouldering for hours on a powder keg of bad temper. I also knew the sight of me would be the spark that would blow the roof off the house when I eventually got home, whenever that might be. I did not fear the bamboo cane. I had outgrown that long ago. And here's the irony: I was much more scared of the lashing of the tongue than the swishing of the rod.

As I had expected, my bike was where I had left it in the town square of Buckie, the largest town in Banffshire. It never entered my mind that it would not still be there when I got back. These were civilised times. Furthermore, no comedian had let down the tyres or even stolen the pump. That was good because it was already a long bike-ride back, the bulk of it so steep that it was less effort to get off and walk and an enforced walk all the way home would take much, much longer and I was already seriously late. I threw my leg over the bar and pedalled off at once to face this apocalyptic appointment with my mother's wrath.

It was a *braw moonlicht nicht* as the parodists of a Scottish accent never tire of trotting out, and once off the main road, on the hill of Maud, I disengaged the dynamo to lessen the resistance as I toiled up the steep hill. I could see perfectly clearly. Not once on the entire journey did I encounter another vehicle. It was a time when all respectable citizens were safely tucked up in bed and only this doomed youth was abroad. Apart from rabbits, the only other living road user I encountered was a hedgehog with a death wish, curled up in the middle of the road not far from the track up to Jim's house. What a stupid place to chose for a bed, I thought.

I dismounted and gingerly picked up the prickly fellow before laying him gently in the grass by the side of the road. At that time I had not thought deeply about religion, merely saw it as an irritant in my life but it did cross my mind then that *if* there was a God in heaven and He was watching now, He being so omniscient and all, He might intervene and persuade my mother to show some similar compassion and spare me the worst of her wrath.

I can't say for sure what time it was when I eventually got home but my guess is that it was about 2 am. The back door was unlocked. That was a good sign. This prodigal son would not have been unduly surprised to find the door bolted and barred. I crept in as quietly as any penitent sinner could—but it was to no avail. My mother, I am sure, had been lying awake, waiting for this moment and down the stairs she materialized in her nightdress, like a galleon in full sail. As far as I could tell, she was not armed with a rolling pin or any other instrument of correction. She was certainly not armed to the teeth as she didn't have them in.

"Where have *you* been?" she gummed, incandescent with rage.

No answer was necessary of course. She had worked it all out hours ago of course. She was not exactly stupid. I absolve myself entirely from the idea that she had spent a sleepless night, fearing the worst, that her first-born had been abducted by aliens. (Thank God she had another child, a good, obedient and dutiful daughter.) No, she knew exactly where I had been all this time, but needed to hear me condemn myself from my own mouth.

"You're a wicked, wicked boy!" she pronounced. "Get to your bed. *And* you had better get up in the morning!" she threatened darkly.

I never saw my father that night. I would be amazed if he had been sleeping peacefully, gently snoring throughout this drama. I think he was just staying out of it. Maybe he was even secretly pleased that I had shown a bit of spunk, even if it did mean that Grandpa Tate's prediction had come to pass. But of course I had been demonstrating that in less obvious ways for a long time. I *was* a bad bugger, and getting worse. God knows what depths I might yet sink to.

I don't remember how much I slept that night but I do know that I went to bed feeling as fresh as a daisy. Maybe it was the adrenaline. One thing I knew, it would be utter madness to irritate my mother an inch further than necessary and the next morning I knew the sooner I got off to school and put some time and distance between us the better.

Chapter Thirty-seven

When I had Fears

School, by the time of that exploit, was Fordyce, over the hill and quite far enough away when you are not much inclined to get up in the morning and when you rely on pedal power to get you there before 9 am. Once again the topography did not suit me, for the hardest part of the journey by far was the beginning—a long, hard slog uphill followed by a merciful few hundred yards of flat which allowed me to regain my breath before tackling a more gradual uphill gradient relieved by some downhill stretches which only flattered to deceive as I could not make the crest of the next rise without more pedalling. But then finally, I could begin the long, gradual descent into Fordyce. There was a final sting in the tail however. There was a short, steep climb into the village before I finally reached the Academy. If only the journey had been reversed, I could have spent another half hour in bed.

But it doesn't really matter now. It was good for my health, or so I believe. Should I ever achieve a really old age and if anyone were to ask me to what I attributed the secret of my longevity, and just in case this hypothetical interview should never take place, I would like to record it here, whilst being of sound mind and body: "Building up a healthy heart when I was young and pickling it in alcohol ever since". And that is "all ye need to know" as Keats put it, should you wish a long life. If you are fat and forty and never did any exercise when you were young, unfortunately for you, you read these words too late. The exercise has to be done when you are young.

Believe it or not, there were one or two other things I did not know when I was but fifteen years towards heaven. One of them was that the farm of Cairnton which I passed twice daily was where the wife of my grandfather's brother, James Addison, was born. Her name was Charlotte Patricia Hendry, known as "Lottie". She was one of eight daughters born to William Hendry and Hannah Clark. Imagine that! Eight daughters! If they didn't call him Hendry the Eight they should have. Or Hendry the Poor, with all those weddings to pay for. And here's another interesting thing. Hannah was the sister of Peter Clark who happened to be married to Maggie Ann, my grandfather Charles Addison's sister! This means that their daughters, Lottie and Jenny, were doubly related to their Uncle Peter at Birkenbog Home Farm. And maybe this is the most remarkable thing of all: when William went off to the tea planting in India, he left his wife Hannah to manage Cairnton until he came back.

I also did not know that the bones of my ancestors, both Addisons and Munros, lay in the old churchyard adjacent to the picturesque old castle, while at the other side of the Academy's playing field wall, in the new cemetery and into which I once hit a mighty six, lay the remains of these other relations I have just mentioned.

My grandfather's brother, James Wright Addison, lies in the same grave as his in-laws. His father-in-law, William Hendry, died at Cairnton on May 27th 1921 aged 65. When he died, Hannah moved into Portsoy.

She lived for nearly twenty more years before she died at Aird House on March 5th 1941 aged 83. Her son-in-law, James, did not survive her for very long. He died on April 23rd 1945 aged only 57. Lottie, his wife, followed him to the grave on January 23rd 1961. She was 69.

At the time of their deaths, James and Lottie were living at Auchip, a mile-and-a-half southwest of Fordyce. In 1901, James's father and mother, William and Jane Wright, had moved the family there from Summertown, with the exception of my grandfather who would have been twenty-seven or eight at the time and stayed on at Summertown. It was just a mere three-quarters of a mile away as the crow flies. I can imagine the corbie from the ballad asking his wife, "Whaur shall we gang an' dine the day? Summertown or Auchip?"

Maggie Ann, who, may I remind you, brought up her brother William's two-year-old daughter, Netta, after her mother died, sleeps the Big Sleep along with her husband, Peter Clark, nearby. Their home and farm of Birkenbog was not far from the schoolhouse in Deskford and we passed within a mile of it every Saturday when we went to Cullen for my mother to do the shopping and my father to go to the bank on school business. But there would have been no point in calling in. By then Maggie Ann and Peter were no longer there. She died on 24th February 1959 aged 82. He predeceased her on 8th May 1952 aged 81. Sharing the grave is their son, William, who died on 31st May 1971 aged only 57 and his wife, Dorothy Jack, who followed him on 15th February 1987. She was 69.

As a boy, I never heard Maggie Ann's name mentioned, at least not that I remember. In fact I did not even know that my grandfather *had* a sister, let alone three brothers. It was only my father's siblings whom I knew, but ironically I did know Maggie Ann's granddaughter Beatrice. She was at Fordyce with me, the daughter of William and Dorothy above. She did happen to mention to me that she was a cousin of mine but it never occurred to me to ask her to explain the connection. On my recent trip back to the North-East to conduct my researches, I was saddened, not to say shocked, to find the grave of her husband, James Barclay, who died aged only 64 on 10th July 2010. There are few things more calculated to concentrate the mind on your mortality than to see people of your own age with their name on a tombstone.

But there was one day I remember my mind was very much concentrated on my mortality. I was only fifteen, and as I set off for Fordyce that morning, I remember looking at my parents and my sister and wondering if it would be the last time I would ever see them alive. It was as undramatic and as unemotional as that. I didn't feel fear, I didn't think I was too young to die, nor do I remember picking up any vibes from my parents that the end was nigh. It was October 25th 1962 and the Cuban missile crisis was in its seventh day. Three days previously, President Kennedy had told the world and released photographs to prove that the Russians had been installing missiles on America's doorstep and demanded their withdrawal forthwith. He also imposed a blockade on the island.

As I left for school that morning, Russian ships with what looked suspiciously like missiles on the upper deck, were steaming towards the quarantine zone. Would they stop and turn back? What if they didn't? The Americans would be sure to fire warning shots across the bows. What if the Russians ignored them? Would the Americans actually fire on the ships? You can imagine they would have to, and if that happened, Kruschev would have to retaliate. He would not like to lose face in front of the world. Even to instruct the ships to turn back would seem too much of a climb-down.

The world held its breath but school seemed to carry on as usual. Maybe the rector had his ear to the radio, ready to send us home if hostilities had started. Would it go nuclear right from the start? Would Kruschev use his Cuban missiles in a pre-emptive attack? Well of course we all know now that war was averted, but that was the hottest day of the Cold War and the closest the world had come to World War Three that day or since.

My daily trips to Fordyce were not without incident and danger too, though nothing like that of course. I seem to have got a free passage on the way to school, but as I came closer and closer to home, my heart began beating faster and faster. After the long coast downhill I knew it had nothing to do with pushing the pedals but everything to do with the mad dog that rushed out to bite me as I entered Kirkton. No matter how hard I tried to kick the mutt in the muzzle, I never connected, and far from discouraging the brute from taking a pound of flesh from my leg, for all I know that may even have encouraged it, given it a sense of sporting danger.

One day it did succeed in sinking its teeth in me which necessitated a trip to the doctor for an anti-tetanus jag. I got that in the bum which was even more painful. For a start, it was embarrassing to have to stick your bum in the air in front of a perfect stranger (well it would be in front of anyone really), but even that was nothing compared to the pain as the fluid penetrated the muscle.

After this incident, my father did protest to the dog's owners and it was muzzled. That did nothing to stop its attacks however, and even through the muzzle it still managed to give me a nip, while for my part, I never succeeded in making my foot connect with its jaws. You would have thought that the owners would have chained the brute up, or at least kept it under control, but I am convinced they let it loose deliberately. I remember seeing them standing at their front door as I cycled past and they never once called the brute to heel. It followed me up the road a bit, snapping its jaws as much as the muzzle would allow, before turning away of its own accord. Perhaps they didn't like me for some reason, though I can't think why since they didn't know me, only who I was. Maybe that was it. I'm glad however, for the entertainment I provided them with: it was certainly better than watching some kid's programme on black-and-white TV. There was not a wide selection of programmes in those days.

And so, at the close of every day of my school career at Fordyce, as I mounted my trusty steed to begin my homeward journey, I knew I had that unwelcoming prospect to look forward to. But one day, there was for me, especially, an even more hair-raising moment, one that gave me goose bumps, literally. Unexpectedly, rounding a corner, I came across a goose and a gander leading the very young goslings across the road. What well-behaved children! They were strung out in single file in a perfectly straight formation. I would challenge a teacher today to get their charges across the road in such an orderly fashion. And then the gander detached himself from the end of the line and came charging at me with outspread wings and hissing the foulest language I have ever heard a bird utter. I had already come to a halt and I stood there, rooted to the spot, too terrified to move lest it was misinterpreted, thinking that all I could do to protect myself would be to put my steed betwixt it and me.

Fortunately the aggressive fellow came to a halt within a few feet of me. His wings seemed to span the width of the road whilst he continued to tell me in no uncertain terms that I was to go nowhere near the weans. When I found my voice, I told him as kindly as I could that I had absolutely no intention of harming them. On hearing this, he lowered his wings a little, looked over his shoulder at where his Missus by now had completed her manoeuvre, followed by the obedient children, and hissed a final warning at me to keep my distance before he strutted off to join them, his chest puffed out with righteous self-importance. "That was him tellt!" he told the wife, ruffling his feathers.

I waited until they were well and truly in the farmyard before remounting my bike. I had heard it said, and I don't know how true it is, that a swan can break your arm or leg with its wings and I could see no reason why a goose could not do the same, but it was certainly not something I wanted to put to the test. I also knew that the Romans kept geese as so-called "watchdogs". This was my closest encounter with a goose since I ate one of this one's relatives, the one that the Macs gave us for Christmas, and if I could well

410

understand the reason for the Romans' preference for this form of attack alarm, I could not fathom, for the life of me, how Mr Mac, I presume, rather than Mrs, could go anywhere near a goose, let alone take it by the neck and wring the life out of it.

Chapter Thirty-eight

The Fordyce Saga: Part One

If the journey to and from school had its dangers, the school itself was a haven. Such a difference from Keith Grammar! It was rather like being transported from hell to heaven. For a start there was absolutely no bullying and the class sizes were small. If I remember correctly, just over twenty in the larger, compulsory classes such as English and Maths and only three in my German class: Mary Gardiner, Irene Sandeson and me. With practically individual attention, one may have thought that I would have ended up speaking German like a native, there being absolutely no chance of daydreaming, for like the Ancient Mariner, our teacher questioned one of the three of us, each in our turn, and there was absolutely no possibility of escape. When he wanted to make a particular point he would say, "Now listen, people," as if we were a multitude.

Now forty years later I can scarcely remember a word of German apart from the German equivalent of *the sixth sick sheik's sixth sheep's sick* which is—*In Ulm, um Ulm und um Ulm herum*. To me the English tongue twister makes the German sound like infant babbling, but I'm sure they must have stronger contenders. But then, maybe it is not our strongest either. So given the years without putting it into practice, it's not surprising that my German rusted up like a Crusader's wife's chastity belt.

The other thing I remember which had nothing to do with German except that it was told by our German teacher, was a joke about Queen Victoria who apparently thoroughly enjoyed a bowl of Scotch Broth either when she was staying at Balmoral or travelling in those airts and addressed the creator of this culinary delight thus: "This is a lovely soup. Tell me, my good man, what is it made of?"

Our teacher, Mr McIver, or "Dodie", did the voices: a very posh one for Queen Victoria and a very Doric one for the other. When he told us jokes, his nose would wrinkle, pushing his glasses further up his face so he had to blink them down again. Meanwhile, the top of his bald head would grow pink with the hilarity of it. This is the only joke of his I remember and this is how the rest of it goes.

"Weel, your majesty, there's neeps in t'ill't, an' carrots in t'ill't, an' ingins in t'ill't, an' barley in t'ill't, an'—"

"Quite so," interrupted the monarch impatiently, "but what I would like to know is what is 'in t'ill't?'"

"Weel, your majesty," repeated the other patiently, "there's neeps in t'ill't, an' carrots in t'ill't, an' ingins in t'ill't, an' barley in t'ill't—"

"Yes, yes, you've told me all that before," interrupted the head of the British Empire in exasperation, but what I want to know is: WHAT IS IN T'ILL'T?'"

Taking a deep breath, the unlucky vassal began all over again, hiding *his* exasperation as best he could.

"Weel ma'm, there's neeps in t'ill't, an . . ."

As with all his jokes, at this point Dodie's entire head would turn a deeper shade of pink and he would study our faces closely to see how much we had enjoyed the pleasantry. We were well-brought up kids and had the grace to smile, then when he looked down at his book again prior to proceeding with the lesson after this hilarious interlude, we would lift quizzical eyebrows at each other and shake our heads imperceptibly lest he caught us, as if to say, "Poor sod, he's quite mad!" But we knew he was quite harmless really and we really liked him.

Why he was called "Dodie" I have no idea. Maybe someone found out his name was George but he didn't look like a "George", far less a "Dod". Imagine an older sort of Mr Pickwick and you have him exactly. He lived across the road from the school and I remember he scored lots of runs in the pupils versus teachers cricket match, probably their leading scorer, and I remember feeling sorry for him going home to his lonely flat and with no-one to boast to of his exploits, though I was probably wasting my sympathy. He must have been very happy indeed to have been a teacher at Fordyce Academy, as surely all the other teachers must have been, with small classes and if not all pupils were thirsting for knowledge exactly, at least there were no disruptive ones at all.

Dodie was supported in the Modern Languages department by Nell. That was her name and her nickname. She was a spinster and lived in Cullen with her sister Hannah who was in the Maths department. Never did you see such different siblings. Hannah was the archetypal sweet old lady with snow-white hair tied back in a bun and the most piercing blue eyes you ever saw, though dimmed somewhat with age. In the year oatcake she had been dux of the Academy where she now taught and had never taught anywhere else.

Never was the phrase "in with the bricks" more true. But Nell was a different kettle of fish. She too had the same gimlet blue eyes but they looked out of you from a brown and wrinkled face that looked as if it could do with a good iron. She looked as fierce as a bulldog and had a voice to match, but her bark was worse than her bite.

One day, someone, I can't remember who, but it wasn't me, was sitting in the row in front of Nell's desk when his foot accidentally brushed against Nell's. She stopped the lesson at once.

"Young man, stop playing footsie footsie with me," she commanded, then giving a big sniff, she looked round the room at us as if morally outraged.

On another occasion, and again the perpetrator wisnae me, she astonished us by saying, "It's no good looking at me like that. I am impervious to the looks of young men." (Sniff. Look of indignant outrage.) I have no idea what had occurred to give rise to this remark (being so closely engaged in my studies) but the idea that any one of us could have ever given Nell anything like what could have been remotely misconstrued as what used to be called a "come hither" look was just so preposterous (as she well knew) that it had the desired effect of producing gales of mirth from us and heaping cringe-making confusion and embarrassment on the unlucky perpetrator.

One guilty person I will name and shame is Jimmy Cowie (pronounced Cooee). I am sure he will forgive me if ever he reads this. One of the exercises we had to do was to write a short story, in French, based on the events depicted in a panel of four pictures. It was a progressive story about a dog walking along the street past the baker's and so on. There was a woman coming out of the butcher's with a link of sausages trailing from her basket. The dog seized the sausages and ran off pursued by an angry crowd crying "Arrêt, voleur!" or at least they did in my tale.

The embarrassing thing about this exercise is that Nell would read our efforts out for the edification of the class, together with an explanation of our *fautes*. And so it came to poor Jimmy Cowie's effort.

"Le chien, qui s'apelle Frou-Frou—" and here Nell broke off, extending Jimmy's jotter at arm's length and retaining as little contact with the jotter as she must in order to defy the forces of gravity. You might have thought the way she was holding it that it was her shoe after she had stepped in dog poo or some other foul-smelling substance rather than an inoffensive jotter, albeit rather dog-eared (appropriately enough). What on earth could Jimmy Cowie have written that Nell found herself incapable of proceeding with the story? We were soon to find out.

"James Cowie," sneered Nell. "Does this dog *look* like a 'Frou-Frou'? (Deep sniff followed by a look round the room in search of approval for her point.)

And she did have a point really. It did not look anything like a "Frou-Frou", for the dog in question was, without any shadow of a doubt, not a poodle which you imagine *would* rejoice under such a handle, but of full-blooded Scots heritage, a terrier, from Aberdeen to be precise. He would certainly rather have died than answer to "Frou-Frou" Nell must have thought—and she was probably right.

Hannah was a dedicated teacher who cared deeply about her pupils, which is not to say Nell didn't. For the first time in three years I had some Maths tuition at last. Patiently and painstakingly, Hannah would try to explain the mysteries of Maths to me but it was an uphill struggle and I had too much ground to make up for instant results. I remember once, after her spending a long time trying to explain something to me, my failure to still not see the light brought tears to her eyes and her whole being to the brink of despair. My desk was at the front of the class, she was standing in front of me and after I failed to give the correct answer, or indeed any answer at all, it practically brought to her knees. In a totally spontaneous gesture, she slapped her hands on her thighs, her knees bent in a posture of supplication, and with tears brimming in her eyes she pleaded, "Can you *not* see that, David?"

It broke my heart just as much as hers to have to let her down like this. It felt like a betrayal. I would have done anything to have been able to see, but for the life of me, I just couldn't. I am sure if I had had kind-hearted Hannah from the start, I would have had twenty-twenty vision in Maths, but alas I didn't.

I was not the only person to break poor Hannah's heart. There was another boy who did a far, far worse thing. It came to Hannah's attention that Ronnie (not his real name), was not giving her his undivided attention. In a casual manner, she made her way up the aisle and like a cat who pretends it couldn't care less about its prey before it suddenly pounces, Hannah sprang her trap and seized from under the desk, where Ronnie had been poring over it—a magazine of ladies so poor they could not afford any clothes.

Oh, what a sigh was there, as Hannah needed only the briefest of glimpses to see, and dismiss, what Ronnie had found so absorbing. In fact it was not so much a sigh, more a cry, but not one of disgust as you may have expected from a spinster lady of a certain age. I'm sure Miss Marple, who never turned a hair at all those dead bodies who had been most foully murdered and whom she kept stumbling over everywhere she went, would have swooned straight away at the sight of all those bare bosoms. (Those magazines were not very explicit in those days—or so I have been told.) But not Hannah. She was made of much sterner stuff.

There were tears in her eyes as she held up the open magazine to afford us a glimpse, too brief a glimpse regrettably, of the evidence, and nothing like as distastefully as Nell did Jimmy Cowie's French jotter.

"You see, class, *this* is what Ronnie is interested in!" she said, waving the offending literature about in front of us. "Oh, Ronnie! Ronnie!" she cried in despair before handing it back to him. She knew she was fighting a lost cause, even more lost than trying to make David Addison understand the basics of quadrilateral equations, although she probably did not realise what we boys knew for certain—that Ronnie was very highly-sexed—and coming from fifteen and sixteen-year old adolescents who thought of sex morning, noon and night, even in our dreams, that was saying something.

The worst thing I remember we did, though I was only a bystander, was the prank we played on the French *assistant*. I remember nothing about him, not his name or where he came from exactly, or any of his lessons. All I remember was that he had one of those ridiculous Citroën Deux Chevaux, the thing that looks like an upturned pram, and deservedly an object of ridicule for something that was meant to be a motor vehicle. Having said that, it had managed to get him from wherever he lived in France to civilisation in the North-East of Scotland.

He had parked it at the front of the school, locked it, left the handbrake on as the Highway Code says you should, and I didn't know you could do this, but it is possible to move a car by rocking it and bouncing it and that's what my colleagues did, bounced it foot by foot to the back of the school. Of course, for something that looks like a pram, that was relatively easy to do. It practically begged to be rocked in fact. All it needed was a baby in the front seat. It would have taken a whole lot more effort to move a proper car I suppose but as it happens, there was a precedent for this, before my time. The music teacher's car, a proper car (I believe it may have been a Vauxhall, belonging to a certain Mr Hutcheson), was bounced so tightly against two walls that the only way to get it out again was to bounce it back out.

Great was the consternation of Monsieur when he emerged from the school, great was the scratching of the head and even greater the Gallic wrath when he finally traced his beloved buggy to where it had been left at the rear of the school, none the worse for its bumpy journey one hopes. I don't remember if the perpetrators were ever traced, or if they were, what punishment they received for their enthusiastic efforts to derail the entente cordiale. Probably they were school leavers and this was their leaving statement.

"Bomber" Thomson was our PE teacher (and erstwhile coach of Buckie Thistle). There was something of the gypsy about him with his tight, raven-black curls and skin as tanned as leather. At the start of a lesson he would warm us up by making us stand in a line and with amazing dexterity and speed, he would move down the line slapping us on the bum, then he would point to the left or right and as we were instinctively deceived into turning the other cheek, like Jesus told us to do, he would also slap that, then before you knew it, he would slap that other cheek again, the one you sat on, before moving on to the next boy. It was all over in seconds. Greased lightning could have taken lessons in speed from him.

A teacher could never get off with that nowadays but it wasn't sore and none of us ever thought of complaining. If we had, no doubt he would have said it was to sharpen our reactions. To me it smacks of the armed services and one of the milder forms of humiliation doled out by bullying sergeants to the National Service conscripts and which was fortunately abandoned just in time for me to miss it. I wouldn't be surprised if Bomber had been at the receiving end of this himself and his nickname derived from his wartime activities.

I was never much addicted to sport, apart from cricket, which did not demand a great deal of high octane energy, though as you may remember, I was a pretty fair runner, especially over long distances. However, when it came to cross-country running, something I may possibly have excelled at, some other non-exercise addicts and I would find a place to hide and while away the time before panting in after a suitable length of time had elapsed, allowing the keen ones to finish far ahead of us.

I'm not sure what Bomber did whilst we were "running"—maybe he put his feet up in the staff room and puffed away himself on a fag. Nice work if you can get it and certainly better than marking a score and more of English or History essays, (the teaching profession was always unequal) but we did see him once from our hiding place scouting for slackers, though mercifully, he did not spot us. I was scared of the consequences if he had caught us, but I felt absolutely no feelings of guilt. What need had I of compulsory exercise? I was probably the fittest boy in the school after cycling ten miles a day over hill and dale.

"Stretchy" was our Latin teacher, so-called for the obvious reason that he was so short he was in need of a good stretch. That's what we called him, though he was known to the rest of the world as Jack Forsyth. He had an unusual method of literally knocking the extinct language of the Romans into us. A complete contrast to Beak in every way, he had a long forelock which he had to keep pushing back into place, a hooked nose and a curling lip which some might have thought gave him rather a cruel expression, especially when you take into account the unorthodoxy of his teaching methods. He would pace up and down the classroom, then make a sudden lunge and punch some poor boy in the belly. It was a very dynamic way of teaching and kept us all on our toes, though not even I needed to stand on mine to see over the top of his head.

I'll never forgot the day when we were all standing at our desks and he did one of his lightning strikes, suddenly pivoting on his heel and smashing his fist into Harold Stewart's solar plexus. We were, of course, accustomed to his methods and constantly on our guard to protect our midriffs as assiduously as footballers are to protect the family jewels during a free kick, but this caught poor Harold completely unawares. He folded up like a penknife and went reeling back, scattering desks everywhere until he came to a full stop at the wall at the back of the room.

If ever there was an aftermath to this, I never heard of it, but I doubt if there was. And if Stretchy felt that he had overstepped the mark on this occasion, then he showed no signs of it. He was no doubt as surprised as the rest of us at the scale of devastation that this "little" punch had caused. As for Harold, he was a good-natured lumbering sort of loon, an embryonic farmer if ever I saw one and who bore no ill will, but once he had got his breath back, merely grinned and up-righted his desk again while the rest of us put the room to rights again.

It seems to me that Stretchy couldn't help but lash out like a cobra. He was like a tightly-coiled spring and once wound up, he had to unwind or burst. Or, a more appropriate simile comes to mind—he was like a piece of elastic that had been stretched to its limit and he had to release the pent-up energy and let fly a punch at whoever was nearest. I don't know if he ever tried this in the pub or not, but I wouldn't have thought it was a very good idea unless he could run very fast.

And I once saw him do exactly that and it was one of the funniest things I have ever seen, his little legs a blur as he had to keep running in order to keep upright. It was on a mountain somewhere in Kintail. Every year he took a party of boys camping and hill walking in those parts, a fact which I was careful not to bring to my parents' attention.

"You didn't tell us about the hill-walking camp in Kintail," they confronted me with one Saturday.

I know it was a Saturday because they had happened to bump into Stretchy in Cullen on their habitual visit to the metropolis. (Maybe he was so small they hadn't seen him coming.) Unfortunately he was one of my father's acquaintances. Just another example of how the cards can be stacked up against you when your father is a teacher.

"No."

"Why not?"

"'cos I don't want to go."

"You're going and that's final!"

Which is exactly why I hadn't told them. They were always trying to make a man of me. I bet they were sorry that National Service had stopped and they couldn't send me there to be toughened up. They had to go to the expense of buying me a pair of boots which, being new, were as tough, inflexible and unyielding as their hearts. (I don't know why the simile equates toughness with old boots: new boots would be more like the thing.) They caused my feet no end of grief: blisters and bleeding.

Those boots, like Nancy Sinatra sang a few years later, were made for walking, and they tramped all over Kintail, including the Seven Sisters. The only thing is I wasn't in them: I had loaned them to someone else. That was because I had developed very sore guts. Dismiss the "gastro enteritis" episode at Keith Grammar from your mind. This was real. In fact I suspected it could be appendicitis. Stretchy examined me, putting his hand down the front of my trousers and having a feel but he couldn't be sure. Neither was I . . .

It was decided that I had better stay in the camp. I can't remember if I spent the day there alone or not,

423

but what would have happened I wonder, if it really had been appendicitis? We were in the back of beyond, miles from anywhere. I could have been the third member of the family to die of peritonitis, though of course I didn't know then about my antecedents.

We travelled like cattle to our destination in the back of a covered truck that was open at the back and it was there that the boy who was lucky enough to benefit from my boots (and I do remember his name, but will spare his blushes) was the winner of an unusual competition which helped speed us merrily on our bone-shaking and rattling journey, not to mention the motorists coming behind who also would have witnessed this edifying spectacle. I never knew that you could set fire to a fart, let alone that if you do (as you might) it burns with a blue flame. Boots Boy's contribution was very impressive, like a blowtorch, and for the seconds that it lasted, must have propelled us more speedily towards our destination, like a rocket.

This was the very same person who Fate decreed should be sitting in front of me with his girlfriend on the school's outing to my first-ever live Shakespeare production, *The Merchant of Venice,* at Her Majesty's Theatre, Aberdeen. (Stretchy would have been perfect as Shylock.) They spent the whole time snogging. It was hard enough to concentrate on the Bard's immortal words without that alternative show, more interesting than blank verse, going on in front of my innocent eyes.

There was something that went on during that camping trip to Kintail that I did not see, thank God. It wasn't a spectator sport: it was a competition that went on in one of the tents, maybe even my tent, but I was only told about it later. The contestants pored over the sort of literature that Ronnie was much addicted to and the winner was he who came first in both senses of the expression.

I understand that sort of thing is rife in the Public schools of England and from whence historically, come our political masters, and still do today—which should give us pause for thought when we hear and see them pontificating. Our English teacher (Norman Emanuel Faid, remember?), told us that Fordyce Academy was like Eton. What he had in mind, I am supposing, was the size of the classes, not this. I do not know who won this competition, but of the contestants, one is now dead and another has cancer. Intimations of mortality again as Wordsworth didn't quite put it. Another, the winner, has to have his wrist permanently in a sling. [No, not really.]

From a misquotation to a proper quotation— *Abandon hope all ye who enter here*—as Dante did say, at least in translation. These words were inscribed in rude letters on a piece of cardboard at the entrance to the latrine which we dug out ourselves, of course. Oh, the fun we had! But only Stretchy would have had the erudition to think of such an apposite caveat, so I presume he was responsible for the wit. It was only years later that I, for one, realised where the words came from, but what I knew instantly, without the need for the brain to move into second gear, was that you got out of that hell hole just as soon as you possibly could and it was definitely not the sort of a place you would take a book in with you.

But that day, up that mountain, Stretchy stumbled and nearly fell and the only way to remain on his feet was to keep up the momentum he had been precipitated into and thus he began running downhill. It was a long time before he could apply the brakes and come safely to a halt. Of course we should not have laughed as it could have had potentially serious consequences, but it was a very funny sight and fortunately only his dignity was hurt.

He will certainly be dead long ago but I saw Stretchy once again long after this when I was on my teaching practice at Banff Academy. By that time he had become Speech and Drama advisor for Banffshire. He was, in fact, a keen amateur thespian and although I don't remember him teaching it at Fordyce, he did put on a production of *The Pirates of Penzance* in collaboration with the music teacher aforesaid, Mr Hutcheson, who found his car immobolised. He was a cause célèbre at the time because he married one of his pupils, (not anyone I knew) just like Peter Addison and Bente, and I reckon, just about the same time. As a matter of fact, I had "Hutchy" as we called him, when I was at Keith Grammar.

I don't remember any of his lessons, not even singing *Non Nos Domine,* the school song, but I do remember clearly what he looked like. He wore gold-rimmed glasses and had very short hair, long before the fashion of shaving one's head down to the wood became an ugliness statement among young men. His whole face and head looked as if he had been highly polished, and like Robin at Keith, he seemed to suffer from a surfeit of saliva. I could only guess at his age but I would have thought somewhere in the region of thirty.

And that is all I remember about the teachers at Fordyce Academy, apart from my friend Michael's father, the aforementioned English and History teacher, Norman Emanuel Faid. As I knew him better than any of the other teachers, I will keep him to the next and succeeding chapters.

What I have to tell you will amaze you. If my parents had ever found out, they would have killed me. But that was later, when I had him in Banff.

Chapter Thirty-nine

The Fordyce Saga: Part Two

When I transferred to Fordyce Academy, I already slightly knew Michael, Norman Emanuel's son, but I suppose we would have been friends anyway, for apart from both having teachers as parents, we both shared a love of crime novels. He did not much care for *The Saint* though and thought that the humour was misplaced in the genre. He was much more addicted to the hard-bitten American school of crime fiction such as Mickey Spillane and Ed McBain's *Precinct* novels, and although I read them dutifully, I was not much taken with them, firstly I think because they were set in a culture that was alien to me, but mainly because I did not like the style. I did not think they were at all well-written. Thus spake the pubescent literary critic.

We also shared a love of writing our own short stories and novels in that genre. I was extremely jealous when in 1963 he had literary success when he had a short story published in the *Sexton Blake Magazine*, but it was not too long after that that my short story *The Rebel* was published and for which I received the princely sum of twenty-one shillings or a guinea, if you prefer. This was indeed riches to me, far easier than the backbreaking howking of tatties and a marvel to me to think that you could actually be paid for doing something you liked.

A writer's life for me, I thought, and began writing the further adventures of *The Rebel*, a sort of hybrid between William Brown and junior Saint (who was alternatively known as a "modern-day Robin Hood"). The difference between William and The Rebel was that William never seemed to go to school, whereas my stories were more school-based and the sort of wrong the Rebel righted was excessive amounts of homework imposed by tyrannical teachers. Needless to say, he always emerged victorious and what's more, got the girl, which would have shaken the misogynistic William to his very roots. But he was only eleven, whereas my character, or alter ego, was fifteen, and packed to the eyebrows with hormones.

One of my most admired writers, Robert Louis Stevenson, when an aspiring writer, described himself as a "sedulous ape", by which he meant he honed his craft by imitating the style of other writers and although I was not aware of this until my University days, it is in fact what I did, albeit with much less dedication and intensity.

The Rebel's adventures were humorous in a contemporary setting, but the exploits of my other hero, Nigel, were thrilling tales of derring-do, set in the time of the English Civil War, and about which I knew practically nothing, apart from, in my view, the Cavaliers were dashing, romantic figures who wore nice clothes and long hair with cascades of ringlets falling to their shoulders—a style I would have emulated if only my parents had allowed me. To my mind the Roundheads were a boring lot of killjoys. They deserved to die and that was the basis of my plot. Nigel went about slaying every Roundhead in sight but he gave them a chance first, defeating them through his skill with his rapier, the inspiration for that, I am sure, being *The Three Musketeers*.

But my hero's premise that the only good Roundhead was a dead Roundhead (which owed much to the TV Westerns mentioned in earlier chapters and a genre in which I also dabbled), met with severe disapproval from my father who did not like Nigel's psychopathic tendencies one bit and suspected that I may be tarred with the same brush, considering the way I wallowed in death with all those crime mysteries I devoured.

I tried my hand at them too. My hero was a private detective called Paul Marshall. I thought that an appropriate name for someone on the side of righting wrongs against the ungodly, but I am sure, also tipping more than a nod in the direction of Raymond Chandler's Philip Marlowe—the one American crime writer whom I thought had a very fine literary style, but inimitable, and which I therefore did not attempt to ape.

It was the only full-length manuscript I ever completed and although it seemed long to me, I am sure it would actually have been very short. I remember making my handwriting bigger and bigger in the school exercise book in which I recorded my hero's exploits in order to make the novel seem longer, but apart from that, all I can remember about it now was it was called *The Bus Murder* and there was one scene, set in a clairvoyant's tent, and Paul was very angry indeed with the flatfooted policemen who walked all over the place, destroying clues in the process. The source for this, I am sure, was Enid Blyton's *Famous Five*, or Fatty in the *Five Find-Outers*, precocious little brats who were always much smarter than the professionals who appeared educationally subnormal by comparison.

Alas, all these embryonic works of literature are lost to the world, wilfully and knowingly destroyed by some person very well known to me—me. But if, by some miraculous event, one of these long-lost gems somehow escaped destruction and was to be found, let's say in someone's attic, it would be interesting for me to find out if I would die laughing or die of embarrassment.

I wouldn't say that it was Norman Emanuel who inspired me to put words down on the page for others to read—that was something that had been with me for as long as I can remember, but like all the other teachers at Fordyce, I considered him a very good teacher. He was prone to practising his golf swing with his pointer during his expositions and when none of us knew the answer to something, he would launch into: *You blocks, you stones, you worse than senseless things* from *Julius Caesar* which is as good a way as any of dinning the immortal words of the Bard into thick skulls.

If Ronnie read titillating magazines under his desk, I can't cast any stones at him as I remember reading a Hammond Innes novel beneath *my* desk whilst Norman Emanuel wittered on about something of much more literary merit. I could have written about it in my 'O' Grade exam, but one was required to write about two different genres and I wrote about *Captain Blood* by Rafael Sabatini instead and since neither poetry nor drama formed part of my private reading, I was forced to fall back on something taught by Norman Emanuel for my second answer. And despite my scorning of his pearls of wisdom, I still managed to pass my 'O' Grade

English. I would have liked to say with flying colours, but all you got was a pass or a fail.

It's a funny thing, but I don't remember what I got for any of my English essays, or whether Michael and I vied for top spot, but it would not surprise me if that honour went to Mary Inglis who was so bright you could have called her gifted, or Jim Goodall, who was similarly blessed with brains. But then there were so many others who were brainy that you may have been forgiven for thinking that Fordyce Academy only selected *la crème de la crème*, like Eton, only dispensing with the entrance exam and the enormous annual fee.

As far as History was concerned, we studied the French Revolution and the Napoleonic Wars which is a pretty interesting period of history anyway but 'O' Grade History was a doddle since we were well practised and prepared for the exam which we were told would certainly include *The Causes of the French Revolution* and *Who made the greater contribution to Napoleon's defeat— Nelson or Wellington? Discuss.*

A sad day it was for us all when Fordyce Academy closed its doors to secondary pupils in 1964. With some teachers, we transferred to Banff Academy, all but two of us—two girls who perversely elected to go to Keith. I don't know why, but they did not like me very much. One of them hit me with a hockey stick and split my eye open. Not because she didn't like me, I hasten to add—it was purely accidental. If it hadn't been, she would have aimed her stick lower down. I can't remember if it was an official game under Bomber command or whether it was an official boys versus girls match as part of school sports day, or whether we were just "playing". Despite the fact that my assailant did not do it deliberately, it was a foul act in the sense that she lifted the stick well over her shoulder before contact with my eyebrow put a stop to her back swing.

Copious amounts of blood sprang forth instantly and refused to stop and it was Norman Emanuel who took me down to the doctor's in Portsoy whilst I tried to staunch the flow with a towel. I won't divulge the GP's name but he was notorious in the town for his alcoholic tendencies. When we got to his surgery, he was unsteady on his feet and after he had examined the gash he pronounced in heavily slurred tones: "Thasgonnaneesomestitches." Naturally this gave me some cause for alarm. Breathing in the whisky fumes from his breath was enough to make *me* light-headed, unaccustomed as I was then, to our national beverage.

But I need not have worried. Dr Who diagnosed himself incapable of performing such a delicate operation in such a vital area and instead I was patched up with wads of cotton wool and Elastoplast and sent back to school looking like a latter-day pirate. I thought that gave me a certain cachet, like the time in Ternemny when I sported a bandage on each knee although the second was more for effect than necessity. A little bit of Elastoplast, if anything, was all that was strictly required to deal with the second wound.

I was just in time for lunch. The dining room was in the assembly hall and we sat on benches at long tables like at a medieval banquet. Happenchance should place Michael and me opposite the perpetrator of the deed and her pal. Not a word was said, not a note of apology, not an iota of sympathy was uttered as the food to my mouth I carried. And when they departed, one unto the other said something I could not quite catch but I knew from the tone was uncomplimentary at best, but probably something sneering about what a big cissy I was, making such a big fuss over nothing.

What I had done to deserve such opprobrium I could not say, but what I can say is that incident did not endear me to them either, especially the one who clobbered me with the stick. She was the little one, her friend the lanky one, was her familiar. Funny that I should remember her name but not the one who struck the blow.

As a footnote to this tale, I thought it incredibly interesting and ironic that these two should be the only two in the entire school when it finally closed, who elected not to go to Banff Academy, but instead chose to go to my most hated institution, the one from which I had strived most assiduously to escape—Keith Grammar. Now, all these years later, I have come to the conclusion that perhaps I was being a bit conceited if I singled myself out as being the sole object of Little & Lanky's displeasure: they probably disliked everyone, apart from each other. I often wonder, and would love to know, what they made of KGS. I can imagine them in the playground in a little huddle of two and on the bus home, in their little clique, discussing the demerits of their new comrades and congratulating themselves on their choice as they had found so many more new people to disapprove of.

Their decision involved no small sacrifice on their part. Like me, they got free transport, but only from the limit of the catchment area, ironically, just two hundred yards from my front door. They must have known when they elected to go Keith rather than Banff they were voting for their feet to undertake a four-mile march to and from school every day, in all weathers. But it would have been the getting-up at least an hour earlier in the mornings that would have put me off, especially in the dark winter days, and as I have said before, we had plenty of snow in Banffshire in those days.

Our paths never crossed in the mornings but I used to meet them on my homeward journey as I biked home. The moment that I rounded a particular bend I knew I would see them as midgets in the distance, growing larger as I bore down upon them, until finally, they became as large as life until the convergence and then, in an instant, it was over.

I only once stopped to speak to them, out of politeness, to ask how they were getting on at their new school, but predictably the answer was monosyllabic and in future I just passed them with the traditional North-East greeting of "Aye, aye" and continued on my way without stopping.

As for the teachers who were forced to find employment elsewhere as a result of the closure of Fordyce, "The Boss", Mr Cruickshank (a nephew of the celebrated actor Andrew Cruickshank who played Dr Cameron in the TV series *Dr Finlay's Casebook*), was demoted to teaching classics at Banff though I imagine his salary was conserved. Hannah and Nell retired. Hannah looked as if she was well past retiring age by the time I arrived at Fordyce anyway, but I bet if the school had carried on, so too would she. Nell must not have been far off retirement either if her wrinkles were anything to judge by. Stretchy might have continued to teach some Latin but I would say that was probably when his Speech and Drama career took off. Where Bomber went I could not say, nor Dodie. Perhaps he retired too. He certainly looked old enough. The only one who taught me at Banff as well as Fordyce was Norman Emanuel.

I think he was the only person who would have let me off with the incredibly bad thing that I did at Banff Academy. Just what that was you will find out in the course of the next chapter, if you will.

Chapter Forty

The Late and Lovestruck Loon

Although I was very disappointed indeed at the demise of Fordyce Academy and if ever there was any sort of closing ceremony for this centre of excellence (and I hope there was) I am not aware of it. But there was one positive thing for me about its closure and my enforced transfer to Banff Academy: my bicycle journey became much, much easier. All I had to do was cycle four miles to the outskirts of Cullen where I hid my bike in the coppice where, like a tuning fork, the road divided, the direction I came from, from Keith, and the other to Banff.

It was a long, slow haul the last half-mile or so from Lintmill to where I stowed my bike but nothing like the hill I had to climb on my way to Fordyce, while the majority of the rest of the journey was relatively flat.

Despite this easier route to school, it did not improve my timekeeping. I was often late to Fordyce, often missing assemblies, but a little application of oil from my bicycle chain was sufficient to convince my first period teacher that the darned thing had come off again. On the occasions when I did make the assembly on time and by the skin of my teeth, I felt so giddy and faint, I had to be taken out before I crumpled into a pool of perspiration on the floor.

At Banff however, I was either incredibly early or incredibly late. I was a familiar sight on the A98 in those days, hitch-hiking to school as I would often miss the school bus. I had my regular lifts, most notably the Mother's Pride bread van, and there's an irony for you, if ever there was one! I never knew my benefactor's name although we became good friends and I could always rely on a lift from him, and what's more, we would beat the bus to school—which is why I would be so incredibly early. But if I missed him, and as long as I could get a lift as far as Portsoy in time, then I knew I could get a lift from Mrs Masson in her Renault.

I remember it was a Renault because her husband owned the Renault garage. She was a teacher at the Academy so when I got a lift from her, it was right to the school door and of course, arrived well ahead of the school bus. She taught domestic science so I never had her as a teacher. She was a very nice lady indeed and naturally, although I thanked her profusely for saving my bacon at the time (and many a time and oft were they), I would like to take this opportunity to express my gratitude again. Just how kind she was to me can be seen by the fact that although she had a son in the year above me, she never once gave *him* a lift to school.

But if I failed to catch Mrs Masson's taxi I was in deep trouble. There was no telling if and when I might get a lift. Too much stress and pressure to begin the day you may have thought, yet some days even the fear of missing my two regular lifts was an insufficient crowbar to prise me out of bed. My parents had long since given up calling me, warning me I was going to be late and issuing dire threats if I did not get up. I just was not born for mornings.

I think I was born after midday which must have something to do with it; that would seem the natural time for me to begin the day. I wouldn't be losing anything, wouldn't be wasting my life by getting up as late as the body dictated—I'd still fit in just as many waking hours a day as the next man; it's just my biorhythms are different. I don't think that's so odd. After all, such an arrangement exists in nature. An owl stays up all night and I would too if I could, for I am nocturnal by nature. My mother always said that I should have been a night watchman. But whereas an owl doesn't give a hoot what other birds do, I have to do my best to fit in with the way the world is ordered around the diurnal and thus I find myself out of kilter with most of society.

Another thing about me (some would say "peculiarity"), is I hate arriving really early for anything and having to waste time hanging about, especially when I could have been curled up in bed. It has been a guiding principle of my life and drives my wife nuts, but usually she gets her way and we are usually hours early for everything. She just can't see it's much more exciting to arrive just in the nick of time for things such as flights. Furthermore, this modus vivendi has resulted in disaster only twice, once when having spent our last *sou*, we arrived in Calais to see the ferry sailing out of the harbour, and when we missed our flight to New Zealand. But those occasions weren't my fault. Not really. Other things conspired.

I did manage to catch the bus to school on quite a number of occasions and if the thought of being late was not enough inducement to make me get up, then the shame of my parents being told that I had not done my homework was. Accordingly, I had to make the supreme effort to catch the bus on the days when homework was due, in order to copy my homework.

I enjoyed Banff Academy almost as much as Fordyce though it was a lot bigger and did not quite have the same feeling of exclusiveness that Fordyce had. And when I say Banff, I am of course referring to the old school at the bottom of the hill and not the new one at the top. That was where I went for teaching practice. The old school *looks* like an Academy with its frontage of Doric columns, whereas the new building is as tasteless, architecturally speaking, as practically everything else that came out of the Seventies.

The rector was Baillie T. Ruthven who left Banff Academy at the same time as I did, in 1965, to become rector at the Royal High School in Edinburgh, once a candidate for the Scottish Parliament building and a very fitting one too I would have thought, architecturally speaking, and about a million light years better than the disfigured carbuncle we are now lumbered with, not to mention the millions we could have saved after the farcical story of the new building's escalating cost made us the laughing-stock of Europe.

Baillie T. had another connection with me in that like me, he began his career in Kirkcudbrightshire or, as I prefer to call it, The Stewartry of Kirkcudbright. He went on to become Professor of Education at Stirling University before becoming principal of Moray House College of Education in 1975. He also chaired the committee that revolutionised teaching in Secondary Schools in Scotland and which bore his name—the Ruthven report. And so, when I became a purveyor of education, as opposed to a consumer of it, Baillie T.'s influence continued still. But all I remember of him is his bald pate and gown which streamed behind him as he made the rounds of his domain.

But it was as a history teacher that he began and it was because of a History teacher that I did a very bad thing indeed, the worst thing I ever did in school and it still staggers me today that I did and, what's more, that I got away with it.

I did not get on with my Higher History teacher at all. I don't know why he did not like me, but he did not (like quite a few others, as you know). He had much of the Nazi Camp Commandant in his make-up—silver, short-cropped hair and gold glasses behind which little eyes glinted malevolently as hard as flint. At least so they appeared to me, but to others, and one boy in particular who I think was in 6th year, they twinkled with benevolence and bonhomie. You might have thought they were the best of mates, he and him. They could even have been drinking partners, for you would never have guessed that he was a schoolboy if you saw him out of school uniform, whereas I would never have been served in a bar in a month of Sundays, and let me say it before you do, it was not only in appearance that I was immature.

The favoured ones sat at the front of the class and enjoyed a lively repartee, whilst for me (and I suspect I was not the only one), he had nothing but the basest contempt which he made blindingly obvious. To be at the receiving end of his caustic tongue and range of vitriolic vocabulary was to be ritually and publicly humiliated and after one dressing-down in particular, for no crime other than giving a wrong answer, I decided enough was enough and I decided there and then, at that precise moment, Higher History and me were a thing of the past.

There was no consultation with my parents: I knew what they would say. Nor were there any such things as parents' evenings. Oh, bliss was it to be a teacher in those days! Baillie T.'s recommendations were still a long way off. There were report cards of course, but nothing like the sort of essays which teachers are required to fill in nowadays. I don't remember what any of my reports said and mercifully none has survived, unlike those of my father and my Aunt Gina's, which must have made their parents extremely proud, just as my parents must have been very disappointed with mine.

I expect there was some compensation in the form of my sister, brighter than me, but who worked her socks off into the bargain—as girls tend to do. Boys tend to have other things on their mind at a certain age, something they can't help thinking about at least every three minutes, or so studies would have us believe, and I was normal in that respect at least: I was madly, deeply, in love.

So there I was with five extra periods a week after I had given up History. What was I going to do with the free time? I could have gone down town and had a fag in the Italian café, only I didn't smoke, and I was too impecunious to buy coffee. Besides I didn't particularly care for it anyway. But the real reason was I was too scared I would be caught by one of Baillie T.'s deputies on the prowl, rounding up strays.

I found a much more cunning way to hide and while away all those hours which seem interminable when you have nothing to do and especially when you know you are doing something wrong, like at Fordyce when I hid in a haystack sheltering from a potential Bomber raid. I am indebted to G. K. Chesterton in one of his *Father*

Brown stories for the inspired solution. In *The Sign of the Broken Sword* a conversation between Father Brown and Flambeau reveals the best place to hide anything: a leaf in a forest, a pebble on a beach and so forth. So, where would you least expect to find a pupil dogging a class? In a classroom of course! And that's what I did. I enrolled for extra English with Norman Emanuel so I could sit beside the Best Beloved: the unexpected benefit of being addicted to reading crime fiction.

I dare say I was the only person in the whole of Banff Academy who could have carried off this daring plot. After all, was I not his son's friend, possibly even his best friend, and had Norman Emanuel not known me since I was in short trousers, and perhaps long before then, because I cannot say when and how my father and he became friends. What Norman Emanuel himself made of this arrangement I do not know. Perhaps he assumed I had a free period at these times (and which I did now) and more than likely he asked Michael if he knew the reason for this eccentric behaviour. Michael would certainly have been able to enlighten him, and yet I was allowed to continue my extra studies.

On the other hand, it was no skin off his nose. I was not any bother, maybe even an attribute to the class since I already had 'O' Grade English under my belt and was able to answer questions, which, as any teacher will tell you, is a great asset in the classroom. Of course I also took what I was meant to be studying—Higher English—where, amongst other literary delights, Norman Emanuel regaled us with Chaucer's best jokes in the *Prologue to the Canterbury Tales*. Actually, I loved Chaucer and still am a great fan.

David M. Addison

Fortuitously I made this transition to extra English after the report cards were issued and so there was no immediate danger of my being found out. I was safe in the knowledge that the Commandant would not report me for he would have been as glad to see the back of me as I was to see the end of him. My biggest fear of discovery came from Norman Emanuel himself but he did not betray me and this is where I got lucky, where events conspired to contribute to the success of my deception. By this time the relationship between the families had cooled after a holiday we spent together camping at Loch Morlich in the Cairngorms. It suited Michael and me all right but I don't think it did anyone else particularly. We climbed Cairngorm together at our own pace and I dare say so did my father and Norman Emmanuel, but I think my mother and sister, and Michael's mother and sister, stayed at base camp.

That, I imagine, was not a meeting of minds as, with hindsight, it seemed to my parents that the real reason we were invited on this holiday was for my sister to keep Michael's sister company. They would have been roughly the same age. My parents found her insufferable and my sister didn't care much for her either.

"Aren't the mountains picturesque?" my sister remarked to her opposite number.

"Pictureek, my dear girl," responded the other, looking down her nose at her.

You see what I mean. Anyway, the traditional Scottish rain and drizzle in the Highlands came to my parents' (and my sister's) rescue. They bailed out their tent and out of the holiday entirely and we came home again. That was probably the last time we saw them socially. I don't recall us ever going to visit them more

444

than once. My parents felt little need for friends and socialising, being so wrapped up in each other, which did nothing at all to help my mother cope with my father's untimely death. Maybe the Faids were sociable people and just had an appalling sense of timing, but they were afflicted with the habit of what the Gaels call *sgiomlaireachd* (but don't ask me to pronounce it)—the habit of dropping in at meal times. I vividly recall the time my mother was in the very act of spreading the tablecloth, then seeing their car draw up, with the same flowing movement, whipping it off again and stowing it out of sight. My parents sat them out. I don't think they were even offered a cup of tea, but I could be wrong about that. In any case they did not get a meal and never tried that ruse again.

Doomsday, of course, was looming nearer every day, yet I cannot say that it concentrated my mind unduly on what I would do when the exam results came out. I went to school as usual on the day of the history exam: it was just another day. There was no such thing as study leave then, though I would have appreciated it for the extra holidays it would have brought.

And when Doomsday finally dawned and I opened the brown envelope which contained my less than spectacular results, History not being among them of course, I merely said I must have failed it so badly that it had not registered even a tremor on the Richter scale of results. I don't remember, but I am sure I must have prepared my parents for this eventuality as they must have asked me after the exam, how I felt it had gone, and I must have said that I had found it very difficult indeed, in tones of abject despondency of course.

You see, I was a bad, bad boy all right, but even worse, cunning with it. That shows a certain level of intelligence does it not? My parents went to their graves never knowing the real reason why I failed History, never realised just how bad and deceitful I really was. It is one thing to break your mother's heart: it is another thing entirely to shatter it, so I am glad she just thought I was thick.

The Best Beloved's mother, the would-be future mother-in-law, did rumble me however, and one day I found myself in deep, deep trouble . . .

Chapter Forty-one

Love's Labour Lost

I suppose you could say it was all my best friend Jim's fault, though I wouldn't, not for a minute.

He was very musical, as I said, and on this never-to-be forgotten evening, like the owl in Lear's nonsense rhyme, was singing to the accompaniment of his own guitar in the Ship Inn at Banff. Being in want of his own pussycat at that time, he asked me, if I had nothing better to do, if I would come along and give him support such as applauding enthusiastically, or even just clapping, at the end of every number. I think it might have been his premiere since he needed no such support in the future. I was happy to oblige. The Best Beloved and I were intending to go to Banff anyway, to the cinema, not because there was a film we desperately wanted to see, but you had to have a purpose, a reason for going out, a destination that her parents would approve of, not the nearest lay-by.

It was no skin off my nose, or so I thought. Three hours in a lay-by, even then, was probably beyond my stamina, so we did give Jim the applause he sought. On the way home, we drove past the Picture House to see what we had supposedly seen and I deposited the Best Beloved back home without stopping in any lay-bys or any of that nonsense. Naturally we were asked what film we had seen and what we thought about it. Easy. We were prepared. Had all the answers.

The next day, totally unprepared for what was just about to happen, I wheeled up at Beauty's castle to find it had been transmogrified into a Dragon's Den and the chatelaine was laboriously scraping flaking paint from the windows. It didn't seem to have occurred to her that she could have removed it much more easily by breathing on it. In response to my cheery greeting, she stopped what she was doing and gave me such a frosty look (amazing for a dragon) that my heart did a sudden somersault. Even worse, she said nothing at all, turning her head away and devoting her attention to her labours. I felt my heart thud. Something was seriously amiss.

I carried on through the open door to find the Best Beloved perched on the edge of the sofa, wringing a handkerchief and sobbing. Her face was bloated, her eyes red and puffy. If I hadn't known better, I would have thought something calamitous had happened like she had just discovered she was pregnant but my conscience was perfectly clear on that score, and I still had no inkling of what could have caused this outpouring of grief on the one hand and overt hostility from the mother on the other.

There was no time to exchange any words which would have demystified me before in came She, the Best Beloved's mother. She was only the size of tuppence but as scary as she was short. As a parent she was extremely strict, kept her oldest daughter, especially, on the tightest of reins. Curfews were imposed and once she even sent the Best Beloved's father down to the Town Hall to hoick her out of a dance as she, too embarrassed to have to admit this shame to her friends, stayed on beyond the allotted hour. But that was nothing to the humiliation she was about to undergo as her father, wild-eyed and furious, his hair dishevelled, his pyjama bottoms showing beneath his coat, appeared at the door to drag his daughter back home by Order of Ayesha, She Who Must Be Obeyed.

I could begin to imagine how she must have felt as Ayesha waved the *Banffie* in front of me, open at the page where next week's cinematic extravaganzas were advertised, including of course, the film we had just "seen" last night and simultaneously accompanied by such a blistering and coruscating attack on my character that I felt like a louse which had been subjected to such a heavy dose of DDT that it was squirming in its death throes before her very eyes. If only I had thought to drive past the cinema *before* we had gone to The Ship! I thought I was good at being bad, but I had much to learn, obviously.

When I finally got a chance to speak and somehow found enough spit to lubricate the utterance of the inadequate words, there was no point in explaining that no drinking had gone on (oh, how I could do with one now!) and that we were only there to support Jim. She already knew that: the Best Beloved had already explained that but it did not alter the fact that we had lied and we were both under age to enter licensed premises.

"I was never in a pub until I was twenty-one," Ayesha wailed, then to my horror, tears began to well up in her eyes and her voice began to quiver as she told me again what an evil influence I was. Thank God her husband was not there, I thought. Things could conceivably have been even worse. I might just get out of here without my head in my hands to play with.

"You've brought shame and disgrace on this family," Ayesha sobbed. "You two are finished. She's never getting out with you again."

The Best Beloved's face was buried in her hands but I could tell from the way her shoulders were heaving that she was silently sobbing. I hoped that it was at the thought of the loss of me, but it might just have been at the shame and the humiliation of it all. Even if it was the former, a fat lot of good it was going to do me, but at least I would be able to get out of this hellhole whilst the Best Beloved would not hear the end of it for days. There was nothing more to be said. Silently, she got up from the settee to escort me off the premises.

We knew She would be watching us. We dared not have "ae fond kiss" before we severed, did not even hold hands, the Best Beloved still wringing the life out of that innocent (and sodden) handkerchief. I now knew precisely how Burns felt when "Clarinda" left him and Scotland for ever when she set sail for Jamaica, which at that time must have felt like the ends of the earth. It felt like the end of my world too.

So this is what it was like to be Romeo! But there was some comfort in the fact that she appeared to be my Juliet. Better to have loved and lost than never to have loved at all. I knew the phrase of course, but did not know, not then, that it came from Tennyson's *In Memoriam,* but I thought it very apposite for the way we young lovers were being forced to part.

And then it was that I discovered something I never would have believed possible, something that took me utterly by surprise, a complete epiphany. What I discovered was that poetry, which I had not had a great deal of time for up to now, Chaucer excepted, had a *use.*

I felt quite the tragic hero as I left the Best Beloved pining at the garden gate for the love that was not allowed to be.

Of course in the cold light of the next school day, things were not as bad as they had seemed. Ayesha could not prevent us from meeting at school, in English classes and on the school bus. It was only weekends that were out of bounds. And finally it came to pass that that ban was lifted too. I don't remember how long it was before I was free again to lead the Best Beloved astray but I set about doing it almost right away. It seemed a good idea at the time, a good laugh, but it turned into a nightmare.

We had been to see *The Sound of Music* in Aberdeen with my mother and sister, and at some stage, dropped into Woolies in Union Street. As most people of a certain age know, the Piggy-wig sold for a shilling, the ring at the end of his nose so that unlikely pairing, the owl and the pussycat, could celebrate their nuptials. We had no intention of taking such a drastic step, at least not then, but in Woolies our attention was captured by a very bright and sparkling engagement ring, price sixpence, or was it one-and-sixpence? It was a bargain anyway. Why would you want to spend a fortune on real diamonds when you could have something as sparkly as this? I don't remember whose idea it was, mine or hers, or maybe it struck us simultaneously: what a laugh it would be if we pretended to be engaged, just to see what the parents' reaction would be!

My mother's reaction was a huge disappointment. Just a shrug of the shoulders and a *que sera, sera* sort of look. Certainly no congratulations. I don't know what I expected, but certainly nothing as devoid of emotion as

451

this. Maybe she had already seen through the "joke" and was not giving us the satisfaction of a reaction. It was the dampest of damp squibs. But when I returned the Best Beloved to her house, oh, there were fireworks all right.

I can see it as if it were yesterday. Her father on the left of the fireplace, us together on the sofa in the middle, her mother on the right. Everything was all right at first but that was because no-one had noticed the ring. At last, impatient with her parents' lack of observational skills, the Best Beloved picked up their little brown toy Poodle, placed it on her lap and began stroking it. That provoked a response all right.

Her mother let out a scream and buried her face in her apron from which the muffled plea, "No! No! Tell me it's no' true! Tell me it's no true!" were just audible enough before the hysterical sobbing began. Whilst I knew that Ayesha did not approve of me a great deal, I presumed any boyfriend would have been treated with the same suspicion of harbouring dishonourable intentions towards her daughter. All the same I was rather staggered, not to say a mite insulted, to find I was considered such an undesirable prospective son-in-law as all that. Mind you, I wouldn't have picked *her* for a mother-in-law either, but there's not much you can do about that. You can't have the one you want without the other, like a hangover the next day after a night of carousing.

I was aware that there was always the risk that the Best Beloved would turn out like her mother. But I thought not. There were three daughters (poor man amongst that regiment of women) but the sixteen-year old philosopher reckoned it would be the middle one who would take after the mother. The other two were like their father, the youngest a blonde version of the original (and best) and only six. I loved her to bits too. I liked the father. Felt sorry for him actually under the thumb of Ayesha. A mild-mannered man, a real gentleman. Just the sort of father-in-law I would have chosen had I had any say in the matter.

But he did have huge hands and I only took a size thirteen collar. That's what I thought as I saw him throw his newly-lit fag into the fire. He was not a rich man and this sacrifice of James the Sixth's "pernicious weed" was no small thing for him. I remember thanking God we weren't telling them we were pregnant. If this was the reaction to a "wee joke", I could never have imagined a better antidote to ripping off the Best Beloved's knickers.

So many things happened at once. At the same time as the apron was attempting to shut out the horror, the dog was pitched on the floor, followed by the ring as the Best Beloved tearfully explained that it was only a "joke" and as the fag was cast to the flames, her father spat out: "Well it wasn't very funny!" What else was he expected to say? As for me, I just sat there, felt the colour drain from my face and wished I was somewhere else, far, far away.

"It had better be!" came from behind the apron, a cry of anguish rather than a threat.

Time seemed suspended. The only sound was the sniffing and snuffling from behind the apron underscoring the awkwardness of the moment. My head down, I stared straight ahead at the fire. A surreptitious glimpse at the mouse of the house told me he was doing the same. Ayesha's face reappeared from behind

453

the apron, the eyes red-rimmed. And still no-one said anything.

At last someone spoke. It was a timid, croaky little voice which I did not recognise at first, then I realised it came from me. "Well I think I had better be going . . ." I had been with the Best Beloved for most of the day, after all. No-one disagreed with me. No-one pleaded with me to stay. No-one said anything. The Best Beloved got up to see me out.

"Phone me tomorrow," I said at the garden gate and did not tarry.

A few years later we did get engaged for real. It was my twenty-first birthday, as it happens, which is why I remember the exact date. I don't know what Ayesha's reaction was this time since the deed was done in Deskford, but I doubt if she was over the moon about it. But she needn't have worried. It was an engagement that did not quite last a year because, reader, I did not marry her. We fell out for the last time in May 1969, the day before my Advanced English degree exam, as it happened. Not exactly the best of timings but that was just the way it was and I don't think that it had a particularly negative effect on my results. I passed the exam anyway.

So ended the romance of my life that had started at the school dance in June 1965. A musical memory helps me remember it well because that underrated group of the Sixties, The Hollies, got their first Number One with *I'm Alive*. We danced to that, maybe it was our first dance together. It was certainly a metaphor for how I felt at the time. I had admired her for some time, and now she was my girlfriend. Yippee! I could not believe my luck. It was a life-changing moment and I still associate her with that song.

Since I lived out in the boondocks, it had been arranged that my father would come to take me home and I asked him to give the Best Beloved and her friend, who happened to live next door, a lift too. I wonder how they would have got home otherwise. I expect the Best Beloved's father would have come for her but how we alerted him to the fact that he need not put his coat on over his pyjamas and drive the eight miles to Banff, I do not know, for incredible as it must seem to younger readers in this age of the ubiquitous mobile phone, they did not even have a phone in the house. There was a phone box just across the street so it was very convenient for the Best Beloved to phone me and if I wanted to get in touch with her, I would ring the box at a prearranged time or, if there were no prior arrangement, I would ring the box and hope that some passing soul would answer it and go and fetch her.

Living in the back of beyond as I did, passing your driving test was a prerequisite for initiating and furthering a romance. Unfortunately for me, but like all the best drivers, I only passed my test at the second attempt. Back then it took weeks and weeks after you had sent in your application before you got a test date, so when, unexpectedly, a cancellation turned up, I did not hesitate for long. What did cause me a moment's hesitation was that the test was in Buckie, whereas I had done all my practising in Keith. I believe I might have passed it first time, had it not been for this change of location, for Buckie had a dual carriageway, something which I had never come across before, and I didn't know that in order to turn right across the central reservation you had to drive on the right. That didn't seem right to me. We drive on the left in this country. I did know *that* much of the Highway Code at least.

I was a tad jealous of my classmates who did not dwell among the "untrodden ways" like Wordsworth's Lucy and I did, but more jealous still of those who had passed their tests, like Jimmy Cowie. His father had an Austin Vanden Plas, the very top of the range, a luxurious car with all the trimmings and a back seat as roomy as a sofa, the most desirable feature of all from the point of view of a teenage youth on a trapping expedition. It would seem, however, that Jimmy's father thought it was just the right size for transporting a sheep, as you do, if you are a farmer.

Whilst that did little for the upholstery or interior of the Vanden Plas, the sheep could not be blamed for the car's mechanical condition. On the very same evening that the Best Beloved and I began our love affair, Jimmy and some other friends arrived at the school dance in style in the Vanden Plas. Not quite to the school gates though. They had to walk the last part of the way as the luxury machine was lacking any brakes other than the handbrake (a condition they knew existed before they set out), and rather inconveniently, the school was situated at the bottom of a hill. Incredibly, they made both legs of the journey safely without so much as a bump.

Unfortunately I could not say the same thing a while later, not long after I had passed my test. I was taking the Best Beloved and another couple to The Two Red Shoes in Elgin. I had been introduced to this place, a sort of upper class cattle market, by my friend Ian from Keith Grammar days, who, after he had passed his test, was allowed the use of his father's A40 van which normally took eggs to customers all over Banffshire and beyond, but which on Saturday evenings, took us to Morayshire.

Going to such a far-flung venue meant that there was absolutely no chance of my ever meeting or getting off with the Best Beloved and I was glad of Ayesha's strictness as it meant at best, that she might be confined to barracks for the weekend, or if she were allowed out, it would be on a curfew, and any other predatory male would say "sod that for a lark" and try and get off with some other bird instead.

In that kind of a mission, Ian and I had varying degrees of success. We hunted together since the girls danced in pairs and since our sort of dancing did not require us to actually touch the other person unless it was a smoochy dance, well-brought up girls, such as those who frequented The Two Red Shoes, would normally agree to grant you at least one dance, no matter how repulsive they thought you. They didn't even have to look at you if they didn't want to. Conversation over the noise was difficult. I had never taken a course in chat-up lines and could never think of anything banal to shout. The tricky part was when the music stopped. That was when you had to say something, preferably witty, before you were dismissed with a "thank you" and you had to sling your hook and make another circuit of the hall to begin fishing all over again.

It was an unwritten law back then that every pretty girl had an ugly friend as a partner and maybe it's still the case today. Ian and I would look at the dancing girls and one of us would say "I fancy her" and the other's duty was to dance with the ugly duckling. And if that person was granted a second dance, it was the duty of the other to keep dancing with her pal, for you knew that female etiquette required that no swan would leave an ugly duckling to dance on her own.

Likewise, according to our unwritten constitution, if one of us did manage to clip the wings of the swan and a date was set for the following week, the other was free to hunt alone and a fat chance you had—but friendship has its limits. Troglodytes we may not have been, but the primitive urge to pass on our genes nevertheless seemed very urgent indeed. But what generally happened, if you did manage to string a few dances together and you began to think that there was a possibility that you might just be getting somewhere, the swan and the ugly duckling would excuse themselves to preen their feathers and on their return, when you asked them to dance again, they would just shake their heads. Clearly, the swan was hoping for a better offer, or the duckling was not prepared to be lumbered with that person with a face like a half-chewed caramel any longer. (Talk about the pot calling the kettle black!)

After one spectacularly unsuccessful evening when we failed to find any dancing partners at all, Ian suggested we split up and hunted as lone wolves for a change. He went one way, I went the other until, after a circumnavigation of the hall, we eventually met up again.

"How did you get on?" I asked.

"Well, the first one reclined, then the next reclined and so did the next," he said glumly.

What a talent! What skill! Why would you bother asking them to dance if you could just get them to roll over and lie on their backs as easily as that? What would be the point?

Things change, life moves on, and once I had passed my driving test, it meant I was no longer dependent on Ian, and of course hunting expeditions were no longer necessary once the Best Beloved and I became an item as the modern parlance has it, or "going steady" as we used to say. But I did want to show her where I had been hiding out every weekend and after which Sam Cooke's 1963 hit, *Another Saturday Night (and I ain't got Nobody)*, seemed so apposite a refrain that it could have been my theme tune, and which I hoped was hers too, as she danced part of the night away at Portsoy Town Hall.

I admit I had been driving fast to impress the Best Beloved, not at what an idiot I was, but what a skilful and fearless driver I was. We had just reached the outskirts of Elgin and in the distance I could see a red traffic light and a queue of traffic. Too late, I applied the brakes and too late I remembered my father's last words to me before I left: "Remember the brakes are spongy."

It was like trying to rein in a horse as I pulled back on the steering wheel, but the horses beneath my bonnet would not obey as I smashed into the back of a Morris Oxford so hard the boot handle of the Oxford was embedded in the radiator of my father's Wolseley 1500 and this in the era before seatbelts. To make matters worse, the driver of the other car was taking his wife to Gray's Hospital where she was being treated for her nerves, but it was my nerves that were bothering me as I phoned my father from the petrol station opposite to make my confession. Not so long previously I had got a right rollicking after I had backed into a barbed wire fence and scratched the bodywork while attempting to negotiate a three-point turn in the track up to Jim's farm. What he was going to say when I told him about this crumpled, tangled mass of metal I dreaded to think.

Funnily enough, he was very good about it indeed. He didn't shout and yell at me and tell me what a stupid little fool I was. He had no reason to suspect I had been driving fast before the accident and anyway, by the time I saw the lights of Elgin, I had already slowed down— only not enough and not soon enough. Inexperience, rather than speed, was the real cause of the accident, but perhaps he felt partly responsible because of the brakes or it might just have been he was relieved that no-one was hurt, just a little shaken, like one of James Bond's perfect Martinis.

A long time later my father arrived with a friend in his car to take us all home. What the Best Beloved's parents made of this latest and worst escapade I had involved their daughter in I can only hazard a guess, but it would hardly have done much to boost my approval ratings in their eyes. The fact that I have no recollection of this event is no doubt due to the slings and arrows of Ayesha's outrage being deflected by the shield of my father's presence. What I can say with more certainty is my weekend activities must have been severely curtailed while the car underwent surgery. But that wasn't a bad thing entirely as it also put some distance between the Best Beloved's mother and me . . .

I volunteered to pay the excess, an offer which my father did not refuse. I am sure his thinking was to make me more careful in future but I needed no such penance. I was not alone. It was a sort of rite of passage, for it seems most of my friends had a bump or a crash of varying severity in the months after passing their tests. No wonder insurance premiums are as high as they are for young male drivers, but in my naivety it never occurred to me that merely listing me as a driver on the policy would have increased the premium, let alone this accident putting it through the roof, and to his credit, my father never mentioned it.

I was getting off lightly therefore, when I withdrew the money from my account, though it broke my heart at the time. It would have been birthday money and other offerings and earnings going back to the time of my birth and now it was all gone. It was the first £50 note I had ever seen (and I have seen precious few of them since) and this at a time when a £20 note was something of a rarity.

After the car was restored to full health and returned, there was the knotty problem of asking my father if I could borrow it again. I tested the water by asking my mother what she thought his reaction would be.

"Ask him yourself," she replied and would not be drawn.

I found him in the garden, digging.

"Erm . . . erm . . . Do you think I could borrow the car, please?"

He must have known that this question was going to arise one of these days and must have given it some thought. He did not stop his toil to answer me straight away however, as if he were turning the idea over with

David M. Addison

the soil. But after what seemed an age, he straightened up and looked at me.

"Try and bring it back in one piece this time," he said, his face as straight as the furrow he was digging.

Chapter Forty-two

On Food, Fighting and Filming

Despite my reluctance to get up in the morning and my dislike of the History teacher aforementioned, not least my aversion to studying anything, apart from English literature, I really enjoyed Banff Academy. I even finally managed to pass 'O' Grade Maths and Arithmetic thanks to the dedication, patience and skills of another very good teacher whose name, regrettably, I have forgotten, otherwise I would very happily have given him a mention here.

For French and German, I had Miss Robertson, unflatteringly known as "Creep" for some reason. She never induced in me even the slightest tingling of the spine as the name might suggest. Maybe the sobriquet had something to do with creeping up on people in order to catch them doing something they didn't oughter but I never saw her do that either. Years later, when I returned to my alma mater as a student and was allowed into the inner sanctum of the staffroom, I was astonished to hear the teachers refer to her as "Creep" too.

I remember nothing about her classes at all except that there was a girl from some obscure religious persuasion or other who was much addicted to kirby grips. I don't know how many of these come in a packet, maybe as many as twenty, and she must have invested in at least a couple of packets to put in her hair. My guess is her religion had a great deal of misery in its philosophy and she was terrified of letting her hair down lest she was whisked straight off to hell. But if she had happened to walk under an electromagnet, she would have been amazed to find herself swept suddenly heavenward and her not even dead yet.

Sometimes we had PE in the playing fields by Duff House, quite a little distance away. The atmosphere in the changing room was a severe trial to the nostrils, but if you could perfect the skill of blocking your nose off long enough to allow the eager beavers to strip off and get changed and charge down to the playing fields ahead of you in their frantic desire to kick the hell out of the blameless ball, the physical fitness fanatic in charge of us would get tired of hanging around and after admonishing us to get a move on, would leave us to our own devices. Bomber would just have skelped our backsides and that would have been us, out on the field of battle with the rest of them. No messing about.

By the time the other reluctant exercisers and I had strolled down to the place of combat, the teams had been picked and we would watch them strive and strain and sweat over the kicking and possession and passing of the leather-clad inflated pig's bladder. I'm sure Oscar Wilde would have had a name for it, something like "the unwashed in full pursuit of the uneatable". It seemed to me much more sensible and hygienic to hang around doing nothing instead of all that rushing about, getting sweaty and out of breath. I don't remember any showers at Banff, or Fordyce for that matter. When we were sure the teacher (I can't remember his name) was engrossed in the bellowing of instructions and the blowing of his whistle, we would melt away and while away the time away more comfortably in the premises of the nearby golf club.

It was not possible to avoid normal PE lessons or, as Christmas approached, the dreaded dancing lessons. Dancing to me, you will remember, ever since the Dingwall days, was an anathema. I was just about to have that opinion brutally reinforced—not that I needed it.

I don't remember what kind of dance it was and I don't remember the name of the young lady either. I was doing my best not to step on her toes or do anything else wrong but at last she could contain her frustration and impatience no longer.

"Have you *no* sense of rhythm?" she snapped.

I suppose if there are boys who get passionate about kicking a ball about, there must be girls who take skipping the light fandango just as seriously. What could I say other than I was sorry, but guilty as charged. I should have gone on to thank her for this insight into my hatred of dancing but I was too taken aback at her forthrightness. Could that really be it? Had she put her finger on it, that my non-musical ear was responsible for my leaden feet? The real reason for my aversion to dancing was because I just couldn't do it. Like Maths.

And just like some, bizarrely, think the height of entertainment on a Saturday night is to prance around a ballroom doing the Lancers or the Military Two-step and other manoeuvres of that ilk, there is nothing some others like even better than to transform the ballroom into a battlefield by having a jolly good punch-up. Tribal warfare was forever breaking out at the dances: Macduff boys against Banff boys; Cullen boys against Portsoy boys and variations thereof, just because. The room could sway from end to end with the fray and although I had no allegiance to any of these, albeit being a native of Banff, I feared being caught up in the fracas, for fighting was not my idea of fun. I had never forgotten the lesson Harry had taught me and I was not in any hurry to get into another fight: I was a coward first, a pacifist second and a preserver of my looks third.

But one day, unexpectedly, just as I was leaving the outdoor toilets, apropos of nothing, I was stopped by a boy and challenged to a fight. He was not a big bruiser, if anything he was smaller than me and younger, and all I knew about him was that he came from a family of brothers with a reputation as trouble-makers, tough guys who instigated fights whenever and wherever they could. I had no axe to grind with him, nor as far as I knew, did he with me, so the reason for this challenge had purely to do, I can only surmise, with his perceiving me as something of a soft target which would allow him to hone his pugilistic skills and perhaps earn him some kudos in the eyes of his brothers.

I declined his kind offer and stepped to the side to pass him by, but this pacifist strategy failed to deflect my would-be pugilist from his designs. A string of unfounded allegations pertaining to my parentage was hurled at my back followed by a blow to my shoulder and I knew that for good or ill, I had no choice but to retaliate. To think was to act. Spinning on my heel, I sank my left fist into his unguarded midriff, then as he began to straighten up again, I unleashed a right hook to his jaw, just like you see in the movies. All those hours I spent watching the fisticuffs in those Westerns turned out not to be wasted hours after all. There was no-one more astonished than me, unless it was him, to see him lying the next moment, flat on his back on the floor of the toilets. It was all over in seconds.

I did not wait for him to get up or pursue my advantage by giving *him* a lesson he would never forget. Instead I strolled out of the toilets as cool as The Saint would have done, as if I were accustomed to dealing with assailants like him every day, as if they were no more than irritating insects that I could bat away without batting an eyelid, so to speak. At any moment I expected him to come after me and jump on my back but I couldn't ruin my sang-froid appearance by as much as a glance behind me, and to my relief, he did not launch a further attack. It was a greater relief still when the bell sounded, signalling the return to classes.

In the following days, and when there were no more repercussions, I hoped that the ease with which I had despatched him had given me, like our national emblem, the Thistle, a warning to all, but him especially, that I was such an expert in the martial arts that it would be very unwise indeed to *daur meddle wi' me*. There was one heart-stopping moment when I saw him in the town the next day with his two elder brothers who had left school and I feared that they were in town for the express purpose of "getting" me. I would have slunk back to the safety of the school but that would have been a craven retreat in front of others, and so the lunch hour was spent looking over my shoulder in fear of an attack whilst I tried to act oh, so nonchalant. There would have been no humiliation in being beaten up by two seasoned fighters, but apart from the pain, which I imagined would be severe, what worried me just as much was that my face would be permanently rearranged in a style that would no longer be to the Best Beloved's taste.

There was a café we used to meet sometimes but it was not a place where you would sit and have a quiet cup of coffee together, but a rough sort of joint run by a poor, demented Italian who was run ragged by a certain number of his clientele. I think his name was Guilio. Perhaps he had been a prisoner of war and if so, it would not have surprised me to learn he would have seen that as a much easier berth, since here he was a hostage to all kinds of bad behaviour that would not have been tolerated in school, and as far as I know, did not happen in Banff Academy at all, unlike Keith Grammar, where teacher-baiting was a daily occurrence and as rampant then as I found it at the end of my career.

Here the sport was to bait poor Guilio instead, to wind him up to the extent that he lost his temper and he would bodily throw offenders out the door to the accompaniment of his heavily-accented English. One sure way of achieving this result was to be caught turning the jukebox up to the maximum volume. He was just a little guy too. Maybe if he had been built like Bluto, no-one would have dared give him any cheek.

His premises were opposite St Mary's where I had previous, you may remember, for bloodying a boy's nose, and to where we will come back presently. It must have been the very café where I spent the illicit penny though I do not think Guilio was the proprietor then. I don't remember actually buying anything at Guilio's but it would have been surprising if I had not had the odd ice cream, Italians being masters of the art, and I wouldn't mind betting Guilio's ice creams sold like hot cakes.

I do remember well however, the stampede for the baker's van at "playtime" where, for a penny, you could buy a massive slab of cake covered in pink icing. It was a conglomerate of all sorts of leftover cakes, somehow welded together and given this topping of icing to make it more enticing. We were mad for it, the best bargain in Banff, and better than feeding the leftovers to the pigs, as must have happened to the barrels of tapioca. But if they still feed that lumpy wallpaper paste to kids nowadays, it will sadly all go to waste as it is considered unfit for even pigs' consumption in these "enlightened" times of health and safety.

I did have school dinners though and I don't remember them either—at least, not like at Keith Grammar, where on tapioca days or "frogspawn" as we preferred to call it (and that is exactly what it looked like, and remember I had a close affinity with that in my carefree, younger days), the slop dish was full and running over, and *still* they persisted in serving it up to us.

I was never a fastidious eater (as long as you gave me what I liked)—apart from frogspawn and cabbage and skin. I was made to eat the skin on the custard even if I hated it and my sister loved it. My parents seemingly, had never heard of Jack Spratt and his wife. She would gladly have had more of it, I none of it at all, would gladly have donated my entire share to my sister, but was not allowed to. I was also made to eat the skin on the chicken though I could scarcely force it down for gagging. But there was no-one standing over me making me eat the tapioca and like the majority of my contemporaries, I didn't.

There was great excitement in 1964 when the BBC came to call at St Mary's to broadcast *Songs of Praise*. In those days to appear on TV was a bit of a novelty. Nowadays you see people being interviewed in the street and passers-by never break their step or even glance in the direction of the cameras. I can never understand that. I have seen such things happen, even come across a couple of movies being made and an advert and I can never tear myself away. I want to stop and watch, find out what's going on. If I were a cat, I would have been killed by curiosity long ago.

The Rev. Wilkie was the school chaplain and he later went on to be one of the lecturers at Aberdeen College of Education though I never had him, theology being one of the subjects I did not study. I would have liked to very much, although I am not a believer, maybe *because* I am not a believer, but unfortunately there just was not time enough. The minimum number of degree subject passes required was seven and I took ten, definitely more than anyone before me and since, as far as I know. I had really got the study habit at last and as they say about smokers and those who get religion, there is nothing worse than the converted.

It was one of the difficulties with the Best Beloved: I was always studying. I craved knowledge. I regarded being a student as the best job in the world. What a privilege I thought, to be educated for free, to have your books paid for you, to say nothing of the accommodation. What's more, with a judicious choice of subjects, the first lectures did not begin until 11 am and sometimes I could not even make them if I was feeling exceptionally tired. After a hard night's studying of course. I had finally found my vocation in life, but that too had to end when I graduated. I would have been the perpetual student if anyone would first have put up the funds.

But I get too far ahead of myself. Back to the BBC. It must have been a Baillie T. Ruthven suggestion and must have done him no harm at all, when it came to his interview for the Royal High School. Just look at us! Fresh-faced and groomed and scrubbed and looking as pure as angels in our white shirts and ties and blazers. The choir of course, featured rather more than most and especially my friend Pat whose signature in my autograph book has more crosses for kisses than a football coupon. The irony of her angelic face, as depicted on TV, would, of course, be lost on an audience not in the know, but little angel Pat certainly was not. She looked very good on TV though, and obviously the cameraman could spot a looker.

But nothing was left to chance in that department. As we were herded into the church, the best-looking pupils were put at the front and the best-looking of all made to sit in the aisle seats in order to be picked out more easily by the camera's roving eye. Well, that's where I found myself anyway and like the photo of me taken in a similarly prominent position when I was in Primary One, such vital matters would not have been left to chance, would they? Once maybe, but not twice!

Unfortunately this was well before the era of the video recorder and I doubt very much if a recording of this televisual feast is still in existence, otherwise you would be able to judge the truth of my words for yourself. What fun it would be to see ourselves now, the way we were then. But, sad to say, for those who are no longer with us, if they did happen to have been picked

David M. Addison

out by the camera, that would probably be the only way that they would appear to live again since the ancestor of the now ubiquitous camcorder, the cine-camera, was affordable only by the very rich.

My days at Banff Academy were drawing to a close and so too is my tale, but first I must mention my music teacher, Miss Anton, not only because she is one of the few teachers I remember at Banff, but because it was she who alerted my cousins, George and Evelyn, then the occupants of Clayfolds, that there was a connection between it and Erik Satie, best remembered nowadays for his *Gymnopédies*.

But just how could the famous French composer, born in Honfleur in 1866, possibly be connected to the ancestral home of the Addisons, at least from the early twentieth century? Unfortunately my cousins could not remember the details and I set myself the task to find out. Obviously the place to start was with Miss Anton but even more unfortunately, by this time, she had passed on to playing the harp in heaven.

Little did I know that when I began this quest, I was to turn the perceived knowledge of Satie on its head and make discoveries that even eminent Satie scholars were unaware of. The credit should really go to Miss Anton, but I'm not sure just how deeply she went into it. In any case it seems she did not pass on her findings to the experts but which I now have. Just what they were, you can find out in the next chapter.

Chapter Forty-three

Goodbye to the Boondocks

Miss Anton—"Phantom Anton" some called her, (but not me) because she was so thin it was said that if she stood sideways on to you, you wouldn't realise that she was there and walk right through her. Monica, to give her the moniker her parents bestowed upon her, was a Hannah-type figure, just as dedicated to her pupils and her subject, and the only music teacher who ever, as far as I remember, did not just make us sing songs by way of music lessons. She tried to instil some musical culture in us by exposing us to some of the great composers. It was at Banff Academy for instance, that I heard *The Planets* for the first time. It was certainly a lot better to my ear than *The Pirates of Penzance* or *D'ye ken John Peel?*

Whilst our house was crammed with books which did a great deal to further my knowledge of literature, my knowledge of music was hardly advanced by there not being a single record on the premises. Apart from some old 78s that I saw at Jim's house, and which I believe belonged to his grandfather—Scottish tunes in which the pipes featured prominently and hardly to my taste—the first record I ever recall hearing as a record, as opposed to on the radio, was *Walkin' back to Happiness.* I heard it on one of our Saturday visits to Clayfolds on their new-fangled record player which my cousins jointly owned and I remember being astounded that it was sung not by a man, but by Helen Shapiro, who, even more astonishingly, was about my own age.

When I tell you that Erik Satie's mother was Jane Leslie Anton, you may not be astounded exactly, but you will automatically make a connection between Monica and her. She was born in Lambeth in 1838 and a bit of a composer in her own right. She met Alfred Satie while she was at boarding school in Honfleur and married him in London on July 19th 1865. They spent their honeymoon in Scotland. Since Erik was born the following May, even I can do the maths, and conclude that Erik must have been conceived in Scotland. It would be nice to think that Clayfolds was the exact place, but alas, we will never know.

Jane had three other children: Louise-Olga-Jeannie (1868); Conrad (1869) and Diane (1871). Poor Diane died in the summer of the following year and tragically, Jane herself died soon after, in October, aged only 33. The children were sent back to Honfleur, where Erik was born, to live with his paternal grandparents. And there he lived for the next six years until the sudden and mysterious death of his grandmother, who, although a good swimmer, somehow drowned at Honfleur in 1878. After this calamity, Erik and Conrad moved to Paris to live with their father.

These events in Erik's early life are well known to Satie scholars but next to nothing was known about his Scottish ancestry, apart from the fact that Erik was very proud of it. According to his biographer, Templier, Erik had an "English" grandfather and his mother, Jane, lost her father at "an early age". As a matter of fact, Templier was wrong on both counts.

Although Jane was born in London, her father was Scottish and he was more than three score years and ten when he died—a good innings. His name was George Anton and his wife was Elsie Davidson, born in Aberdeen in 1818. Since Templier got that so badly wrong, it is no wonder that so little is known about Erik's Scottish ancestry. When Jane was born, George, the boy from the boondocks of Banffshire, had found that the streets of London were paved with golden corn. He was a corn factor at the Stock Exchange.

Now here's the connection with Clayfolds. Perhaps Monica started out by researching her ancestry, I couldn't say, but she became a bit of a local historian and wrote a booklet, *Monumental Inscriptions in Alvah Old Churchyard*, in which it is recorded that George Anton died at Clayfolds on October 20th 1881 aged 74. I presume Monica is some sort of a descendant but I regret to say I have not been able to find the link. (It's actually easier for the genealogist to find out things in the distant past, as long as it is not remotely distant, than the recent past.) She certainly seems to have inherited the musical genes anyway.

Also recorded on the stone is a William Anton who also died at Clayfolds on January 4th 1883 aged 77. From their resting place, in the cemetery at Alvah, they have a grand view of Clayfolds.

So thanks to Monica (and that very useful tombstone—remember the foreword), I set off on the trail of finding out more about the Antons. The Old Parish Records for Alvah show that George was born in 1808 to James Anton and Jean Ellis at Muiryhill and that his brother William was born in 1806. Muiryhill is only a matter of miles from Clayfolds, probably not

David M. Addison

much more than an hour's walk by road though if you were a crow you could be there in minutes.

It would seem that William moved to Clayfolds sometime in the early 19th century. The family was certainly there by 1841. George, meanwhile, was in London, seeking his fortune. *The Farmer's Magazine* of 1836 contains a learned treatise entitled *Estimate of the Late Harvest in Great Britain and Ireland* which I heartily recommend to sufferers of insomnia, but by 10th August 1841, he was declared bankrupt.

Over the next forty years he plied his trade, living in various addresses in Lambeth, but in 1881 he pops up again at Clayfolds. There is no knowing when he arrived there—it could have been at any time in the previous ten years. However, sometime between 1851 and 1861, he and Elsie split up. Since we know that Jane met Alfred Satie sometime before 1865, it seems a reasonable conjecture that she was sent to finish off her eduction in Honfleur around 1859 when she would have been 21. Maybe she was packed off there not so much to improve her French, but to distance her from the trouble and strife at home, a bit like my mother, only she was much younger. The separation therefore, was more likely to have been nearer 1861 than 1851—a time too when George was also more likely to have been able to afford the fees after his financial collapse of twenty years previously.

After the rift with George, Elsie became a companion to her sister who was married to a certain Mr MacCombay, a rich Puritan zealot, much given to handing out tracts at theatres and other dens of iniquity, in a selfless and unsparing effort to save the souls of poor sinners. Poor Elsie! But what's a poor abandoned

476

woman to do? It was better than being homeless and so she threw herself on the mercy of the good Christian gentleman that he was.

As we know from the tombstone, George died at Clayfolds in 1881 but he was not 74 as the stone states, but 72. He died just six months after the census was taken. As for Elsie, she certainly outlived George as she and their only surviving son were responsible for erecting the headstone at Alvah, which, as well as recording the demise of George and his brother William, who never married, also says this: *and in loving memory of Jeannie (Jane Leslie) his dau. Wife of M. Satie of Paris, died there, Oct. 8, 1872 aged 33.*

So there you have it. But who could George and Elsie's "surviving son" be? There is no mention of any siblings at Lambeth when Jane was twelve. I wouldn't have thought that they would have started having more children at that stage, especially if the marriage was starting to fall apart. So, if we are to assume that Jane's siblings were younger—where were they and who were they? Monica might have been able to tell me. It seems likely that one of them could have been her ancestor, but at the moment that remains a mystery and an untidy loose end, but that it is not really my concern. All I set out to do was discover the connection between Clayfolds and Erik Satie. The Satie scholars can tie up those loose ends if they wish.

There just remains the loose ends of my tale to tie up and my job is done too.

Whilst I waited, not too hopefully, for my exam results in the summer of 1965, I was faced with the dreadful realisation that I had reached a milestone in my life. I had now left school. I had to do something with my life. But what? I could think of nothing. There was nothing I really wanted to be. I didn't know if the mattress makers employed testers or not, but one thing I couldn't do was to lie "rotting in bed" as my father put it, whilst he maintained me for the rest of his life. As it happens, he had only a little over four years of that left, though I could have made it seem like an eternity: four months was more than enough of me mooching around unemployed.

Since I had no interest in a career of any sorts, my parents suggested the Civil Service. A job for life they said, with a good (and non-contributory) pension. Might as well, thought I. What else is there anyway and it did not involve getting up in all weathers at the crack of dawn to attend to doubly incontinent cows. A nice warm job pushing a pen in an office sounded about the best I could hope for. But there were so many departments! Which to choose?

I liked the sound of the Diplomatic Service. Whilst it would be a wrench to leave the Best Beloved behind, I reasoned that since I would have to leave home anyway, why not let it be far, far away and somewhere exotic. The idea of living in a foreign country appealed to me. I might even be able to put my Higher German and French to use (if I passed them). So that was what I had decided on.

Then one Sunday, a lay preacher came to Deskford. In a former life he had been in the Diplomatic Service and he advised against it. With my paltry qualifications, he said, I would merely be a dogsbody or a go-for. I wouldn't like it at all. Those with the degrees, he said, (like him) were the ones who had the good jobs, the interesting jobs. It never occurred to me that I might have enough Highers to go to University and I could join this elite: I was not yet in love with studying. Besides, I had no strong desire to be a career diplomat. I already was a diplomat and didn't think much of it, trying to preserve my parents' sanity by keeping a low profile and trying to be good.

So I listened to the advice and as I was later to discover, it was a huge mistake, and one which altered the course of my life. Since that was out, the next best I thought, would be a department which involved meeting people. That was bound to be more interesting than being stuck behind a desk from nine till five, so I plumped for the Ministry of Pensions and National Insurance. That too was a mistake, on two counts. Firstly, the only sort of people I met were ex-jailbirds or irate members of the public who were already upset at being refused benefits and were further enraged when they demanded to see the supervisor and refused to believe that this fresh-faced loon could possibly be him and proceeded to tell me so in no uncertain terms. Put it politely, they did not. I had never met such hostility before.

Secondly, after my training, I found myself in charge of a section of a dozen people, most of them not only older than me, but some as old as my parents, and I was expected to tell *them* what to do if they had a problem they could not solve. The irony is, if they, who had been doing the job for longer than I had been born, couldn't do it, how on earth could I? They quite rightly resented me being their boss only by virtue of my Highers and not for any skill or expertise I was supposed to have, despite my training.

I hated it, which is why I gave it up. I was in Dundee at that time, living in a flat with some other exiles from Banff when Jim from Deskford, who had just completed his first year at Aberdeen University, came to spend some of his long summer holidays with me. It was during that visit that he told me about a new B.Ed degree.

So that was how I became a teacher. But that was still years in the future. First I had to pass the Civil Service interview. Amongst the questions they asked me were ones on current affairs and what I was reading at the moment. The interview was held in Edinburgh and anticipating the first of the questions, on the way down in the train, I read a newspaper so I knew all about the former, while the second of course, was never a problem, except in the sense that my parents sometimes wished I would stop reading and get out, get some fresh air and do *something*. They asked about my hobbies and never mind the others, I was able to tell them that I was a published author. I had expected them to ask me why I wanted to join the Civil Service and safely negotiated my way around that, did not say it was my parents' idea and if I didn't get some sort of a job soon, my mother would take the bread knife to me, and what's more, no court in the land would have convicted her as she would have pled insanity due to me.

I was put up in the Waverley Hotel, in the garret, and from my porthole of a window I could look directly down on the Scott Monument. Edinburgh seemed very strange, very exotic to a boy from Banff and very big. I felt very small and lost, nervous about the interview.

In the next week or so, the result came out. I was never in much doubt that I had got in. Whether there was any suspense on the part of my parents I couldn't say, but I am sure there was a great deal of relief. I was told to report to Edinburgh for nineteen weeks' training, after which time I could be posted absolutely anywhere.

The Civil Service recommended digs in Gilmore Place. The landlady turned out to be a shrewish alcoholic. My room, which I shared with another new recruit, was vast and bitterly cold. Those early days in Edinburgh were like being scooped suddenly out of the warm bath I was accustomed to (I *had* started washing by this time) and being plunged into a swimming pool of cold water in which I was completely out of my depth—and what's more, I did not know how to swim.

It is just as well I did not know what lay before me, merely had a natural apprehension of the unknown, but my mother—did she have some instinct that things were going to be difficult, that unhappy times lay ahead? Or was it just the natural response of a mother, despite all the hard times I had put her through, to see her first-born launched upon the world? At any rate, as my father backed the Wolseley out of the drive and my mother stood watching us at the garden gate, I was astonished to see tears streaming down her face.

"Stop!" said my sister, who had been sitting in the back seat, and she clambered out to comfort her by throwing her arms around her.

There was a lump in my throat as we set off to catch the bus that would take me to Aberdeen to catch the train that would take me to Edinburgh, along that route that I had cycled many, many times to my rendezvous with the Mother's Pride van.

I knew I could not get off with that sort of nonsense any longer. If any moment more than any other could be said to be a moment of transition from boyhood to adulthood, then this was it. It was time for the Banffshire loon to grow up and to leave Banffshire behind. What life held for me in the future I could not possibly know, but for the moment I knew it lay in Edinburgh.

APPENDIX

Crow Family Tree

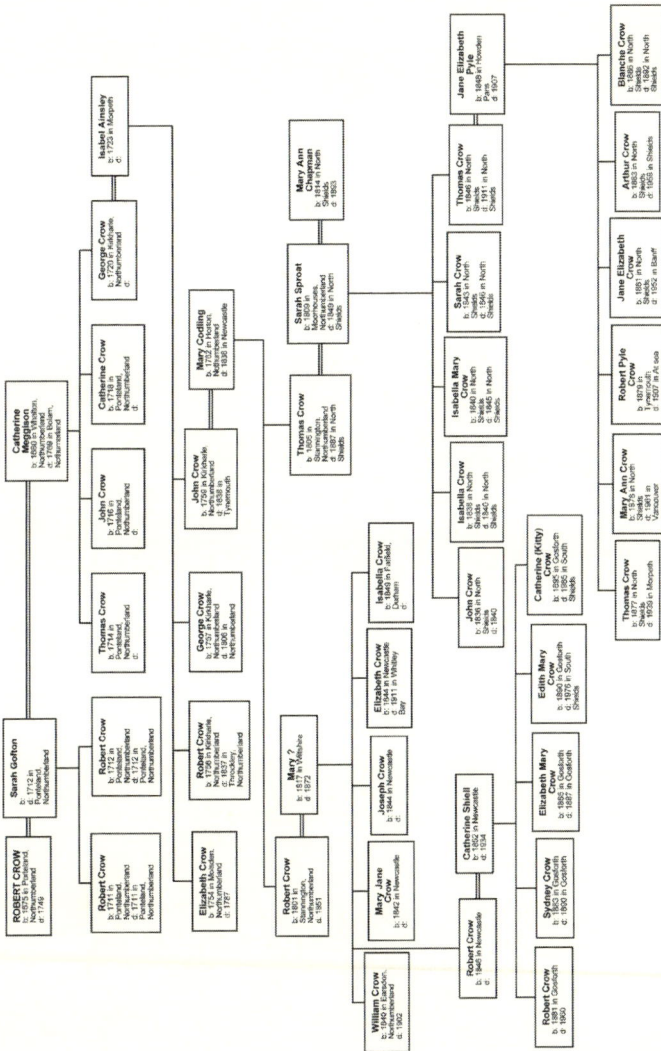

ROBERT CROW b: 1675 in Ponteland Northumberland d: 1749
Sarah Gofton d: 1675 in Ponteland Northumberland
Catherine Meggison b: 1692 in Whalton, Northumberland d: 1768 in Bolam, Northumberland

- **Robert Crow** b: 1741 in Ponteland, Northumberland d: 1711 in Ponteland, Northumberland
- **Robert Crow** b: 1712 in Ponteland, Northumberland d: 1712 in Ponteland, Northumberland
- **Thomas Crow** b: 1714 in Ponteland, Northumberland d:
- **John Crow** b: 1746 in Ponteland, Northumberland d:
- **Catherine Crow** b: 1748 in Ponteland, Northumberland d:
- **George Crow** b: 1720 in Kirkharle, Northumberland d:
- **Isabel Aimsley** b: 1723 in Morpeth

Robert Crow b: 1736 in Kirkharle, Northumberland d: 1837 in Throckley, Northumberland
Elizabeth Crow d: 1787
Mary Codling b: 1752 in Horton, Northumberland d: 1836 in Newcastle
George Crow b: 1757 in Kirkharle, Northumberland

John Crow b: 1796 in Kirkharle Northumberland d: 1858 in Tynemouth
Thomas Crow b: 1838 in Stannington Northumberland d: 1887 in North Shields
Sarah Sproat b: 1809 in Moormousses, Northumberland d: 1849 in North Shields
Mary Ann Chapman b: 1814 in North Shields d: 1863

Robert Crow b: 1801 in Stannington, Northumberland d: 1851
Mary ? b: 1817 in Wiltshire d: 1872

- **William Crow** b: 1842 in Earsdon, Northumberland d: 1902
- **Robert Crow** b: 1846 in Newcastle
- **Mary Jane Crow** b: 1842 in Newcastle d:
- **Joseph Crow** b: 1844 in Newcastle d:
- **Catherine Shiell** b: 1852 in Newcastle d: 1934
- **Elizabeth Crow** b: 1844 in Whitley Bay
- **Isabella Crow** b: 1846 in Fatfield, Durham

- **Robert Crow** b: 1881 in Gosforth d: 1880
- **Sydney Crow** b: 1863 in Gosforth d: 1866 in Gosforth
- **Elizabeth Mary Crow** b: 1860 in Gosforth d: 1887 in Gosforth
- **Edith Mary Crow** b: 1866 in Gosforth d: 1876 in South Shields
- **Catherine (Kitty) Crow** b: 1856 in Gosforth d: 1940
- **John Crow** b: 1858 in North Shields d: 1940
- **Isabella Crow** b: 1838 in North Shields d: 1840 in North Shields
- **Isabella Mary Crow** b: 1840 in North Shields d: 1840 in North Shields
- **Sarah Crow** b: 1840 in North Shields d: 1846 in North Shields
- **Thomas Crow** b: 1846 in North Shields d: 1941 in North Shields
- **Jane Elizabeth Pyle** b: 1846 in Hendon Paris d: 1907

- **Thomas Crow** b: 1877 in North Shields d: 1939 in Morpeth
- **Mary Ann Crow** b: 1875 in North Shields d: 1941 in Vancouver
- **Robert Pyle** b: 1879 in Tynemouth d: 1937 at sea
- **Jane Elizabeth Crow** b: 1881 in Staiths d: 1952 in Staiths
- **Arthur Crow** b: 1883 in North Shields d: 1955 in Shields
- **Blanche Crow** b: 1885 in North Shields d: 1942 in North Shields

Tate Family Tree

- Jasper Tate — b: 1734 in Berwick, d: 1800 in Alnwick
- Rachell Wardell — b: 1734 in Alnwick
- Jasper Tate — b: 1774 in Bedlington, d: 1814 in Alnwick
- Ann Short — b: 1773 in King's Lynn, d: 1840
- Rachel Tate — b: 1777 in Alnwick
- Mary Tate — b: 1771 in Alnwick
- Robert Tate — b: 1769 in Alnwick
- James Tate — b: 1769 in Alnwick
- James Tate — b: 1769, d: 1769
- James Tate — b: 1810 in Blyth, d: 1881 in Blyth
- William Tate — b: 1803 in Bedlington, d: 1881 in Blyth
- Jasper Tate — b: 1801 in Blyth, d: 1838 in Blyth
- Margaret Montgomery — b: 1814 in Glasgow, d: 1899 in Blyth
- Charles Tate — b: 1838, d: 1843
- James Tate — b: 1836 in Blyth, d: 1866 in Chilliwack, BC
- John Tate — b: 1840 in Blyth, d: 1914
- Isaac Tate — b: 1847 in Blyth, d: 1927 in Blyth
- Margaret Ann Tate — b: 1848 in Blyth, d: 1924 in Merritt, BC
- Samuel Tate — b: 1853 in Blyth, d: 1918 in Blyth
- Thomas Tate — b: 1859 in Blyth, d: 1918 in At sea
- Daniel Carmichael Tate — b: 1869 in Blyth, d: 1937 in Vancouver Park, Surrey
- Charles Montgomery Tate — b: 1851 in Blyth, d: 1933 in Vancouver
- Caroline Sarah Knott — b: 1809 in Bloomsbury, Middlesex
- Margaret Liddle — b: 1854 in Cramlington, Northumberland, d: 1807 in Blyth
- William Tate — b: 1853 in Blyth, d: 1891 in Cardiff
- Jasper Tate — b: 1835 in Blyth, d: 1887 in Blyth
- Nicholas Tate — b: 1858 in Newcastle, d: 1921 in Northumberland
- Eleanor Ann Fenwick — b: 1838 in North Shields, d: 1877 in Wallsdon, Northumberland
- Gertrude Maria Huntman — b: 1871 in Isle of Wight, d: 1908 in Isle of Wight
- Jasper Tate — b: 1871 in Blyth, d: 1928 in South Shields
- Marian Tate — b: 1897 in South Shields
- Alexander Tate — b: 1842 in Blyth, d: 1924 in South Shields
- Chicken Ann (Annie) Lee Laidler — b: 1838 in Newcastle, d: 1929
- Alexander Tate — b: 1879 in South Shields
- Jane Crow — b: 1862 in North Shields, d: 1952 in Banff
- Jane Elizabeth Tate — b: 1900 in Blyth, d: 1952 in Thornaby
- Thomas Crow Tate — b: 1907 in North Shields
- George Gibb
- Thomas Gibb — b: 1905
- William Laidler Tate — b: 1869 in Blyth, d: 1948 in South Shields
- Sarah Rewcastle — b: 1870 in South Shields, d: 1945 in South Shields
- Ann Tate — b: Blyth, d: About 8
- Alexander (Alec) Tate
- Ruth Worsley — d: 1967
- Clara Lillian Tate — b: 1872 in Blyth
- John Thomson — b: 1942 in South Shields, d: 1919 in South Shields
- Edith (Edie) Frances Tate — b: 1904 in South Shields, d: 1916 in South Shields
- John Alexander Thomson — b: 1935
- Stillborn Son — b: 1938, d: 1938
- Gillian Rewcastle Thomson — b: 1941 in Dalton, Northumberland
- Edith Margaret Thom — b: 1938 in Jesmond, Northumberland
- Alexander Gibb — b: 1902 in South Shields, d: 1989 in Blackpool
- Ethel Thomson Shields — b: 1906 in Great Broadwin, d: 1989 in Great Broadwin
- George Gibb — b: 1900
- Lillian Gibb — b: 1897
- Herbert Gibb — b: 1895
- Thomas Gibb — b: 1905

Gordons of Letterfourie Family Tree

JOSEPH ADDISON (1803-1877) Family Tree

The Portknockie Addisons

- Joseph Addison b: 1803 in Rathven d: 1877 in Fordyce
- Janet Croll b: 1810 in Rathven d: 1888 in Fordyce

- John Addison b: 1833 d: 1904 in Buckie
- Elizabeth (Betsey) Bruce b: 1833 in d: 1910 in Portknockie
- William Addison b: 1847 in Portknockie d: 1921 in Fordyce
- Jane Wright b: 1849 in Deskford d: 1915 in Fordyce

- JOSEPH ADDISON b: 1853 in GRANGE d: 1921 in PORTKNOCKIE
- Louisa Sutherland b: 1853 in Portknockie d: 1947 in Portknockie
- Mary Jane Addison b: 1859 d: 1869
- Jessie Ann Addison b: 1876 d:
- George Bruce Addison b: 1871 d:
- Mary Louisa Addison b: 1903 in Portknockie d: 1987 in Portknockie
- Joseph (Joffy) Addison b: 1895 in Portknockie d: 1917 in Roeux
- Jessie Ann (Shan) Reid b: 1902 d: 1960 in Portknockie
- Jessie Ann (Janet) Fraser b: 1888 d: 1923 in Aberdeen
- Alexander John Wright Addison b: 1894 in Fordyce d: 1935 in Colombo
- Lilian Mair b: 1898 in Portknockie d: 1972 in Buckie
- Peggy Cowie b: Portknockie d:

- Elizabeth (Bessie) Addison b: 1882 d:
- Bessie Addison b: 1886 in Portknockie d: 1889 in Portknockie
- George Addison b: 1883 in Portknockie d: 1951 in Portknockie
- Margaret (Maggie) Mair b: 1887 in Portknockie d: 1968 in Portknockie
- Louisa Addison b: 1893 in Portknockie d: 1894 in Portknockie
- William Addison b: 1882 in Fordyce d: 1948 in Portknockie

- Alexander (Alecky) Addison b: 1891 in Portknockie d: 1945 in Portknockie
- Mary Bruce Mair b: 1894 in Portknockie d: 1934 in Portknockie
- Mary Bruce b: 1914 d: 2001 in Banchory
- William (Willie) Addison b: Portknockie d:

- Bessie Addison b: Portknockie d:
- Joseph Addison b: Portknockie d:
- Mary Louisa (Louie) Addison b: 1920 in Portknockie d: 1930 in Portknockie

- Alexander (Sandy) Addison b: 1930 in Travancore, India
- Joan Wood b: 1933 in Portknockie d:
- William (Willie) Addison b: 1931 in Carnations, India d: 2008 in Brisbane

- Jean W. Addison b: 1918 in Portknockie d: 1976
- James Petrie Calder b: 1910 d: 1994 in Elgin
- Margaret Addison b: 1916 in d: 1997 in Elgin
- William Mair Slater b: 1917 in d: 2000 in Buckie
- Jessie Ann (Netta) Addison b: 1921 in Portknockie d: 2007 in Buckie

Munro Family Tree

"Heligoland" Joseph's Family Tree

Joseph Coull
b: 1803 in Rathven
d: 1877 in Fordyce

Janet Coull
b: 1810 in Rathven
d: 1888 in Fordyce

Catherina Denker
b: 1837 in Niendorf, Schleswig-Holstein
d:

George Addison
b: 1838 in Portknockie
d:

Joseph Addison
b: 1835 in Niendorf
d:

Helen Cormack Wood
b: 1874 in Cove, Kincardineshire
d: 1917 in Aberdeen

Agnes Freeland
b: 1868 in Niag
d:

JOSEPH ADDISON
b: 1866 in HELIGOLAND
d: 1919 in Aberdeen

Joseph (Dovey) Addison
b: 1895 in Niag
d:

Tina Addison
b: 1895 in Niag
d: 1909 in Toronto

Mary Agnes (Aggie) Addison
b: 1893 in Aberdeen
d: 1947 in Toronto

Agnes Banks Murison

George Addison
b: 1860 in Cullen
d:

Agnes ?
b: 1865 in Niag
d:

Tina Addison
b: 1868 in Lossiemouth
d:

Jemima Addison
b: 1866 in Peterhead
d:

Helen Stella Marriot
b: 1913 in Kintrasity, Aberdeenshire
d:

Charles Addison
b: 1915 in Niag
d: 1978 in NSW

Andrew (Andy) Leiper Addison
b: 1906 in Aberdeen
d: 1960 in Toronto

Irene Thomasina Beatrice Tyrell
b: 1909 in Argentina
d: 1931 in Toronto

John Wood Addison
b: 1903 in Aberdeen
d: 1985 in Toronto

John Tyrell Addison
b: 1928
d: 1962 in Verona, Ontario

Fred Cikut (Cyde)
b: 1898 in Romania
d:

Boris Addison
b: 1940

Joseph Addison
b: 1943

John (Jack) Blackhall Stephen
b: Portlethen, Kincardineshire
d:

Helen (Nellie) Wood Addison
b: 1906 in Aberdeen
d: 1938 in Toronto

Thomas (Tommy) Stephen
b: 1931

George Stephen
b: 1934
d: 1936 in Toronto

William John Whitford
b: 1893 in Hayle, Cornwall
d: 1966 in Carlton, Michigan

Jane Freeland Addison
b: 1922 in Aberdeen
d: 1987 in Carlton, Michigan

Bonnie Helen Jean Whitford
b: 1930 in Detroit
d:

Agnes Irene Whitford
b: 1933 in Detroit
d: 1935 in Detroit

Joseph John Whitford
b: 1941 in Detroit
d:

Florence Whitford
b: 1926 in Detroit
d:

Muriel Whitford
b: 1924 in Detroit
d:

Rodney Murison Addison
b: 1922
d: 1966

Mary Isobel Kean
b:
d:

George Murison Addison
b: 1921
d: 1980

George Murison Addison
b: 1891 in Niag
d: 1966 in Aberdeen

Jessie, Louisa and Charles Addison Family Tree

Joseph Addison b: 1809 in Rathven d: 1877 in Fordyce

Janet Coull b: 1810 d: 1880 in Fordyce

Jessie (Janet) Addison b: 1836 in Portknockie

John Forbes b: 1828 in Cullen d: 1896 in Cullen

William Forbes b: 1867

James Forbes b: 1869

John Thom Forbes b: 1873 d: 1894

Mary Ann Forbes b: 1879 in Cullen

Alexander Forbes b: 1863 d: 1865

Elizabeth Bruce Forbes b: 1859 d: 1866

Catherstine Murphy Forbes b: d:

Janet (Jessie) Forbes b: 1835 d:

John Parr b: 1855 d:

Janet Parr b: 1869 in Rathven

Isabella Parr b: 1888 in Cullen

Joan Parr b: 1860 in Inverurie

Alfred Parr b: 1894 in Inverurie

James Parr b: 1896 in Inverurie

Jeannie Frances Mann Parr b: 1897 in Inverurie

John Mitchell

Annie Parr b: 1900 in Inverurie

Louisa Addison b: 1849 in Portknockie

William Seivewright d:

Jessie Ann Seivewright b: 1873

Alexander Coull Seivewright b: 1875

Louisa Seivewright b: 1877 d:

William Seivewright b: 1878 d:

George Seivewright b: 1880 d:

James Seivewright b: 1882

Anna Seivewright b: 1883 d:

Charles Seivewright b: 1885 d:

John Seivewright b: 1887 d:

Frank Seivewright b: 1889

Mary Seivewright b: 1891

Charles Addison b: 1851 in Portknockie

Mary Angus b: 1852 in Fraserburgh

Jessie Addison b: 1876 in Aberdeen d:

Margaret (Maggie) Addison b: 1877 in Aberdeen d:

Helen (Nellie) Addison b: 1879 in Fraserburgh d:

Charles Addison b: 1881 in Fraserburgh d:

Charlotte (Lottie) Addison b: 1883 in Fraserburgh d:

Alexander Howat Addison b: 1885 in Fraserburgh d: 1910 in Fraserburgh

William Addison b: 1887 in Fraserburgh d:

John Addison b: 1889 in Fraserburgh d:

George Addison b: 1865 in Fraserburgh d: 1945 in Glasgow

The Canadian Addisons

John Addison
b. 1763 in Rathwen
d.

Ann McClelland
b. 1763 in Rathwen
d.

George Addison
b. 1815 in Rathwen
d. 1878 in Fordyce

Elizabeth Stainton
b.
d.

GEORGE ADDISON
b. 1840 in Boyndie Banffshire
d. 1921 in Hullett, Ontario

JANE WEBSTER
b. 1836 in Murroch, Blyth
d. 1921 in Hullett, Ontario

William Walker
d. Clinton

Jennie Addison
b. 1865 in Clinton
d. 1940 in Clinton, Ontario

George Addison
b. 1869 in Alwin
d. 1873 in Hullett, Ontario

Louisa Addison
b. 1872 in Hullett, Ontario
d. 1947 in Clinton, Ontario

William Addison
b. Abt. 1874 in Clinton, Ontario
d. 1957 in Clinton, Ontario

Annie Grace Maude Beatrice Addison
b. 1877 in Clinton, Ontario
d. in Clinton, Ontario

Joseph Addison
b. 1878 in Clinton, Ontario
d. 1941 in Clinton, Ontario

Dora Jemima Ruddell Addison
b. 1885 in Saunders, Ontario
d. 1959 in Clinton, Ontario

Jennie Addison
b. 1865 in Clinton
d. 1940 in Clinton, Ontario

John Cartwright (JC) Addison
b. 1888 in Brandon, Ontario

Annie Grace Maud
b. 1891 in Toronto
d. 1969 in Orillia, Ontario

Beatrice Maud Ego
b. 1894 in Orillia, Ontario
d. 1956 in Orillia, Ontario

Claude Addison
b. 1912 in Orillia, Ontario
d. 1998 in Orillia, Ontario

Velma Irene Addison
b. 1914 in Orillia, Ontario
d. 1914 in Orillia, Ontario

Edith Cavell Addison
b. 1919 in Orillia, Ontario
d. 1919 in Orillia, Ontario

Audrey Addison
b. 1920 in Orillia, Ontario
d. 2002 in Orillia, Ontario

Oswald Addison
b. 1921 in Orillia, Ontario
d. 1995 in Orillia, Ontario

Emory Addison
b. 1930 in Thomas, Ontario
d. 1969 in California

Thomas Carlyle (Carl) Addison
b. 1906 in Orillia, Ontario
d. 1972 in Huntsville, Ontario

Myrtle Elizabeth Lamb (Bobbie)
b. 1909 in Gravenhurst, Ontario
d. 2009 in Huntsville, Ontario

George Edward Addison
b. 1908 in Orillia, Ontario
d. 1995 in Paris, Ontario

Isobel Ann Addison
b. 1915 in South River, Ontario
d. 1978 in Paris, Ontario

Rebecca (Becky) Addison
b. 1985 in Deep River, Ontario
d.

Peter George Addison
b. 1939 in Paris, Ontario
d.

Bente Clara Nielsen
b. 1943 in Copenhagen

Timothy George Addison
b. 1966 in Deep River, Ontario
d.

Ann Laura Henderson
b. 1950
d.

Patricia (Pat) Ellen Malone
b. 1950 in Peterborough, Ontario
d.

Andrew Arthur Addison
b. 1981 in Calgary

Julia Mary Isobel Addison
b. 1983 in Calgary

Mary Elizabeth Addison
b. 1941 in Brantford, Ontario
d.

Margaret Anne Addison
b. 1944 in Brantford
d.

About the Author

The author's origins and early years is documented within these covers. He went on to find someone who has been keeping him off the primrose path and on the straight and narrow for the past forty-two years. He has two children and five grandchildren to show for it and has decided to call it a day at that.

Now happily (and mercifully) spared from having to teach any more English literature and language to generations of young Scots, when he is not at his laptop, he can often be found indulging in a bit of garden taming or preferably quenching his thirst at his local hostelry. But more often than not he will be somewhere else, satisfying his masochistic tendencies for more travel misadventures and possibly gathering more material for another book.

Printed in Great Britain
by Amazon.co.uk, Ltd.,
Marston Gate.